CONTENT LITERACY FOR SECONDARY TEACHERS

CONTENT LITERACY FOR SECONDARY TEACHERS

Christine J. Gordon
University of Calgary

Mary E. Sheridan

W. James Paul
University of Calgary

HARCOURT BRACE
CANADA

Harcourt Brace & Company, Canada

Toronto Montreal Fort Worth New York Orlando
Philadelphia San Diego London Sydney Tokyo

Canadian Cataloguing in Publication Data

Gordon, Christine J. (Christine Joanna), 1940–
    Content literacy for Secondary teachers

Includes bibliographical references and index.
ISBN 0-7747-3402-7

1. Language arts — Correlation with content subjects. 2. Language arts (Secondary).
3. English language — Study and teaching (Secondary). I. Sheridan, Mary E. (Mary Evelyn), 1942–   . II. Paul, William James, 1953–   . III. Title.

LB1631.G672 1998   428'.0071'2   C97-931061-X

Acquisitions Editor: Joanna Cotton
Senior Developmental Editor: Laura Paterson Pratt
Production Editor: Stacey Roderick
Production Coordinator: Sheila Barry
Assistant Production Coordinator: Shalini Babbar

Copy Editor: James Leahy
Permissions Editor: Nicole Fowler
Cover and Interior Design: The Brookview Group Inc.
Typesetting and Assembly: Bookman Typesetting Co.
Technical Art: Bookman Typesetting Co.
Printing and Binding: Hignell Printing Limited

This book was printed in Canada.

1 2 3 4 5   02 01 00 99 98

To our children, all fervent readers of the world

Tyler and Christopher
— C.J.G.

Pamela
— M.E.S.

Janay and Shelayne
— W.J.P.

PREFACE

Most content area textbooks are strongly rooted in cognitive psychology and heavily prescriptive in application of reading and writing (more so than speaking and listening) strategies in the subject areas. This textbook differs, conceptually and philosophically, in that it combines transactional theory (Rosenblatt, 1989) and interdisciplinary emphases in content area learning. Transactional theory purports that learners transact with text to create a unique interpretation while taking stances depending on their purposes: either to take away information from the text (efferent) or to become part of the world created in the text (aesthetic). The reader can also shift stances when transacting with any one text. Interdisciplinary emphases focus on integrating different aspects of lived experience in a specific discipline with different domains of knowledge. As one reviewer commented, this textbook reflects an instructional road "less travelled" in the content areas. My experiences in teaching literacy across the curriculum courses and my observations in junior and senior high-school classrooms have convinced me that inundating students with page upon page of strategies has not resulted in more than isolated change both in teacher practice and in the way secondary students learn/read/write/view their subject areas. Subject specialists are often so overwhelmed by the number of strategies to be mastered that they abandon any concerted efforts to enhance content literacy; they can relate few of the strategies to their own experience and have difficulty developing a content literacy philosophy that resonates with what they already know and do in literacy activities. As one of the reviewers of this text wrote, *Content Literacy for Secondary Teachers* aims to "win over not just the minds, but the hearts" of readers. With this philosophy in mind, this book consists of four underlying thrusts.

First, this book is about learning. To be literate in any discipline one should be able to talk, read, and write about the subject area and, in turn, to be able to use talking, reading, writing, and viewing as means of learning more about it.

The second thrust is that affective dimensions of learning should not be seen as separate from cognitive dimensions. More attention should be paid to the affective domain — that is, to the "hearts" of secondary students. Affective responses are often the first steps in learning how to make meaning. Learning to transact with text from an efferent stance rather than an aesthetic stance has in the past been the sole focus of all content areas except for English language arts. Such an overemphasis has lessened students' enjoyment in transacting with text. This book intends to show the importance of adopting different stances for reading, writing, viewing, and discussing and to show how changing stances is essential to active and independent learning of content.

The third aim of this book is to develop the framework, provide appropriate examples, and then give "space" to specialists in each of the content areas to make content-specific applications based on the philosophy and concepts presented. For example, how can the skill of writing a research report be used in art, music, mathematics, science, or drama? The focus is more on presenting general content literacy skills that can be applied to a number of specific disciplines. Some attention is given to literacy skills specific to each content area through examples in the chapters. In other words, there will be no separate chapters devoted to "literacy in science" or "literacy in mathematics." We will rely on subject area specialists to use their knowledge of the nature and logic of a discipline — its inherent text structure, its vocabulary, and its concepts — to develop content-specific skills applying the framework and concepts in this book.

The fourth aim of *Content Literacy for Secondary Teachers* is to show teachers how to encourage interdisciplinary transactions across the traditional content area specializations. Students need to connect their specific knowledge of a discipline to their knowledge of other disciplines rather than segregate or departmentalize what they learn. An emphasis on interdisciplinary transactions is particularly important in the secondary-school classroom, where traditional subject area divisions (and the knowledge and belief that such organizational structures should continue) lead to a fragmentation rather than an integration of knowledge.

This book is intended first for pre-service teachers and, second, for experienced classroom teachers who may never have had a course in content literacy or who might wish to use a different approach to developing content literacy.

The foundational and philosophical chapters are presented in Part I. Part II consists of chapters integrating theory and practice, with an emphasis on practical teaching/learning suggestions. Part III concludes the book, with chapters on assessment of students and texts.

Chapters 1, 2, 5, 6, 8, 11, and 12 were written by me, the senior author. Mary Sheridan was invited to write Chapters 3 and 4 and to co-write Chapter 7 with me because her theoretical stance is in harmony with the philosophy underpinning this book. Her contribution has strengthened the book. Chapters 9 and 10 were written by Jim Paul, who graciously accepted the invitation to be part of the project at a later date; his contribution has added much to the collaborative effort!

Several special features characterize this text. Each chapter begins with a series of questions that require the learners to bring their own experiences to the reading. These are followed by an overview, which serves as an advance organizer. Throughout the chapters, several "hands-on" activities for the reader as well as boxed "reflection exercises" promote active learning through aesthetic, efferent, and interdisciplinary transactions. Each chapter concludes with a summary, to review key concepts, and questions for further reflection, which invite learners to integrate new learnings with previous experiences and to share them with others.

In a 1991 study in which I was a co-investigator, pre-service teachers were asked to write a weekly response journal commenting on course content, ideas, and activities. In this way, these pre-service teachers contributed insights and anecdotes about what worked for them as learners. Some of these "stories" are used to support several important concepts in this textbook. Our hope is that future pre-service and in-service content area teachers will adopt the theoretical underpinnings of this book, and then apply, modify, and/or discard the ideas, as necessary, in their disciplines.

Acknowledgements

Since this book was a collaborative effort, I extend thanks first to the two contributors — Mary Sheridan and Jim Paul. Also special thanks to the pre-service student teachers in content literacy courses from whom we have learned so much as teachers.

Special thanks to the reviewers for their careful attention to the manuscript and their detailed suggestions for improving the text. The reviewers include Deborah Begoray, University of Winnipeg; Marg Iveson, University of Alberta; Joanne McGowan, University of Saskatchewan; Roderick Wm. McLeod, Lakehead University; Judith Robertson, University of Ottawa; and Warren Wilde, University of Alberta.

I gratefully acknowledge the support of the Izaak Walton Killam Memorial Awards and thank the Killam Resident Fellowship Committee for awarding me the Killam Resident Fellowship, Fall 1995, to work toward the completion of this book. I also extend gratitude to the Faculty of Education, University of Calgary, for granting me a Sabbatical Fellowship, from August 1996 to July 1997, which enabled me to attend to the revisions and the numerous editorial matters related to the book.

For her steadfast support, unflagging friendship, and expert secretarial assistance, special thanks go to Barbara Rennie. For her good sense of humour, her computer and graphic skills, and her extraordinary efficiency, special thanks go to Barbara Howe — she truly was my rock of Gibraltar in this endeavour.

Last but not least I wish to acknowledge the role of a number of editors at Harcourt Brace & Company, Canada. My sincere gratitude to Joanna Cotton, Acquisitions Editor, for her keen interest in the project; to Laura Paterson Pratt,

Senior Developmental Editor, for her constant support, expert guidance, and unstinting encouragement throughout this project; to James Leahy, Copy Editor, for his meticulous attention to detail; to Nicole Fowler, Permissions Editor, for her resolve in securing reprint permissions; and finally to Stacey Roderick, Production Editor, for her infectious enthusiasm and adherence to a tight, but not unreasonable, schedule in the final stages of production.

Christine J. Gordon
University of Calgary

A Note from the Publisher

Thank you for selecting *Content Literacy for Secondary Teachers* by Christine J. Gordon, Mary E. Sheridan, and W. James Paul. The authors and publisher have devoted considerable time to the careful development of this book. We appreciate your recognition of this effort and accomplishment.

We want to hear what you think about *Content Literacy for Secondary Teachers*. Please take a few minutes to fill in the stamped reader reply card at the back of the book. Your comments and suggestions will be valuable to us as we prepare new editions and other books.

BRIEF CONTENTS

CONTENTS

Chapter Two
Literacy Processes   **40**

Chapter Three
Aesthetic and Efferent Reading:
Concepts and Strategies   **71**

Chapter Four
Crossing the Boundaries between Content Areas:
Interdisciplinary Transactions   93

PART TWO
Successful Learning in the Content Areas   123

Chapter Five
Talking and Discussing to Enhance
Content Comprehension   124

Chapter Six
Reading and Writing to Enhance
Vocabulary Development   **165**

Chapter Seven
Enhancing Content Comprehension
and Metacomprehension   **209**

Chapter Eight
The Role of Writing in Developing Content Literacy   238

Chapter Nine
Strategic Learning for Life: Learning to Learn   277

Chapter Ten
Media Literacy: Learning from Electronic
Image-Texts   304

PART THREE
Assessing and Evaluating in the Content Areas   331

Chapter Eleven
Assessing and Evaluating Students'
Content Literacy   332

Chapter Twelve
Evaluating Text to Bridge the Gap between Reader and Author   370

PART ONE

Introduction to Content Literacy

CHAPTER ONE

Content Literacy: The Framework

Questions to Consider for this Chapter

1. What is content literacy?
2. What roles do the subject area teachers play in developing content literacy?
3. What is a text?
4. How are the language processes interrelated?
5. What is the difference between reading-to-learn and learning to read? writing-to-learn and learning to write?
6. What are the effects of talking-to-learn?
7. Why is viewing-to-learn an important literacy activity?
8. What are ways to "integrate across the curriculum"?

Overview

This chapter begins with a discussion of the meaning of content literacy. It also provides a rationale for developing content literacy or literacy in each subject area. An expanded definition of "text" is provided as is a review of the development of language and literacy processes. Talking-to-learn, reading-to-learn, viewing-to-learn, writing-to-learn, and representing-to-learn are then discussed as means to learn in a content area. Because content literacy calls for holistic approaches such as the interrelationship of the communication arts, teaching learning strategies along with content, and integrating themes across the curriculum, several forms of integration in the curriculum are discussed.

What Is Content Literacy?

To be literate in any discipline is to be able to read, write, and talk about the discipline, and to use reading, writing, talking, listening, and viewing as effective ways of learning still more about the subject area. That is, being literate is to be better able to use one's **content literacy** as a means of extending one's knowledge of a discipline even after a particular course or subject has been completed. Students can best become literate in any given subject area if reading, writing, talking, and viewing are an integral part of content learning and of the subject area curriculum. Talking, reading, writing, and viewing in the subject areas are known as **talking-**, **reading-**, **writing-**, and **viewing-to-learn** activities, and are ways to maximize the learning of content. The teaching of processing strategies (talking-to-learn, reading-to-learn, writing-to-learn, and viewing-to-learn strategies) is not seen as separate from the content (McKenna & Robinson, 1990); nor are affective dimensions of learning seen to be separate from cognitive dimensions. That is, content literacy students' responses to content area texts may vary — from an intent to take away information to a variety of feelings that are evoked by the associations to the text (Frager, 1993; Rosenblatt, 1989) — or include all of these responses. The variance will depend on purposes for the reading, viewing, speaking, or writing and on the "texts" read. Students should learn that "responding to the author means experiencing the feelings generated by the words as well as thinking about the concepts" (Frager, 1993, p. 621). "To isolate [emotion and cognition] is like studying the planes of crystal separately, losing sight of the crystal that gives them being" (Bruner, 1986, p. 17).

Defining Content Literacy

What is literacy? How is "content" literacy defined? In conducting a semester-long research study with students in a literacy across the curriculum course (Gordon & Hunsberger, 1990–91), pre-service teachers were asked to write once a week in their response journals their reactions to course content, ideas, and activities. As part of the research, journal entries were analyzed and re-analyzed for emerging themes (Glaser & Strauss, 1967). Some of these entries will be used where relevant in the first two chapters to support concepts. We will start with pre-service teachers' definitions of literacy. The majority of pre-service teachers, when asked to define literacy, wrote that it was the ability to speak, read, and write according to the social norms of and/or the ability to function in a particular society (to read the newspaper, to do the banking, to read directions and labels, or to read to carry out one's job). Several teachers noted types of literacies such as computer literacy. A much smaller number (all subject area specialists) touched on content literacy. For example, one teacher-education student stated,

> I believe it [literacy] must not only include reading and writing but also the ability to read and write in the subjects and to have a general understanding of the content. It's being able to read and write with understanding in the subject area at hand. (Sarah)

In Western society, the definition of **literacy** includes more than having literacy skills such as decoding letters and words, and comprehending the explicitly stated main ideas. According to Heath (1991), being literate means that

> individuals can compare, sequence, argue with, interpret, and create extended chunks of spoken or written language in response to a written text in which communication, reflection, and interpretation are grounded. (p. 3)

Content literacy is not synonymous with content knowledge. "Content literacy represents skills needed to acquire knowledge of content" (McKenna & Robinson, 1990, p. 184). Some of these skills are general and can be applied to learning across the curriculum. Others are more specific to a particular discipline by virtue of the nature and logic of the discipline itself, the text structures used in presenting information, the skills needed to read specialized symbols, or the ability to integrate graphic information with information in running text. These **content-specific** skills are best applied by subject area specialists. McKenna and Robinson (1990) define content literacy as

> the ability to use reading and writing for the acquisition of new content in a given discipline. Such ability includes three principal cognitive components: general literacy skills, content-specific literacy skills (such as map reading in the social studies) and prior knowledge of content. (p. 184)

A paraphrase of McKenna and Robinson's discussion of the three components is now presented.

While a general ability to read and write is obviously required for students to function in any subject area, it is not the responsibility of the content area teacher to instruct students in the mechanics of reading and writing. Content area teachers should not be teachers of reading and writing in the traditional and idealistic sense of teaching the basic skills in order that a student may learn to read and write. Learning to read and learning to write are not the same as reading-to-learn and writing-to-learn (Myers, 1984; Vacca & Vacca, 1989). Reading- and writing-to-learn focus on retention or expansion of knowledge.

To be literate in any subject area is to have content- or subject-specific literacy skills as well (McKenna & Robinson, 1990). For example, it may involve reading graphs and formulaic equations in mathematics, writing up scientific experiments in science, following verbal and written directions, or interpreting the rules for playing a particular sport in physical education.

Finally, just as important to the concept of literacy is the amount of prior knowledge of the subject area that one possesses. The more prior knowledge of the content, the more likely that such knowledge will enable the integration of additional knowledge, given the same general literacy skill level. Because content literacy contains these three components (McKenna & Robinson, 1990), increasing it has the potential to maximize content aquisition.

Active and Passive Learning

In order to become literate in a content area, students must also become active, independent learners in today's print-oriented society. To encourage independence, content area literacy instruction should focus on developing self-guided **strategic readers** and writers (learners who are aware of their strengths and difficulties and use a variety of strategies/skills in literacy activities). Such learners are capable of successfully controlling and monitoring their own cognitive actions as they use reading and writing to comprehend subject matter content (Baker & Brown, 1984; Bonds, Gant Bonds, & Peach, 1992; Miholic, 1994). Content area teachers should also help students monitor their feelings, emotions, and other affective elements during reading (Frager, 1993). Thus, not only cognitive and affective but also metacognitive aspects of reading and writing need to be monitored. **Metacognitive theory** holds that active readers and writers not only construct meaning but rely on various metacognitive resources to maintain awareness and exercise control over the processes (Garner, 1987). Active readers are always in the process of predicting, hypothesizing, questioning, reflecting, interpreting, feeling, associating, and bringing in their personal knowledge. These are the literate behaviours described by Heath earlier. Active learning can be a solitary activity but it can also be done in collaboration with peers. Here is what two pre-service teachers wrote in their response journals about active and passive learning (Gordon & Hunsberger, 1991):

> This lesson has made me do a little more metacognitive analysis. I realize that I am much more passive when I summarized my chapters. I don't even think about the headings that I am writing down and in fact do minimal thinking when I write any of it down. (Hans)

> My co-op [co-operating teacher] continually allows the class to be active in their learning process. Instead of making the students work individually (read and answer the problems), he guides the class (orally) and allows them to work through their problems (reading, interpreting) together. The students are not only keen on voicing their own opinions and explanations but also maintain their

interest and really seem to understand better when another student makes things
more clear. This method of active learning just seems so different than/from my
day of learning because we were always passive learners. (Joan)

In general, most new teachers in the research reflected that their learning
experiences in secondary school had been passive rather than active but that
their exposure to active learning in the course was beginning to change their
approaches to learning.

Content area teachers cannot teach students everything there is to know
in a content area, but they can instil in their students a desire to learn and provide them with tools for learning independently. This is the mark of a literate individual. However, in order to reach that end, students need to be
shown how. Many present models of reading and writing therefore view readers and writers as active learners who possess a variety of strategies to direct
their own cognitive resources to learn from text. Learning is thus affected not
only by the type of text being studied, the tasks being performed, the strategies used by the learner, and the contexts in which learning occurs, but also
by learner characteristics such as learning style, background knowledge, confidence, interest, motivation, and attitude (Brown, Campione, & Day, 1981;
Jenkins, 1979). Learning is also affected by a reader's personal experience, feelings, images, and associations (Rosenblatt, 1978).

Why a Course in Content Literacy?

Because some teacher-education students come into a course on content literacy without understanding what content literacy is, they can have negative
attitudes, or at the very least feelings of ambivalence, toward the concept of
literacy across the curriculum. Not uncommon are such reactions as those
found in Gordon and Hunsberger (1990–91, 1990). These reactions question the use of printed material and/or the need to teach students how to read
and write content materials.

> I expect to learn how to present material from appropriate textbooks along
> with the other usual resources in such a way that the written material will be
> just as relevant as anything I could show them. Kids don't expect, or necessarily
> want, to read in their art classes — they want to "get their hands dirty." I real-
> ize that there are some wonderful textbooks out there for me to use but, partly
> since I never used texts myself in art class, I'm not sure where, or how to fit
> them in! (Valerie)

> To be quite honest I don't know how valuable this course will be to me. My
> area of specialization is mathematics. This is a discipline that does not really

deal in language but in numbers. A given problem, say $3 \times 5 + 6x + 4 = 0$, is not open to the ambiguities of language, nor the problems of interpretations. There is only one correct answer. (Devon, quoted from Gordon & Hunsberger, 1991, p. 401)

Such attitudes may reflect some of your own attitudes, beliefs, and feelings since you too may consider yourself a subject area specialist whose responsibility is to teach only the content of your discipline, not how to read- or write-to-learn the content. Yet students who have completed elementary schooling do not already know how to read and write the content of junior and senior high-school courses. Many of you may feel that you have support in your beliefs from the teaching staff already in the schools. Yet it has been our experience that many teachers, even without such course work, seem to provide content literacy instruction intuitively because they have come to know that students should read and write as a way of mastering content. Too, research has shown that teachers' attitudes toward teaching literacy across the curriculum improve by course end (Allen, 1987; Bean & Zulich, 1990; Crowhurst, 1989; Gordon & Hunsberger, 1991).

What Is Text?

Although we most frequently think of **text** as printed text rather than oral or visual text, and even more frequently think of text as being drawn from a textbook, text "can be anything from a riddle to a road sign, from a newspaper article to a whole book" (Tierney, Mosenthal, & Kantor, 1984, p. 139). It can be a soup can label or a chart posted in a high-school classroom. A person speaking can be a text. Text can also be a lecture, a piece of music, or any oral presentation, such as the text of a film. Text can be a picture, a drawing, or a mural. Text can be the mountain scenes you are studying as you drive through the Rockies. All of these texts can be read in some way. Texts can be student-constructed or teacher-constructed, taking on many forms different from those in textbooks (O'Brien, Stewart, & Moje, 1995). The form of printed texts themselves is changing with the advent of hypertext and multimedia text. Hypertext is electronically enhanced text designed to help students understand text through the addition of examples, definitions, and questions. Multimedia text uses print in conjunction with graphics, video, and other accompanying multilayered technologies (Tierney, 1994). Most commonly, however, we think of texts as the reading materials (be they fiction or nonfiction) students encounter in their content area textbooks. The primary emphasis in this book is on content area text as presented in textbooks, although other types of texts are not neglected in our discussions.

For Reflection 1.1

At this point, you might ask yourself, What do I understand by the term literacy? the term "content literacy" or "literacy in a subject area"? You might also reflect on how your own secondary-school teachers taught students to better learn the content of the subject areas. Too, you might reflect on your definition of "text" in relationship to your definition of literacy.

Content Area Instruction for Diverse Learners

In today's inclusive classrooms, you will find a number of different types of learners and special students: ESL, gifted, or at-risk students (those lacking requisite learning skills and/or family and community support to fully succeed at their grade levels). The fabric of today's classroom is much more diverse than in the past — not only because of inclusion policies but because of the language, cultural, and socio-economic diversity in North American society. Content area teachers need to adapt instruction to the needs of **diverse learners** and to capitalize on the knowledge and interests brought to the classroom by different ethnic groups. There are five principles for adaptive instruction (Alvermann & Phelps, 1994; Strother, 1985):

1. Provide instruction based on students' strengths rather than their weaknesses.
2. Choose materials and approaches/methods on the basis of students' interests.
3. Involve students by giving them active roles in setting goals and evaluating their own progress.
4. Make available alternative materials, activities, and assignments for students who need additional help.
5. Use co-operative and **collaborative approaches** to learning.

Alvermann and Phelps (1994, p. 20) also provide specific guidelines for respecting diversity:

1. Teach students to think critically.
2. Recognize and celebrate language differences.
3. Build an understanding of how students from different cultures view the world and make sense of it.

4. Consider what "schooling" means to those with different language and cultural backgrounds and develop students' sense of ownership and pride within that meaning.

A more extended discussion of student diversity is provided in Chapter 5.

Oral Language Development: An Overview

Talking, listening, reading, and writing are all related **language processes**. At this point, it is important to explore the nature of oral language development (talking/speaking) because of the relationship of language to literacy development (reading, writing, viewing). This discussion draws heavily on Ruddell and Rapp-Ruddell (1994), who trace the complexity of language acquisition and review the research on which this summary is based. In summary, children learn to become expert users of their native language at a very early age and continue their language development throughout their school years. They actively create rules about how oral language works on the basis of models and responses of adults around them, test the rules for "match," and modify the rules accordingly.

Investigations (cited in Ruddell & Rapp-Ruddell, 1994) provide evidence that in similar fashion children construct rules and test hypotheses in written language development (reading and writing). The impetus of these types of language growth is to make meaning, to make sense of the world around them. To make sense of the world, they need to make sense of the language system. When constructing oral (and written) language, children gradually increase their control over **phonology** (oral and written sound symbol combinations), **morphology** (combination of letters [sounds] that carry meaning), **syntax** (grammar, the order of words in sentences, sentence complexity which shapes meaning), and **semantics** (the cognitive and affective repertoire of concepts and their labels). Semantic development generally moves from concrete thinking (*chair, girl*) to abstract thinking (*democracy, atom*). Acquisition of complex syntactical structures and semantics continues throughout the secondary-school years.

The acquisition of language behaviours that allow children to function in the home, the school, and the community is another important facet of language development (Ruddell & Rapp-Ruddell, 1994). Seven language functions (Halliday, 1978) permit communication: instrumental (*I want*), regulatory (*Do as I say*), interactional (*Me and you*), personal (*Here I come*), imaginative (*Let's pretend*), heuristic (*Tell me why*), and informative (*I have something to tell you*). Eventually children are able to switch registers, that is, to use appropriate functions in different situations. Literacy development unfolds as language users become fluent in the oral mode (Gambell, 1989).

Developing Literacy Processes

Beginning with scribbling and picture representations, children then connect oral language with written language and begin to understand the relationship of printed symbols to sounds. Beginning writers progress from scribblings and drawings to writing using invented spellings and finally to conventional spellings. Young children generally make few distinctions between spoken and written language. However, children's writing increases in complexity and sophistication so that by secondary school sentence complexity in written expression is superior to that in oral expression. Children's knowledge of written language functions also increases, giving them the ability to switch writing registers (see Table 1.1 for language registers common in classroom interactions).

With respect to reading, children also progress through developmental stages in ability to read words (word analysis and word recognition) (Ehri, 1991; Ruddell & Rapp-Ruddell, 1994) and in learning that there are relationships between print and oral language. The foundation for reading comprehension is built on oral language development, early writing experiences, and early reading experiences of "texts" in the environment. It is also based on the many social interactions that provide opportunities for dialogue that expands language growth, the ability to develop understandings of the real world and the world of print, and the ability to construct and negotiate meanings on the basis of cognitive and affective dimensions. In short, children and older learners are "active participants in their own language and literacy development" (Ruddell & Rapp-Ruddell, 1994, p. 96).

Researchers have learned that literacy development moves along a continuum with children actively constructing oral and written understandings in interactions mediated by more knowledgeable others. We have such evidence from developmental studies. Loban (1963) conducted a thirteen-year longitudinal study of oral and written language development by following students from kindergarten through Grade 12. Collecting oral language samples (beginning in kindergarten) and written language samples (beginning in Grade 4) twice yearly, Loban aimed to establish which language features contribute to language proficiency. He found that in both oral and written language development, the key was elaboration or modification within the main clause. Older and stronger language learners used longer units for communication, elaborating the subject and predicate (verb); embedded more units; and used many kinds of dependent clauses. Research focussing solely on the complexity of children's writing (Harrell, 1957) also showed that, as with oral

Table 1.1

Registers Common in Classroom Interactions

CLASSROOM LANGUAGE REGISTERS	ORAL FORM	WRITTEN FORM
Informal personal exchange	• greetings (inter-actional, personal) • communication of feelings (instrumental, interactional, personal) • control of other's behaviour (instrumental, regulatory)	• personal notes to friends • newsy letters and notes • memos and directions
Formal information exchange	• classroom discussion (informational, heuristic) • classroom lectures (informational) • public talks (informational)	• edited stories, narratives, and accounts • edited reports and essays • school textbooks
Literary exchange	• drama, theatre (imaginative, informational, heuristic)	• poetry, narrative, drama

Source: From "Language Acquisition and Literacy Processes," by R.B. Ruddell and M. Rapp-Ruddell, in R.B. Ruddell, M. Rapp-Ruddell, and H. Singer (Eds.), 1994, *Theoretical Models and Processes of Reading.* Newark, DE: International Reading Association, p. 91. Copyright © 1994 by International Reading Association. All rights reserved.

language development, children developed the ability to use embedded sentences, increased their length of clauses and compositions, and used more subordinate clauses as they grew older (e.g., by ages 13–15). Based on the research, Moffat (1968) developed curriculum on principles of language development rather than on divisions in subject matter.

Britton and his colleagues (1975), in research on 11–18 year olds, attempted to base a model of language development on the principles of intellectual/cognitive development. Britton et al. viewed the learner as working in a context where the language is **expressive** (highly contextualized so speaker or writer can assume that the listener or reader has similar background and interests). With maturity, the language learner can move to **transactional language** (for purposes of informing or persuading) or toward **poetic language** (consisting of jokes, anecdotes, novels, poems, or plays). In transactional language the speaker or writer must provide context and anticipate audience needs. Poetic language permits speakers/readers to take on the "spectator" role. Britton et al.'s research showed that schools stifled students by placing transactional demands on them in all subjects with the exception of English (and even in English the emphasis on the expressive was minimal). According to the model, the research team proposed that the starting point for more formalized written language in a variety of subject areas was expressive language. The premise that informal, speechlike writing is a starting point for more formal (transactional) writing became the foundation of the language across the curriculum movement influencing subject area writing in North America and the United Kingdom. Further, the inclusion of a focus on the writing process (where students are guided through several drafts) in English language arts classes has helped to make "writing across the curriculum" (referred to as "writing in the content areas" in North America) a reality in secondary-school classrooms (Simmons, 1991; Newkirk, 1991).

Traditional Approaches to Learning to Read and Write

Even though many children learn to read and write in a fairly holistic and natural way, there are more traditional ways in which children acquire literacy. The traditional approach generally consists of teaching children to read and spell before they write so that they know the conventions and proceed by writing "correctly" from the outset. Reading and writing begin first with smaller units such as letters, words, and sentences, and then progress to larger units such as paragraphs and whole selections (narrative and expository). This bottom-up approach is now thought to develop literacy in a piecemeal, linear fashion that then requires children to integrate and transfer learnings on their own. The traditional approach falls under the **transmission perspective**. Transmission adherents contend that meaning rests outside the reader and that the purpose of reading is to determine the author's intended meaning (Straw, 1990).

Development of Language, Thought, and Learning

Wood's *How Children Think and Learn* (1988) offers a complete review of theories about learning and thinking. However, a brief summary of Vygotsky's (1934/1962, 1978, 1986) ideas is presented here because some of the guiding principles for learning in the content areas will be based on his socially based theory of language development, learning, and cognition.

Vygotsky (1962, 1978) places language and communication at the heart of intellectual and personal development. He also places instruction in the forefront because he defines intelligence as the capacity of an individual to learn through instruction. In Vygotsky's view, social interaction has an important role to play in learning. In a **mediation** process, children and students learn and shape their cognitive processes in verbal interaction with more expert members (adults, parents, caregivers); they learn as a result of a joint construction of meaning. In this expert–novice participation, experts serve as mediators by assisting novices with any aspects of the text or situation the novice cannot perform. These experts, or "others," then provide the necessary **scaffolding** (Vygotsky, 1978; Wertsch, 1984).

In instructional scaffolding, the "teacher" initially provides verbal support and guidance — a "scaffold" — to help students comprehend materials or perform tasks that are beyond unassisted efforts (Lehr, 1985; Wood, Bruner, & Ross, 1976). Gradually the structure (hierarchical formats, focussing attention, demonstrations, provision of critical features or information, clarification, and extension) is withdrawn as students become increasingly able to build these types of conceptual structures themselves. Teachers in the content areas operate as "scaffolders" in the same way. In a type of collaboration, following initial teacher guidance, the students begin to assume more and more of the roles or responsibilities in their own literacy events because they no longer require some of the earlier support and guidance. Given initial and appropriate teacher direction and support, students progress on the continuum in literacy learning and eventually can do independently what they previously did with assistance. They take ownership for their own learning. They have learned to use the strategies that teachers had used earlier to support their learning. Students then can provide their own **self-mediation**. Given familiar tasks and appropriate content, students serve as their own mediators. They do so during solitary literacy events (Gordon, 1991a) or during moments of reflection, private reading, or intentional study. In other words, students "take on literacy for themselves" (Gordon, 1991a, p. 32).

To summarize, according to Vygotsky, students' potential for learning is revealed in interactions with others who are more knowledgeable than they are — others like parents, teachers, and peers who have expertise, knowledge, and ability the students may not possess. One important contribution to learning theory from Vygotsky's thinking therefore is the concept of the "zone of proximal development." The **zone of proximal development** refers to the distance or space that exists for a child, a student, or an adult between what he or she is able to do independently and what he or she can accomplish with assistance from someone who is more knowledgeable. Thus readiness for learning, in the Vygotskian sense, "involves not only the state of . . .

For Reflection 1.2
Reflect on what you remember about learning to speak, learning to read, and learning to write before and after you entered school. What do you remember about talking-to-learn, reading-to-learn, writing-to-learn, and viewing-to-learn after you started school?

---

existing knowledge but also . . . [the] capacity to learn with help" (Wood, 1988, p. 25). Individual differences in learning are explained by the fact that one of two individuals at the same level of existing knowledge or performance may have a "larger" zone of proximal development. Thus, given the same amount of instruction, the individual with greater capacity or potential to learn (given certain tasks or certain domains [disciplines] of learning) benefits more. Bearing in mind the role of mediation, we now need to examine talking-to-learn, reading-to-learn, viewing-to-learn, and writing-to-learn.

Talking-to-Learn

As stated earlier, oral language can be used as a medium of learning (Barnes, 1972, 1973, 1976; Britton, 1970), and learning takes place through expressive language or informal talk. As early as 1976, the National Association for the Teaching of English advocated a language across the curriculum movement. Studies of talk in elementary and secondary classrooms viewed language as a window on students' learning and development (Barnes, Britton, & Rosen, 1971; Barnes, 1976). Marland (1977) stated that if secondary schools assisted in language development, "learning in all areas will be helped; if attention is given to language in the content and skill subjects, language development will be assisted powerfully by the context and purpose of those subjects" (p. 3).

Implicit in Marland's statement is the need to engage students in classroom talk, in small-group discussion, and in dialogue with teachers so that students use talking as a means of understanding content. In such discussion, students formulate for themselves their understanding. Even through several digressions in any discussion, students learn to return to the main point or topic under discussion and to control and monitor their discussions and each other's contribution to the talk. Talk is active learning, rather than the kind of passive learning generally found in teacher-directed, information-giving classrooms. Students learn by talking and writing (since written discourse also is "language") as effectively as, if not more effectively than, they do by listening and reading. Pre-service teachers made the following representative entries in their journals with respect to talking-to-learn in Gordon and Hunsberger's (1991) study. As can be seen, they felt that talk promoted both understanding and enjoyment.

> After reading a piece of text, I love to discuss it with others to share different interpretations. Often I feel I learn more about the text in the discussion than in the actual reading of the material. (Aaron)

> Yes!! *When I'm finished reading I love to talk it over!* I want to tell everyone all the neat things I've learned. Especially if the other person has read the text it's interesting to listen to someone else — because often they clarify points I thought were already clear. So with my own students I hope to encourage group discussions of readings, even in the science field. I know this would be useful. (Greg)

Fillion (1979) suggests two good questions that teachers should ask themselves (from a list of eight directed at school administrators implementing a language across the curriculum policy):

1. How many teachers encourage students' "exploratory talk," to put new ideas and information into students' own language?
2. In an average day (or week) . . . , how much opportunity will an average student have to question, to talk, to write about the things she or he is expected to learn? How much opportunity does he or she have to use and apply knowledge (except on tests)? (p. 51)

Talk among students enables them to learn, to come to grips with new ideas and feelings, and to remember what they themselves have formulated. Talk also enables students to communicate: to tell others what they think or feel or what they have learned. Using oral language for learning is similar to using written language for learning (rather than using writing only for expressing what has been learned). Thought written down without much attention paid to correctness is similar to **expressive talk** (as opposed to transactional language and writing, which are more polished, more organized, more precise).

As the pre-service teachers' journal entries quoted in this chapter show, both students and teachers can determine whether students have learned, what they have learned, and how they have learned it if the students' expressive language is used as a means to gain these insights. "Language is the exposed edge of the learning process" (Fillion, 1983, p. 702). Expressive talk and expressive writing do not include such activities as verbatim oral recall or direct note-copying. They do include undirected writing activities and expressive talk:

a. *for various purposes* such as explaining, interpreting, describing, defining, giving an opinion, inferring, speculating, predicting, paraphrasing, summarizing, comparing and contrasting, giving examples and inquiring;

b. *for various results* such as developing understanding, informing, recording or reporting, reflecting, evaluating, persuading or entertaining; and,

c. *for various audiences* such as themselves, their peers, students in lower grades, adults, the outside community and, as traditionally, the teacher as the evaluator. (Fillion, 1983)

The subject areas lend themselves much better to such language use than does any language arts or English class.

Expressive talk, just like students' writing, can be not only a medium for students' learning, but also a window to students' processing; it gives teachers insights into students' thinking and learning. When students are encouraged to talk (and write), to share their questions with teachers and with their peers, to reflect on what they are doing, to reflect on what they have learned and what they still do not know, they reveal the "routes" they are following to make meaning. They reveal much more than can be inferred from products (performances, outcomes) of learning. In summary, expressive language that is informal and personal first of all prompts involvement with text and enhances motivation, and, second, helps establish relationships between the new and the known. Expressive language (talking and writing) is seen as the most powerful way of learning.

Reading-to-Learn

Learning to read and reading-to-learn are not the same, although they can be complementary (Myers, 1984). Learning to read focusses on acquiring the skills to be able to read. One reason for learning to read in the first place is to be able to read-to-learn from books and thus further enhance intellectual growth. The essence of reading-to-learn is improving one's knowledge of content. The readers who know how to read-to-learn effectively have learned and actively engage (before, during, and after reading) in mental activities to enhance their comprehension and mastery of content. When reading-to-learn, readers also respond

---

For Reflection 1.3

Stubbs (1976) observed that in secondary-school English classrooms, classroom talk was "asymmetrical . . . almost never used by students." Recall the types of activities you were involved in at the secondary-school level that would be considered talking-to-learn.

affectively and critically to the texts that they read. Successful readers have learned to "live" in some texts, or parts of texts (to respond with emotion, pleasure, or displeasure, bringing themselves into the reading).

Exercise 1.1
A Reading-to-Learn Activity

To help you clearly understand the essence of reading-to-learn (as opposed to learning to read), try this short reading-to-learn activity.

In this instance, your main aim is to read the information in such a way that you remember information after the reading. However, that does not preclude some affective responses during the reading. Let's suppose you are studying a unit on physical fitness and the systems of the body associated with it, in particular the muscular system. You have learned that in order to function efficiently muscles need both strength and endurance. You probably know that to develop strength and endurance, one must exercise. But what forms of exercise are needed? Read the following passage to learn about the kinds of exercises that develop strength and endurance.

Isometrics and Isotonics

These words are often used in reference to forms of exercise. Depending on the actual exercise, there are advantages and disadvantages to both.

Isometrics are exercises that use pressure rather than movement. Muscles contract as parts of the body are pressed against themselves or an immovable object. Isometrics include activities such as pressing arms down on tables or against walls or against themselves. The purpose of most isometric exercises is to build strength, not endurance. Muscles are used briefly to their fullest potential. The exercises take a very short period of time, which makes them appealing to some people. However, isometrics do not exercise the heart or lungs and may, in some cases, actually strain the heart.

Isotonics are exercises that involve moving an object or resistance, even your own body. The muscles contract and relax throughout the exercise. When a heavy object is moved, muscle strength is increased. For example, lifting a heavy set of weights develops strength. When a small object is used and the exercise is done many times, endurance is increased. A cyclist does an isotonic exercise when the pedals of a bicycle are moved. There is little resistance but the repetitions increase endurance.

Weight-lifters are an example of isotonic strength building when they lift the weight and isometric strength building when they hold the weight in position.

Source: From *Lifestyle 3,* by J. Campbell, 1986, Markham, ON: Globe/Modern Curriculum Press, p. 105. Reproduced with permission of Prentice Hall Inc.

Suppose, having read the passage, you understand that isometrics are exercises that build strength and isotonics are exercises that build endurance. But you are still not clear on how the muscles are exercised to develop each of these — not clear partly because you may not have the relevant background in physical education. What are you going to do to learn the differences? Likely you will reread the passage and apply some other strategies. As a reading-to-learn activity, reread the passage and monitor what you do to read-to-learn the differences.

Having reread the passage, summarize the strategies you used when you reread. Now let me share with you what I did when I reread-to-learn. First I reread parts of each paragraph. Second, as I reread parts of each paragraph, I tried to sort out my confusion by stopping and sifting through, paraphrasing what I was learning and comparing the two types of exercises. I read and responded in this way:

```
"Isometrics ... use pressure rather than movement." "Isotonics
... involve moving an object or resistance." In isometrics "mus-
cles contract." In isotonics "muscles contract and relax." What
kinds of activities are isometric and what kinds are isotonic? That
may help me see the differences. Let me go back and read.
"Isometrics include activities such as pressing arms down on
tables or against walls or against themselves." An example of iso-
tonics, hmm ... lifting a set of weights ... moving the pedals of
a bicycle ... ah, so there is movement ... and there is little resis-
tance ... but many repetitions. Actually, I think I like isotonic
exercises better probably because I tend to associate them with
sports activities I do. OK, I think I've got the content.
```

How did you and I compare? Did we use the same or different strategies to read-to-learn, strategies such as self-questioning, comparing and contrasting, and rereading to confirm understanding? Was there any emotional response to the text? Our strategies need not be identical, as expert readers are flexible in their use of strategies, using some from a repertoire, and discarding those that do not serve them effectively. Our affective responses to the text might also be the result of different associations and experiences with isotonic and isometric exercises.

———————————

Students' ability to read-to-learn should not be taken for granted just because they have reached junior or senior high school. First, the fact that students have learned to read in the elementary grades does not mean they have learned to read content area materials and to use the kinds of strategies for learning and remembering that I used (or you used) when reading the text on isometric and isotonic exercises. Although students study science, social studies, and other subjects in the elementary grades, some subject areas have no specific textbooks, and much of the reading in the content areas in the elementary school is done from a variety of library sources as part of individual and small-group research projects. Seldom do the reading-to-learn activities involve class use of textbooks. Often the difficulty in attempting to teach students how to learn to read textbooks stems from the fact that multiple sets (let alone class sets) of textbooks are not available for subject areas in the elementary school. Thus the elementary school generally does not prepare the students to read-to-learn from textbooks, and the transition to junior high school, with its intensified emphasis on, and use of, textbooks is not an easy one for students. In fact, if students are to improve their knowledge of content in the subject areas through reading, they often require new and vital skills and strategies to meet the demands of reading-to-learn the content in their junior and senior high-school textbooks.

Second, if students have learned to read expository (informational) elementary-school text, this does not mean that they can consistently apply that knowledge to text in the junior and senior high-school content areas. Reading in the subject areas at the higher levels places new and different kinds of demands on students when they are reading-to-learn. While students already possess basic reading skills, they need to use these skills in reading situations where more complex demands are made on their reading abilities. These demands are due not only to the increased difficulty level of the materials to be read, but also to the differences in the demands placed on the reader because of the way text is written in the content areas in general and in each discipline specifically. Different content area texts use pictures, charts, diagrams, equations, and special formats and require the reading of visuals as well as much integration of text and diagrams in the descriptions and explanations provided. They use discipline-specific vocabulary, concepts, and conceptual frameworks. Different subject areas require different emphases in reading different texts, be they oral, written, or visual.

Expository (explanatory) text, the main genre of all subject areas other than English, introduces information in a way that is different from **narrative text**. First, reading expository text often makes demands on prior knowledge that a reader does not possess. Much of the knowledge of the content of science, social studies, or mathematics is not part of students' everyday experiences, and therefore students have little **prior knowledge** and no personal experiences in which to anchor new and incoming oral, written, and visual information in the content areas. It is often through reading expository text and writing about it that students begin to build their background knowledge in a subject area. Second, many of the concepts that appear in any one subject area are abstract rather than concrete. The more abstract a concept, the more difficult it is to comprehend. At times, students acquire the vocabulary of a discipline without having any real understanding of the underlying concepts.

The third possible difference is that expository materials may also contain extensive, specialized vocabulary of each particular field; alternatively, these materials may use common words in new ways or in technical contexts. In addition, expository text is very compact, with large numbers of ideas and basic concepts relevant to any discipline compressed into each sentence.

Regardless of the amount of prior knowledge a reader may have, the sheer volume of concepts confronting the reader at any one time is a complicating factor. Expository materials in the content areas also have particular organizational structures for organizing and expressing information. These structures are not as readily discernible as they are in narratives; nor have students had sufficient practice in reading content materials in the elementary grades to acquire an implicit knowledge of the ways authors in each discipline organize and present the information.

Bearing in mind what has been stated in the foregoing paragraphs, you need to reflect on the question "Who better to deal with the teaching of relevant reading strategies than the subject area teacher?" Is the English teacher in a better position to teach students how to read science or mathematics texts than the subject area specialist? Conversely, if your area of specialization is social studies or science (or any other), do you feel adequately prepared to teach reading-to-learn strategies in a course such as English or mathematics? Added to that, remember the difficulties students have with independently transferring and applying across disciplines learning strategies that are common to several disciplines. The locus of instruction for reading-to-learn activities must then be each content area classroom, with the students using the actual content area materials. The aim of reading-to-learn is a functional one: to enhance the learning of content. Witness the positive comments of students in a literacy across the curriculum course with respect to the usefulness of reading-to-learn activities (Gordon & Hunsberger, 1991):

> When I began studying music at the university, I struggled in my attempts to read the music history text. I was not familiar with a lot of the terminology and really had no idea what types of things were or were not important. Only through trial and error did I learn what to read for. (Elijah)

> I find it hard to believe that some teachers (in particular the teachers I had in school) don't share strategies to help their students understand their texts and don't help students use/apply these techniques to other reading material that they encounter. (Kim)

Viewing- and Representing-to-Learn

If there is a human sense dominating contemporary society, it is the sense of sight. We take pride in being seen, seeing ahead, and looking back. The sense of sight, with its powerful telescopic, microscopic, projectionist, and virtual technologies, has come to the fore as visual thinking. Visual thinking defines what it means to be a successful, literate language user today. Certainly, oral language — listening and speaking — is the foundation of literacy. We are

---

For Reflection 1.4
Describe your recollections of reading-to-learn activities in the different subjects you studied in high school.

---

born hearing the world long before we image it, speak it, read it, or write it. However, living in the world requires the rapid acquisition of reading and writing. But reading and writing are still grounded in visual sign systems. Therefore, it is important to study visual language and thinking — viewing and representing. Viewing-to-learn enables learners to understand the historic and contemporary tensions between images and words as embedded in visual, auditory, spoken, performative, or print texts. Viewing-to-learn provides learners with a critical opportunity to see, and not just look at, such texts.

If viewing-to-learn shows the relationship between human thought and action and the senses, primarily the sense of sight, then representing is those human responses — texts — primarily featuring the sense of sight. Representing-to-learn enables learners to functionally and aesthetically respond to texts in a variety of ways (such as visually, orally, and through performance). When learners construct a responsive representation, it enables them to demonstrate understanding of and accomplishment with visual texts as having particular ways of constructing reality and influencing the perceptions of others. Representing-to-learn is a learner's specific response to a (re)presented text, which in turn becomes a viewing-to-learn text for others.

Writing-to-Learn

Writing-to-learn in the subject areas is not the same as learning to write for English composition. In writing-to-learn, the focus is on (1) the use of writing to learn content (for example, the content read), and (2) how to write the content of each subject area (e.g., reports in science, problems in mathematics).

Using Writing to Learn Content

Writing-to-learn fosters the ability to think analytically and critically (Langer & Applebee, 1987) in the subject area being studied (remember Heath's definition earlier?). "Writing is how we think our way into a subject and make it our own. Writing enables us to find out what we know and what we don't know — about whatever we're trying to learn" (Zinsser, 1988, p. 16). Yet research has shown (Applebee, 1981) that at secondary school the writing opportunities provided often restrict students by not engaging them intellectually or socially in the process. Some content area teachers also stifle reasoning through writing by focussing on the surface features of writing and not valuing writing as learning (Newell, 1986). Further, they often see writing as time lost for "covering content-area material" (p. 301).

In writing-to-learn, the focus is not solely on the writing skills themselves. Hence, if some of the conventions of written language (e.g., handwriting, capitalization, spelling, punctuation) do not interfere with meaning, content area teachers tend not to correct them or teach to improve them. However, while teachers may select and point out specific error types to students, evaluation of writing in the content areas generally is based on ability to show completeness and clarity of thought and to present the information in the logic of the discipline.

The theoretical base for the writing-to-learn movement comes from the language and learning theories of Britton (1970), Martin, D'Arcy, Newton, & Parker (1976), and Barnes (1976) in England, supported by the theoretical tenets of Vygotsky (1978) and the schema theorists (Anderson, 1994; Piaget, 1926). Schema theorists propose that learning is a process of acquiring knowledge through experience and through **assimilation** or **accommodation** (or restructuring) of knowledge structures (schemata). Assimilation requires adjustment of incoming information to fit schemata, while accommodation requires adjusting the schemata to fit new information. The latter occurs over a longer period of time and is critical, for example, to the correction of **misconceptions**. Language and learning theory states that one of the vehicles by which these types of learnings take place is through language, especially expressive language, or talk. Expressive language (talk that occurs naturally in groups of people, the most natural form of language) should thus be the vehicle by which learnings are acquired in the classroom. Expressive language (both talk and writing) is informal, personal, speculative, exploratory, searching, and digressive (Britton, 1970). It enables students to discover ideas more independently. By contrast, transactional language (formal, impersonal talk and writing) is much more prompted or directed by teacher instructions and assignment specifications (Britton, 1970). It is used not only to instruct but also to inform and to communicate to others a knowledge of content. Expressive language can be found in conjunction with transactional language, and vice versa. Writing can function in a manner similar to talk (expressive language) in the classroom (Britton, 1970).

Writing externalizes thinking and enables learners to examine and modify links made between aspects of new knowledge, between new knowledge and already possessed knowledge, and between new knowledge and learners' own world views. Writing also induces a personal involvement or engagement in learning (Emig, 1983). The experience of using writing with adolescents has confirmed that written responses go deeper than students' talk (Atwell, 1987). Writing-to-learn also enhances the process of correcting one's information if knowledge held is based on misconceptions (Schumacher & Nash, 1991).

Exercise 1.2
A Writing-to-Learn Activity

To understand more clearly writing-to-learn, try this simple activity. There are, of course, many types of writing-to-learn activities (you may, for example, be familiar with a learning log or a response journal; other activities will be suggested in chapters that follow).

Let's continue with the topic of physical fitness. You may think you know a fair amount about the topic, but let's get more specific. Think not of muscular, circulatory, or respiratory fitness. Think about cardiovascular fitness, even more specifically about aerobic fitness. Now try a simple exercise. *Before* reading the text below, write down everything you know about cardiovascular fitness. Having done that, read the following text. After reading, write on the topic again, this time integrating what you knew with what you learned.

Cardiovascular Fitness

The cardiovascular system is a term that describes the working condition of the lungs, blood vessels, and heart. With cardiovascular fitness, the body learns to take in large quantities of oxygen and use it efficiently. Cardiovascular fitness can come from aerobic exercise.

AEROBIC EXERCISE

Aerobic exercise requires your body to increase the amount of oxygen it takes in over a period of time. (*Aerobic* means "with oxygen.") This type of exercise pushes your body to increase its capacity for oxygen. It works your lungs, and, in turn, your heart works to circulate oxygen-carrying blood quickly through your body. Your heart rate is increased for a length of time so that your cardiovascular system is working at its peak. Fuel and oxygen are combined and used in your body during aerobic exercise. Your body increases its ability to process oxygen.

The purpose of aerobic exercise is to establish a balance of oxygen need and oxygen supply in your body. When you are sitting still and breathing easily, your body is in an aerobic steady state. You are getting all the oxygen you need for the activity of sitting. The goal of aerobic exercise is to have this steady state while exercising or doing a physical activity. For example, a jogger who is getting all the needed oxygen fairly easily is in an aerobic steady state. Oxygen is being provided to the body as it is required.

Aerobics are endurance-type exercises that require the body to work for a length of time. There is no rest period during the actual exercise. The physical activity is steady and continuous but not too fast.

Aerobics are moderate, rather than high, activity level exercises. This way, the heart can supply all the oxygen the muscles need for the exercise. Large muscle groups of the body are used. Walking, cycling, and swimming are aerobic exercises. Short bursts of energy and speed are not aerobic.

Regular aerobic exercise can improve the efficiency of the heart and lungs. Three to five aerobic activity sessions a week will give your body an opportunity to develop cardiovascular fitness. Each session should have 15 to 20 minutes of actual aerobic exercise with a good warm-up and cool-down in addition to that time. If you allow yourself one hour for aerobic exercise every other day, you will be well on your way to a fit cardiovascular system.

It is important to begin with mild aerobic exercise and build on this as your body becomes more fit. Aerobic exercise should make you breathe more deeply and more quickly but you should be able to talk while exercising. Know your own limit and slow down if you cannot talk during the exercise.

Walking is a good mild aerobic exercise. In fact, people should walk every day. For aerobic exercise, walk until you begin to feel tired. Do not overtire your body. Increase the distance slightly every day. Speeding up your walking will exercise your lungs.

Swimming, cycling, cross-country skiing, skating, snow-shoeing, and jogging are moderate aerobic exercises. Strenuous aerobic exercises can include racquet sports, ball games such as football and soccer, and hockey. These activities must be continual to be aerobic. Stops and starts in an activity are not aerobic. Of course, the level of activity can affect the strenuousness of an exercise. Jogging for long distances and jumping rope can be very strenuous activities.

Source: From *Lifestyle 3,* by J. Campbell, 1986, Markham, ON: Globe/Modern Curriculum Press, pp. 110–13. Reproduced with permission of Prentice Hall Inc.

You may have noticed that, while writing was a way for you to show what you already knew or what you have just learned, it was also a tool for learning. When students put their thoughts on paper in the course of the composing process, they set their purpose for writing. As they write, they tend to

1. clarify their thinking,
2. become actively engaged in dealing with the facts and generalizations, and
3. have to decide what ideas to emphasize or highlight, which ones to omit, and what relationships to make.

Often students generate new insights about the topics, and often they discover relationships about what they knew and what they learned in the reading or in the class presentation. Different feelings and associations may become evident during the process of writing.

Writing activities improve students' knowledge of topics (schemata) encountered in the content areas. Students can organize, through writing, the information presented in class or in textbooks and connect it to their prior knowledge of content. Writing in the content area classroom can be done for several purposes: to think through a concept, to clarify one's thinking, to generate ideas, to communicate to others, to aid retention, to respond aesthetically, or to express what one has learned. First-draft writing or writing-to-learn allows students to "think on paper" and to bring knowledge to consciousness. Writing is also a way to monitor one's learning.

A growing body of research and opinion concludes that writing is a powerful **strategy** for learning content (Stotsky, 1983). If a writer already knows exactly what he or she wants to say, there is no need to write about it; often writers/learners need to write before they know what they want to say (Murray, 1982). Representative entries made in training teachers' weekly journals about writing-to-learn and even about their own journal writing provide a **lived experience** of writing-to-learn (Gordon & Hunsberger, 1991) as well as support for the need to write to enhance learning.

> When I reach the end of a session of writing I find that the sequence of events I had envisioned has taken my ideas somewhere new that I did not anticipate. I may begin writing on a topic with a direction but find the facts that occur and information I have presented have led me in a new direction that I could not see when I began. In other words the beginning of the text does not match the middle or the end of it. My first log entry is such an example. When I started writing I was going to state how I felt that the course would be of little value and arranged my ideas to support that point of view. But I found, as I wrote, that my view began to change as I considered each new idea I presented. Since this is a journal I didn't go back and rewrite the beginning, but rather left it to show you my thought process. Where you start does not always match where you end up when you write. (Devon, as quoted in Gordon & Hunsberger, 1991, p. 403)

> Writing is a very personal experience for me. I often write simply to clarify what and how I think. Nobody listens to me the way my pen does and nobody reveals me the way that paper does. (Melanie)

Learning How to Write the Content of Each Discipline

Writing-to-learn can be used as a way of learning to write the content of the discipline. Some believe that as students engage more frequently in writing-to-learn activities across the subject areas, their writing skills will improve as a secondary benefit. Increased amounts of writing, however, do not necessarily lead to improved writing abilities, but informed instruction in writing will. When students are learning how to write the content of each subject area, the content area teacher is in the best position to teach the special kinds of writing required in each of the disciplines. "Who knows better than the scientist knows the kinds of writing needed in scientific endeavors?" (Walker, 1988, p. 99). It seems logical then that writing cannot remain the exclusive domain of the language arts teacher or the English composition teacher. Content area teachers need to know about the types of texts written and read in their subject area specializations as well as the most effective methods of teaching writing in their subject areas. For example, what types of texts are read and written in science as opposed to physical education, art, or mathematics? What are the best ways to guide students to read and write those texts?

A representative testimonial (from Gordon & Hunsberger, 1991) shows the value of teaching students how to write the content of a discipline:

> We were discussing types of writing we'd done in our high school classes when I suddenly remembered the perfect example from my school days to use to teach students how to write the content. In Grade 8 in a family life (living) option we had an assignment to write a paper. To do this we took notes from readings and placed the ideas we found onto cue cards. We then organized the cards and wrote our paper. This "cue card" technique is used by a lot of researchers. Last year when I was doing my honors research, it was recommended to use this strategy that I actually had learned in Grade 8 — and it wasn't learned in a language arts class. (Gustaf)

In holistic approaches to instruction such as talking, listening, and reading-, viewing-, writing-, and representing-to-learn across the curriculum, students integrate many skills and strategies to master the content. Integration is an important concept to keep in mind as you think about everything stated thus far about improving literacy across the curriculum, about improving knowledge of content through reading-to-learn and writing-to-learn activities, about expressive talk, about viewing and representing, and about transferring skills and strategies across the curriculum.

Integration

Integration can take several forms in the development of literacy across the curriculum: integration of the communication processes, integration of content and process, and integration across the curriculum (using an interdisciplinary approach).

Integration of the Communication Processes

The best-known form of integration is the use of reading, writing, speaking, and listening in a combined form for a communicative or learning purpose, not as separate subjects or as ends to be practised for their own sake.

There are many instances of integration in the language arts at the elementary-school level, where reading, writing, speaking, and listening are considered within the context of communication. Viewing is often added to this integrated communication model. Grammar, spelling, and phonics are integrated with reading and writing instead of being taught as separate subjects or in isolation from meaningful language-use situations. Some integrated activities might be built around a theme and include relevant materials, ideas, and tasks as natural and necessary elements. Some integrated activities occur in other subject areas in the elementary school. For example, when students develop a dictionary for a unit of science by interviewing others to determine the meanings of technical words, they use talking, writing, listening, and reading.

For language to play a critical role in the junior and senior high-school curriculum, you must create and encourage in your classrooms a context similar to that in the elementary classroom — a context in which there is a wide range of language use through speaking, reading, listening, and writing activities — so that students develop thinking skills and master the concepts in each content area. The balance between activities that require students to talk and write (student-centred) and those in which students listen and read (teacher-directed) has to be rethought. Teacher-directed classrooms tend to predominate in secondary schools, where students listen passively to lectures and then regurgitate the text verbatim. Student-centred classrooms tend to be more prevalent in the elementary grades, where students talk, listen, write, and read to interact with text more actively through peer–peer and teacher–student interactions, and through the use of various teaching/learning activities.

One activity that uses language in an integrated way is Extending Concepts through Language Activities, or ECOLA (Smith-Burke, 1982). ECOLA presents a snapshot view both of language use in a subject area and of integration because of its use of (1) language to develop concepts/understanding through talk and understanding through listening, (2) processing strategies for reading text, and (3) writing to clarify one's thinking. ECOLA involves all the communication processes in one activity. (While such integration is not always possible within specific activities, many learning/teaching activities incorporate at least two or three of the communication skills.) An activity such as ECOLA reinforces the central role of language in the learning process. The movement between linguistic forms and functions is natural, and the language users (the students) are often not even aware of the interfacing and crossovers that occur among the communication skills.

ECOLA exemplifies a student-centred activity involving active use of language rather than passive reception.

ECOLA focusses on improving comprehension of content and, in addition, "is designed to aid junior and senior high school students in becoming independent comprehenders [of content materials]" (Smith-Burke, 1982, p. 164). Based on research in comprehension and **metacognition** (thinking about one's thinking), ECOLA was developed by Smith-Burke for use in content area classrooms. It can be used with narrative, descriptive, or informational (expository) text. ECOLA employs language as it is used in settings that demand communication for real social purposes. Students are encouraged to talk with one another, read, write, and listen as naturally as they would outside formal school settings. They engage in relating reading and other language activities so that they can understand and communicate. In the context of this learning activity, integrated use of all the language arts is required.

The purpose for using ECOLA in this chapter is to demonstrate how talking, reading, writing, and listening can be integrated in one activity to promote active rather than passive learning.

Exercise 1.3
ECOLA

Read the following portion of a chapter on probability. Then follow the five steps that constitute the ECOLA procedure.

Probability

Probability is a subject that plays an increasingly important role in our lives. For example, in recent years, Environment Canada has made rain predictions in terms of probability. On any day, you can turn on the radio or television and hear the weather forecaster say something like ". . . The probability of rain is 50% today, rising to 80% tomorrow . . . ." Correct interpretation of this statement is important to farmers, construction managers, tour operators, and many others whose activities depend on the weather.

Many other disciplines use probability to describe uncertainty. For example, in approving the construction of a nuclear power station, regulatory agencies estimate the probability of major disasters at the proposed station, such as earthquakes, fires and other accidents. These probabilities must be sufficiently small before construction is approved. Applications of probability also arise in medicine, computer science, geology and many other fields.

Another way probability is encountered is through games of chance such as dice and cards, lotteries, prize draws, horse races and so on. For example, if you study a lottery ticket you will find printed on it a statement like, "The odds against winning the grand prize are approximately 688 424 to 1, but will vary with the number of tickets sold." The probability of winning the grand prize corresponding to those odds is 1/688 425. (Note that games of chance and lotteries are used in this book only to teach and explain concepts in statistics and probability. The authors certainly do not advocate gambling in any form.)

In this chapter, we shall develop a mathematical description of probability, which is called a probability model, and look at some applications. There are many very important uses for such models. Unfortunately, the most useful examples are too complex for this text, but a thorough understanding of the concepts in this chapter will enable you to master more advanced applications in a future course.

PROBABILITY MODELS

A probability model is used to describe a situation in which the outcome is uncertain. For example, suppose a die is rolled, and the topmost face is observed. The possible outcomes are 1, 2, 3, 4, 5, and 6, and it is not certain which face will occur. We list the possible outcomes in a set *S*, called the *sample space.*

$$S = \{1, 2, 3, 4, 5, 6\}$$

Since the die is symmetric, if it is rolled a large number of times, each face will probably occur about one-sixth of the time. This behaviour is described by assigning probabilities 1/6 to each outcome in the sample space.

The sample space and the associated probabilities define a probability model. Note that in any roll of the die, one and only one of the outcomes in *S* can occur. Also, the probabilities are all between 0 and 1, and their sum is 1.

A *probability model* consists of a sample of outcomes. To each outcome, the probability of the outcome, a real number between 0 and 1, is assigned. The sum of these probabilities is 1.

An *event A* is a subset of the sample space. The probability that *A* occurs, denoted by *P(A)*, is the sum of the probabilities of the outcomes in *A*.

We are often interested in specific events such as an even-numbered face being topmost. This event corresponds to the subset *A* of the sample space, where

$$A = \{2, 4, 6\}$$

The subset

$$B = \{1, 2, 3, 4, 5\}$$

corresponds to the event that 6 does not appear when the die is rolled.

An event occurs if one of the outcomes in the event occurs. The probability that the event A occurs, denoted by *P(A)*, is the sum of the probabilities of the outcomes in *A*, so

$$P(A) = 1/6 + 1/6 + 1/6$$
$$= 1/2$$

Source: From *Finite Mathematics*, by R.G. Dunkley, 1988, Toronto: Holt, Rinehart and Winston, pp. 203–204. Reproduced by permission.

Now that you have read the text on "Probability," follow the steps set out for teachers.

Step 1: Setting a communicative purpose. First, you need to determine what the students should glean from the text (i.e., set the general purpose for reading). Also you must decide what type of support the students need. For example, it may be necessary to discuss important ideas or brainstorm on the topic. Finally, you must determine the actual task to which the students will respond (e.g., several questions for reading might be subsumed under the general purpose).

Step 2: Silent reading for a purpose and a criterion task. Students should be reminded of their purpose(s) for reading and be able to support their understandings with background knowledge, ideas from text, and/or reasoning.

Step 3: Crystallizing comprehension through writing. At this step students develop the ability to self-monitor and verbalize what they do not understand. Each student *and the teacher* write a response to commit themselves to an interpretation and write down what they find confusing. For clarification, they are urged to ask other students.

Step 4: Discussing the lesson. Organized into groups of about four, students are expected to discuss interpretations, compare responses, and challenge conclusions within a given time limit.

Step 5: Writing and comparing. The final step is to have students write, in small groups or individually, a second interpretation. In a group, a consensus must be reached by discussion. Following completion of the revised interpretation, students are encouraged to discuss the changes made and to talk about the strategies they found useful in understanding the text.

I have set the overall communicative purpose for you in step 1. It focusses on learning and recall of content. Nevertheless, your response in the course of reading for content may also be a personal or emotional one. While it is not possible for me to discuss with you key ideas or thoughts and feelings about the topic, you might now do this independently. Think about everything you know about probability from reading, watching television, playing board games, and talking with others. Thus step 1 includes generating an overall purpose or question and some sub-questions to guide the reader. These are provided for you below so that you may proceed with the exercises.

1. Overall Purpose: What roles does the concept of probability play in our lives?
2. Sub-Tasks/Sub-Questions:
   a. What is a probability model?
   b. What is a sample space? Give an example. What is the probability of any outcome in the sample space you used as an example?
   c. What is the probability that event *A* occurs in your example?

In order to build student independence, the responsibility for setting the purpose (following such teacher-modelled questions as listed above) is eventually placed on the students.

Find a partner or two and, using the text on probability, work your way through the ECOLA procedure beginning with step 2.

When you have finished the activity, think about the responses to the following questions:

- What images/pictures did this text portray to individuals?
- What feelings and associations did each reader bring to the reading?
- Did your examples and interpretations vary even on material that leaves less room for different interpretations than does narrative text?
- How much did you already know about probability before you read the text?
- How did reading, writing, listening, and talking to others help you answer the questions and make sense of the explanation?
- How much information came from the text and how much from each person's background knowledge?

Let's review what has ensued in ECOLA. As you worked through the steps, beginning with step 2, you read silently for the outlined purposes, then, based on your own experiences, associations, examples, and knowledge, wrote your understandings of the text in response to the questions. In step 3, you discussed the questions in small groups, where you listened to clarify and support your interpretations with justification from text, background, or reasoning. In step 4, you shared, through talk, your interpretations in small groups to sort out your confusions, to raise questions, to note similarities and differences in your understandings, and to alter your ideas if new insights were gleaned. Finally, in step 5, you wrote a second (and consensual) interpretation of the text in small groups, or individually if consensus could not be reached. After completing the revised interpretation, your metacognitive awareness of how you thought and what you did was heightened through discussion of your prior knowledge, feelings, questioning strategies, associations, inferential strategies, comprehension monitoring techniques, and fix-up or repair strategies used during ECOLA.

It is, of course, your task to model effective learning strategies and to provide feedback for students who are experiencing some difficulty comprehending materials and/or making interpretations. The integration of reading, writing, and talking with and listening to others in an integrated activity such as ECOLA helps students focus not only on the constructive nature of the comprehension process but also on the need to constantly monitor their understanding against text and background knowledge, and to understand the perception and interpretation of others to make sure that their interpretation of content also makes sense. The following journal responses made by teachers-in-training (Gordon & Hunsberger, 1991) provide some insight into the positive value of integration of the communication processes:

> I detest the idea of assigned reading . . . just like some of the other students I have spoken to. I have become an expert at avoiding texts at all costs. Maybe if teachers turned reading into an activity, where there is an interaction and explanation from the teacher and fellow peers on the process of reading, assigned reading might lose its stigma. Such a strategy may very well provide the social interaction with which readers can test, confirm or reject ideas gained from reading. If I read for my own knowledge and enjoyment or with the idea that some activity will arise from it, my whole perspective changes. I begin to interact with the text more, formulating ideas, searching for answers, and making predictions. (George)

> The group discussions were very effective and made me realize the amount of resources we have between a few group members on such a vague topic. What I found amusing was the number of students giving their explanations for the short text on the elephant hunters and giving detailed examples about the topography and elephants in western Congo . . . But I learnt that not everybody perceives things the way I do and it makes you realize the importance of communication between peers. (Jingha)

Integration of Content and Process

In many secondary-school classrooms, teachers concentrate only on teaching the content of the discipline and on the quality "end" product (i.e., the knowledge of content) as measured by tests and examinations. It has been found that the more difficulty a student has in trying to understand a text, the more likely the teacher will try to explain the content of the text rather than show the student how to figure out what is in the text (MacGinitie, 1984). Teachers who emphasize content assume that students have a solid understanding of techniques and apply them for comprehension of text.

Other educators believe that the main emphasis should be on teaching students to make sense of the content — that is, on teaching the process used to learn content — downplaying the quality of the end-product. Those who emphasize process assume that students, especially the average and below average, need to be taught how to make sense of the text in order to better learn the content.

Neither approach is satisfactory. Process should not be separated from content nor from expectations with respect to the product. The intent should be to teach content at the same time as teaching students how to process the content they are reading for maximal mastery of content. The intent is to integrate content and process instruction for the best result. The focus then is to develop specific strategies to understand the content. Many of these strategies involve talking-, listening-, reading-, viewing-, and writing-to-learn. The processing strategies are integrated as part of the lesson so that the learning of content is maximized. The subject area lessons will contain content objectives (the essential ideas), process objectives (how one acquires the ideas and understandings), and product expectations (criteria to be met in reading, writing, listening, and viewing of content) as essential ingredients.

Moore, Readence, and Rickelman (1986) present two arguments for helping students improve their reading and writing skills in conjunction with learning content: motivation and transfer. If the skills and strategies are integrated with content matter, students are motivated to use them to learn the content because they can see their usefulness. In addition, if skills and strategies are presented in the subject area classrooms, immediate application on, or transfer to, the content area can be made.

Just as we need to consider the integration of reading, writing, speaking, viewing, and listening for concept development (as in ECOLA), we need to consider integration of the process and the product goals or the process and content objectives. Roehler, Duffy, and Meloth (1984) refer to such an approach as the **process-into-content** approach to direct instruction. They stress that content is the context in which process knowledge is applied. In other words, teachers cannot teach processing strategies in isolation (see section on "situated cognition," p. 49). Based on what we now know from research in metacognition (Brown, 1980; Brown et al., 1981) and from the strategic behaviours employed by good readers (Roehler, Duffy, & Meloth, 1984), teachers should first share with students the knowledge of how one reads to be a good comprehender so that they can become aware of these strategies. Second, students should be taught how to apply these behaviours.

The integration of content and process can be operationalized in any individual lesson plan (see Box 1.1). One example of teaching a processing strategy at the same time as teaching content in a mathematics lesson is to teach students the tangent of an angle at the same time as teaching them to integrate the reading of text and figures. In other words, to teach the content of mathematics (i.e., the tangent of an angle), emphasis needs to be placed on improving students' skills at using figures to improve their comprehension of written text.

Integration across the Curriculum

The third kind of integration is integration across the subject (content) areas. Although more will be written on this topic in Chapter 4, some introductory

Box 1.1
Parts of the Daily Lesson Plan

Grade Level _____   Subject _____   Lesson Duration _____

1. LESSON PURPOSES

Content (the essential ideas) and process (how one acquires the understanding or ideas) purposes should be stated clearly and precisely. (This part is primarily for the instructor. The more precise teachers are in stating purposes, the better they will be able to plan and teach a successful lesson.)

2. PRELIMINARY PREPARATIONS

This involves any special arrangements needed for carrying out the lesson plan, such as furniture and special equipment or materials.

3. INTRODUCTION

The introduction includes the following three areas:
a) Relating the lesson to the students' past experiences or previous teaching.
b) Using motivating techniques to gain the attention and interest of students.
c) Informing students about the purposes of the lesson in language they can understand. (Students' knowledge of the lesson purposes is important because it helps them to know what they are expected to accomplish.)

4. DEVELOPMENT

This is the heart of the lesson. Each step in the teacher-directed sequence is enumerated. The questions, examples, materials, and activities used to help the students to attain the purposes are stated. Teacher modelling, use of examples, and direct explanation are aspects of this component. Student-directed activities or student involvement should also be included.

5. SUMMARY AND EVALUATION

a) The summary ties the loose ends together and makes sure that learning is complete.
b) The purposes should be restated, and evaluation should provide evidence that the desired outcomes have been achieved.
c) The progress and interest of the students may be noted and standards of work evaluated.

6. FOLLOW-UP ACTIVITIES FOR INDEPENDENT PRACTICE

Assignments based on the lesson are explained and given.

comments need to be made at this point. As mentioned earlier, this type of integration is more readily manageable in the elementary classroom, where (for subject areas other than music and physical education where there may be a subject area specialist who teaches only these subjects to all grades) the homeroom teacher is usually a generalist who teaches all content subjects. This arrangement enables the elementary-school teacher to (1) draw on common themes to plan assignments that transcend subject areas, (2) assist students with integration of content knowledge across subject areas, and (3) teach students to apply similar strategies across the curriculum. Even pre-service secondary-school teachers expressed concerns about students' ability to transfer strategies across subject areas. Note this journal entry (Gordon & Hunsberger, 1991) made by a pre-service teacher who shows a concern for a lack of interdisciplinary approaches at the secondary level.

> . . . students tend to segregate strategies . . . this is for math, this is for science, etc. Thus it would be helpful for the math teacher, say, to coordinate with the LA teacher and have students apply some of these same strategies to math. (Taylor)

The concept of integration in the elementary school has often been expanded to include all of the visual and performing arts (music, drama) as well as the content areas (mathematics, science, or social studies), similar to the idea of the *integrated day*. In the integrated day (a concept from early childhood education), the content areas of language arts, mathematics, and social studies are taught within a theme throughout the school day rather than introduced as separate subjects in particular time slots.

Integration across the curriculum in junior and senior high school requires co-operative planning (and perhaps even co-ordinating class schedules) with teachers who are teaching the other subject areas, since assignments are based on a common theme. One teacher we know reports very successful integration of other subjects with the language arts at the Grade 9 level (Hentze, 1989). Based on common themes and in co-operation with other teachers, her approach integrated social studies and science with the language arts, language arts with the fine arts, and language arts with physical education. In the social studies–language arts integration, for example, students wrote position papers, précis, biographies, character sketches, plays, short stories, descriptive paragraphs, and poetry based on social studies content. Class study of the novel *Oliver Twist* was integrated with a discussion of the Industrial Revolution in social studies. This theme was eventually integrated with the fine arts, resulting in a stage production of *Oliver Twist* involving dance, band, singing, and stage props. Another example of this teacher's integration of language arts with social studies was the use of current world events as motivational devices for creative writing. She used an article from a local newspaper about an Australian family supposedly abducted by a UFO as a springboard for students' short stories, wherein they assumed the role of one of the kidnapped family members. The stories were later displayed at a local shopping mall during Education Week.

Working in collaboration with science teachers, this teacher also integrated science with the language arts. One project in this thematic unit required students to write letters to a professor of cryonics (the freezing and storing of dead bodies). The students needed to grapple not only with the content of science but also with the moral and emotional issues raised by cryonics as well as the mechanics and format of business letters.

In the language arts–physical education integration, this teacher again used the content of a subject area as a launching pad for developing themes and language activities. She often used the school's track and field meet or an interschool basketball game as the basis for short story writing on athletic competitions.

Such an approach encouraged the interaction of the students' knowledge systems as well as the integration of their cognitive and affective responses in their reading and writing. Without this kind of response, teachers create "mechanical readers [and writers] whose ability to perceive nuance, to appreciate analogy, to penetrate metaphor, and to understand implication will be seriously limited" (Eisner, 1978, p. 18). Teachers need to encourage students to strengthen their imaginations (Eisner, 1978). Students "begin to own their learning; in the process, they hone the basic skills of reading, writing, listening, seeing, and yes, feeling and collaborating" (Ricco, 1989, p. 22).

Many other teachers have reported successful integration across subject areas. A good example of an integrated approach is the *thematic unit* (a series of lessons and activities on a theme within a unit of study) developed by Seminoff (1983, pp. 135–58). In these units, students explore topics that are relevant to their lives to develop a deeper understanding of how to explore topics on their own. For example, English and social studies classes can combine a reading of Dickens's *David Copperfield* with the study of industrialization (Ricci, 1985). Students can learn about relevant political and social issues through talk (discussion), reading, and writing. A number of interdisciplinary activities in the social studies involve integrating literature, journalism, and drama, thus creating an interdisciplinary environment (Holbrook, 1987). This type of integration not only combines various aspects of history, geography, and civics but also serves to unify the curriculum (Holbrook, 1987) so that students begin to understand how seemingly separate areas interrelate and how they affect their lives. Ian Kilpatrick (in Korchinski, 1991), a high-school counsellor, maintains that "we need a more holistic approach to education, with cooperative learning programs . . . . Rather than having Social Studies 10, 20, 30, you could have Environmental Concerns 10, 20, 30 . . . which would look at what you're doing in chemistry, in physics" (p. 16). Those concerned with ecological education also want "to go beyond the boxes we call disciplines to see things in their larger context" (Orr, 1993, p. 18). At the senior high-school level, one of the teachers with whom we work teaches a Grade 11 humanities program that offers English, social studies, and art history as one course (MacDonnell, 1992). The program focusses on interconnecting and contextualizing knowledge by covering topics in English literature, art, and social studies, from prehistoric times up to the Renaissance period.

In an integrated approach, one must be careful to respect the different conventions of the subject areas involved. For example, if *David Copperfield* were studied from a historical perspective, the questions asked and the criteria used to judge successful acquisition of learnings would be different than if the novel were studied from a literary perspective or a visual or performance arts perspective. Teachers must also avoid focussing on trivial and conceptually unrelated learning activities in the integration process (the thematic units presented in Chapter 11 are good examples of relevant activities).

Thaiss (1983), an advocate of approaching traditional curriculum in different ways that restructure it away from more coverage of content and away from blocks of time as units to teach a subject, proposes the creation of opportunities to learn through activities such as discussion and in-class writing projects without the strict separation of subject areas. These are new and/or different directions junior and senior high-school education might want to take in the future. Schools themselves need to change philosophically and structurally if learning and teaching are going to change. For integration to be a success, teachers need to reflect more on the complexities of the school culture in which the curriculum (and content literacy) is implemented (O'Brien, Stewart, & Moje, 1995).

Summary

This chapter provided a framework for thinking about how students can become literate in the subject areas by being able to read and write in each discipline and by using reading, writing, talking, listening, and viewing as

---

For Reflection 1.5

Can you recall if integration across the curriculum took place during your terms as teachers or secondary-school students? What school contexts made such changes possible? What types of integration and/or interdisciplinary arrangements were part of those content learning experiences?

ways to think their way into a subject. The main aim of content literacy (or literacy across the curriculum) is knowledge of content. Talking, listening, reading, writing, and viewing are related language processes that develop concurrently over time. Reading-, writing-, talking-, and viewing-to-learn are ways to enhance content literacy and are thus an integral part of the subject area curriculum. Teaching students how to read to comprehend content area text and how to use writing to improve learning of content, as well as involving them in exploratory talk, form the basis of content area literacy instruction. The notion of text is expanded to include pictures, oral presentations, and films. One important guiding learning principle (based on Vygotsky's work) is the mediation provided to novice learners by expert readers, writers, and speakers (e.g., teaching parents). Students gradually assume the mediating role and no longer require earlier support or instruction. In such holistic approaches to instruction as content literacy, the concept of integration becomes important. Students can better learn the content of their subject areas by integrating communication skills (reading, writing, talking, viewing, and listening); integrating the teaching of processing strategies with the teaching of content; and integrating across subject areas by drawing on common themes/topics in language arts, fine arts, academic subjects, and option courses.

Questions for Further Reflection

1. What do you now understand about "being literate in a content area"?
2. What are appropriate "texts" to use in the content areas?
3. Give two examples each of reading-to-learn, writing-to-learn, talking-to-learn, viewing-to-learn, and representing-to-learn activities in your subject area specialization.
4. Begin your own writing-to-learn activity by keeping a response journal in which you reflect on some of the key ideas in each chapter.
5. Give one example in your subject area specialization of (a) integrating communication skills, (b) integrating content with the processing strategies, and (c) integrating themes and learning activities across subject areas.
6. What factors might account for the lack of integration in the teaching of the subject areas?
7. Do you think it is part of your responsibility as a subject area teacher to help your students talk, read, and write content in the subject? Why or why not?

Key Terms

Accommodation
Assimilation
Collaborative approaches
Content literacy
Content-specific
Diverse learners
Expository text
Expressive language
Expressive talk
Integration
Language processes
Literacy
Lived experience
Mediation
Metacognition
Metacognitive theory
Misconceptions
Morphology
Narrative text

Phonology
Poetic language
Prior knowledge
Process-into-content
Reading-to-learn
Scaffolding
Self-mediation
Semantics
Strategic readers
Strategy
Syntax
Talking-to-learn
Text
Transactional language
Transmission perspective
Viewing-to-learn
Writing-to-learn
Zone of proximal development

CHAPTER TWO

Literacy Processes

Questions to Consider for this Chapter

1. How do different conceptions of the reading process underpin the types of literacy activities that teachers use in the content areas?

2. Why can the experience of reading a novel be different from, or similar to, that of reading a chapter in a subject area like science?

3. How is the experience of rereading a text different from the experience of reading it the first time?

4. Why do readers have different interpretations of the same text? How can teachers accommodate them?

5. How do perspectives of writing as process influence the kinds of writing-to-learn tasks used in the content areas?

6. How are reading and writing related? How do these relationships influence instruction in the content area classrooms?

7. If you give your students a writing task in your subject area, how can you guide their writing?

8. How do students develop control of reading and writing processes used in different subject area activities?

Overview

This chapter describes the literacy activities of reading and writing. It focusses first on pre-service teachers' perceptions of the reading process. It then elaborates on conceptions of reading as a cognitive/metacognitive, affective, and transactive activity. The use of trade books to complement the content area textbook by making reading affectively rewarding is discussed. A section on conceptions of writing, obtained from content area students, follows. Writing is then presented as a cognitive, sociocognitive, and transactive activity. Again, through **think-alouds**, writers are assisted in examining their own writing processes. The relationship between reading and writing is then discussed. The chapter concludes with a section on developing independence in learning (reading and writing).

Perceptions of the Reading Process

Chapter 1 pointed out that pre-service teachers are sometimes resistant to content literacy instruction. This resistance may exist partly because of **perceptions** of what occurs during the literacy processes of reading and writing and also because of teachers' beliefs as to their responsibilities in these literacy activities.

Exercise 2.1
Perceptions of the Reading Process

Jot down your definition of reading. Now read the passage that follows and write down what you understand of the content. State your affective response to the passage.

> It is highly unsettling for some to come into close contact with them. Far worse to gain control over them and then to deliberately inflict pain on them. The revulsion caused by this punishment is so strong they will not take part in it at all. Thus there exists a group of people who seem to revel in the contact and punishment as well as the rewards associated with both. Then there is another group of people who shun the whole enterprise: contact, punishment and rewards alike.
>
> Members of the first group share modes of talk, dress, and deportment. Members of the second group, however, are as varied as all humanity.
>
> Then there is a group of others, not previously mentioned, for the sake of whose attention all this activity is undertaken. They, too, harm the victims, though they do it without intention of cruelty. They simply follow their own necessities. However, they may inflict the cruelest punishment of all, sometimes — but not always — they themselves suffer as a result.
>
> *Source:* From Instructor's Manual to accompany *Understanding Reading Problems: Assessment and Instruction*, 2nd ed., by J.W. Gillett and C. Temple, 1986. Copyright © 1986 by J.W. Gillett and C. Temple. Reproduced by permission of Addison Wesley Educational Publishers, Inc.

Did you find the process of reading and summarizing the content an easy task? Why or why not? Could you decode the words? Could you understand the sentences? Could you identify the main topic? What associations and feelings did you bring to the passage? Why? How many ideas could you recall? Did the whole thing make sense to you in such a way that your recall was coherent? How did you feel after you read the passage?

As you experienced in Exercise 2.1, reading is more than decoding (matching sounds to symbols, recognizing whole words, using context to figure out pronunciation), although decoding and attending to what the words and phrases mean is certainly part of the process. In efforts to make sense of the passage or construct meaning, you pronounced the words, you probably anticipated some words in the sequence from your knowledge of word order (syntax), and you understood individual words; even phrases and whole sentences made sense to you, but the text likely did not all fit together in such a way that it had global meaning. If asked what this passage was about, and if asked to recall the key ideas, you would likely experience difficulty answering. In fact, you probably reacted quite negatively to the exercise. When this activity was performed by students, the responses to the question "What is the main topic?" ranged from "It's about teaching" to "It's about gangs" to "It's about prisoners." You, too, probably searched for (and at this moment may still be searching) for some context, some association, some prior knowledge that would help you bring meaning to this passage. What happened in this instance is that you were denied access to your prior knowledge because the title, which gave the topic of the passage, was withheld from you. The title is "Fishing Worms." Now that you can bring your prior knowledge to bear and some of your personal associations and feelings, reread the passage to see what you focus on and/or how much easier the passage is to understand, to remember, and to enjoy. Another factor that obscured the meaning is that the passage is not well structured (organized). Students often encounter reading problems when textbooks are written in unfriendly (inconsiderate) ways. (See Chapter 12 for more on **considerate (friendly)** and **inconsiderate (unfriendly)** text.)

Data collected from students in secondary-school subject area specializations (Gordon & Hunsberger, 1991) provide some insights as to what student teachers initially understood (upon course entry) about reading processes. Their responses revealed several levels of understanding. Some came to the course assuming that reading was **decoding** and/or that reading was a linear, cognitive process with interpretation based solely on information coming from the text. To read was to get the literal meaning of text. Other pre-service teachers broadened their definitions to include implicit meaning. Some representative perceptions from pre-service students are listed below.

Reading is the ability to pronounce words. (Morgan)

To understand/comprehend a collection of letters that make words, words that make phrases, phrases that make sentences, sentences that make up paragraphs. (Jagit)

Some beginning teachers viewed reading as synonymous with **comprehension** or understanding. They wrote the following:

Being able to take from material the key points or message that is trying to be communicated or that the individual wishes to extract from the material. (Marcella)

A few students viewed reading as a much more **interactive**, cognitive process and presented definitions such as:

Reading is the ability to understand the written word and relate it to past experience so that it takes on meaning. (Anwar)

Reading is primarily a solitary activity (though not exclusively) involving an interaction between an individual and a written text and the subsequent interpretation of meaning within that text. (Dexter)

About one-quarter of the teacher-education students added **aesthetic** (or affective) and/or reading-to-learn dimensions to the reading process.

Entails recognition (i.e., of words), understanding, interpretation and evaluation — both objective (what is the author saying *literally*) and subjective (e.g., personal emotional response). (Jan)

A process by which we can entertain ourselves and learn just about anything we wish to learn about. (Mel)

At this point we need to look closely at what is known about the literacy events of reading and writing. Understanding more about the processes of reading and writing may bring an awareness of thoughts, feelings, and associations during these activities. This awareness enables teachers to more readily share ways of processing with students and to discuss with them the feelings experienced from the reading. Understanding more about reading and writing may also enable subject area teachers to plan for and integrate instruction of process with the instruction of content in classrooms and to encourage students to become involved both cognitively and affectively with text.

We turn now to an examination of what theorists and researchers working from several different perspectives tell us about reading. As we experienced in our reading of "Fishing Worms," reading is more than decoding and comprehending individual units of text.

Reading as a Cognitive and Metacognitive Activity

As the excerpts from student teachers in the last section revealed, reading has traditionally been viewed as a linear, routinized activity in which expert readers automatically applied a set of discrete skills and the reading processes were broken down into separate components. The teaching of reading "skills" meant moving from part to whole, sequenced according to a continuum of growth that was believed to characterize the development of readers. As mentioned in Chapter 1, teaching young children (and illiterate adults) to read typically began with teaching letters of the alphabet and their corresponding sounds, followed by blending syllables into words and linking words into sentences and phrases. The curriculum focussed on a series of word identification and comprehension exercises.

In the past fifteen to twenty years, however, researchers in cognitive psychology, reading education, and metacognition (awareness of, and control over, thinking processes) have demonstrated that reading is an interactive, **constructive process** (Garner, 1987; Paris, Lipson, & Wixson, 1983). Expert readers set their purposes and engage in strategic reasoning, which includes accessing relevant prior knowledge and experiences as needed, constructing meaning by combining prior experiences with information from the text, responding or reacting to text as they read, and monitoring their comprehension through awareness of and control over processes. Encounters with text involve thinking processes, which construct meaning. These processes may include predicting, confirming, integrating, attention focussing, discriminating, analyzing, associating, inferring, synthesizing, and generalizing. However, it is the prior knowledge (and prior experiences) that readers possess that is one of the most important variables in the cognitive view of reading.

Background or Prior Knowledge

Much of what we know about the role of prior knowledge in a reading situation comes from schema theory. Schema theory explains how we acquire, store, and use information. According to schema theory (Ruddell & Unrau, 1994), the declarative, procedural, and conditional knowledge structures (schemata) that students bring to any learning situation determine how much will be comprehended and learned from text. **Declarative knowledge** includes the "what" knowledge of language, facts, concepts, theories, and events in the world. **Procedural knowledge** consists of "how to" skills and strategies for application and use of knowledge. **Conditional knowledge** is the awareness of knowledge use; it is the "when" and "why" knowledge that allows for application of declarative and procedural knowledge. **Schemata** (background or prior knowledge) are abstract representations of the knowledge acquired through experience and stored in memory in a hierarchical organization. For example, an overarching schema such as "vehicles" would include more specific schemata such as types of vehicles (cars, trucks) and types of cars (Acura, Honda, Lamborghini). Schemata continue to develop through further experience. In an expanded view of schema theory (Spiro, 1988), "chunks" of knowledge from existing hierarchical structures are used to assemble new meanings representative of "texts" far more complex than those in the hierarchy. In other words, the process of comprehension is much more complex than "filling slots" with specific incoming information.

Personal and world knowledge and experience are believed to be stored as "image" schemata. World knowledge includes texts read and viewed in the past — printed texts, events, oral communications, music, ritual, and gesture (Ruddell & Unrau, 1994). **Intertextuality** (the process of connecting current texts to past texts) then plays an important role in meaning making (Bakhtin, 1981). From the schematheoretic perspective, then, meaning does not reside in the text, but is constructed by the reader on the basis of schemata in memory and in incoming information. Schemata play an active, constructive role in the comprehension of the world and of texts heard, viewed, or read. They may result in a learner ignoring or altering incoming information and may lead to particular interpretations of text. For example, some learners may view *Gulliver's Travels* as a series of adventures rather than as a satire on politics, academia, and society. Experiences and incoming information from text, in turn, shape the schemata that are stored in memory. Reading comprehension, then, is bridging the new and the known, that is, bridging information from a reader's head with information from a text (Pearson & Johnson, 1978). In this interaction, meaning resides not only in the text but also within the reader.

Schema theorists Wilson and Anderson (1986), after reviewing a decade of research on the role of background (or prior) knowledge in comprehension, concluded that "the knowledge that a reader brings to a text is a principal determiner of how that text will be comprehended, and what may be learned and remembered" (p. 32). While it has been shown that well-developed and appropriate prior knowledge has a facilitative effect on comprehension, it has also been shown that such knowledge can inhibit comprehension (Pace, Marshall, Horowitz, Lipson, & Lucido, 1989). Different perspectives, experiences, personal belief systems, and sociocultural backgrounds not only encourage different interpretations of text but can also adversely affect the comprehension and interpretation of text (Pace et al., 1989). Some prior knowledge (schemata) is more cognitive in nature, some is primarily *affective* (affect deals with emotion, attitude, motivation, interest, confidence, beliefs, values, and feelings) (Cowan, 1982). Knowledge structures with affective components tend to be the most resistant to change by incoming information as these concepts tend to be viewed more personally. Misconceptions about natural phenomena (e.g., our climate is warmer in summer because we are closer to the sun) tend to fall in this category of prior knowledge with affective components. Prior knowledge sometimes needs to be fine-tuned, or, as in the case of misconceptions, completely restructured.

Initially, schema theorists established that prior knowledge consisted not only of knowledge of content (the substance of texts) but also of knowledge of structure (an underlying organization of texts). Gradually, however, prior knowledge has emerged as an even more complex and multidimensional construct, one that is idiosyncratic (depending on the learner) and that consists of different facets of knowledge (Valencia & Stallman, 1989). The present schematheoretic view that prior knowledge is much more multidimensional than previously thought (Valencia & Stallman, 1989) brings together two positions, one from cognitive psychology and the other, **reader response theory**, from text interpretation theory. In reader response theory, readers' feelings, subjective responses, and personal, idiosyncratic thoughts (many of which have their roots in prior knowledge) are always considered important and relevant in the reading of text (see the section entitled "Reading as Transaction" below). However, just because a reader, writer, listener, or speaker possesses any or all facets of the requisite prior knowledge does not guarantee that he or she will necessarily access or use that background knowledge in the comprehension/composing processes. Current research (Phillips, 1988; Norris & Phillips, 1994) shows that it is the quality of thinking and not the amount of prior knowledge that distinguishes proficient readers from their less proficient peers. Teachers need not only to develop and/or expand students' store of information on a topic, but also to assist students with activities that teach them strategies to utilize that background knowledge for better comprehension (Pearson, 1982). Such activities might include brainstorming to trigger ideas and issues related to the topic, categorizing the ideas, predicting selection content before reading new information on the topic, and thinking aloud to show them how readers need to reason through their own repertoires of knowledge and strategies to interpret text.

Just as important as background or prior knowledge to the mastery of content through reading is the development of students' knowledge of text structure.

Knowledge of Text Structures

Expository (explanatory) text, the kind of text one finds in most of the content areas, is written to inform the reader about a specific topic. Expository text generally contains an explicit or implicit topic sentence containing the main idea and then subordinate ideas to support the main idea. All the ideas are organized into text structures. Text structures are the author's arrangements of main and subordinate ideas in text. These organizations or patterns include listing of ideas (enumeration), sequencing of ideas according to a time order, comparing and contrasting ideas, describing characteristics of ideas, discussing causes and effects of ideas, and addressing the problems presented by certain ideas as well as their solutions. However, expository text, unlike narrative, has no one recognizable pattern (Mulcahey & Samuels, 1987). Several different organizational patterns may be present in the overall structure of a particular text. For example, any one paragraph may contain elements of description, narrative, problem-solution, and argumentation. Often the writers of texts provide words that signal the organizational pattern. For example, a paragraph or a portion of it organized into a sequence states its main idea in the topic sentence, and to support the main idea the author arranges details in a specific order to carry out the correct meaning of the text. Key or cue words may include *first*, *second*, and *third*, or *next*, *then*, *finally*, *last*, and *after that*. If a reader (or listener) knows how to use the author's structure (capitalizing on the cue words to grasp the underlying organization), he or she is more likely to build a coherent understanding of text. The better the text is organized, the more apparent its structure will be. For example, if a reader or listener is cued by some key words that the text presents a sequence, prior experience with sequence leads the reader or listener to anticipate and search for a time order during the reading. Alternately, if the underlying pattern is a problem-solution, then the problem-solution schema may be activated by the directional words or structure in the text, in turn generating expectations that the problems will be stated and that the reader or listener can anticipate and search for solutions (Meyer, Brandt, & Bluth, 1980). Thus text structure plays a role in text comprehension. Similarly, it plays a role in the composition of text in the content areas, as authors use particular structures to frame their ideas and to elicit associations and feelings.

Research has shown that awareness and use of the patterns that structure expository writing are positively related to the amount and type of information that students recall after reading expository (informational) passages (Richgels, McGee, Lomax, & Sheard, 1987). The general consensus is that learners who are aware of and can use their knowledge of structure search for and recover ideas from text and bind the content to the structure. Such readers thereby weave large chunks of information into a cohesive whole by tying together essential information on the basis of structure. To tie together the most essential information, strategic learners use their knowledge of organizational patterns and their knowledge of words that signal patterns and relationships.

How do listeners, readers, and writers acquire a schema for structure? They do so first through experience with informational (expository) texts (through listening to the reading of such texts, reading expository texts, and writing expository texts). Readers (and writers) also acquire such knowledge through direct instruction in text structure. For example, teachers can work with students to highlight signal words (e.g., *first, finally, on the other hand, consequently*) that cue the reader to organizational patterns in a paragraph or a larger section of text.

Knowledge of content and structure is a prerequisite to the transfer of knowledge across the subject areas and tasks. Knowledge transfer is addressed next as a necessary condition for effective learning.

Knowledge Structures and Knowledge Transfer

Central to learning and cognitive development is the transfer of knowledge. "Far" transfer, which involves moving knowledge across disciplines or subject areas, has been difficult to achieve. Since teaching specific or general metacognitive skills has provided only "near" transfer (transfer to similar tasks), researchers began to study the teaching of strategies or procedures to enhance knowledge access and transfer across domains. "Far" transfer, however, remained elusive. As a result, knowledge organization (schemata), in particular the progression from general to specific structures in cognitive development, has recently been re-examined. Case (1992) has proposed that certain knowledge structures, which he calls **central conceptual structures**, may dominate conventionally defined domains. Each conceptual structure can be used to make sense of new content in a broad yet delineated range of conventionally defined domains. Moreover, if taught, it is believed, the structures can enhance transfer to many tasks that share the same conceptual underpinnings (Case & McKeough, 1990; Case, Bleiker, Henderson, Krohn, & Bushey, 1993). To illustrate, McKeough (1995) has identified a central structure, labelled a *central narrative structure*, which identifies the structural organization of narrative and shows how such a structure enables narrative (as opposed to expository or scientific) comprehension.

Bereiter (1995) offers a *dispositional* view of transfer. In this view, transfer is seen as an event, not an ability. Further, the potential for transfer is thought to reside in whatever has been learned, and not in the learner. Teaching for transfer therefore is not skill or strategy instruction but something akin to character education. Transfer of principle (depth of understanding) and transfer of disposition (incorporation into character or a way of approaching things) become important issues. Bereiter adds that the "full" transfer (or "far" transfer) of a principle is achieved only when it is incorporated into the cognitive system in such a way that it becomes part of a person's personality.

Bereiter's thinking is consistent with a school of thought called "situated cognition" (Brown, Collins, & Duguid, 1989). In **situated cognition**, situations (contexts) are the co-producers of knowledge/learning through a variety of activities. In classrooms, ways of thinking, skills/strategies, and social practices are modelled for the learners. Classrooms in turn are embedded in still larger contexts such as the whole school, the community, the city/town/ rural area, and society as a whole, each context shaping literacy development. The concept of situated cognition works well in teaching/learning situations where learning about comprehension strategies is embedded directly in the reading of text and learning of content. The learning of a comprehension strategy then becomes a secondary outcome in learning content, but it is "situated" in a community of teachers and students discussing the content of texts. In situated cognition people also learn by entering into the "communities of practice" (e.g., a nursing home, a research lab, or an automobile factory) and working toward full participation by acquiring concepts and situation-specific skills.

Since the link between schools and the larger community has not been made in many of our school systems, proponents of situated cognition state that schools should be turned into places of *cognitive apprenticeship* (Collins, Brown, & Newman, 1989) where students enter relevant communities of practice in different scientific and scholarly disciplines. Such a practice would involve a transfer of situations rather than a transfer across situations. Situations that have worked well in the schools would transfer to the workplace with the result that people would know in advance how to function in the workplace.

Cognitive apprenticeship is based on the notion of apprenticeship (Rogoff, 1990) as a model or metaphor in which novices enhance their understandings through participation with more skilled partners such as peers or teachers. It is not unlike the Vygotskian notions of learning and the concept of the zone of proximal development discussed in Chapter 1. The metaphor of apprenticeship focusses on the active role of learners, on the use and support of people in social interaction in tasks and activities, and on the sociocultural nature of institutional and other culturally organized activities. Central features of learning in apprenticeship are: shared problem solving, guided participation, explicit and tacit communication, supportive structuring, and transfer of responsibility to novices for handling skills and strategies. Cognitive development as an apprenticeship reflects a sociocultural view of learning that manifests itself in many schools. In such classrooms, learners are involved in guided participation in activities with peers, teachers, and parents, who support and further the understanding of and skills for using the tools of a culture.

Reading as an Affective Activity

As mentioned earlier, reading is not just a cognitive activity; it is also an affective activity. Both cognitive and affective conditions exist in meaning construction. Affective factors in reading include attitude, motivation, interest, belief, mood, value, and emotions elicited in the reader by the text. Attitudes toward reading, for example, have been described as "mobilizers" (or de-mobilizers) or "energizers" (or de-energizers) that will determine whether a reader will undertake and persist with the reading task (Holmes, 1960; Athey, 1985). For example, students' initial dislike of a content area can affect their attitudes toward learning and in turn their mastery of the content. Affective factors may set cognitive actions in motion. For example, if attitude, interest, and motivation are high, they can facilitate cognitive processes in learning from text; if they are low, learning and retention may be hindered (Dreher & Singer, 1986). Thus affective factors work in conjunction with cognitive factors and are critical to the understanding of text (Athey, 1985; Mathewson, 1985).

It is apparent that teachers must provide classroom activities and reading experiences that promote greater interest in, more positive attitudes toward, and a greater motivation for reading and reading-to-learn instruction. Self-questioning and answering activities during reading, for example, may be motivating for some students since they are able to find answers to their own questions and consequently develop a positive attitude (Singer & Donlan, 1989).

Students also invoke affective criteria when evaluating what they have read. Liking what is read enables readers to more correctly predict their own reading achievement (Singer & Bean, 1986). Additionally, students with positive attitudes may express a greater interest in reading and become sufficiently motivated to read and/or to read-to-learn on their own.

Research in the realm of cognitive outcomes is much more advanced than it is on affective outcomes, although researchers are now seeking answers as to how affect might positively mobilize cognition and vice versa. The general agreement, however, is that the relationship between affect and **cognition** is one of mutual facilitation. If educators are seriously concerned with illiteracy and **aliteracy** (being able to read but unwilling to do so), then priority must be given to affect in reading (Dreher, 1990).

The extent to which reading is experiential, affective, and personally rewarding seems to depend partly on one's purposes for reading and on the types of text read, as pre-service teachers state below. As they reflected on their literacy experiences, some pre-service students in content area classes (Gordon & Hunsberger, 1991) reported that they enjoyed informational materials more than narrative materials. Others reported the opposite.

> The experience of reading is something that I believe is highly dependent upon the type of reading and the text. I find that reading for enjoyment is not my favorite pastime by a longshot, but in an educational setting I find reading and studying a textbook very interesting and informative. (Norman)

> I find reading and writing to be worlds apart. Reading is a torturous experience while on the other hand, I find writing to be quite enjoyable. (Angelique)

> I read for enjoyment or for information. When I read for enjoyment I often picture the scene . . . I become caught up in the story and can often shut out outside noise. I really enjoy it. One the other hand, reading for information is often tedious unless I have a topic I'm enthused about . . . Reading a text-book for me is often hard work. (Thomas)

Instructional approaches that influence the affective aspect of reading should aim to make the reading experience a positive one by having students participate in active comprehension and response activities so that they can play a role in their own learning. For example, the questions they ask are those that are relevant and meaningful to them. Activities in which students' responses to text include their own feelings and interpretations allow them to enter into a "conversation" with the text. Activities that encourage students to monitor their own learning are essential to the development of independent learning. Activities where the locus of control for learning is given to the students allows them to satisfy some of their own curiosity. In addition, when students are so **empowered**, they feel more confident in expressing their ideas and opinions. Positive feelings are instilled when students are successful in their learning. In turn, such student involvement promotes interest. In Part II of this text, you will learn a variety of instructional strategies that promote active comprehension and involve the affective domain in the content areas — strategies that should be instrumental in improving motivation and attitudes toward literacy activities in the content areas.

Reading as Transaction

For over 50 years, one theory dominated the field of literature and had an impact on reading and on the interpretation of text. This approach to text interpretation theory (called **New Criticism**) presented a view of reading texts that stressed the objectivity and autonomy of the information in the text. Unlike reader response theory, the reader's "subjective" responses, feelings, and thoughts were considered unimportant and irrelevant. *Meaning was to be found only in the text.* There was to be one correct reading or interpretation, even of a literary text, and it was the reader's responsibility to discover this meaning through close analysis (Harker, 1990). Variable interpretations were not acceptable despite the fact that literary experts and the New Critics themselves, each reading a piece of text independently and doing the close analysis demanded by the theory, came up with different interpretations. While readers' private responses (and cognitive activities) were acknowledged, they were judged to be acceptable only if they agreed with the correct answer. In this "transmission" perspective, therefore, the teacher was considered the authority on the meaning of text.

Varying interpretations (and even contradictions) eventually led to inquiries into the role of the reader and his or her responses and judgements. In recent years, the roles of text, author, and reader, as well as the process of reading itself, have been re-examined. Reader response theories have emerged, *privileging the role of the reader* by emphasizing that meaning does not come ready-made from the page to the reader, but emerges as the reader transacts with the text. Reader response theories (or "reader-response criticism") focus on the **transaction** between the reader and the text, a transaction that can be unique to each reading and to each reader. In developing the transactional theory of reading, Rosenblatt (1938, 1969, 1978) drew on Dewey and Bentley's (1948) definition of transaction. They defined transaction as an event in which there is a transformation of participating entities. Response theorists such as Rosenblatt see reading as a process of co-creativity involving reader response and direction from the text in the making of meaning. While it is the reader's responsibility to use cues in the text to guide meaning making, the reader's private response is seen as an important component in shaping meaning. Rosenblatt (1978), for example, in her transactional theory of reader response, does not discount the text but views the reading as a lived-through experience, a unique coming-together of a particular person and a particular text at a particular time in a context to create meaning. The reader's social and cultural setting, as part of the context or matrix of the reading event, becomes important in text comprehension. The transaction is viewed as a complex, nonlinear, and often revised constructive process in which the accumulated experience of the reader is brought to bear.

Your reaction might be, "That's fine for literary works of art. That is not the way we read nonliterary texts such as science or mathematics or books on life skills." And you are partly right. But it is not entirely the type of text that determines how the text will be read. What will be "evoked" (Rosenblatt, 1989) depends on the reader's focus of attention. The reader, consciously or unconsciously, adopts a stance or focus of attention that reflects his or her main purpose for reading a text. The reader may also adopt a particular stance because of the directions, instructions, or expectations set out by the teacher. *Stance* is determined by the bringing forward of certain aspects — some private (the experiences, attitudes, personal associations, feelings, and images that are stirred up) and some public (the concepts that the words and sentences point to or their dictionary meanings) — into the scope of selective attention and the pushing of others away. To make meaning, a reader can adopt an "efferent stance," which draws mainly on the public aspect of sense making, or an "aesthetic stance," which includes more of the experiential, private elements. Or the reading stance may fall elsewhere in this efferent–aesthetic continuum.

In **efferent reading**, the reader's attention is paid primarily to public meaning, to the information comprehended and to be remembered *after* the reading. *Efferent* refers to "a nonliterary kind of reading" of a text (Rosenblatt, 1991, p. 444). The reading event itself is secondary, though not necessarily unimportant. The reader is concerned with getting meaning by identifying or analyzing facts, drawing conclusions, or even attending to the writing style and techniques to be retained after the reading. Examples of efferent reading are reading a label, a newspaper, a driver's manual, or a chapter in a textbook.

On the other end of the continuum is the **aesthetic reading**, a type of affective response. The focus of attention in this stance is mainly on what is being "lived through" cognitively and affectively *during* the reading (Rosenblatt, 1989, p. 159). The poem, as Rosenblatt labels it, or the evocation, or the unique experience, is an event. Sensations, feelings, attitudes, images, prior experiences, ideas, associations, and personalities come into play and shape the meaning during reading. Although the reader may recall a lot of information following aesthetic reading, that is not what makes aesthetic reading different from efferent reading. Poems, stories, and plays are most often read this way, but any text can be read either way. Thus, reading a recipe can be an aesthetic experience if the purpose is only to enjoy, to relish each ingredient in turn, to imagine the pleasure of the first warm or cold mouthful, to sense a texture, to react to the perception of the visual appeal of the end product, rather than to determine the nature and amount of each ingredient and the sequence in which one puts the ingredients together. In fact, some of us can read whole cookbooks in an aesthetic way! So there is a difference between a literary and a nonliterary reading — the difference being in the way the reader chooses to read a text and in the direction the text gives the reader, not in the text itself. Verbal elements such as metaphors and stylistic, syntactic, and linguistic conventions contribute to the meaning making, but the experiential contribution of the reader is most important. Efferent and aesthetic readings are not contradictory activities, however; efferent cannot be identified solely with cognition, nor aesthetic with affect or emotion. As Rosenblatt (1991) writes,

We read for information but we are also conscious of emotions about it and feel pleasure when the words we call up arouse vivid images and are rhythmic to the inner ear. Or we experience a poem but are conscious of acquiring some information about, say, Greek warfare. (p. 445)

The reading of many texts, however, does not fall at either end of the continuum. Therefore, "any text can be the occasion for a 'literary' *or* a 'nonliterary' reading" (Rosenblatt, 1991, p. 444). Any text has that potential.

Many texts fall nearer to the middle of the continuum, where both efferent and aesthetic readings can occur on the same text. For example, in the reading of a textbook (predominantly an efferent reading), one or two key ideas can be understood in light of a personal experience associated with them. "Sometimes, the aesthetic is attributed to the presence of emotion, as when students become excited about scientific information" (Rosenblatt, 1991, p. 444). Thus the mix of private and public aspects of meaning occurs in any stance taken. Because readings have just such a mix, readers (and writers) must keep clear their main purposes for engaging in a literacy activity (Rosenblatt, 1991).

The same text can be read either more efferently or more aesthetically on different occasions (Rosenblatt, 1991). If you are reading Robert Frost's poem "Stopping by Woods on a Snowy Evening" because you know you will be tested on its form, structure, and content, you may read to learn facts, key ideas, and rhyme schemes rather than experience it as a literary work of art. Conversely, you may read a science text to savour the pictures of animal life or the elegance of a scientific insight rather than to abstract key information on, say, the classification of the species.

There is likely a close tie between reading as a transaction and reading as an affective activity. It is possible that students exhibit negative attitudes toward content reading because the focus in the content areas is always on efferent reading, with the aesthetic seen as irrelevant or trivial. Perhaps students are not allowed to bring enough of themselves into the readings for positive attitudes to develop. Efferent reading in and of itself can subordinate affect.

Having examined multiple perspectives on reading, we can state that reading is an intermingling of linguistic, cognitive, metacognitive, affective,

---

For Reflection 2.1

What do you now understand about the literacy activity of reading? How would you define reading?

and associational (experiential) reservoirs. "What is brought into awareness, what is pushed into the background, or what is suppressed depends on where the attention is focused" (Rosenblatt, 1989, p. 157). Reading is not simply learning facts; that is, it is never simply efferent reading. Response in reading allows for reflecting, savouring, exploring, interpreting, evaluating, and contemplating, not just summarizing, paraphrasing, and recalling. Aesthetic response is not an add-on; it constitutes the essence of the experience of reading. It is the lifeline to lifelong reading.

In Chapter 1 you read about the kind of integration that can take place across the curriculum, particularly the integration across subject areas like English, science, social studies, art, music, and other subjects. Since more and more of this kind of integration is taking place in the classroom, it seems only sensible to combine aesthetic and efferent reading. Students might be encouraged to study topics in science, math, social studies, or any of the subject areas from a more aesthetic perspective. When students feel, see, hear, and think the topic, a connection is built between the content and the students' lives. One way to add an aesthetic dimension to content area learning is to integrate literature (including poetry writing on content area topics) into content learning. Grade 9 science students we know recently completed writing a myth that incorporated the evolutionary phases (from science) of a chameleon. These types of responses and activities constitute active reading (also described in Chapter 1) and support aesthetic education. In other words, active reading and aesthetic response are connected.

Integrating Literature into the Content Areas

Literature-based materials, called **trade books** (e.g., books of science and historical fiction, diaries, biographies, autobiographies, magazines, newspapers, and paperbacks), are seen as personalizing content area curricula and allowing for more aesthetic transactions with text. Such materials should be seen as complementary to "recommended" textbooks in the content areas (Sanacore, 1993). Table 2.1 (from Sanacore, 1993) provides a comparison of textbooks and literature-based materials in a number of categories. Not only will comprehension of content be improved through transactions with trade books, but the enjoyment created will improve students' attitudes and move students in the direction of lifelong reading in the content areas.

Content area teachers should obtain the help of the school library/media specialist for trade books with the appropriate content and reading levels. Many of the strategies and activities outlined in this book are appropriate for use with trade books. Alternatively, some of the trade books could be read simply for enjoyment and background information.

Table 2.1

Some Comparisons of Textbooks and Literature-Based Materials

FACTORS	TEXTBOOKS	LITERATURE-BASED MATERIALS
Presentation of text	Ideas are organized in a listlike and listless fashion. A large number of concepts are introduced.	Ideas are blended with poignant narration. Fewer concepts and themes are highlighted and dealt with in greater depth.
Short-term, long-term perspective	Immediate information is provided for classroom discussion and related tests.	More opportunities are given for responding both intellectually and emotionally to the text and for developing the lifetime reading habit.
Variability	One source usually dominates instruction.	A variety of "real" resources (trade books, pamphlets, magazines) support instruction.
Comprehensibility	Content is uninteresting and detached from readers' prior knowledge.	Content is more easily personalized and understood by readers.
Applicability across the curriculum	Information is vacuously linked to separate subject areas.	A diversity of themes can easily be adapted to several content areas.
Externally, internally driven curriculum	A single publisher controls the bulk of the curriculum.	Educators and students determine curriculum focus.
Externally, internally driven assessment	Chapter questions dominate quizzes and tests.	Individually selected outcomes (projects, portfolios, interactions) are used to determine progress.
Emulation of home environment	Parents and children rarely read textbooks for pleasure.	Family members are more likely to read, read aloud, and discuss "real" resources.

Source: From "Supporting a Literature-Based Approach across the Curriculum," by J. Sanacore, 1993, *Journal of Reading, 37*(3), pp. 240–44. Reprinted with permission of Joseph Sanacore and the International Reading Association. All rights reserved.

Perceptions of the Writing Process

Before you read any further, jot down your definition of writing. Now read on to see how others have defined writing. Perceptions of writing based on the content literacy study described by Gordon and Hunsberger (1991) show a progression similar to that in perceptions of reading (from cognitive, to interactive, to transactive). However, many more students viewed writing as an interactive, aesthetic, and creative literacy activity than viewed reading in that way. Representative entries include:

> Symbols of a language (letters, symbols, etc.) put together on paper to spell words. Can be phonetically done or like English, not always phonetic. A method of communication which is learned in lower elementary. (Jagit)

> Putting down symbols which have a meaning in the appropriate order includes — spelling, penmanship, paragraphing, putting ideas into words and words into sentences, and grouping ideas into essays, or reports. (Anwar)

> Writing entails the ability to read and understand a written language. Writing is a person's ideas about their life experiences which includes anything they may have read, thoughts and feelings. (Jan)

At this point, let us review some theoretical positions (under which some of these definitions fall) with respect to the writing process.

Writing as a Sociocognitive Activity

Writing can be viewed as an interactive, cognitive process. According to Flower and Hayes (1981), who have conducted research into the cognitive processes of writing, three key elements interact during writing. These are the task environment, the writer's long-term memory, and the elements of the writing process itself. The task environment includes the assignment, the topic, the audience, the writer's interpretation of the assignment (including his or her goals), and the growing text produced to any point. The writer's long-term memory includes all the stored knowledge of topic, of structure to frame content, of audience, of language and print conventions, and of a variety of writing plans. The elements within the writing process itself are planning, translating, and reviewing, all under the control of a monitor. Planning consists of generating ideas, categorizing them, organizing them, and setting goals. Translating means that the writer is putting the ideas into visible language using knowledge of the conventions of writing (e.g., spelling and punctuation). Reviewing consists of evaluating and revising. Along with the overall monitoring that occurs throughout the writing, the subprocesses of evaluating and revising also function as a metacognitive component, exercising executive control over all other processes and operating continuously throughout the writing. The elements of the writing process are explained in more detail as follows.

Writers plan at all stages of writing — before, during, and after they write down sections of their texts. The ideas they express might come from their minds and/or be gathered from external sources. Then writers decide how to organize the ideas (i.e., structure the text) in terms of their goals for writing. Good writers spend more of their writing time planning than do poor writers, and they tend to plan more at the global level than at the local level (which focusses on words and sentences).

Translating is a complex stage as the writer has to co-ordinate many elements at the same time, concentrating on both sense making and mechanics. Good writers, of course, having mastered the mechanical aspects of writing to an automatic level, can devote their attention to higher-level thinking skills, such as analyzing or synthesizing and comparing and contrasting, while writing.

The act of reviewing also occurs at any stage during the writing — to see if the chosen word is appropriate, to ensure that the sentence conveys the message clearly, to see if there are errors in mechanics, to determine if the direction the text is taking needs altering, or to decide if further planning or specific revision is needed. Again, good writers tend to review their writing at the level of clarity, organization, and content, whereas poorer writers only look for mechanical errors.

In revising (as part of reviewing), writers make changes in their compositions. Again, revising can occur at any point in the writing, not only when the first draft has been completed. Although it is described as having "stages," the whole writing process is seen to be **recursive**, not linear. Good writers tend to make more meaning and structural changes (reorganizing or adding content) in revision, while novice writers revise at the level of correcting spelling, capitalization, and punctuation errors.

More recently, the cognitive view of writing has been expanded to a sociocognitive view (Flower, 1994). Writing, like speaking, is seen to be a social, even a conversational act (Bruffee, 1984), and "readers are to writers what listeners are to speakers" (Sperling, 1996, p. 54). Writing, like oral language, is meaning making that is shaped by culture and social interaction (Flower, 1994; Flower et al., 1990; Sperling, 1996). A central tenet in the sociocognitive view of writing — the relationship between writers, texts, and readers — is that meaning does not "reside" in the text or the intentions of the writer but comes from the interaction and assumptions shared by readers and writers (Nystrand, 1989). Writers then must anticipate how their words will be read. Writers and readers construct meaning in the process of bringing to text "the overlapping influences of their social and cultural contexts, language and discourse conventions, and the more immediate influences of their specific purposes and goals" (Sperling, 1996, p. 55).

Instruction that reflects the belief that writing is similar to speaking encourages genuine oral conversations (in discussions) or writing exchanges (such as journal writing) in pairs or small groups with peers and the teacher. In other words, the sociocognitive view of writing encourages a process approach to writing instruction (see the section "Guiding Composition" below).

Writing as Transaction

In this view reading and writing are similar because both readers and writers construct texts (Rosenblatt, 1989). Writing, like reading, is considered a transaction because writers, like readers, "transact" with the text they are writing. Drawing on their past experiences, their linguistic reservoirs, writers begin with what may be vague ideas, associations, and feelings, and then pro-

---

For Reflection 2.4

Reflect at this point on how you would define the literacy activity of writing.

ceed to construct meaning. Writing has been defined as "an event in time, occurring at a particular moment in the writer's biography, in particular circumstances, and under particular external and internal pressures. In short, the writer is always transacting with a personal, social and cultural environment" (Rosenblatt, 1989, p. 163).

In this process, or event, of writing, setting one's purpose as a writer means adopting a stance appropriate to this purpose (just as a stance is adopted in reading), a stance that falls in the efferent–aesthetic continuum. How much of the public and private aspects of the writer's linguistic and/or experiential resources are included will determine which stance the writer will adopt. Through writing, new lines of feeling and new ideas are opened up and new relationships are discovered (Rosenblatt, 1989). "Writing can become a learning process, a process of discovery" (Emig, 1983, p. 166).

In real life, selecting a stance is not an arbitrary decision. "[Stance] is a function of the circumstances, the subject, the writer's motives, and the relations between the writer and prospective reader" (Rosenblatt, 1989, p. 168). For example, in your history course you might like to write about your feelings on the Gulf War, about its sights, sounds, your inner tensions based on T.V. accounts and statements you have read (thus activating more of an aesthetic stance), even though your assignment calls for an efferent stance in which mainly impersonal facts, or the public aspects, need to be elaborated. Under different circumstances or for different purposes (e.g., a soldier writing a letter home to his family, or a teacher asking you for a personal response to the Gulf War), writing on the Gulf War might fall at different points of the efferent–aesthetic continuum.

Exercise 2.2
What Is the Writing Process/Experience Like for You?

To gain insight into the process of writing, try this activity. The task is to write on the topic of "Feelings" in a health option course. Let us set up this exercise so that we compose on the left side of the sheet, and, as we become aware of our writing process and what we are experiencing (as we become metacognitive), we record it on the right side of the sheet. After reading this "talk-as-I-write" account, try your hand at this kind of activity.

Composing   **Think-Aloud**

I think I know a lot about feelings; I certainly have experienced anger, joy, frustration, hope, and love. I'd rather write about those but I guess since this is to be a paragraph for my CALM 20 (Career and Life Management) course

Composing

What are feelings?
- some are instincts (we're born with them)
- some are learned (like grieving in our society for someone who dies, but perhaps feelings of grief are different in other cultures)
- examples are anger, depression, jealousy, embarrassment, love, hate, happiness, fear (is fear a feeling?), (grief — inserted later)

(grief added to earlier examples)

Feelings
           Feelings
        What Are Feelings?
Ever wonder what feelings are?
    I know you have all experienced feelings, like anger, but can you put into words what feelings are?
    Feelings (or emotions) are a natural part of your make-up as a person. You are born with some feelings and these are known as instincts.

Think-Aloud

in Grade 11, I think the teacher will be looking for some key facts, definitions, and generalizations. Let's see. What do I know about feelings? What information do I have to research? How will I organize it? I'll start with a definition. So, I write the title of my first subtopic.

    And I add a few jot notes. I remember reading bits and pieces of this information somewhere.

    I'll give some examples of feelings. I'm not really sure of any of this. I'll have to read some books or articles later to see if I'm on the right track. Maybe I'll add a personal touch and mention some things my friends or I have expressed when it comes to feelings. Might add that as I start writing. Well, let me see where I'm at. I'll reread my notes. I'd better add grief to my list since I mentioned it earlier. Well I'm not sure I'm happy with it but I'll start writing and rethinking what I want to say as I write. How shall I start? Need a catchy line like good authors that I have read use. Need a title and subtitle.

    Title should be centred so I'll erase what I wrote.

    Starting with a question is good.

    Now I'll tie in something personal.

Composing

Think-Aloud

Aha — I can link that to instincts, and animals.

Animals are born with instincts too.
    Humans and animals have instincts like fear, surprise, discomfort, anger. Some of these feelings help them protect themselves in life-threatening situations.

Something might be wrong with my paragraphing. I'll tend to it later. But am I getting off topic? Since I'm not sure, I'd better put "I think" . . . and I'd better start a new paragraph here.
    I reread that sentence and decided to add "particular" before society. That makes better sense.

I think other feelings are more or less learned as part of living in a particular society. These are pride, sympathy, bravery, and maybe even boredom.

As you can see from my think-aloud, I must constantly plan, write, review, and revise. As you can also see, the process is recursive, not linear. As the writer I had to weigh the balance of personal and private elements that would enter into the text in light of the task. Now complete the short composition I started, while at the same time becoming aware of your processes, thoughts, and feelings.

The Relationship between Reading and Writing

Read the following paraphrased explanations to see how differently or similarly the relationship between reading and writing is viewed by the experts.

Reading and writing can both be viewed as composing processes: as essentially similar processes of meaning construction. (Tierney & Pearson, 1983)

During reading the reader's stored knowledge (schemata) interacts with the text in order to communicate with the author. During writing, the writer's knowledge of the world and of language interacts with the text to communicate with the readers. (Tierney & LaZansky, 1980; Tierney, LaZansky, Raphael, & Cohen, 1987)

Reading and writing are both sociopsycholinguistic processes. (Harste, Woodward, & Burke, 1984)

Reading and writing are similar in that both readers and writers construct texts. (Rosenblatt, 1989)

Writing, like reading, is an active strategic recursive process requiring constructive thinking that starts with the intent to convey meaning. (Flower &
Hayes, 1981; Hayes & Flower, 1980; Scardamalia & Bereiter, 1986a, 1986b)

Effective reading and writing are constructive problem-solving processes that
require learner effort, enthusiasm, and perseverance, together with thinking
and strategic reasoning ability. (Hermann, 1990)

A reader comprehends by integrating impressions gleaned from text with models of reality that are personal, cultural, and contextual. A writer composes by
making meaning from incoming information, personal prior knowledge, and
frames based on culture and context. The process of composing occurs as theoretical understandings of processes converge, with the role of human understanding of texts or the world being a central component. (Petrosky, 1982)

The relationships between reading and writing have been perceived mainly
in three different ways, each with its own implications for instruction
(Sternglass, 1987). First, reading and writing have been seen as parallel
processes, each sharing content and process knowledge. The implication, in
this traditional and somewhat outdated view, was that both were to be
planned and taught but that these two literacy activities were discrete and
could be taught as separate subjects. Second, reading and writing are sometimes still viewed as interactive, constructive processes with the interaction
of a learner's prior knowledge and the text being critical to understanding and
composing. In the classroom, the role of reading during writing and the
direct effect of reading on writing are considered important. Classroom activities focus on writing précis and summaries, building awareness of the role
that rereading plays while composing, and discouraging students from pre-
mature editing so as not to interfere with their ideas. Third, in the more recent
transactive perspective, reading and writing are thought to construct meaning, but what results (the transaction) is an event that is "larger than the sum
of its [parts]" (Harste, 1984, p. 22) because learner, environment, and text
affect what understandings emerge. In the classroom, reading and writing are
viewed as social activities, with ideas shared, discussed, and reworked in a way
that encourages thinking and engagement.

Similarities and Differences between Reading and Writing

Because reading and writing are used to convey ideas or messages to others,
both are considered parts of the communicative process. Tierney and Shanahan
(1991) state:

> Writers try to address and satisfy what they project as the response of the reader. . . . Readers as they read text, respond to what they perceive writers are trying to get them to think of, as well as what readers themselves perceive they need to do. (p. 259)

In other words, when reading and writing take place, a transaction occurs between readers and writers (Nystrand, 1986).

Second, both reading and writing are constructive or composing processes. The author produces or constructs a new text as he or she goes through the process of writing and revising ideas mentally and on paper. The reader constructs messages or meaning in a transaction with words already in existence.

Third, reading and writing share a core of knowledge, processes, and strategies (Hansen & Rubin, 1984). Drawing on a pool of language data, readers and writers draw on common cognitive, linguistic, and aesthetic processes (Kucer, 1985). Various thinking strategies are also common to reading and writing: hypothesizing, predicting, inferring, and contextualizing events and concepts through imaging, revising, structuring, questioning, and validating. In the process of constructing meaning when reading and writing, a number of information sources are involved: world knowledge, linguistic knowledge, knowledge of the structure of texts, and knowledge of the processes and subprocesses involved.

Finally, expert writers, like strategic readers, exercise control over the cognitive reasoning processes associated with reading/writing (referred to as metacognition). Metacognitive activities might include setting goals for reading or writing, monitoring one's progress, reviewing and rethinking (revising) what has been read/written, and evaluating one's reading comprehension or written composition.

Tierney and Pearson (1983) have proposed a model of reading based on the features common to reading and writing. These include drafting, aligning, revising, and monitoring. Like writing, reading requires the drafting of an initial picture or impression of what is happening in the text. Like writing, reading involves aligning oneself (or taking a stance) with the author in order for communication to take place. Like writing, readers must be revising texts, or altering their "initial" impressions, as they read. Finally, like writing, reading involves monitoring or keeping track of and control over all the other functions. The model is useful when thinking about some of the similarities and differences between reading and writing.

It is, however, simplistic to think that reading and writing are identical and interchangeable activities simply because they share a common language pool and reasoning strategies (Langer, 1986). Reading and writing involve different patterns of thinking and different approaches to making meaning. Writing requires generating meaning from prior knowledge to put on a blank page, while reading requires the construction of meaning based on one's knowledge and associations as cued by the text. Further, while certain cognitive processes underlie both reading and writing, they are used in differing proportions and patterns. For example, studies have shown there is more planning in writing than in reading and more refining of meaning in reading than in writing (Anderson, 1990). Teachers therefore need to recognize the specific competencies required in each and to take care that differences between reading and writing are not ignored in the current emphasis on integration (Langer, 1986; Malicky, 1990).

Because of their shared knowledge and processes, writing can be learned from reading and reading can be learned from writing. For example, teaching students the underlying structure of text in writing can improve their ability to detect the author's organization when reading text. When readers read, they do not always have to write, but when writers write, they need to read what they have written in order to go on writing. Reading their own writing may improve their ability to read as well as their ability to write. But if readers write, writing has a positive effect on comprehension of the content read. What we know then is that integrating the acts of reading and writing enables one area of literacy to enhance the other area. Thus, using reading and writing together, rather than separately, is more effective in the goal of learning content.

Many of the activities in Part II of this text will use reading and writing in combination to enhance learning and thinking in the content areas, to promote social and collaborative interaction, and to engender aesthetic appreciation.

Based on the processes that have been shown to operate during writing, various classroom approaches to improve students' writing have been developed. One of these approaches, the "writing process approach," is described briefly below and in greater detail in Chapter 8.

Guiding Composition

Process writing is an approach to improving students' writing ability based on the processes that operate in writing (planning, translating, reviewing, and revising) (Flower and Hayes, 1981; Flower, 1994). Although "process writing" has sometimes been used to refer to the "stages" that writers go through as they write (Murray, 1986; Graves, 1983), the cycle of (1) pre-writing, (2) drafting or writing, (3) revising, and (4) publishing corresponds closely to the processes described in the sociocognitive process model of Flower (1994) described previously. The **process approach to writing** includes much sharing and collaboration. It treats writing as a social rather than a solitary activity (Atwell, 1987; Gordon, 1991; Graves, 1983; Sternglass, 1987). It is important to repeat that the writing process is recursive, not linear, with all of the processes operating at any one time. For example, collecting information, writing, reading, and revising can occur at the planning stage; a student may draft (write) and return to planning before revising, and can revise and then return to pre-writing activities. Research on composing shows that the nature of the writing task (for example, type of prose to be written or topic to be covered) has an effect on the different aspects of the composing process (for example, planning or revising) (Applebee et al., 1984). That is, when different modes of discourse or types of writing come into play, a writer may perceive the topic to be more abstract, and may spend more time at the planning stage.

Since Chapter 8 is devoted to discussions of how content area teachers can guide students' writing by using a writing process approach, it is sufficient to mention here that students' writing of content area papers is not likely to improve without teachers guiding students' writing in their areas of specialization. In addition, the process approach to writing enables students to understand the relationship between reading and writing and to consider both as processes of constructing meaning. Including the writing process as a major element in English language arts instruction has helped to make "writing across the curriculum" a reality (Simmons, 1991).

Guiding the writing process is somewhat different from emphasizing writing-to-learn in the content area subjects. Writing-to-learn activities are intended mainly to promote thinking and learning in a subject area and to enhance comprehension of materials read. Making students aware of and guiding them through the subprocesses of writing produces better writers of science, social studies, mathematics, and other subject areas. Practice in writing without teacher guidance and opportunities for writing-to-learn activities *may* improve students' writing of content, but guiding the writing process *will* insure their success when writing in specialized areas.

The following comment made in the literacy across the curriculum research (Gordon & Hunsberger, 1991) supports the notion of having teachers guide students' writing efforts:

> An unfortunate experience in one English course made me paranoid. I tried to get feedback on how to improve my writing, but I could never receive any that I thought was particularly helpful. This put a damper on my subsequent writing. (Susan)

Learner Control and Independence in Learning

Readers and writers need to develop some understanding of the cognitive and affective processes involved in making sense of text and in learning from text.

Readers need to understand that while reading and writing in the content areas (other than English) may be mainly to satisfy efferent demands, students also need to pay attention to their own aesthetic experiences that come into play when reading and writing efferently. Aesthetic reading increases involvement in and enjoyment of informational texts. Affect provides energy for the cognitive domain and therefore plays a key role in reading and writing (Athey, 1985). However, in English language arts and secondary-school English classes, the aesthetic evocation of students' own experiences and feelings is of primary importance.

Readers and writers need to operate at a level of processing that is automatic and unconscious (Brown, 1980). They cannot stay at the level of conscious awareness (demonstrated earlier in the think-alouds) and still learn efficiently. Knowledge of content and processing strategies becomes *internalized* in such a way that they become personal possessions allowing the learner to perform independently in a new context what could previously be accomplished only with assistance (Malczewski, 1991; Vygotsky, 1962).

Good readers use strategic behaviours (Duffy & Roehler, 1987; Gordon, 1994; Paris, Oka, & DeBritto, 1983). **Strategies** are internalized systematic plans or techniques that readers use flexibly (Duffy & Roehler, 1987). Examples of strategies include summarizing, brainstorming, outlining, visualizing, and making analogies. Readers modify and adapt the strategies to particular reading situations or contexts. By their very nature, strategies are generalizable beyond any one task and across subject areas. A comprehension strategy such as SQ3R (survey the text; raise questions; read the text; answer the questions by reciting the answers; then reread or review the text to see points missed or requiring elaboration) can be adapted to meet a variety of comprehension tasks and applied in subjects such as science and social studies. Another strategy is to integrate information presented in text with information presented in figures, diagrams, pictures, graphs, or charts. Other strategies are more specific to particular disciplines, such as improving your comprehension of the explanation sections in mathematics by using your knowledge of the underlying organization or the structure of the explanation pattern.

Strategic readers use not one strategy but a **repertoire** of strategies (Gordon, 1994). They know (perhaps subconsciously) when and where to apply a particular strategy or set of strategies, easily discarding one for another if the strategy is not effective. Readers and writers invoke strategies to make cognitive progress. These strategies can have cognitive, metacognitive, and affective components. Affective factors determine the extent or degree to which strategic readers use particular strategies. Students' attitudes toward, and motivation for, using the strategies (which take time and energy) often determine the extent to which strategies will be implemented (Paris et al., 1983). Awareness and control of affective factors also help students monitor their feelings as they read so that they can overcome any feelings that impact negatively on comprehension (Frager, 1993).

To acquire control over their own efferent reading, students in the content areas should be taught text-processing strategies to enhance the learning of content. They should know how the strategy works and where and when to use it. And they need to eventually internalize and automatize such processing strategies. (Teaching/learning strategies are presented in Part II of this book.) To enhance aesthetic reading such strategies as drawing on prior experience and visualizing (imaging) should be encouraged.

Below are some comments made by pre-service students (Gordon & Hunsberger, 1991) about their awareness and use of strategies during high school and university.

> I remember being in Social Studies 10 and being frustrated because my teacher had asked me to answer an interpretative question the answer to which I could not find in the text. I did not realize it was an interpretative question and was afraid to accept an answer out of my own head. I believed all answers should be found directly in the text. (George)

> I happened to read a couple of books during the Christmas break. I discovered during this time that I am far more aware of my reading experience and processes than I had been previously. (Jagit)

> Most of my knowledge now is intuitive; it's seldom conscious. It stopped being conscious many years ago as my facility with print and understanding grew and became internalized. Now in explaining it to someone else, I have to rethink what I know. (Anwar)

Summary

Several different perspectives contribute to our understanding of reading and writing. Reading and writing are complex composing processes the purpose of which is to construct meaning. Both are active, constructive processes that involve cognitive strategies (predicting, confirming, integrating, analyzing, associating, inferring, and synthesizing) and the use of prior knowledge and an awareness of the organizational structure of text. Both are also affective, experiential activities. For reading to be affectively rewarding, trade books should be used in conjunction with textbooks. In addition, both reading and writing are transactional activities in which readers and writers transact with the texts they are reading and/or writing. Personal feelings and associations become important in interpreting and composing narrative and expository texts. Reading and writing are similar but not identical processes. When reading and writing are used together, rather than separately, content is learned more effectively because one area of literacy is enhanced by the other. Students gradually assume control over the cognitive and affective processes associated with reading and writing and become strategic and independent learners.

Questions for Further Reflection

1. If you have not already done so, think aloud as you read a portion of a text and jot down what you become aware of as you read the content — feelings, reactions, strategies, and personal experiences. Do the same for a writing activity. What cognitive and affective responses transpired? Were there any similarities between reading and writing?
2. As you read a portion of a text in the future, think about what you do, think, feel, and react as you read. Think about what goes through your mind when you write nonfiction as opposed to fiction. How did your purposes for reading or writing include both efferent and aesthetic aspects?
3. Think about how you can use reading and writing together, rather than separately, with your students in your subject area specialization.
4. How did thinking aloud as you read contribute to making you a "strategic reader"? How did thinking aloud as you composed contribute to making you a "strategic writer"? How can one be a "strategic listener"? a "strategic viewer"?
5. When you become consciously aware of your mental processes and your feelings, does this awareness help or hinder your speaking, reading, listening, viewing, and writing activities? In what ways?
6. What are the instructional implications of (a) thinking of reading, writing, and talk as transactions? (b) becoming more aware of your thinking processes?

Key Terms

Aesthetic
Aesthetic reading
Aesthetic stance
Affect
Aliteracy
Central conceptual structures
Cognition
Comprehension

Conditional knowledge
Considerate (friendly) text
Constructive process
Declarative knowledge
Decoding
Efferent reading
Empowered
Inconsiderate (unfriendly) text

Interactive
Intertextuality
New Criticism
Perceptions
Procedural knowledge
Process approach to writing
Reader response theory
Recursive
Repertoire

Schemata
Schema theorists
Situated cognition
Strategic readers
Strategies
Think-aloud
Trade books
Transaction

CHAPTER THREE

Aesthetic and Efferent Reading: Concepts and Strategies

Questions to Consider for this Chapter

1. What is involved in aesthetic reading?

2. How can content area teachers foster learner engagement with texts through aesthetic reading?

3. What is involved in efferent reading?

4. How can content area teachers empower learners to be more successful in their efferent reading?

5. How do you make sense of a difficult text?

6. What is involved in "making meaning" when you read?

7. What strategies can be used for aesthetic reading? For efferent reading?

8. What kind of writing do learners likely engage in when they read aesthetically? When they read efferently?

Overview

Understanding the difference between aesthetic and efferent reading and writing is the main thrust of this chapter. This difference is revealed in the **affective responses** evoked in readers and writers as they attempt to construct meaning about a text. An **efferent reading** or writing event is a cognitive event that entails purposeful disregard of the affective response and requires the reader to "carry away" particular information or knowledge. **Aesthetic reading** allows for the play of both affective and cognitive responses. For both kinds of reading choosing the reading stance is essential for active and independent learning and the achievement of content literacy. Examples of aesthetic and efferent reading and writing are offered in this chapter. We also explore how meaning is made and how meaning making is an ongoing learning process. We show that a reader can change his or her stance during reading or writing and that by changing that stance the reader becomes aware of the difference between aesthetic and efferent reading and writing.

Aesthetic Literacy

As discussed in Chapter 1, affective and cognitive dimensions of reading and writing are not separate. Although research studies have tended to dichotomize these domains, many researchers and teachers now recognize that a response to text involves experiencing feelings generated by the words as well as thinking about the concepts being presented in a text (Frager, 1993).

When asked to describe their response after reading a text such as "Fishing Worms" (Chapter 2, Exercise 2.1), readers describe a range of feelings from annoyance to anxiety, even fear and anger. Their efforts to make sense of the passage are foiled because the language seems deliberately mystifying. "Fishing Worms" is difficult because no title is provided and no topic is clearly defined at the outset. Without such cues, the reader is cut off from the possibility of initiating a conversation with the text.

Many students in our classrooms experience frustration with scientific, technical, and literary text. Teachers know only too well how this frustration can impede the learning process: many students do not understand what they are reading and exhibit anger and fear at having to read or write. Many teachers have asked how they can help these students break through this vicious cycle.

Readers can be helped to understand what they are reading and writing in the following ways. The first step is to recognize the significance of affective or emotional responses in our own reading and writing. The second step is to create opportunities for learners to respond to text through conversation, discussion, and writing that encourage positive experiences of affective response, both with literary texts and with scientific and technical texts. Such opportunities are a starting point for encouraging and supporting aesthetic reading and writing, which can enable readers and writers to become aware of what they are experiencing during their reading and writing. Readers and writers who understand their affective responses can learn to see them as beneficial to the development of self-understanding. This kind of understanding can be linked to aesthetic understanding and to aesthetic literacy.

The development of **aesthetic literacy** makes possible the inclusion of both affective and cognitive responses. A positive affective state can act as a "mobilizer" (see Chapter 2), bringing the reader closer to an understanding of the "possible worlds" (Bruner, 1986) evoked by reading or writing. Aesthetic literacy introduces us to ways of living in and writing about new textual worlds, and enables learners to appreciate new forms of text: for example, visual text or combinations of visual and print text. This view of aesthetic literacy is supported by Boughton's (1986, p. 137) concept of **artistic literacy**, which involves being able to "adopt a variety of intellectual stances" when reading or writing in order to achieve a level of "cultural understanding" across a range of cultural contexts (p. 140).

Engaging in Aesthetic Reading and Writing

Aesthetic reading and writing enable us to make meaning from a text. Creating meaning through aesthetic reading and writing helps readers and writers obtain a new sense of what it means to be literate and "to feel and to create harmony within their daily world" (Heath, 1991, p. 3). This is very different from traditional conceptions of literacy, which include "the ability to read and write" and the achievement of a "value neutral" cognitive state. The "standard picture" of literacy (Winchester, 1990, p. 23), with its emphasis on literacy as a cause of social and economic progress with "the potential to reduce crime, poverty and ignorance," needs to be revised. The definition of literacy cannot be restricted to a causal relationship between language and the world, or to a "self-maintaining and self-propagating" phenomenon. There remain "many deep theoretical and conceptual problems relating to literacy" (p. 37), not the least of which is how we can learn to read and write (actively and independently) about difficult texts across the scientific and artistic disciplines.

The ability to read a text both efferently and aesthetically is the hallmark of the active and independent reader. A reader's sense of being literate derives from his or her ability to exhibit literate behaviours that demonstrate cultural understanding as well as cognitive and affective understanding of a text. Heath's (1991) list of literate behaviours — comparing, sequencing, arguing, interpreting, and creating extended chunks of spoken or written language in response to text — characterize aesthetic response as well as efferent response. Taking a stance to read or write for aesthetic understanding and changing that stance to read or write for efferent understanding are not separate and discrete skills, but, rather, are complementary. When a reader or writer decides to take a stance and becomes aware that new meaning can be created, he or she is learning how to use these different reading positions to understand not only that other "possible worlds" exist, but that our world can be read and written about from a multitude of different cultural stances.

For Reflection 3.1

Some science writers invite their readers to take an aesthetic stance. Among these writers are Stephen Jay Gould, Barry Lopez, and Lewis Thomas. Two such texts are Gould's *The Panda's Thumb: More Reflections in Natural History* and Thomas's *The Medusa and the Snail: More Notes of a Biology Watcher*. With your instructor's help, select an essay from one of these books that interests you. Take an aesthetic reading stance toward one section of the essay and write an aesthetic response.

The Relationship between Aesthetic Reading/Writing and Content Literacy

Understanding the possibilities of transactions between aesthetic and efferent reading and writing is an aspect of content literacy. As stated in Chapter 1, content literacy is not synonymous with content knowledge. One can be knowledgable about particular content but unable to read and learn from new text in the same content area. To know how to read in a content area, we need to be aware of the affective responses we have to text as well as the cognitive processes we use during reading and writing. Becoming aware of and being able to think about our thinking is called **metacognition** (Flavell, 1976, 1979; Garner, 1992; Gordon, 1994). Metacognition is a form of reflection and a way of carrying on a conversation with the text being read (Gordon, 1994). Content literacy requires readers to cultivate the ability to carry on a conversation with the texts they read and write, knowing how to question different texts in different ways so that when they meet a new text this conversation can continue. Learning how to read and write aesthetically is a way to open up a conversation: aesthetic reading and writing begin with the prior knowledge and experience of a particular reader reading a particular text.

Writing an Aesthetic Reading

What follows is an example of a written aesthetic response to the evocative poem "This Is Just to Say," by William Carlos Williams (see Box 3.1).

For Reflection 3.2

Looking back on your own experience of reading, both in school and during leisure time, describe the memories and feelings you experience now as you recall a favourite novel, short story, or poem.

Box 3.1
This Is Just to Say

I have eaten
the plums
that were in
the icebox

and which
you were probably
saving
for breakfast

Forgive me
they were delicious
so sweet
and so cold

Source: From *Collected Poems: 1909–1939, Volume I,* by William Carlos
Williams. Copyright © 1938 by New Directions Publishing Corp. Reprinted by
permission of New Directions Publishing Corp.

This is one of my favourite poems and, though I am not sure why,
I am still delighted with each reading. A surprising depth of
desire is aroused during each reading, as well as something akin
to astonishment at the simplicity of the piece. What is this
desire about and why does such astonishment emerge? How do these
feelings arise? Why does the simplicity of the language evoke wonder and even satisfaction?

The image of the plum-eater indulging in stolen pleasure arouses
the desire to experience a similar act, even though I am not particularly fond of plums. The desire for pleasure is strong. I find
pleasure, at least in part, in my daily living through simple rituals and rites such as taking a hot shower, writing in my journal
at the end of the day, sharing laughter with colleagues at work,
meeting with interesting clients, or walking by the river in the
evening. Occasionally I am surprised by pleasures like a letter
from an old friend or a new insight into a person I thought I knew.

A stolen pleasure is quite different from any of the previous
examples, however. Stolen pleasure is dangerous, risky, open to
legal and moral questions, and the experience of the pleasure as
something stolen is difficult to explain and justify. Still, small
stolen pleasures, like taking an extra bit of time for lunch, can
evoke surprising satisfaction and even wonder. I have discovered
that the experience of even small wonders in everyday living can
be invigorating and regenerative.

Part of the surprise of this poem is its simplicity. Somehow this note works as a poetic piece but I am never sure how or why. Though the form is simple, the experience being related is surely not. And why not? I am not certain why not but each time I read this poem I think I get a little closer to understanding the complexities of relationships, the risks entailed in intimacy. These days neither is easy to achieve or maintain.

The central image of plums so sweet, so cold always intrigues me. I am always drawn first to the image of plums (in my mind, always purple plums on a white plate). Then I see a man eating quickly and quietly so as not to alert the plum-saver. I imagine an icebox small and squat and silent. I always want to provide a time-frame from my own experience — probably the 1930s or 1940s because refrigerators became available in the 1950s.

I know that the poet was a medical doctor, so I imagine that he is the thief who steals the plums either on the way out to visit a patient or on the way to bed after a night at the hospital. I imagine the plum-saver to be his wife asleep, perhaps dreaming of plums.

The fact that the title is also the first line of the poem always intrigues me. Titles of poems sometimes seem irrelevant and even obtuse, but here the title works rather like a lead to a story. I usually read on without disconnecting the title from the main text because the title itself is a poetic line. The first four lines intrigue me because they are such a simple statement of fact, without tension or drama. Perhaps their simplicity arouses desire. Is that all there is, I wonder? Isn't there more here than meets the ear and the eye?

With this reading, I become aware for the first time of the double meaning of the title. It is a simple statement, yet standing by itself the title suggests the poem is a confession; it is an act of domestic justice, an offering required as justification for the stolen pleasure. It *is* just that the plum-thief replace one pleasure with another, that the stolen plums be replaced by a found poem. I am compelled to understand the title in two ways now. I experience competing desires: one, to read the title as a statement about justice, and two, to read the title as a simple statement of intention.

Separated by space but not by punctuation, the second stanza always provokes questions. Who is "you"? Why does the poet acknowledge that the plums were being saved by someone else? Why does the poet eat the plums when he knows they were being saved for breakfast?

The last four lines always surprise me: the simple surprise of the capitalized F in "Forgive" interrupts my reading. I am always stopped in mid-reading by that small surprise, and I am always compelled to ask another question; would I forgive if someone close to me stole one of my pleasures?

This last question brings me back to a favourite memory of catching my father at midnight eating the last piece of a chocolate birthday cake. He grins sheepishly but there is a certain impish elation in his eyes. In his own way he has disrupted the ordinary routine of domestic life and is proud of it! That memory makes me laugh and wonder if I always imagine the plum-thief as a man because of it. I cannot remember my father without also remembering my mother whose concern for conservation and frugality dominated our lives.

Perhaps this poem astonishes and intrigues because I can never reach final answers to any questions, even the simple ones. Perhaps this piece also intrigues me because in my reading there is always an intimation of Adam and Eve, and Eden's stolen apples.

As I move through each line of this piece I experience a multitude of feelings — compassion, annoyance, envy, pleasure, and, yes, the possibility of forgiveness. Feelings, memories, faces from the past, and answerless questions compete with each other, jostling for centre stage yet there is never a finished resolution, never an ending. After reading it, I am always astonished at the simple pleasure of this poem. In the immediacy of this awareness, I am also very aware that this poem is in some way both a gift and a stolen pleasure.

What would you do if someone stole something you were saving? Would you write a note to that person? What would you say in that note?

Here is what I remember of a stolen pleasure:

Careening
a truck lurches
dumps a cardboard box
onto the quiet street

Stopping
in my tracks
I watch
to see if someone watches me

Scooping
shiny cans dented
bright with yellow labels:
Premium Quality Peaches

Pedalling fast
I head straight for home

The Meaning of Meaning

When you look back at my attempt to write about my aesthetic reading of Williams's poem, you can see that I have created a chunk of text out of the associations gathered from my personal experience, as well as from my reading of the text itself. You can also see that an aesthetic response to one piece of text can open up a conscious attempt to create poetic text. Aesthetic reading that becomes a written aesthetic response can lead to a more formal **aesthetic writing**. The images in the poem evoke different meanings as we transact with the poetic text. Our aesthetic reading and writing of such a text make possible new relationships with past experience and knowledge.

Reading Williams's poem for the first time you may be struck with the ordinariness of the language. You may even find this ordinariness annoying or you may be flabbergasted by the simplicity of the text. You may ask questions such as, Why would anyone write about such an insignificant event? You may find that you identify with the poet or the plum-saver or even with both. This identification through response may enable you as a reader to write about your own everyday experience. You may find that aesthetic response is possible even with the most ordinary everyday experience, and that significant meaning can be made about the most ordinary experiences. Meaning is not found simply in our own experience or our own memories or even in the text alone, but somehow somewhere in between.

This is why Louise Rosenblatt argues that we do not find meaning "solely in the text" or "solely in the reader's mind" (1978, p. 14). As she points out, critical theory and practice have failed to recognize that each reader carries on a "dynamic, personal, and unique activity" (p. 15). Aesthetic reading is a "confluence of reader and text" (p. 16) and, therefore, meaning does not reside in either just the reader or just the text. This view has implications for the "meaning of meaning." Philosophers, psychologists, and social scientists have produced theories about meaning. Linguists and literary critics have also attempted to deal with the problem of meaning in relation to an individual reader's consciousness.

Rosenblatt's questioning of the meaning of meaning leads her to adopt the idea of **transaction** as a kind of metaphor for the process of making meaning, a term suggested by John Dewey and Arthur F. Bentley (p. 16). This idea of transacting with text has implications pointing to open-ended meaning making. It is this open-endedness that takes us to the heart of aesthetic reading because it is during this reading process that meaning becomes questionable. The origin and very nature of meaning, whether drawn from text or from reader, is no longer determinable, no longer clear, no longer predictable, and so the very meaning of meaning itself is no longer easily definable.

Where in all of this melange of transacting elements is meaning with which you can make a connection?

Usually we think of meaning as linked to the purpose or intention of the author, that meaning is already determined ahead of time, that meaning is given in certain words or a sentence or a piece of text. But with aesthetic reading and writing, meaning arises somewhere in between the text and the conscious mind of the reader. Rosenblatt calls the meaning that is formed in the space between the reader's mind and the text a "poem." This "poem" is an analogue for the meaning we make during aesthetic reading and writing. In this "space" between the reader and the text are the words we gather together for memories of previous knowledge and experience, and this gathering includes our past experiences of reading other texts. Also included in the "poem" are words put to the conditions already set up by the fact that this is a book being written for a particular audience. Thus, meaning arises as an experience of a particular situation or context and out of a transaction of the affective and the cognitive fused in a domain which is both personal and public. As Rosenblatt has suggested, the "public, dictionary meaning" of words and "their private associations" can be "linked through past reading or life experiences" (1989, pp. 445–46).

"Yes," you may say, "I understand that we can read and write both ways and that the difference in stance can affect the meaning we construct as we read or write, but just what is the meaning of meaning?"

A complete or final answer to this question cannot be given to this question: taking an **aesthetic stance** requires that each time we read or write a text aesthetically we understand it in a new way, not in a totalizing way but in a way that takes on new dimensions that are added to and change the previous understandings we have of our reading and writing. In other words, when reading or writing aesthetically, the meaning shifts and moves, is transformed, altered, even undercut, is sometimes invisible. The text becomes permeable and open. As Rosenblatt argues, when we take an aesthetic stance, we are faced with continuing to question ourselves about "the meaning of meaning" (1978, p. 40). A large part of the immense pleasure of learning to read and write aesthetically is that one can never be sure what meanings will surface during a reading.

Meaning making before, during, and after reading and writing involves cognitive processes, but making meaning also involves affective processes. Conceptualizing activities are involved in the use of language when an aesthetic stance is taken but, at the same time, we are also in the midst of a "stream of feeling." When we focus on what words cause us to see and hear and feel and think, and we put words to what we see and hear and feel and think during readings of a text, we are in the midst of a stream of thought in transaction with a stream of feeling. As readers we are "selective" in the attention to what we are thinking and hearing and seeing and remembering, and we are also conscious that all of these experiences, memories, perceptions are part of a "consciousness of self" (Rosenblatt, 1978, p. 42). There is a difference in my **lived experience** of the text each time, however, and, therefore, a difference in my thoughts and feelings during this particular reading.

The Relationship between Stance and Meaning

Transactional reading theory is concerned with what the reader *does* when he or she takes a stance to read either aesthetically or efferently. The significance of stance is threefold. First, the stance taken sets up a particular relationship between reader and text and, therefore, sets the scene for a particular kind of conversation with a text. Second, changing the stance means the conversation with a text can become an unpredictably broad transaction between the text and the reader's knowledge, experience, and understanding. Third, the choice of stance affects not only how meaning is constructed but also what we understand meaning to be.

Let us use the following example of taking an efferent stance. Suppose we wish to learn how to tie a knot that will not break but is easy to untie. We must first find a book that explains and illustrates how to tie knots, and look specifically for a knot that fits this description. Such a knot is the "bowline." Our efferent reading may be aided by a drawing that shows each step in tying the knot as well as by an explanation of the various uses of the bowline. This "conversation" is sequential: a stringing together of a question-and-answer sequence that follows a predictable path.

Here is another example: we wish to set up an aquarium for a science class, so we turn to a book concerned with this topic. We look for information on choosing an appropriate site in the classroom for the aquarium, selecting the materials, and installing the heater, regulator, and filter. We read this information for the purpose of taking action. This reading again involves gathering items into a list, and constitutes a fairly predictable relationship with the text.

By contrast, aesthetic reading or writing centres on what the reader is "living through during his relationship with a particular text" (Rosenblatt, 1978, p. 25). The reader brings the "resources" of his or her personality to the reading or writing event, and experiences a fusion of the cognitive and the emotive as "facets of the same lived-through experience" (p. 46). By choosing to take an aesthetic stance when reading, we are able to play with the nuances of words and become performers with words. When we allow our reading or writing stance to change, we cross the boundaries between "taking away" information and "living through" language: we learn to allow transactions to occur across the range of our knowledge, experience, and understanding.

We readers may take a certain stance as we begin to read, and then change that stance if we wish to change our focus. At the same time, the stance can change without our being aware of the change. Reading then becomes a process that is neither linear nor random, but a continuing going back and forth to build a complex relationship based on personal experience, knowledge, and understanding. For example, a reader taking an efferent stance with Williams's poem about plums can take away the meaning that someone has written a poem asking forgiveness for eating the plums being saved by another. That stance can be changed to an aesthetic stance that permits the reader's personal experience to become part of the meaning (as mine did in my aesthetic reading of the poem).

Because prior knowledge and experience are multidimensional and idiosyncratic, meanings can be so engrained that they remain inert, and in this state, readers may resist change. One problem with resisting change in stance is that the reader may actually be engaged in re-establishing a misunderstanding of a concept. Misunderstandings can demobilize learning, yet, once raised or brought into a "conversation" with text or with others, they can be changed. By reading and writing aesthetically, learners can be surprised by unexpected associations, images, ideas, thoughts, and questions, resulting in a change in how they understand a concept.

Learners can decide to read or write efferently and then change their stance and read or write about the same passage aesthetically. Learners can also shift back and forth during a reading or writing event from an efferent to an aesthetic stance and then back again. What is important for learners is that they become aware that this shifting of stance in relation to a text is happening, and that the moving back and forth of a reading stance can be immensely beneficial and satisfying in surprising ways.

Some texts will lend themselves to being read and written efferently and aesthetically more readily than others, and this is an area in which teachers can help learners to become more active and independent readers and writers. They can help them to recognize when a change in stance needs to be taken, when the change is likely to provide the reader-as-learner with new or changed understanding, and when a text is likely to lend itself to being read both ways. Teaching our content area learners to switch their intentions before reading is a way of teaching them how to take responsibility for their learning. Helping them to become aware that their stance can change even during reading is a way of helping them to become more active and independent in their construction of meaning during and after reading.

Efferent and aesthetic reading and writing are not contradictory activities. As pointed out in Chapter 2, an aesthetic approach to content area subjects is "very much in line with the emphasis on developing understanding and reasoning abilities" (Rosenblatt, 1978, p. 112). By learning how to read and write aesthetically, learners develop "a sense of self as participant, as inquirer," a sense of self essential to learning because the bedrock of lived experience is at work in the process of understanding.

We will show how both stances can be taken with the same piece of text later in this chapter. At this point we look at what happens when we decide to take an efferent stance with reading.

Engaging in Efferent Reading and Writing

Efferent readers form an intention to take meaning away after reading. They decide to bring specific prior knowledge and experience into play before and during reading. To do this readers must decide, before reading, what they need to focus on: this could include new vocabulary, new concepts, new definitions, or new facts.

One way to position ourselves for effective efferent reading is to note where the piece of text is located in the book we are reading. In the case of the two pieces of text about salt (see Boxes 3.2 and 3.3 below), both are located in the middle of a chapter entitled "Solutions." In previewing the Table of Contents as part of the preparation to take an efferent stance, we note that there are five previous subsections. A **prediction** can be made that the titles of these five subsections will yield information related to the two sections concerning salt. The first subsection, entitled "Solutions," is a one-page introduction outlining the chapter as a whole. Scanning this introductory text provides a summary of vocabulary used throughout the chapter. "Solutions" is given three different interpretations: figuring out a crime, finding out the answer to a math problem, and a chemical mixture. A list of eleven questions outline the main topics of the chapter. Within these eleven questions are key words and phrases: *solution, non-solution, solute, solvent, hard water, soluble, insoluble, dilute solution, concentrated solution, saturation,* and *solubility.* Nine of these words and phrases are nouns, and the other two are adjectives; if we can make some sense of a few of the root words such as *solution, solute,* and *solvent,* we can deduce meanings for the compound words and the adjectives that use the same root words.

Here, as you can see, an efferent stance is being taken in order to carry away meanings about salt in the narratives that appear later in the chapter.

The two passages are given a main heading, "Getting the Solute Out of the Solvent," and a subheading, "The Salt Industry." Locating the two texts within the larger text helps the reader to anticipate that both these texts are concerned with the chemical process of extracting a solute from a solvent because the main heading signals that a solute is derived from a solvent.

As we take an efferent stance, however, we need to summon up our prior understanding of "solute" and "solvent." If we are unsure what these two terms mean, we can turn back to the section entitled "Parts of a Solution — Solutes and Solvents." Here we find definitions for "solvent" and "solute." A review of these definitions will help to make connections between the processes of making a solution and extracting a solute from a solvent. This is a review procedure for making the connection between what I already know and what will be new knowledge of content.

In this review procedure, smaller bits of text emphasize exactly the information I need. In a small blue box in the upper right corner of the page are two short sentences: "The *solvent* dissolves the solute. The *solute* dissolves *in* the *solvent.*" The bright blue colour attracts the eye. As well, the words stand out against the blue background because they are black and in *italics.* The italicized words are *solvent, solute, in,* and *solvent.* The solvent is something bigger that contains the solute: the solvent contains the solute and, therefore, "dissolves" the solute. The second sentence gives me the reverse as a correlative fact. The solute is contained *in* the solvent. The solute "dissolves in" the solvent.

A **think-aloud**, which here appears as a **write-aloud**, helps to create a link between old and new knowledge and understanding. We get used to new words and begin to live with them and feel at home with them. We then begin to make meaning of the new: So the solvent is something the solute is *in*. The solute is spread about inside or with the solvent. The solute disappears into the solvent. This process of disappearing is called "dissolving." So what could act as a solvent? The solvent would likely be a liquid or a gas, and not so likely be a solid. What could act as a solute? A solute could be a liquid or a gas or a solid.

If we now make a prediction about the two texts we are about to read to "carry away" information, we can say with some certainty that they will be about two different processes for making a solute reappear from out of a solvent. Further, we can make a prediction about what the solute is: we can predict that salt is the solute. Now we need to look for what is common to both processes and be alert to the possibility that there may be differences between the two processes. Begin by reading Box 3.2.

Box 3.2
Making Salt

___

Cibwa salt is found mainly in the country of Zambia. This kind of salt is found in a sort of grass.

In August the grass is collected using hoes and spread on the ground to dry. This grass may remain there for about two months. When it is dry it turns brown in color.

In September and October the Cibwa salt is extracted from the grass. People go to the place where they left the grass to dry, and there they build shelters which are for temporary use. Two days later they start the burning of the dry grass which turns it into ash. The salt is in the ash.

The ash is put on a filter made of grass and water is added to the ash. The water dissolves the salt and leaves behind the insoluble impurities of the ash on the filter.

The solution is poured into a clay pot which is placed on a fire. During the boiling, the water evaporates away.

When the water has all evaporated, the salt is in the bottom of the pot in solid form.

The people in this part of Zambia still make salt the same way.

Source: From "Making Salt," by Michael Nosenge and John Bavalya, in C.P. McFadden and E.S. Morrison, 1990, *Science Plus: Technology and Society (8)*, Toronto: Harcourt Brace, p. 101. Reprinted by permission.

The writers in Box 3.2 report the time of the year when the grass is gathered and the month when the salt makers begin their process of getting the salt out of the grass. There is a chronology for the procedure. This time order means that a summary of the process can be constructed by numbering the steps.

```
First, the grass is collected in August and then the grass is left
to dry. Second, in September or October the people who will do
the extracting of salt from the grass build shelters. Third, when
the grass is dry, they burn the grass, and fourth, they place the
ash left after burning the grass on more grass, which acts as a
filter. The fifth step is to add water to the ash. Next, the water
containing the salt from the burned grass is poured into a clay
pot. This is the sixth step, the step that enables the salt to
be separated from the impurities in the ash. The seventh step is
to boil the water until nothing but salt is left.
```

The sequence can be inferred from the text, and a numerical order can be composed in writing. Here is the sequence of steps:

1. In August grass containing salt is collected and left to dry.
2. In September or October shelters are built near the drying grass.
3. The grass is then burned.
4. The ash is placed on more grass.
5. Water is added to the ash, which dissolves the salt and leaves impurities behind.
6. The water–salt solution is placed in a clay pot.
7. The water–salt solution is boiled until the water has evaporated and only the salt is left.

What would you do to carry away the information about getting the solute (salt) out of the solvent (the water)? Some suggestions are to make a calendar to show the stages in this process, or to illustrate the process by drawing a picture of each step. Even before you read a second piece of text on extracting a solute from a solvent, you can predict that the processes of extracting salt described in these two texts will not be the same. The title of the second passage reveals that this process takes place in Nova Scotia, a province in eastern Canada. Prior knowledge of the area's geography assists in making the prediction that the process for extracting salt is likely to be different in a significant way from the process of making Cibwa salt in Zambia. Box 3.3 contains the second text.

This process of salt extraction is done with the help of technology. The last step in this process is essentially the same, however, as the last step in the process of obtaining Cibwa salt: the solvent (water) is evaporated so that the solute (salt) can be used. One important difference is that the salt comes from under the earth. To understand the difference in the process, we can evoke

---

Box 3.3
The Salt Plant at Nappan, Nova Scotia

Much of our area has large salt deposits deep underground. It is believed that these salt beds were formed millions of years ago when salt seas evaporated, leaving the salt behind. In some areas, the salt is mined using tunnels. However, at Nappan a different method is used.

First a hole is drilled down to the salt bed. Water is pumped down through the pipe. This water dissolves some of the salt, making an underground cavern full of salt water. This salt water is forced back to the surface where the water is evaporated leaving the salt behind.

Source: From *Science Plus: Technology and Society (8)*, by C.P. McFadden and E.S. Morrison, 1990, Toronto: Harcourt Brace Jovanovich, p. 102. Reprinted by permission.

---

an image of what a salt bed might look like. Visualize a layer of white salt underground so far down that the salt cannot be dug up by hand, then make a comparison between getting oil out of the ground and getting salt out of the ground. Getting oil out of the earth is difficult and costly because oil deposits are usually found deep underground. The Nappan salt deposits are also deep underground, but salt is a solid, unlike oil. By visualizing these deep salt beds, we can get a picture of building tunnels to get the salt out. Picturing the building of these tunnels helps us infer that the process of extracting salt is difficult and dangerous. This difficulty means that Nappan salt recovery requires the use of technology.

Even if the technology cannot be visualized in detail, the reader is positioned to understand how the Nappan salt plant works. The steps in the process can be identified just as they were in the Cibwa salt-making process. A numerical order can be constructed:

1. A hole is drilled down into the salt bed.
2. Water is piped underground.
3. The water dissolves the salt, making salt water.
4. The salt water is forced back up to the surface.
5. The water is evaporated, leaving the salt behind.

Seeing an order in both processes enables the reader to compare the two. The Cibwa salt extraction process seems to be a longer and less efficient process than the extraction of Nappan salt. There are fewer steps in the Nappan process, but the salt plant at Nappan depends entirely on technology. The machines needed to do the work are large and complex; if the machines break down, there is a

---

For Reflection 3.3

There is much more that can be "carried away" from these two passages about making salt. What else can you "take away" from your reading? Can you take away new information about the people who make Cibwa salt in Africa when you take an efferent stance with this text? Can you visualize what the salt plant at Nappan looks like? What hypotheses can you make about differences between the way of life in Zambia and the way of life in Nappan? What social differences do you think might exist between these two places? What similarities might we find in these people who live in two different parts of the world?

---

work stoppage, which interferes with production. The Cibwa salt makers, on the other hand, are dependent on the natural growing process of the grass from which they extract the salt. If the grass does not grow, they will have no salt.

Changing Our Stance: The Benefits of Difference

The difference between taking an efferent stance and taking an aesthetic stance for reading may be clearer at this point. When an efferent stance is selected, personal associations, imaginings, and feelings are set aside. On the other hand, taking an aesthetic stance about the making of Cibwa salt opens up the possibility of visualizing families joining together to build shelters, picturing the burning grass, and imagining the smell of the salt after the water has boiled away. A reader could speculate about how these people dress, or about the celebrations they might have after the long process of making salt. A reader might conclude that while making Cibwa salt takes more time than the technological process at Nappan, there might be a stronger social coherence in that part of Zambia. A reader might also wonder if the salt plant at Nappan has created environmental problems.

Knowing that one's reading stance can change, the reader is aware that thinking about environmental problems involves feelings and associations that arise during reading. As we now know, paying attention to what we experience during reading means changing our stance from an efferent reading to an aesthetic reading. With efferent reading the reader must try to set aside the questions, associations, and feelings that arise during reading. Yet the reader is always aware that he or she can return to an aesthetic stance or back to an efferent stance. Deciding what stance to take before reading means that we act differently as we read. Understanding how to change our stance during reading is important if we are to become lifelong learners.

For Reflection 3.4

Four different kinds of reading and writing strategies were used here to "carry away" meaning from the reading of the two texts on salt: previewing for vocabulary, predicting, questioning, and summarizing. Can you identify other strategies which could be used?

For Reflection 3.5

In your exploration of efferent and aesthetic reading stances, which position have you found more comfortable? Why do you think this is? What value can you see in changing your reading stance?

How Meaning Changes When We Change Our Reading Stance

To show that learning to read and write efferently and aesthetically is both possible and desirable, this section contains a sample response to a piece of text called "The 'Bay'" (see Box 3.4).

The first word in this text, "I," is big and black. Behind the "I" is a grey background. Yet two authors are named. Who is the "I"? Who is the writer? The names Annaqtuusi Tulurialik suggest that the writer is an Inuk who has told a story to someone named David, and that David is translating her story into English. The phrase "coming in" from the land to the "Bay" seems strange. Why? The difficulty can be linked to the reference to the "Bay." This is a body of water we see as the watery fist of the Arctic plunged deep into every map of Canada. "The Bay" is known also as the retail department store where Canadians buy clothing and housewares.

When we speak of travelling from land to sea, we usually say we are going *out* to sea, not coming *in* to sea. But the "Bay" could mean the trading company that was founded early in Canadian history: the trading post may be the topic here because you would have to "come in" to the Hudson's Bay trading post to get food or supplies. The narrator is telling about coming in to the "Bay" to trade for food. The "Bay" in this narrative is necessary to the survival of the Inuit.

With an efferent stance we can take away the conclusion that the land of the far north is a place so vast, so cold, so difficult that you must learn how to live *with* the land. If you were to live off the land carelessly, you would not be able to live at all. There is also a stark elegance in this way of life: build-

Box 3.4

The "Bay"

by Ruth Annaqtuusi Tulurialik and David F. Pelly

I remember when people used to come in from the land to trade at the Hudson's Bay post, about 1949. Very few of us lived here near the post. Most people lived out on the land, coming in to the Bay only once or twice a year, spring and fall—usually May and October when they could travel by dog teams. Normally the men came in from the camps by themselves, with their foxes, but sometimes they were accompanied by a few women.

Only at Christmas did whole families come in from the land. Then everybody stayed for the celebration. There were lots of *iglus* [snow houses], all along the shore from the rock in front of the Bay to the Catholic mission, and many dogs.

In May the shelves in the Bay were nearly empty. There were no planes then. All the things came in on the ship in the summer. The people traded for biscuits, flour, baking powder, lard, tea, sugar, dried beans, molasses, cigarettes and tobacco, bullets, and rifles. They could get more for five foxes than we would get today for the money paid for five fox skins. The people pointed at what they wanted and the Bay manager took it off the shelf—not like today when we go around and pick things we want by ourselves. There was no heat in the building, so it was really freezing. The Bay manager just came over from his house when people arrived.

A man brings in one dried fox skin and two frozen foxes. They used to trade both, but the dried skin was more valuable. There was an old *Inuk* [person] working for the Bay manager to prepare all the skins from the frozen foxes. He worked very hard. Sometimes a hunter brought in 40 foxes at a time, which the old man had to skin, dry, and clean. The hunter's wife also brought some caribou clothing, which she made, to trade at the Bay.

In counting out the value of the skins, the Bay manager put some wooden tokens on the counter instead of money. The people will point out the things they want until all the wooden tokens are gone.

Another man and woman are just arriving at the Bay. He is carrying lots of foxes. His wife is following, thinking quietly about the box of biscuits she will get from the trader.

While these people have come in to the Bay, most of the people stayed out on the land, far away. In camp one woman is cooking a big pot of caribou soup over a fire built in the shelter of a skin, to block the wind. Several hungry people are waiting to eat. The rest of the camp is playing, enjoying themselves, except for one woman sitting off at the edge of camp chewing some caribou skin, to make it soft in preparation for some *kamiik* [skin boots]. They will all be happy when the people return from trading at the Bay, with a fresh supply of flour, tea, and other things.

It was a lot different even that short time ago.

Source: From "Qikaaluktut," by David F. Pelly and Ruth Annaqtuusi Tulurialik. Reprinted by permission of the author.

ing your own snow house, "thinking quietly" about a box of biscuits, cooking soup over a fire with only a skin to hold back the wind, people waiting in the wind to eat, the lone woman chewing caribou skin — all this appears simple but is not. Being unable to do these things would mean slow starvation and death. The image of forty frozen foxes piled upon a counter beside hand-made caribou clothing indicates this life could not possibly be simple. The image of a woman cooking over a fire with only a skin to shelter her from the wind reveals that her life is a struggle. The image of a woman chewing caribou skin also tells us that life in the north requires the will to make use of everything, to waste nothing.

When the narrator tells about a man bringing one dried fox skin and two frozen foxes, the narrative changes to the present tense. The time frame shifts, moves from remembering to reliving. The reader moves with the narrator into the lived experience of being an Inuk: the woman thinking only of biscuits, and a woman cooking soup over an open fire. Each image is as clear as cold air and just as shocking. These people live each moment carefully, using every bit of the caribou, chewing the skin, making clothes from the softened skin, trapping foxes, skinning them, trading all of this careful work for food and hunting equipment.

By the end of the memoir we know with certainty that the ones telling this story cannot live this way anymore. The life of living carefully is gone, and with it the way of life of an entire civilization.

Becoming aware that the world of Arctic peoples lives on in the text we have just read helps me to change my reading stance. Seeing a lived world through the text shows that reading and writing in response to the text is not separate from lived experience. Becoming aware of text as a world also helps the reader to know that the reading and writing position in relation to this text has shifted in the midst of this reading and writing. Using visualization as a strategy to "see" into this textual world, the reader can engage in questioning the text so that we might find a way to live *through* the world of each text.

What other strategies would you use to reveal how you live through your reading of "The 'Bay'"?

Another strategy employed here in order to respond to this text is to draw into our conversation another text about travelling in the north. The reader can activate past experience with "The 'Bay.'" Drawing on lived world experience and reading experience, the reader can arrive at an awareness that the lives of Arctic people have changed greatly since 1949. This understanding, which brings associations, experience, and knowledge together with the experiences and knowledge of others, empowers the reader to take an efferent position to "carry away" information about an earlier period of Canadian history. Reading other texts about the north will lead to other questions or confirm that changes have indeed occurred.

What other texts can you draw upon to create a picture of the north?

When we reread the "chunk of text" on "The 'Bay,'" we can note that, as in the text about getting salt out of Cibwa grass in Zambia, a time order has been given. The year is marked by three passages "from the land" to the trading post: once in the spring, once in the fall, and once at Christmas. Only during one of these passages — at Christmas — does the whole family come to the trading post known as "the Bay." No information about how Christmas is celebrated is given, but the reader can infer that the Catholic mission was an influence in this area of the north. With this information, the reader can make some predictions about the celebrations that take place at Christmas. A reader could seek other sources that tell about the history of the Catholic church in the north, and could test predictions by reading further, by checking how Christmas was celebrated in northern Catholic missions. This research could become an interesting social studies project that might involve research into Inuit culture, including art and religious beliefs, as well as other content areas such as visual art and Canadian literature.

From this same part of the text the reader can also infer that the people who came to celebrate Christmas knew how to make their own houses out of snow. We can also deduce that dogs were an important part of the life of people in the north because they pulled the sleds that carried people and supplies. There were no komatiks, or snowmobiles, at that time. The people built their own sleds and trained the dogs that pulled the sleds just as they built their own snow houses. Notice that reading in this way entails inferring and predicting to construct meaning about this text.

There are three times of the year when the people come from the land to trade at the Bay. From the paragraph that begins with "In May," the reader can predict that the information given at this point will tell about trading in the spring, and that this period was different from the celebration at Christmas. The rest of the sentence can lead to other predictions: "the shelves of the Bay were nearly empty." The spring was a difficult time of year for northern peoples because supplies at the trading post were depleted. The next sentence tells why: all supplies were brought in by ship during the summer. There were no other means of transportation.

Of the list of supplies in this paragraph, we note that eight items were food, two items were for "entertainment," and the other items were for hunting. From this short summary we can also infer that these northern peoples expended most of their energy on survival.

Doing business was different at the Bay than it is today. The differences can be summarized as follows:

1. Hunters got more money for furs then than they do now.
2. The Bay manager controlled the trading process.
3. Tokens were used instead of money.
4. Fox fur was the most valuable trading item.

For Reflection 3.6

Four strategies were used to help "carry away" information from this reading of "The 'Bay.'" Can you identify and describe these strategies? What other reading-to-learn strategies would help readers to take information away from this piece of text?

The last paragraph allows us enough information to picture the hardships and difficulties experienced by these hardy people. In camp, one woman cooks for everyone. People are often hungry for some time before they get food. The Inuit waste nothing. The women make the soup out of caribou meat and they chew the skin of the same animal to make clothing. We can infer from these details that the roles of men and women are different: men hunt and women cook and make clothing. Finally, we can carry away as the two central ideas of this text that: (1) the Bay was an essential source of food for the Inuit, and (2) the way of life of the Inuit has changed greatly since 1949.

Summary

Understanding the difference between efferent and aesthetic reading and writing as well as the possibility of a transactional relationship between the two is essential to active and independent learning. Efferent reading and writing entail the retrieval of information, while aesthetic reading and writing mobilize the construction of meaning. The affective response to reading is significant because the struggle to create meaning from previous personal experience and knowledge is the first step in making sense of a text. Aesthetic reading and writing demand of the reader the ability to maintain a "conversation" with text across a range of knowledge, experience, and understanding. Aesthetic and efferent reading and writing can be experienced as interrelated processes that enable readers and writers to add to content knowledge through content literacy. Examples of aesthetic written response and the creation of poetic text show aesthetic reading and writing to be ways of "living through" a text. Efferent reading and writing, on the other hand, constitute a purposeful, cognitive conversation with a text that concentrates on the information to be retrieved from a text. Following from Rosenblatt's (1978) questioning of "the meaning of meaning," we see that the intention to learn through reading and writing is itself a shifting and sometimes unpredictable state of mind. In order to link knowledge and experience, a reader or writer can actively choose to make a shift in stance. Becoming aware of the shifts and changes in our reading or writing stance is part of the metacognitive process of reading and writing. Metacognitive awareness shows how reading and writing involve a three-way conversation among the self as a reader of the lived world, the self in conversation with other readers and writers, and the self as a reader of the world of a text.

Questions for Further Reflection

1. Select a favourite piece of poetry or prose about any subject and do a think-aloud to share with others.
2. Select a difficult piece of expository writing and compose a summary that you can share with others.
3. Go to a favourite place and spend at least fifteen minutes just looking and listening and thinking about what you experience. Find words for what you hear, see, think, and feel. Write them down. Then arrange them on a page in a way that seems to match the experience of being there. Share your poetic piece with others.
4. Go back in time to a frightening experience and find words to picture what happened. Write down as many words as you can that vividly show the terror of the experience. Tell others about this experience.
5. Select a difficult piece of text. Read the title and write as many questions as you can before you begin reading. Write down every question that comes to mind during your reading. After reading, write any other questions that come to mind. Attempt a conversation in which you share these questions with others.

Key Terms

Aesthetic literacy
Aesthetic reading
Aesthetic stance
Aesthetic writing
Affective responses
Artistic literacy
Efferent reading

Lived experience
Metacognition
Prediction
Think-aloud
Transaction
Transactional reading theory
Write-aloud

CHAPTER FOUR

Crossing the Boundaries between Content Areas: Interdisciplinary Transactions

Questions to Consider for this Chapter

1. How would you define "interdisciplinary" in relation to teaching and learning?

2. How might interdisciplinary learning and teaching be applied to particular disciplines?

3. What is an "integrated curriculum"?

4. What content area issues or problems might teachers of social studies and language arts have in common with teachers in math, physical education, or the fine arts?

5. What interdisciplinary instructional issues or topics might benefit teachers in these different disciplines?

6. What kinds of text might be used in a secondary classroom to provide overlaps for interdisciplinary teaching and learning?

Overview

This chapter begins with a review of recent literature concerned with integrated curriculum to show why integrated interdisciplinary programs are considered a legitimate alternative to the traditional curriculum. Examples of integrated interdisciplinary programs in Canada and the United States are offered. Louise Rosenblatt's (1978) concept of "transaction" is applied as a method of engagement with text in an integrated interdisciplinary curriculum. Transaction with text is explained as an act of integrating different aspects of a learner's lived experience with different domains of knowledge. This process broadens and deepens the meaning of literacy and resists "the decisive confinement of science, morality and art to autonomous spheres separated from the life-world and administered by experts" (Habermas, 1983, p. 14). Since much of what learners do in almost every discipline entails reading text and writing about what they are reading, reading and writing are essential learning and teaching processes. Further, reading and writing can be complementary processes: what one learns through reading can be understood more clearly through writing; when a learner writes about a topic, prior knowledge and understanding are more readily integrated when he or she reads new texts. The idea of learning through transacting with text across disciplinary boundaries is reinforced by an examination of sociosemiotic theory, which is concerned with the social significance of language. Gardner's concept of "multiple intelligences" further shows how the concept of an integrated interdisciplinary curriculum supports and promotes the idea of content literacy. Five examples of interdisciplinary transactions with text are featured in this chapter.

A Platform for Reconceptualizing Curriculum

Educational practitioners, working to integrate **whole language theory** and philosophy into classroom practice, are helping to reconceptualize curriculum and instruction as both *integrated* and *interdisciplinary*. Rooted in almost a half-century of language research, the concept of *whole language* embraces a "hands-on approach" to language learning that is a "philosophy of literacy acquisition" (Mickelson, 1992, p. 121). Whole language programs begin with "knowledge, language, and thoughts of the child," and when language skills need to be taught, they are an "extension" and "refinement" of the learner's language (p. 112). Opportunities to listen, speak, read, view, and write about images in different contexts are provided, and text is used as the basis for teaching and learning how to read and write across the disciplines. Individual differences are respected, language is taught and learned across the curriculum, and evaluation is integral and ongoing. Whole language philosophy acknowledges that children already have "considerable mastery over the syntactic and semantic" linguistic structures when they come to school, but have varying degrees of mastery over graphophonemic language structure (p. 113). The basis of whole language instruction is to acknowledge the "transactive nature of human learning" (p. 115). In general, whole language theory shifts the emphasis from "conventions" to "meaning," particularly in relation to writing (Berghoff, 1993, p. 217), and conceptualizes reading "less as a matter of extracting sound from print than of bringing meaning to print" (Smith, 1971, p. 2).

Since language is also a sign system, laden with social meanings, language learning is a "communal activity" (Bruner, 1986). Sociosemiotic theory helps us to see that visual art, music, and science are all sign systems that are part of our language, and that learning these sign systems means learning how knowledge in each domain can be learned as part of an understandable and interrelated whole. *Semiotics* is "the systematic study of signs" (Eagleton, 1983, p. 100) that interprets words or gestures as signs or symbols of both personal and cultural knowledge (Berghoff, 1993, p. 217). The words and images learners use as signs to express meaning when they communicate as social beings work in relationship with all other existing sign systems, including sounds, electronic imaging, and body movements.

Berghoff suggests that both whole language and sociosemiotic theory could serve as a framework to reconceptualize curriculum, particularly the process of learning to read and write (p. 217). Drawing on the work of Harste and Eisner and others, Berghoff proposes a double-edged concept of literacy: as a development "involving multiple sign systems simultaneously" (p. 217) and as an acquisition of "aesthetic literacy," since literacy "from this perspective is a whole literacy, comprised of multiple systems of expression" (p. 217). When language learning is viewed in this way, it can be seen that working in multiple sign systems simultaneously enables learners to "prolong thinking and consider multiple perspectives" (p. 225). Creating a curriculum in which "a range of sign systems" is available for learning and teaching in each content area would enable learners to mediate their thinking by using the multiple sign systems available through math, visual art, science, and language arts.

Berghoff's (1993) research shows that visual signs can be learned together with letters and words as learners read and write. Individual learners create their systems of meaning through a recursive and "complex flow" of multiple signs — "visual, emotional, musical, and dramatic" (p. 223). Some learners may draw single images in great detail with a single word as a descriptor. Others may create extended pieces of written text as companions to detailed drawings. Many learners discover ways to evoke responses from others: they use what they understand of various sign systems "to create artifacts of experiences" and to "invite conversation and comment from others" (p. 224). Sign systems can be used to "transmediate" social responses and understanding. This means that learners can learn to change, alter, enlarge, and enrich their reading and writing responses by attending to and becoming aware of social responses and understanding. Learners can use sign systems to make sense of part-whole relationships, and to recognize and create a "place" that invites "world-making" and a "sense of agency" (p. 224).

Berghoff's conclusions point to the idea of "interdisciplinary transactions." Transactions with text, whether visual, auditory, or print, can be a way of gathering together various sign systems. Therefore, viewing learning from

For Reflection 4.1

Howard Gardner (1983) proposes the argument that each of us learns through "multiple intelligences" such as linguistic intelligence, spatial intelligence, bodily-kinesthetic intelligence, and logical intelligence. What different kinds of "intelligences" have you experienced in your learning? How would you describe these "multiple intelligences"? Read Gardner's book, *Frames of Mind: Teaching for Multiple Intelligences,* and compare your idea of "multiple intelligences" with his.

text as a sociosemiotic process helps to reconceptualize curriculum at the secondary level as both "integrated" and "interdisciplinary."

It has been shown that both children and adults are able to learn in many different ways: through words, numbers, and reasoning; via images and pictures; by listening to rhythms, tones, and timbres in music; by observing and using the movement of the body and the hands; and through social understanding, self-knowledge, and self-understanding (Armstrong, 1994). According to Perkins's theory of **understanding performances,** *understanding* can be differentiated from *knowing,* however, because understanding "goes beyond stored information" (1991, p. 4) into lived experience. Further, self-understanding and social understanding involve "action more than possession." To be active in their understanding, learners need to be able to explain, exemplify, make analogies, and generalize, and be "actively engaged in understanding performances" (p. 5).

By linking sociosemiotic theory, transactional reading theory, and Perkins's concept of understanding performances, this chapter offers a platform for conceptualizing an integrated interdisciplinary curriculum. This platform supports Jacobs's (1991) four-phase action plan for curriculum integration:

1. internal research by small groups of teachers by grade level, department, or interdisciplinary team;
2. action-oriented proposal development;
3. implementation and monitoring of a pilot project; and
4. adoption of a program as a permanent part of the curriculum. (pp. 27–28)

This chapter adds to this plan by suggesting that conceptualizing curriculum integration needs to begin with planning and carrying out interdisciplinary reading and writing "transactions" in our classrooms. By offering opportunities for reading and writing that require multiple viewpoints and analogies among subject matters, teachers can help learners to engage in "understanding performances." And by asking learners to generalize about concepts by drawing examples from different subject areas, teachers enable students to mobilize what Gardner (1983) has called their "multiple intelligences."

With this view of language learning and curriculum in mind, this chapter offers five examples of transactions with text. These texts have been selected because they are conducive to planning and implementing reading and writing activities in different subject areas. Strategies for integrating reading and writing transactions with these texts are suggested. Teachers are also shown how they might initiate integrated interdisciplinary reading and writing activities for texts in their own classrooms.

What Is an Integrated Interdisciplinary Curriculum?

"Interdisciplinary" describes curriculum that combines traditional disciplines. Many postsecondary institutions offer interdisciplinary courses and teaching faculty: for example, technical education often combines the study of theoretical mathematics and physics, and art schools often combine art history and literature with the practice of studio art.

Chapter 1 explained that integration of content areas is more readily manageable in the elementary classroom, where the teacher is usually a generalist. In the elementary classroom, the teacher can draw on themes common to a number of content areas to plan assignments, assistance can be given to students to actively integrate content knowledge from different subjects, and learners can use reading and writing strategies to help them integrate content from different content areas. Integration across the curriculum in junior and senior high school requires co-operative planning and even co-ordinating class schedules. Successful integration of social studies with science, science with language arts, language arts with fine arts, and language arts with physical education has already occurred in some schools.

There are arguments for and against the integrated curriculum in junior and senior high schools. Arguments for an integrated curriculum include:

1. exploration within single disciplines can be retained;
2. explicit connections within a discipline can be made;
3. natural combinations of disciplines can be planned so that links between concepts and practical applications can be made, for example, a lesson on the circulatory system could target the concept of systems;
4. topics can be arranged in individual disciplines so that similar units coincide, for example, a study of the stock market in math could coincide with study of the Great Depression; and
5. concepts or themes can be overlapped across different disciplines, for example, the concept of argument and evidence can be applied in math, science, language arts, and social studies. (Fogarty, 1991, pp. 61–65)

Arguments against an integrated curriculum include:

1. activities designed for an integrated curriculum may lack educational value in a particular subject matter;
2. integration activities may distort content;
3. activities may disrupt or nullify the accomplishment of major goals in the subject areas involved; and
4. activities may be educationally insignificant. (Brophy and Alleman, 1991, p. 66)

There is also a growing consensus that the **Cartesian philosophy** underlying modern education needs to be dismantled (Orr, 1993, p. 17). Cartesian philosophy refers to the ideas developed by the seventeenth-century French philosopher René Descartes and rests on four declarations:

1. that which is true knowledge is that which can be proven to be evident;
2. problems presented by such evidential knowledge can be solved by being reduced to the smallest parts;
3. knowledge proceeds from learning the easiest and simplest and rising to the most complex; and
4. knowledge is measurable and, therefore, requires complete enumeration. (Descartes, 1980, p. 10)

Applications of this philosophy have resulted in a separation of knowledge and experience. The "scaffolding of ideas, philosophies, and ideologies that constitutes the modern curriculum" divides education from lived experience by maintaining a separation of humanity from the natural world and by segregating mind from body (Wertheim, 1995, p. 17). The separation of personal knowledge and experience from subject matter knowledge may present serious barriers to learning for certain groups of learners. One implication of this separation is that one form of knowledge is superior to the other, and therefore has a higher value than the other. Most often it is personal experience and knowledge that are regarded as inferior. Another implication is that prior knowledge and experience gained outside of school actually impedes learning. We know through educational research that prior knowledge and experience is always involved in new learning whether negatively or positively. Yet another implication is that maintaining separation reinforces the dominant idea that knowledge is by nature hierarchical, that school knowledge is of great social and economic value and personal knowledge is not. The ethical problems with such a continued separation are perhaps the most difficult issue for teachers and educational researchers.

Many teachers are collaborating on developing integrated curricula for practical reasons: curricular changes are driven by concern for the particular

For Reflection 4.2
Why do you think maintaining a traditional disciplinary approach to teaching and learning could be of value? What would be the benefits of adding interdisciplinary teaching and learning strategies? How do you think an interdisciplinary approach to your own discipline might help you as a learner?

groups of adolescents attending a school, and small changes have frequently become a motive for school-wide change. One example of acting on a concern for a particular group of adolescents is the creation of arts schools where special emphasis is placed on drama, music, visual art, and creative writing. Another is the establishment of "alternative" schools for adolescents who have difficulty coping in large mainstream schools. In these schools, class sizes are small and there is evidence of greater accountability for time on tasks from the individual students than in larger schools.

The middle school, or junior high school, is a logical place to implement integrative curriculum, even though the "subject approach" is still "deeply entrenched in our schooling" (Beane, 1991, p. 12). An **integrative curriculum** for the middle school is built on three concepts: (1) the need for a general education focussing on the "shared concerns of early adolescents"; (2) the need to "serve the early adolescents who attend school"; and (3) the need to understand adolescents as "real human beings" who are "participants in the larger world" (p. 10). The number of middle schools has grown in the United States because of a growing awareness of the "need to provide school programs specifically designed for younger adolescents" (Wood & Muth, 1991, p. 84).

Many secondary schools in both Canada and the United States have recently attempted to move closer to a form of interdisciplinary education: English or language arts being combined with social studies and named "humanities studies" is one example. Interdisciplinary, thematic, and team-based humanities programs have been set up at St. Francis High School in Calgary, Alberta, as well as in the Los Angeles Unified School District in the United States. Typically, teams are composed of English, social studies, and art teachers, but some teams have included math, science, and dance instructors as well (Aschbacher, 1991, p. 16).

In New Richmond, Wisconsin, biology and agriculture teachers collaborate in order to design biotechnology curricula, and at Humboldt High School in St. Paul, Minnesota, teachers of industrial technology, college preparatory English, and geometry bring their students together for peer tutoring by graphic arts students in the school's computer laboratory. In the same school a teaching team from home economics and general mathematics/general science have joined forces to study world protein distribution (Beck, Copa, & Pease, 1991, p. 30). Science teachers at Littleton High

School in Colorado have integrated the study of the life, earth, and physical sciences to focus on developing scientific literacy. Students are required to study "every science, every year" and to demonstrate such skills as observing, comparing, categorizing, inferring, and applying (Crane, 1991, p. 40).

Collaboration across disciplines is a difficult and time-consuming process, and requires of individual teachers a willingness to listen to different points of view. A group of Ontario teachers interested in an integrated curriculum reported experiencing a "letting go" of their hold on the familiar boundaries of their disciplines (Drake, 1991, p. 20). Each participant had to find "personal meaning at every stage of the curriculum design" (p. 20). The team, consisting of teachers in the fields of English, history, geography, science, graphic arts, intermediate special education, physical and health education, and environmental studies, saw that gaps in their planning of the integrated curriculum were usually due to gaps in the team members' knowledge base and experience. They recommended that "as many different subject areas as possible be involved in curriculum building" (p. 22).

Although interdisciplinary studies are not always integrated in the sense that each discipline is given "equal time" or the same emphasis, the intention usually is to enable learners to study problems, concepts, procedures, and questions from multiple points of view. Such practice supports learning that makes use of the various learning styles of both teachers and learners.

The concept of integration is not new. Evidence of **integrated core curriculum**, which attempts to integrate a set of core disciplines, can be found as early as the mid-1800s (Vars, 1991, p. 14). In the United States the progressive education movement emphasized integrative approaches to education. Since that time, "more than 80 studies" of these approaches show that students in "various types of integrative/interdisciplinary programs have performed as well as or better on standardized achievement tests than students enrolled in the usual separate subjects" (pp. 14–15).

In spite of the history of advocacy for integrated interdisciplinary education, however, the **interdisciplinary curriculum** is difficult to implement. Heidi Hayes Jacobs offers three reasons for this: (1) "time barriers," (2) "personal barriers," and (3) trying "to do too much at once" (Brandt, 1991, p. 24). Because teachers in secondary schools identify strongly with their subjects and are protective of their departments' "cultures," Jacobs (1991) suggests looking for some "natural overlaps between subjects" and providing

For Reflection 4.3
What gaps can you identify in your acquisition of knowledge of different disciplines? In which of these disciplines are you most interested in building knowledge? What other disciplines seem most obviously related to your own?

"common planning time" for teams of teachers to build a two- to three-year plan (Brandt, 1991, p. 25).

Why Engage in Interdisciplinary Transactions with Text?

Before forming a team of teachers to plan an integrated interdisciplinary curriculum, individual teachers need to adopt interdisciplinary reading and writing tasks in the instructional practices of their own classrooms. Teachers should have experience using texts that are suitable to interdisciplinary reading and writing activities, and need to be able to make judgements about the limits of such texts. Integrated interdisciplinary reading and writing activities can be carried out in any secondary classroom where a teacher wishes to provide opportunities for "understanding performances" for his or her learners. Transacting with text that is interdisciplinary in content enables learners to experience problems or concepts in different ways; the "multiple intelligences" of learners are drawn into the reading and writing process.

The reading and writing activities suggested in this chapter use the concept that language learning is a transaction of multiple sign systems. These activities are also transactions that involve the readers' experience, understanding, and knowledge of the sign systems of different content areas. Thus, we call these reading and writing activities **interdisciplinary transactions**.

Urging teachers in secondary classrooms to work with interdisciplinary texts may sound like an impossible task. Yet, in our lived experience, many of us develop a range of interests or avocations in other disciplines or fields of knowledge. However, the time has come to think about and act on the idea of interdisciplinary transactions so that learners and teachers alike may become lifelong learners.

Our introduction to the idea of interdisciplinary transactions has emphasized reading and writing, but it also includes viewing, discussing, and listening. Viewing a scientific documentary produced for television or on CD-ROM can be enhanced with an accompanying written scientific text. Listening to and discussing music from different countries or different historical periods can become part of a unit that includes written and visual text related to those countries or periods. Discussion of any or all forms of text enhances learning by providing opportunities to make visible the aesthetic and efferent responses of individual learners.

Understanding the connection between the ideas of content literacy and those of interdisciplinary transaction can clarify the concept of integrated interdisciplinary learning. As shown in Chapter 1, content literacy is the ability to use reading and writing for the acquisition of new content in a given discipline (McKenna & Robinson, 1990). This ability includes general and content-specific literacy skills (Chapter 1 offers the example of map reading in social studies) and prior knowledge of content (McKenna & Robinson, 1990, p. 184). The main aim of a curriculum that supports content literacy and interdisciplinary learning is the active and independent acquisition of new knowledge of content by learners. To achieve content literacy across all the disciplines, learners must go beyond "technical literacy" (p. 186).

The difference between technical literacy and content literacy across the disciplines is an important one. Technical literacy does not necessarily provide evidence of understanding because such literacy relies on the skills expected in the particular context of a single discipline. To be technically literate, learners need only satisfy the "literacy demands of the instructional setting" (p. 186). To be content literate, however, learners must be able to show that they can organize and accommodate new knowledge of content as they clarify, refine, and extend prior knowledge of content through reading and writing tasks.

Chapter 2 showed the importance of reading as an aesthetic activity, and that integrating the acts of reading and writing enables one area of literacy to enhance the other. Chapter 3 discussed how integrating efferent and aesthetic reading and writing assists in active and independent learning. In becoming literate in one content area and across both cognitive and affective domains, learners are motivated to make connections between what is known in one content area and what can be learned in another content area, between prior lived experience and new experience.

As Orr (1993) has suggested, we recover the connections that already exist between experience and education. We enable our learners and ourselves to draw on prior experience, on what we have already understood and "performed" as part of our lived experience, our social understanding, our self-understanding.

Learning is more likely to occur when a learner is motivated to write about a text that is presented as belonging not just to one content area (that is, closed off to other subject matters) but as open to interpretation by mediating understanding from different subjects. The positive motivation derived from learning in one content area can be transferred to the traditionally less valued disciplines (such as music and drama) through the practice of integrated interdisciplinary reading and writing activities.

Talking and planning with teachers in different content areas works against the polarities created by "subject isolation" (Jacobs in Brandt, 1991, p. 24). The team approach to building an integrated interdisciplinary curriculum helps to support the growth of an "ecological imagination" and the development of a vision of "ecological education" to "heal the breach between humanity and its habitat" (Orr, 1993, p. 18). We do not lose the "great ideas" or "grand conversations" of the past; rather, we bring them to the horizons of our present understanding and knowledge.

To illustrate what we mean by supporting the growth of an ecological imagination and a vision of ecological education, the next sections offer examples of transactions with text that could be suitable for integrated activities in English and social studies and in science and social studies.

Exercise 4.1
An Interdisciplinary Transaction with Text:
English and Social Studies

Reading and writing about *The Diary of a Young Girl* in social studies and English classes in a **collaborative unit** brings together knowledge of World War II and the literary aspects of historical autobiography. Questions can be asked and discussed regarding the nature and effect of ideologies and the features of fascist movements in Europe at the time of the Second World War. Reading and writing about the diary of a young victim of the Holocaust could encourage an understanding of the text as well as the social and historical context in which the writing takes place.

The following is a passage from *The Diary of a Young Girl* by Anne Frank. Following this excerpt is an example of an interdisciplinary transaction with the text.

> As you can no doubt imagine, we often say in despair "What's the point of the war? Why, oh, why can't people live together peacefully? Why all this destruction?"
>
> The question is understandable, but so far no one has come up with a satisfactory answer. Why is England manufacturing bigger and better aeroplanes and bombs and at the same time churning out new houses for reconstruction? Why are millions spent on the war each day, while not a penny is available for medical science, artists or the poor? Why do people have to starve when mountains of food are rotting away in other parts of the world? Oh, why are people so crazy?
>
> I don't believe the war is simply the work of politicians and capitalists. Oh no, the common man is every bit as guilty; otherwise, people and nations would have rebelled long ago! There's a destructive urge in people, the urge to rage, murder and kill. And until all of humanity, without exception, undergoes a metamorphosis, wars will continue to be waged, and everything that has been carefully built up, cultivated and grown will be cut down and destroyed, only to start all over again!
>
> I've often been down in the dumps, but never desperate. I look upon our life in hiding as an interesting adventure, full of danger and romance, and every privation as an amusing addition to my diary. I've made up my mind to lead a different life from other girls, and not to become an ordinary housewife later on. What I'm experiencing here is a good beginning to an interesting life, and that's the reason — the only reason — why I have to laugh at the humorous side of the most dangerous moments.

I'm young and have many hidden qualities; I'm young and strong and living through a big adventure; I'm right in the middle of it and can't spend all day complaining because it's impossible to have any fun! I'm blessed with many things: happiness, a cheerful disposition and strength. Every day I feel myself maturing. I feel liberation drawing near, I feel the beauty of nature and the goodness of the people around me. Every day I think what a fascinating and amusing adventure this is! With all that, why should I despair?

Yours, Anne M. Frank

Source: From *The Diary of a Young Girl: The Definitive Edition* by Anne Frank. Otto H. Frank and Mirjam Pressler, eds. Translated by Susan Massotty. Translation copyright © 1995 by Doubleday, a division of Bantam Doubleday Dell Publishing Group, Inc. Used by permission of Doubleday Dell Publishing Group Inc.

When I attempt an aesthetic reading of this text, I find that certain passages and words cause me to stop. I experience a resistance to continuing to read. The narrator's reflections are very personal and the author's experience of fear of imprisonment and death causes strong emotions. I experience deep discomfort about these feelings. I also want to avoid feelings of guilt and responsibility, to avoid asking myself questions about why I am doing little or nothing to contribute to solving problems related to war, or social inequality or racism.

I note, however, that in my aesthetic reading of this passage the questions in the opening paragraphs seem to generate little emotional response perhaps because they are rhetorical questions. Without an answer being given in the text, these questions seem futile. I find myself looking to economics and political science for answers: for example, "to extend territory" or "to defend territory." I can also retrieve prior content area knowledge about the causes of war. Such generalizations do not require me to draw on my own experience of the lived world, so my answers to these questions ignore the terrible human experience of war.

As I read on to discover Anne's thoughts about her future, however, my own memories of being a young girl looking ahead into a bright future are called forth. These thoughts turn me inward because I must now draw on past lived experience and memory. But as I turn inward, I seem to plod, to drag myself heavily from one word to the next. When I stop reading, I wonder about this sensation of being slowed in my reading. I ask myself why the reading has become "weighty."

When Anne sings of the beauty of nature and the goodness of the people around her, I am thrown into the middle of an imagining that is composed of violence and mass murder. I see again the image of the little girl in the red coat running from Nazi soldiers in the film *Schindler's List* and remember catching just a glimpse of the red coat later under a heap of bodies in a cart. I bring to this reading what I remember feeling when I first saw photographs of the mounds of dead bodies at Dachau and Auschwitz.

When I position myself to read this passage efferently, I return to the first half of this diary entry, to the questions about why we continue to build more and heavier bombs instead of houses, about why money is spent on war instead of in support of artists and the poor. These questions are invitations to debate because they continue to demand discussion and solution today.

For Reflection 4.4

Learners can "live in" or inhabit the story of Anne Frank as an interdisciplinary text in many ways. What experiences or other texts could you draw on in thinking about a unit related to war?

Here are some questions derived from my efferent reading that could be discussed both as social studies and as science questions: Is there indeed an inborn urge in all of us to destroy, to kill, to murder? Is war the result of natural aggression in humankind? Can anyone prove that violence is part of human nature? What can scientists tell us about the effects of war? What institutions or movements contribute to peacemaking?

Questions that link aesthetic reading to efferent reading can be asked. For example, "What do your parents or grandparents remember about the year 1944?" Or, "Who could we ask to come to class to tell us about the war in 1944?" Learners might wish to find out what was happening in their town or city or country during May 1944. These activities could entail interviewing veterans and then reporting on the findings.

The activities described above can generate even more questions: What was happening in England in May 1944? in France? in Germany? in other parts of Canada? in the United States? in Japan? What other writing about World War II is available? What films? What music was popular in this period? What were the newspapers and magazines of different countries telling us about the war?

Integrated reading and writing activities like the ones described here enable students to experience reading and writing as border crossings between their prior knowledge and experience and new content area knowledge. The experience of reading and writing about a text using knowledge from more than one content area enables learners to carry on different conversations with the same text. Integrated reading and writing activities support the **practice of metacognition** or the ability to be intentional when reading and writing to "make sense of the text and the world" (Gordon, 1994, p. 116).

Exercise 4.2
An Interdisciplinary Transaction with Text:
Science and Social Studies

Further illustrating the nature of interdisciplinary transactions with text is the following excerpt entitled "Views and Values" by Canadian science writer David Suzuki. This text was originally a newspaper article, and it is expository in style, compared with the narrative form of the excerpt from Anne Frank's diary. An interdisciplinary transaction with this text follows.

Each of us is first and foremost a human being, with all of the attendant foibles and idiosyncrasies. We are products of the genes we received from our parents, our personal experiences, and the culture we grew up in. From the earliest part of our lives, we learn to "see" the world through the value and belief system of people around us. I'm impressed by this each time my young daughters squeal with delight at the same things *I* love and turn their backs on those *I'm* indifferent to. They've learned their lessons from me very well.

We acquire genetic and cultural "filters" through which we perceive the world around us. I was struck with the power of those filters last Labour Day weekend when I visited the Stein River Valley, a watershed supporting one of the last great virgin forests in British Columbia.

I was flown by helicopter up into the valley with my host, a Lillooet Indian. He pointed out the burial grounds of his ancestors, the battle site between his people and the neighbouring tribes, and their ancient hunting grounds. Our pilot told me that a week before he had taken a load of "foresters" over the same area and all they spoke of were the number of jobs, the years' worth of logging and the enormous profits those trees represented. The foresters and the natives were looking at the same things, but what they "saw" were worlds apart.

Source: From an article originally entitled "Network Needed with Views and Values of Native People," by David Suzuki. Reprinted by permission of David Suzuki.

The textbook from which this passage is taken is used in language arts and English classrooms, yet the vocabulary requires the reader to draw on his or her knowledge of science and social studies in order to construct meaning about the text.

If I begin with an efferent reading using a strategy aimed at constructing meaning through vocabulary, I can select from this passage a few words that I usually associate with the study of science and list beside them a few words associated with social studies. This listing process is a strategy called a **word sort**. Here is an example of a "word sort":

Science	**Social Studies**
genes	culture
genetic	belief system
watershed	Lillooet
genetic "filter"	cultural "filter"
virgin forest	Stein River Valley
	British Columbia

Even though the lists in Exercise 4.2 are short and incomplete, it is possible to construct relationships between some of the words in the two different lists. For example, the Stein River Valley is a "virgin forest" and also a "watershed"; the same valley is also a site rich in the native Lillooet culture and history. This relationship has biological, ecological, geographical, and cultural dimensions; thus, the topic "Stein River Valley," as encountered in this text, draws on knowledge from at least four disciplines.

Yet another relationship exists, the relationship between the Lillooet people and the foresters, which poses a contradiction in viewpoints about the same place. The same environment can be seen, suggests Suzuki, through different but related filters or viewpoints. Still another relationship presents itself in these lists, acting as a link between science and social studies. The relationship between the topics "genes" and "culture" can be seen if I use them to create an overarching topic for an entire unit. For example, an interdisciplinary unit topic might be "Nature or Nurture — What's in a Gene?" or "Nature or Nurture — How Does Our Culture Affect an Individual's Point of View?" Interdisciplinary questions can be formulated to guide reading and writing activities: What are genes? Do they determine behaviour? What are "genetic filters"? What do we mean by "culture"? How is it formed? Is there such a thing as a "cultural filter"? How might a "cultural filter" work? How might we change our "cultural filters"?

When I ask such questions I can begin to see how Suzuki's text can be linked to Anne Frank's diary. Learners could read and write about "cultural filters" that cause us to see different races or cultures as inferior or superior. Learners might ask questions such as: Can "cultural filters" be understood in scientific terms? How do we acquire our "cultural filters"? What "cultural filters" are at work in North American society?

After reading this text, one student teacher suggested that a debate between students representing the foresters and others representing the Lillooet Indians would be useful. Suzuki's report of the foresters' concern for jobs and profits could lead learners into research on the pulp and paper industry in British Columbia, or anywhere else in Canada. Inquiry into Lillooet culture could direct learners to search out Native art, information covering Native beliefs about nature, and the relationship between Native culture and the natural world. A debate could involve the entire class in an interdisciplinary unit aimed at integrating learning about Native art and culture, religious beliefs, geography, history, the pulp and paper industry, and the study of cultural filters at work in our society.

If I take an aesthetic reading stance with this text, I can ask myself questions that lead into interdisciplinary topics in a different way. When I read the first paragraph, I experience conflict: on the one hand, I can see myself as an individual yet I can also see myself as an inheritor of parental values. This experience of conflict is uncomfortable, so I try to find a balance between seeing myself as a unique person and seeing myself as an extension of my parents, conditioned by the values of the social group into which I was born.

Each claim rings true, and yet each seems to contradict the other. Living through this text involves contradiction and uncertainty about meaning, and shows the reader that truth does necessarily come to us as the result of reduction of meaning.

An Interdisciplinary Transaction with Text: Science and Mathematics

In this section we focus on a text that can be used for a unit that combines biology and mathematics. "Organ Transplants: Achieving the Impossible," in Box 4.1, offers an opportunity to study organ transplant procedures in conjunction with a class survey on attitudes toward organ transplants.

An efferent reading of this text produces a number of facts:

1. the dates of the first successful transplants;
2. the organs that were transplanted during these operations;
3. the names of the doctors who performed these operations;
4. the major problem with organ transplants: rejection of the transplanted organ;
5. the most commonly transplanted organ: kidneys;
6. the most recent live-donor transplant of part of a liver from a mother to her infant son; and
7. the acute shortage of suitable transplant organs.

When readers change to an aesthetic reading stance, they place themselves in the position of living through these facts as a series of narratives. First, there is the story of the initial operations, then the story of the invention of a drug to prevent organ rejection; next, the story of kidney transplants, and then, the story of a mother donating part of her liver to her infant son. The final story is about the shortage of organs available for transplant.

Changing one's stance from efferent to aesthetic enables readers to see the multi-faceted nature of this text. The facts do not stand alone as scientific truths, but, rather, add up to a very particular problem that is not scientific in nature, but social, or psychological, or moral, or all of these.

Let us review the different interdisciplinary directions that have been opened up by efferent reading and the composing of **efferent writing** responses. The first paragraph gives a brief history of transplant operations, but while this history is informative, it acts mainly as an introduction. The topic of the second paragraph is stated in the first sentence: the "major problem" with organ transplants. The problem — rejection of donated organs —

Box 4.1
Organ Transplants: Achieving the Impossible

Transplant operations have come a long way since 1954, when American doctor Joseph Murray performed the first successful organ transplant (a kidney from one identical twin to the other), which lasted 24 years. Two years later, Dr. E. Donnall Thomas performed the first bone-marrow transplant, which has become the standard treatment for leukemia. The first heart transplant was performed in 1967 by South African doctor Christiaan Barnard. Many years later, in 1990, Drs. Murray and Thomas received the Nobel prize in medicine for their pioneering work.

The major problem with organ transplants is rejection by the recipient. In 1980, tests showed that the drug cyclosporine could effectively suppress the body's natural tendency to reject foreign tissue. Subsequently, transplants of the kidney, liver, lung, heart, pancreas, and bone-marrow tissue became increasingly common. These operations have saved many lives, but not without controversy over the ethical issues involved, especially the selling of body parts — as opposed to donating — and the use of fetal tissue.

Kidneys are the most commonly transplanted organs. Because the human body can function with only one of its kidneys, live donors are sometimes used. The operation is less expensive than long-term dialysis, the only other treatment for kidney failure. Despite the advances in organ transplantation, not all transplants are successful, and the recipient must fully recover from the traumatic operation before it can be attempted again.

We cannot survive without a liver, yet doctors in Australia recently used a live donor in a liver transplant operation. They removed one quarter of a woman's liver and transplanted the piece to replace her 17-month-old son's defective liver; without the transplant, the child would have died. Because the liver can regenerate itself, the transplanted portion should grow normally along with the child, while the mother should regrow her own liver.

Unfortunately, there is an acute shortage of suitable organs available. Although many Canadians say that they would be willing to have their organs used to save someone else's life, only 27% actually sign the organ donor card on their driver's licence. Even if this card has been signed, most doctors will not use an organ without the permission of surviving relatives, and many doctors are reluctant to approach grieving relatives. Even if all parties agree, there is not always enough time to transplant the organ before it deteriorates. The increasing use of national and international computer database systems to keep track of suitable organs may help solve this problem, but people will continue to die while they wait for a suitable organ.

Source: From *Biology in Action*, by M.C. Poole, G. Pilkey, and E.C. Johnson, 1992, Toronto: Harcourt Brace, p. 185. Reprinted by permission.

can be controlled by the drug cyclosporine; however, the increase in organ transplants resulting from the drug's success has brought to light another problem: the selling of body parts. Scientific advance is shown in this case to be accompanied by social problems.

The third paragraph focusses on the kidneys, but this paragraph tells me that the success of organ transplants is countered by yet another problem: the fact that not all transplants are successful even with the help of new drugs. The next paragraph tells of the transplant of a part of a mother's liver to her baby. Compelled to change my reading stance to an aesthetic position, I visualize a tiny child lying on a surgical table while his mother lies nearby as a live donor. Then I remember my daughter as a newborn. As a mother, I identify very strongly with the mother who gives part of her own body to her infant son. I feel great emotional pain at the thought of my child dying, and so I can empathize with this mother whose son will die without the liver transplant. I can begin to understand the dilemma described in this text because I can live through the difficulties related to organ transplants.

In the last paragraph I learn that only 27 percent of Canadians sign the organ donor cards on their driver's licences. Living through this text engenders an experience of deep fear: What if I or someone I loved needed an organ transplant and there was none available? What prohibits so many of us from donating our organs?

Several possibilities for interdisciplinary reading and writing activities present themselves when we ask questions about this text. Learners could study the organs of the human body from a scientific point of view. Visual text is useful here in showing the function and composition of each organ. Since there is an enormous amount of information to be learned about the organs, independent and/or group research projects could help individuals focus on the study of a particular organ. Charting helps to organize this information.

Another direction for group work is the traditional dissection procedure followed by a report. This kind of activity belongs traditionally to the biology lab and requires laboratory facilities and a teacher with the skills and experience to undertake such a procedure. The biology report could be carried out in written and oral form providing other learners with the information gathered in each group.

Diseases of the organs can also be learned and added to the chart. Charting also provides an opportunity to identify new vocabulary. Vocabulary study will be necessary in the acquisition of understanding about the organs of the human body.

What is most unique in regard to interdisciplinary transaction with this text, however, is the possibility of collaborating with math and social studies teachers in order to help students carry out a survey of attitudes toward organ donation. Designing and conducting a survey requires the following steps:

1. Deciding on a survey topic.
2. Brainstorming the type of information desired, for example:

   - number of students who are for and against organ donation
   - number of students against for religious reasons
   - number of students in favour for scientific reasons
   - number of male students for and against
   - number of female students for and against
   - most common reasons for and against
   - number of students refraining from taking a position for or against.

3. Deciding on the size and nature of the sample group(s).
4. Creating clear, answerable questions for the survey.
5. Working as a team to collect the data.
6. Calculating the results and expressing the findings in percentages.
7. Deciding on the best way to communicate results: by charts, graphs, computer program with graphics, video, or newspaper article. (Here collaboration with other teachers and students in other disciplines is desirable.)
8. Evaluating the significance of the results.

A survey such as this would entail careful organization, but the rewards would be considerable for both teachers and students. Learners would have the opportunity to discover what is required when working as a team. They would have the opportunity to learn how to work with computer math software and could even learn definitions of "fractions," "decimals," and "percent." Learners could also use this unit to learn about spreadsheets.

An example of an interdisciplinary approach to this text would be to collect information from newspaper, television, or magazine surveys. This opens up an opportunity to explore mass media as a subject matter. Connecting learners to the world of print and visual media offers an opportunity to use our "multiple intelligences" and our prior knowledge of popular culture. Learners can also engage in critiquing the value of surveys in general, and applying this experience to evaluating the methods and results of other surveys.

An Interdisciplinary Transaction Combining Visual and Written Text

One of the most exciting possibilities of interdisciplinary transactions is crossing the borders between visual and written text and, as in the following examples, between literary art and the science of biology. In this transaction I use a visual text of the brain (see Figure 4.1), which is accompanied by a written text.

Figure 4.1

Sagittal View of the Central Nervous System

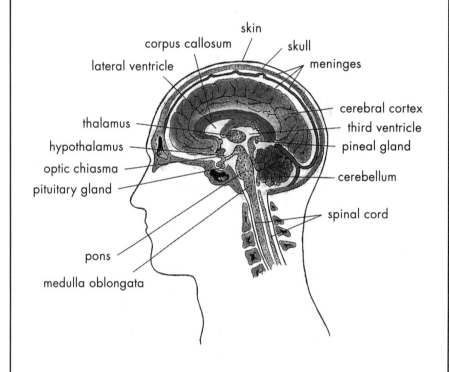

Source: From "Organ Transplants: Achieving the Impossible," by M.C. Poole, G. Pilkey, and E.C. Johnson, 1992, in *Biology in Action,* Toronto: Harcourt Brace, p. 366, Figure 19.5. Reproduced by permission.

Surrounding the visual text of the central nervous system are sixteen vocabulary items I will need to understand if I am to take away knowledge about the central nervous system. The words or terms are not defined on the actual diagram, but the captions do show the various locations of the parts. I can read the visual text, therefore, to identify the spatial relationships among the parts of the central nervous system.

To begin this process of reading the visual text for comprehension, I will note the terms I am already familiar with. In this case, I find three: skin, skull, spinal cord. I know that skin covers my whole body and that it is an organ. I can touch the skin that covers my scalp, and when I do this I can feel the hard shell under my scalp that we call the skull. When I move my hands to the back of my head and down to the back of my neck, I can actually feel from the outside where my spinal column meets my skull. If I return to read the visual text, I see that there appears to be no connection between the spinal cord and the skull. Instead, the spinal cord enters the centre of the central nervous system inside the skull, and becomes something like a tree with branches off a main trunk. Working from what I know and can experience about my own body, I begin to understand that the spinal cord is the connection between the central nervous system and the rest of my body.

I can now find another set of terms for which I can associate a meaning but cannot give a full definition. The words are: optic, cerebral, and gland. Working from "optic," which I associate with vision or sight, I can predict that the "optic chiasma" has something to do with my eyes, with how I see. When I look at my eyes in a mirror, and then look back at the visual text, I begin to understand that my eyes are my outer connection to the world: the inner connection to the world of my central nervous system is that small branch off the spinal column called the optic chiasma. I can now formulate questions to guide my search to understand the function of the optic chiasma. How does the optic chiasma help to make my eyes work? How does it work in relation to the rest of the central nervous system?

Now I turn to the word "cerebral." This word is familiar to me as an adjective to describe a personality or way of looking at the world: "She is a cerebral sort of person." I understand this word to mean "intellectual" or "thoughtful" in the sense of being analytical and reflective. Since I am not certain about the meaning of cortex, I have to return to the visual representation offered of the cerebral cortex in order to begin to make sense of this term. The cerebral cortex is a large, coiled mass occupying nearly the entire area between the front of the skull and the back. It looks like a helmet or, to use my tree metaphor, a solid mass of leaves spread about the top of the trunk formed by the spinal cord. It is the largest part of the central nervous system. Now I can ask more questions: Why is the cerebral cortex so large? What is its function? How does it work?

When I turn to the word "gland," I note that there are two glands shown in the drawing of the central nervous system: the pituitary gland is located at the front just above the optic chiasma and the pineal gland is located in the centre of the nervous system at the top of the spinal cord but opposite to the pituitary gland. I can now ask more questions: What are the functions of these glands? Are their functions related? If so, how?

Reading this visual text by starting with my prior knowledge of the meanings of words and my lived experience of my own body, I have used a succession of strategies to aid in my efferent reading of the text that accompanies the diagram. When I search the text for those four terms, I find the following definitions:

pituitary gland or hypophysis — called the master gland because it controls the release of hormones from other endocrine glands in the body.
pineal gland — in amphibians called the third eye because it controls skin colour to allow animals to blend with their surroundings; in humans it is indirectly connected to the eyes but its function is not yet understood.
cerebral cortex — the major centre for co-ordination and motor functions, 85 percent water, soft, almost jellylike.

I can find no definition for optic chiasma so I will have to search elsewhere for an explanation. I now have nine terms left. They are: medulla oblongata, pons, hypothalamus, thalamus, lateral ventricle, corpus callosum, meninges, third ventricle, and cerebellum. Without rereading the visual text, I can predict that the hypothalamus and the thalamus are likely to be related because "thalamus" is the root word of "hypothalamus." When I do return to the visual text, I see that the "thalamus" is larger than the "hypothalamus" but that both images are textured to look like connected parts of the spinal cord. This visual similarity would indicate a relationship. When I check for definitions I find these:

thalamus — the main relay station of the brain.
hypothalamus — where nervous and hormonal systems interact to regulate body temperature, growth, sexual function, hunger, thirst, blood pressure, salt balance, and water balance; interacts with the pituitary gland.

I infer that the hypothalamus is a smaller, more specific kind of relay station handling signals that move outward to other organs of the body. For example, it regulates skin temperature and interacts with glands throughout the body. I can deduce that the thalamus deals with signals going into the brain whereas the hypothalamus deals with signals going outward to other bodily functions.

I now have seven terms left. I can make a prediction about the lateral ventricle and the third ventricle because I understand that "ventricle" refers to a cavity or space. The lateral ventricle and third ventricle must refer to spaces or cavities in the central nervous system. Sure enough, when I check the diagram, the lines drawn from the term point to a white space. Still, the function of these cavities is a mystery, and I wonder why there is no "second ventricle." There is no information in the index or in the chapter on the central nervous system, so I will have to look elsewhere for information about function. This leaves me with five terms. I search the text for definitions for medulla oblongata and pons first because they are the only parts I have not yet investigated. This is what I find in the text:

medulla oblongata — located at the anterior end of the spinal cord; controls reflex functions such as breathing, swallowing, vomiting, and heartbeat.

I can find no definition for pons, so I will have to search elsewhere. Three terms remain: corpus callosum, meninges, and cerebellum. Here is what I find in the accompanying written text:

corpus callosum — a thick junction joining the cerebral hemispheres of the brain, through which there is a constant flow of information to allow the hemispheres to co-ordinate activities on both sides of the body.
meninges — the three membranes that cover the central nervous system.

When I return to the visual text to check on the cerebellum, I see that it is pictured as a green, leafy area, a bundle smaller than the mass of the brain itself, but similar in its appearance of being coiled and thick. Here is the definition:

cerebellum — control centre for motor co-ordination and posture: co-ordinates body movements on orders from the new brain.

The mention of "new" here helps me to see that the human brain is composed, in a sense, of two brains: a "primitive" or old brain, and a new brain. Mammals such as humans have a primitive brain much like fish and reptiles, but humans also have a new brain that is thought to control conscious thought. The old brain is believed to control basic emotions such as anger.

In reviewing the strategies I have used to make sense of this visual text and the names of the parts of the central nervous system, I began with prior knowledge, with an understanding of language I am familiar with in my lived experience. My next step was to use my hands to locate my own spinal cord and the bottom of my skull. In a sense I did what might be called a "body reading." I then compared this reading with a reading of the visual text and saw that although my spine seemed to disappear at the junction with my skull, in fact, it continues deep into the interior of my head. I then used analogy to see that the spinal column is like a tree in the sense that it branches out once it is inside my skull. I then formulated questions to guide me in my search for information about these parts of the central nervous system. I approached the individual parts of the system that I did not know as branches of the spinal cord, locating each branch visually and then listing and defining each in writing. I drew on multiple intelligences such as linguistic intelligence, spatial intelligence, and bodily-kinesthetic intelligence. I also used logical intelligence, or my ability to reason, to make connections between one kind of intelligence and another.

Can you identify other strategies that I used? Did you notice that I moved back and forth, placed the two texts in transaction with each other in order to construct meaning about both?

An Interdisciplinary Transaction between a Science Text and a Literary Text

Joy Kogawa's poem "What Do I Remember of the Evacuation?" can be read in transaction with the previous text on the central nervous system with interesting results (see Box 4.2).

In developing her theory of transaction with literary text, Rosenblatt (1978) urges us to attend to what we "live through" as fully as possible during each reading. Since I have just carried out a lengthy transaction with scientific text from an efferent stance in the previous section, I am bringing to my aesthetic reading of Kogawa's poem a new and growing understanding of the possibilities of how the central nervous system affects human behaviour.

What has been carried away from the scientific text is not the detailed differences among each part of the central nervous system but a "big picture" of the new brain interacting with the old brain. The old brain I picture as the seat of emotional energy and basic drives; the new brain I see as an electrified beehive of activity, an efficient power plant composed of millions of floors, corridors, and processing rooms that generate, maintain, and store our memories and conscious thought. The old brain is where I experience emotions such as love or rage, whereas the new brain does the thinking and planning.

As I read this poem from an aesthetic stance, I live through the words and letters as signs with which I am already familiar. The images used in the poem are familiar to me for they are made of the letters and words of my mother tongue. Still, I can predict from my past experience of reading poetry that these familiar signs will likely be placed in relationship with each other in ways that will surprise me, making me stop to question my previous experience of a word or phrase.

As I position myself to "live through" this poem, I remember that my central nervous system is processing every one of these signs. I am unsure where in my central nervous system each phase of this activity of living through my reading will take place, but I am fairly certain that some activity will occur in the old brain and some in the new brain. It is likely, for example, that the dozens of images that I live through as I read this poem will evoke memories from my past, accompanied by feelings and thoughts associated with those memories. Because the poet is writing about her memories of being taken away from her home as a small child, I will be living through my own memories of leaving or departing when I did not wish to do so. It is a transaction between the lived experiences of two very different lives.

As I begin to draw on my memories of childhood, somewhere in my "new brain" and somewhere along the corpus callosum dozens of messages are flowing back and forth to create the images I call my traces of memories. To

Box 4.2
What Do I Remember of the Evacuation?

What do I remember of the evacuation?
I remember my father telling Tim and me
About the mountains and the train
And the excitement of going on a trip.
What do I remember of the evacuation?
I remember my mother wrapping
A blanket around me and my
Pretending to fall asleep so she would be happy
Though I was so excited I couldn't sleep
(I hear there were people herded
Into the Hastings Park like cattle.
Families made to move in two hours
Abandoning everything, leaving pets
And possessions at gun point.
I hear families were broken up
Men were forced to work. I heard
It whispered late at night
That there was suffering) and
I missed my dolls.
What do I remember of the evacuation?
I remember Miss Foster and Miss Tucker
Who still live in Vancouver
And who did what they could
And loved the children and who gave me
A puzzle to play with on the train.
And I remember the mountains and I was
Six years old and I swear I saw a giant
Gulliver of Gulliver's Travels scanning the horizon
And when I told my mother she believed it too
And I remember how careful my parents were
Not to bruise us with bitterness
And I remember the puzzle of Lorraine Life
Who said "Don't insult me" when I
Proudly wrote my name in Japanese
And Tim flew the Union Jack
When the war was over but Lorraine
And her friends spat on us anyway
And I prayed to the God who loves
All the children in his sight
That I might be white.

Source: From *A Chance of Dreams*, by Joy Kogawa. Reprinted by permission of the author.

help me select and focus on these remembered images as they correspond to the images in the poem, I slow down the retrieval process by returning to the text and fixing on the images that stand out for me. Here are a few of them:

> . . . my father telling Tim and me . . .
> . . . the mountains and the train . . .
> . . . people herded . . . like cattle . . .
> . . . at gun point . . .
> . . . bruise . . . with bitterness . . .
> . . . prayed . . . that I might be white . . .

Notice how a few images are being "carried away" from the poem, and that combining these parts of the poem produces an abridged version of the original poem. If I were to merge some of my own memories I might have something like this:

> lighting a cigarette
> my father launches his story
> of the conquered French
> my father telling Tim and me
> how the British
> herded people like cattle
> at gun point
> praying for their lives

Somewhere in my cerebral cortex visual signs are sparked. To live through my reading of "my father launches his story," I construct a fragmented image of my dead father's face. Telling stories was not something my father did very often, but once he told a story about the expulsion of the Acadians. As I try to reconstruct his telling of families being sent away from their homes on boats, of children being separated from their parents, of wives being torn from their husbands, I am astonished to realize that, like the evacuation of "Tim and me" and their parents, the expulsion of the Acadians was also an "evacuation." Unbidden come the words "elimination" and "extermination" and a remembrance of Anne Frank and the evacuation of her family.

How have these connections happened? Are words stored in one particular place in the cerebral cortex? In what form do these words live? Why do they seem to link themselves so readily? Is it just that they begin with the same letter? Or because I remember just enough Latin to know that these words all refer to being "kept out" or "sent away" or "wiped out"?

I return to the diagram of the central nervous system, reread the names for the parts of the system, and then locate them once more in the visual text. The parts all appear to be interconnected, coiled neatly about each other, designed to fit together like parts of a carefully designed system. But how could such a clever system be designed so that a person learns to see others as enemies, as cattle to be herded, as objects to be evacuated, eliminated, exterminated? I have only a partial answer, which isn't much of an answer at all: a system is just that, a physical plant waiting to be put into action. Something must fill the storage rooms of the plant, and drive its generating stations. That something must be the individual's lived experience, knowledge, and understanding of his or her experience — something we call self-definition or, better, self-understanding. We can understand ourselves as human beings in contradictory and sometimes disturbing ways: as murderers and caregivers, as builders and destroyers, as artists and scientists.

Somewhere in the central nervous system we make decisions, sometimes without being conscious of making them. Some of us store lived experience and knowledge about caring for offspring, and try to make decisions that ensure our children grow and live well. Some of us learn how to love and protect, and some of us learn how to hate, eliminate, and exterminate. Most of us are capable of all of these actions.

Engaging in an interdisciplinary transaction with these texts leads me to reflect that the hatred that drives us to eliminate and exterminate co-exists with our ability to care, to love, to nurture. I am willing to predict that some day we will understand how this is so, but I have inferred from my reading about the central nervous system that there is still much that we do not understand about how the system works. We might be tempted to think that if we could locate where our emotions and desires reside, we could simply turn one off and the other on. Or we might think it desirable to eliminate the destructive aspects of human behaviour and allow only our good side to direct our choices. But how are we to determine laws defining which human actions are universally good or bad? And, just as important, who will make and enforce these laws?

Another reflection that might arise as we allow readings of these texts to transact with each other is the extent to which the human brain has evolved. Is the old brain so old that it is dying? If it dies, will it take with it all the emotions, the "good" and the "bad"? Or perhaps the old and new brains are designed to "converse" with each other, to struggle over decisions and actions. Perhaps a poem such as Kogawa's is the product of such a struggle.

In trying to sum up, I begin to think that is what I have lived through as I read this poem — the writer's ongoing struggle to understand her experience of fear and hatred, and her continuing struggle to find ways to live graciously and magnanimously in spite of the fear and hatred of others. This revelation opens up an awareness that each of us can learn to struggle to understand this experience of fear and hatred. Each of us can gain insight into what it means to live bravely, not only by living through a reading of poetry like Kogawa's, but also by conversing with others and writing about what we

---

For Reflection 4.5

Picture three or four fields of green grass dotted with a few old trees spreading shade under leafy branches, and picture these fields with walls built between them. Picture also small groups of people in each field: in the first meadow a group of painters, in the second a group of biologists, in the third a group playing soccer or field hockey, in the fourth, a group doing something different again. Describe what you see happening in the first field, in the second, and then in the third and fourth. Then compose a conversation that might occur between any two or three groups of these people coming together to share their experience and knowledge.

---

understand as we construct meaning from the texts of those who work in separate fields.

This conclusion returns me to the value of being able to read and write through interdisciplinary understanding, and of helping our learners cross the "borders" between the arts and the sciences. We need to become aware of how our readings of textual worlds can be both scientific and aesthetic. When we have experienced the pleasure of seeing the same world in different ways, and when we have learned how to communicate these differences in our perceptions and understandings through talk, through reading, and through writing, we will have learned something about the joy of creating "possible worlds" out of "actual minds" (Bruner, 1986).

Summary

This chapter describes what is meant by integrated interdisciplinary curriculum and explains why interdisciplinary transactions with text within such a curriculum are desirable. By linking the idea of transaction with sociosemiotic theory and Perkins's theory of understanding performances, the chapter supports the conceptualizing and planning of such a curriculum at both junior and senior high-school levels. The need for teachers to transact with interdisciplinary texts so that they can implement such transactions in their own classrooms is emphasized. Learning how to transact with texts across different disciplines helps learners to use the knowledge and understanding they have of the different disciplines being learned in schools, to build on their comprehension of text, and, in the process, to become more content literate. Five examples of interdisciplinary transactions with texts demonstrated how readers can construct meaning across a range of content areas.

Questions for Further Reflection

Select two or three pieces of text that you and your learners read as part of your curriculum, and then answer the following questions.

1. Make a list of words you find in these texts that you think might be encountered in content areas other than your own.
2. Make a word web (showing how the words are associated) for each of any two or three of these words, using any associated words that come to mind. (See Chapter 6 for examples of word webs).
3. From among the words you use in your word webs, select another two or three and brainstorm on what you think they might mean in other content areas.
4. Plan a word scavenger hunt for your learners using all the original words you selected from the texts you chose in question 1.
5. Find a picture or an object to match one or two of these words and write about what you see in the picture and why the object is a good match for the word.
6. Go to an art gallery or see a film or video, and afterwards write down words and/or images that were used in the work and that could be linked to a content area in which you teach.

Key Terms

Cartesian philosophy
Collaborative unit
Efferent writing
Integrated core curriculum
Integrative curriculum
Interdisciplinary curriculum

Interdisciplinary transactions
Practice of metacognition
Understanding performances
Whole language theory
Word sort

PART TWO

Successful Learning in the Content Areas

CHAPTER FIVE

Talking and Discussing to Enhance Content Comprehension

Questions to Consider for this Chapter

1. What does the concept of "transaction" mean to you?

2. What is the difference between transaction with text and transaction with peers?

3. How does talk/discussion (oracy) provide support for reading and writing (literacy) activities?

4. What does it mean to hold a discussion? What is the teacher's role in a "true" discussion?

5. How can you teach students the process of discussion?

6. What types of questions need to be posed by teachers and students to enable transactions with texts (textbooks or student-composed texts) and fellow students?

7. How do you honour and encourage cultural and language diversity in discussions?

8. What do you think is meant by "being a good listener"?

9. How do you teach the participants in a discussion to be good listeners?

10. How do you assess the effectiveness of classroom talk/discussion?

11. What is the relationship between talk/discussion and collaborative and co-operative activities?

Overview

The chapter begins by discussing students' talk with one another as valuable transactions. Discussion (classroom talk) is then defined as an open exchange of ideas, sometimes on topics or themes for which there are no "right" answers. Methods for teaching the process of discussion are outlined. Several categories of questions (to be posed by teachers or students) are then developed to focus discussions; it is also acknowledged that discussion can be sustained through student and teacher comments and statements. Since today's classrooms are rich with differences in abilities and cultural backgrounds, linguistic and ethnic diversity is also addressed. Strategies for "teaching to diversity" are elaborated. The chapter then outlines specific techniques for facilitating effective discussions. Two holistic approaches for reflecting on and evaluating discussion are also provided. The chapter then contains a section on collaborative/co-operative learning, both of which are crucial to discussion/classroom talk. First, a differentiation is made between collaborative and co-operative learning; then, suggestions are provided for peer collaborative and peer tutoring activities as discussion activities.

The Value of Classroom Talk

Earlier chapters focussed on how students can transact with texts; this chapter deals with transactions during classroom talk. When students talk they transact with text and with one another. The transactions that occur among students, teachers, and peers within a social environment are called "events" (Almasi, 1996). Events can occur in whole-class or small-group discussions. Meaning is socially constructed and students can improve comprehension, critical thinking skills, and metalinguistic abilities (Rosenblatt, 1989). By sharing their thoughts, students learn how their evocations differ from those of other students. Writers also learn to better understand their transactional relationship with their readers when they read and discuss each other's texts (Rosenblatt, 1989). Such sharing by readers, writers, listeners, and viewers contributes to a **metalinguistic awareness** because students become more aware of and more critical of their selection and synthesis processes as they think about their interpretations (Rosenblatt, 1989; Newton, 1991). In the English language arts, in particular, discussion of different interpretations leads to group interpretation, to criticism of one's own interpretations, and, in turn, to the development of criteria to validate interpretations. Students need to read, write, and talk about texts from both an efferent and an aesthetic stance.

As discussed in Chapters 1 and 2, language is a process set in the social world and is linked to cognitive development (Vygotsky, 1962). Language is also linked to the ongoing dialogues among individuals in different social interactions (Bakhtin, 1981). On the basis of these two premises, Sperling (1996) asserts that an understanding of how language makes sense in a social

---

For Reflection 5.1
Think about how talking about a subject with others in everyday experiences
helps you to understand it.

---

context lies at the heart of learning. In **social contexts**, "readers always **negotiate meaning** with an unseen author and often with a visibly present group
of peers (along with a teacher) in a discussion group" (Pearson, 1993, p. 503;
Bakhtin, 1981). Such activities are transactional because they are determined
jointly by students and the teacher and because interpretations of the text also
are determined jointly.

Language serves for the expression of thought (Chomsky, 1977) and for
achieving higher-level thought and learning through interaction (Vygotsky,
1962, 1978). Bruner (1966) and Britton (1970, 1984) thus support the idea
of students reading, talking, and learning together in small groups. Since talk
plays an essential role in learning (Vygotsky, 1978), those who do not participate in talk miss opportunities for learning. Mentioned in earlier chapters was the value of expressive talk as a way of thinking one's way into a
content area. Talking through things helps us explain concepts to ourselves
and to others. At the same time, there are opportunities to listen to others
and to learn by listening. The term **oracy** has been used to describe ability in
listening and speaking (Wilkinson, 1965), while literacy refers to reading and
writing abilities.

Unfortunately, in many content area classrooms, it is silence that is
equated with thinking and productivity (Cullinan, 1993). Silence denies students opportunities to become competent language users who can "talk" the
content of each content area. Silence denies students opportunities to transact with text and with each other.

There are several reasons to encourage talk (and discussion) in the classroom (Cullinan, 1993; Gambrell, 1996):

- Talk develops deeper understandings of content and process.
- Talk helps clarify thinking and increases higher-level thinking and problem-
solving ability.
- Talk improves communication skills.
- Talk aids comprehension.
- Talk before writing supports writing and leads to effective composition.
- Talk develops students' confidence.
- Talk provides insight into students' thinking.

Almasi (1996) adds that discussion has not only cognitive value but social-
emotional and affective benefits as well. Students assume control of their own
learning, increase their self-esteem, judge their own competence, and develop

For Reflection 5.2
Think back to how talk and discussion were used in large and small groups in the content area classroom when you were in secondary school. What kind of instruction was provided in how to carry on a discussion?

positive attitudes toward others in discussion groups. They also have opportunities to respond aesthetically during the talk.

For talk to develop, practice must be provided in a variety of situations and activities. Among these activities are discussions, **literature circles**, storytelling, creative drama, and Readers Theatre (Wilkinson, 1965). However, discussion is the most frequently used vehicle in classrooms, particularly content area classrooms, for developing and extending oral language, stimulating thinking, identifying and clarifying comprehension of informational texts, assessing comprehension, generating ideas for writing, and problem solving (Mazzoni & Gambrell, 1996; Smith & Smith, 1994).

Research with teachers and students at the secondary level provides evidence that discussion enhances the learning of content (Alvermann, 1986; Alvermann, O'Brien, & Dillon, 1990; Alvermann & Hayes, 1989). In peer-led discussions, students recognize and clear up their misunderstandings because "cognitive unrest" is shared, exposed, and confronted in social transactions (Almasi & Gambrell, 1994). Small-group discussions of content materials enable students to increase and clarify their understandings (McMahon, 1992; Mazzoni & Gambrell, 1996).

Defining Discussion

What constitutes **discussion**? "True discussion is an open exchange of ideas and opinions about topics that may not have easy answers" (Kletzien & Baloche, 1994, p. 540, citing Cintorino, 1993). With difficult or complex topics there may be more than one right answer and there may be many facets to an answer. In discussion, students, not just teachers, ask questions and interact or transact with other students. Students clarify and expand their thinking as they listen to different understandings.

While the terms conversation and discussion are sometimes used interchangeably in the professional literature, discussion combines conversational aspects (responsive dialogue among participants) with instructional aspects to enhance learning of content and thinking skills (Walker, 1996). This type of discourse is based on the **constructivist model**, in which talk (which encourages participants to manipulate ideas and make connections with what they already know) is a stimulus for understanding text (read, heard, or viewed) and for creating meaning (Wertsch, 1991; Gaskins, Satlow, Hyson, Osterlag, & Six, 1994).

Discussions are not **recitations**, in which teachers predetermine the structure by controlling student turn-taking, asking most or all of the questions, doing the majority of the talking, and allowing students only two- to three-word answers (Alvermann, Dillon, & O'Brien, 1987). Discussion differs from recitation in at least three main ways (Alvermann, Dillon, & O'Brien, 1987):

1. Participants must present multiple viewpoints and be prepared to change their minds on the basis of other arguments presented.
2. Participants must interact (or in our view, transact) with one another (at least 40 percent of the time, according to Dillon, 1981) as well as with the teacher.
3. The verbal interactions must be longer than the typical two- or three-word phrases.

Recitations tend to occur mostly in whole-class settings. In discussion, questions are more exploratory and open-ended than in recitation events. Requesting short answers to specific questions will suggest efferent responses at their simplest levels, whereas open-ended discussions will encourage aesthetic responses. The focus in recitations is students' performance *evaluation* rather than the *promotion of comprehension*. Such traditional recitation and lecture formats do not foster a regenerative exchange of ideas or allow students to take control of their own learning.

Traditional IRE approaches (teacher *initiates* talk, a student *responds*, and the teacher *evaluates* the response) result in "inert knowledge — possessed but not usable" (Bereiter & Scardamalia, 1985; Gaskins et al., 1994). However, in discussions, both students and teachers assume to varying degrees a number of roles: inquisitor, facilitator (both of the transactions that occur among students and of the interpretations/understandings developed), respondent, and evaluator (Almasi, 1996).

Because students are not empowered in teacher-dominated or -controlled discussions, whether in large- or small-group settings, active and critical thought does not occur. But "meaningful conversations will occur among students and teachers if contexts are created where students feel their ideas are respected and valued by teachers and peers and where time is taken to reflect on and talk about discussion expectations and strategies" (Villaume et al., 1994, p. 487).

It is important to take the time to model for students how to hold a discussion. Students need to see and experience the kind of discussion that can be sustained by multiple transactions involving students, texts, and teachers.

Teaching the Process of Discussion

Content area teachers need to learn practical approaches to and techniques for teaching students how to carry on a discussion and how to evaluate the process of discussion in order to improve the oral transaction and learn from it (Smith & Smith, 1994). Students will not intuitively "learn the art and skill of the process" (p. 582) of discussion, a process that involves listening, speaking, and thinking skills. But students can be taught the art and science of discussion. Once learned in a whole-class setting, skills in holding and sustaining a discussion can be applied in smaller groups. The following **simulation** or model (Smith & Smith, 1994) can be applied in content classrooms.

The simulation consists of two concurrent processes: (1) a discussion of an assigned text, and (2) role-playing discussion styles and behaviours (for example, making declarative or reflective statements and encouraging elaboration) likely to be experienced in real communication events. Role-playing provides opportunities for students to examine their own roles and the roles of others, and to experience types of sustaining and obstructing behaviours in negotiating, reaching consensus, accommodating, and problem solving (Smith and Smith, 1994). Several purposes (stances), including both aesthetic and/or efferent stances, should be taken by participants when discussing content area texts.

Before a simulation can be a success, students must be aware of the following:

1. Some roles will be exaggerated for learning purposes.
2. Teachers must be involved to motivate and, at times, refocus the discussion.
3. Coaching of individual students may be necessary.
4. Topics, chosen by teachers (with the help of students) from students' curriculum materials, should be debatable, and students should have some basic knowledge of the topic. (Smith & Smith, 1994)

A Discussion Simulation

The suggested procedure for a discussion simulation (Smith & Smith, 1994) is as follows:

1. All class members must participate in the 30–35 minute discussion and in the debriefing.
2. Before the discussion, one-third of the class take a "role behaviour card" (see Box 5.1) and contribute to the discussion as outlined on the card.

3. Several students are named as observers. Their task is to evaluate the process and content of the discussion during the debriefing. (Teachers should provide observer guideline cards [see Box 5.2] if students are not experienced observers.)
4. Participants sit in a circle so they can make eye contact.
5. The teacher informs the class that several participants will be role-playing during the discussion (according to the cards they drew).
6. Besides participating in the discussion, all members attempt to ascertain what roles were played, how discussion was blocked or supported, and how participants remained impartial in the course of discussion.
7. Teachers forewarn students that they are to act out their roles throughout the discussion and not discuss the roles with others in the discussion group.
8. The discussion stops when closure occurs naturally or all roles have been played out.
9. The debriefing period follows, and the discussion process is evaluated in terms of the suggested list in Box 5.2. (Note: The questions used for debriefing are the same as those used by observers to evaluate the discussion.)
10. Evaluation of the content of the discussion might include an assessment of the accuracy of information provided, pertinent elaborations and extensions, reference to examples in the texts read, and personal stories and experiences.

Variations of the Model/Simulation

Variations for playing out the simulations (Smith and Smith, 1994) include:

1. having students suggest discussion topics;
2. redistributing role cards during the discussion or giving students several roles to play;
3. using a fishbowl environment, wherein the group in the inner circle carries on the discussion while students in the outer circle observe the process and evaluate; and
4. videotaping the discussions for future analysis.

If the discussion involves only text-based questions, a teacher-dominated conversation, or an efferent stance, the opportunities for learning are lessened. By taking an aesthetic stance, students can open up ways of thinking about different topics: by learning to "live through" a topic by talking about it, by learning to ask questions of each other, and by learning to take hold of (to view or understand) a topic in different ways. When we think we understand a topic or idea completely, we may see that someone else

Box 5.1
Sample Role Behaviour Cards

CARD 1   Try to get the group to compromise or agree with an idea.

CARD 2   Criticize the group for not making progress — for example, not enough participating, not discussing the real issues related to the topic.

CARD 3   Say anything that is not related to the subject but is of interest to you.

CARD 4   Mention one or more of your life experiences related to the topic.

CARD 5   Suggest that a committee be formed to study the main points or suggest the group move on to other issues.

CARD 6   Repeat someone's opinion as if it were your own idea.

CARD 7   Suggest that more research or information is needed in the area, e.g., "We need more information to make the decision."

CARD 8   Suggest that discussion should end — for example, "This group will never reach complete agreement."

CARD 9   Summarize the discussion for the group and assume a leadership role. This can be done by calling on certain members for their comments. Tell participants to raise their hands to be recognized.

CARD 10   Go along with any idea — for example, be very agreeable, especially when new points of view are introduced.

CARD 11   Agree without giving a reason — for example, say "Good idea!"

CARD 12   Take a conservative position — for example, "Let's continue to do it the way we have always done it," or "It's just fine the way it is."

CARD 13   Make a supportive comment — for example, say something that another group member wants to hear: "Greg, that's a great idea."

CARD 14   Explain your point of view to the person sitting beside you and solicit his/her opinion. Do it in such a way that it distracts the group.

CARD 15   Ask questions to clarify the issue — for example, "Would you elaborate, explain in more detail, or could you give an example?"

CARD 16   Praise the group for their progress — for example, "This is a good discussion. We are making progress."

CARD 17   Take a liberal viewpoint — for example, "Let's change what we are doing," or "Let's give it a try."

(continued)

(continued)

CARD 18   You're bored! Act it out nonverbally. Look at a book or out the window.

CARD 19   Lead the discussion as much as possible. Ask members for opinions or ask participants to repeat opinions to ensure that you have accurate notes.

CARD 20   Ask someone to support your point of view — for example, call them by name: "Jane, don't you agree?"

CARD 21   Call for a vote on the issues — for example, keep reminding the group that they should remember that the majority rules.

CARD 22   Evaluate others' comments — for example, call them good, fair, or unrealistic.

CARD 23   Express disagreement with nonverbal behaviour by nodding your head, rolling your eyes, etc.

CARD 24   Express agreement with nonverbal behaviour by nodding your head, giving the OK sign, etc.

Source: From "The Discussion Process: A Simulation," by L.J. Smith and D.L. Smith, 1994, *Journal of Reading, 37*(7), pp. 582–85. Reprinted by permission of Lorna J. Smith and the International Reading Association. All rights reserved.

Box 5.2
Sample Observer Guideline Cards or Debriefing Questions

1. What were some of the role behaviours observed?
2. For role participants: How did you feel about the role you portrayed? Was the role you?
3. What behaviours were real or not real?
4. Which behaviours facilitated the discussion process? Hindered the process? Were neutral?
5. What are the relationships between this simulated discussion and a real discussion?
6. What experiences have you had with some of these behaviours?
7. What could you do in a discussion to counter nonproductive group discussions?

Source: From "The Discussion Process: A Simulation," by L.J. Smith and D.L. Smith, 1994, *Journal of Reading, 37*(7), pp. 582–85. Reprinted by permission of Lorna J. Smith and the International Reading Association. All rights reserved.

has more to add to our stock of knowledge about that topic. Questions, asked by the teacher or by peers, are nevertheless the foundation of many discussions.

Questions and Responses as the Foundation of Discussion

Questions stimulate thought and increase students' awareness of processing (Denner & Rickards, 1987; Alvermann & Moore, 1991). A large portion of discussion in the content areas will always centre on questions that elicit efferent responses, that is, responses focussing primarily on the information in the text. Learners will be expected to study the concepts in texts and concentrate on the knowledge to be retained. However, using Noden and Moss's (1994) framework, which consists of several categories of student responses (an aesthetic response, a rhetorical response, a metacognitive response, and a shared inquiry response), and drawing from Barton's (1995) continuum of discussion questions (transfer questions, academic knowledge questions, and life knowledge questions), we can broaden the "paradigm for interaction with students" (Noden & Moss, 1994, p. 504) into a "paradigm for transaction."

Discussion has the power to engage students at all levels by moving back and forth between efferent and aesthetic stances (Rosenblatt, 1991). Discussion has the power to get students to apply knowledge, to connect information from one subject area to another, and to relate subject area knowledge to their own lives. Different types of questions can trigger different stances (we use the term *stance* here to mean all of the types of responses listed above). In the following examples, questions that stimulate different types of responses are presented. Although different texts are used, some question types or discussions on any one text would normally be centred on questions from several categories.

Aesthetic Responses

As stated earlier, teachers and students can enhance their discussion of content area texts by focussing on the experience of reading the text itself. A list of questions (adapted from Noden & Moss, 1994, p. 504, based on Probst, 1990, pp. 170–71) designed to elicit aesthetic response follows. The questions can be used to discuss the text entitled "How the Body Uses Food — The Great Breakdown" (see Box 5.3).

Box 5.3

7 How the Body Uses Food

The Great Breakdown— A Three-Act Play

The Scenario

On June 6, 1822, an 18-year-old Canadian named Alexis St. Martin was accidentally shot. His doctor, William Beaumont, was able to reinsert the part of the lung that protruded through St. Martin's wound, but he could not repair the wound to the stomach. A permanent hole remained. Beaumont was able to observe the temperature within St. Martin's stomach, and the movement of his stomach, and the changes the food he ate underwent as it was digested. What Beaumont observed over the next 11 years changed the way people thought about what happens to food after it is eaten. What did he find/discover? Read the following three-act play to find out.

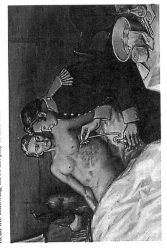

The Principal Characters

What principal "characters" do you think are involved in digestion? Write down your ideas and then read the following descriptions.

The Mouth: The starting place. Here the food is chopped up into smaller bits in preparation for the processes to come.

The Salivary Glands: Located at the back of the mouth, they start producing saliva even at the thought of food. The smell and taste of food makes them work even harder.

The Stomach: Things start getting interesting here. This bag-shaped region can hold 2.4 L of food. Most food passes from the stomach in 2.5 h, but some kinds remain much longer. The stomach acts like a churn, first mixing the food with juices, and then forcing the mixture into the small intestine.

The Liver: This character is referred to as the clearing house for the body. It removes poisons from the blood. It also produces a substance called bile, which is necessary for digestion. Its most deadly enemy is alcohol. Too much over a long period of time causes the liver to become enlarged with yellow fat—a disease called *cirrhosis*. However, once the intake of alcohol is stopped, the liver can regenerate itself.

The Gall Bladder: It is located just below the liver and stores the bile produced by the liver until it is needed.

The Pancreas: Located just below the stomach, it produces enzymes needed for digestion. These enter the play during the climax.

The Small Intestine: It is not very small! It is the longest of all the characters, consisting of 600–700 cm of 4-cm wide tubing coiled below the stomach and between parts of the large intestine. Because its interior is folded into thousands of projections, it has the same area as a tennis court. This large area is covered with hair-like projections called *villi*. These absorb and pass water-soluble nutrients into the bloodstream, which flows past just inside its interior walls.

The Large Intestine: Our story of digestion ends with the large intestine, a 6.5-cm wide tube about 180–190 cm long, from which the food that cannot be digested is passed on, eventually leaving the body as a waste product.

Now you have met the characters. Read the summary of the play and observe each character in action.

Act I: Digestion Begins

Even at the mere thought of food, the salivary glands start producing. In one day, they can produce 1.5 L of saliva. Saliva contains an essential enzyme called *amylase*, which is needed to start digesting the carbohydrates in the food. Get into the act by doing the following Exploration to discover more about this stage of digestion.

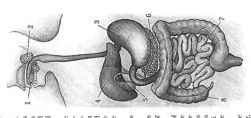

Match the numbers on the diagram to the names of the principal characters.

Source: From "How the Body Uses Food — The Great Breakdown," in *Science Plus 9*, Toronto: Harcourt Brace Canada, pp. 384–85.

First Reaction

What is your first reaction or response to the text? Briefly describe or explain your reactions.

Feelings

What feelings did the text awaken in you? What emotions did you live through as you read the text?

Visual Images

What image was called to mind by the description of the hole in St. Martin's stomach? Describe it briefly.

Associations

What memories — of people, places, events, sights, smells — feelings, or attitudes does the description of the liver call to mind?

Thoughts, Ideas

What idea or thought was suggested by the text on the role of food itself? Explain it briefly.

Evolution of Your Reading

How did your understanding of the whole text or your living through it change as you talked? How does this topic lend itself to being experienced as a drama? How could the author have presented the same information in a different format?

Evaluations

Do you think the text is a good one? Why or why not?

Rhetorical Responses

Questions that centre discussion on rhetorical responses are most appropriate for texts in subject areas like English, social studies, and art appreciation. In rhetorical responses, discussion centres on "how the author uses words to evoke emotional response" (Noden & Moss, 1994, p. 505). Building such an

awareness of the author's artistry or craft becomes progressively more important as students progress through secondary school.

Typical rhetorical questions for the selection "Driver's TV" in Box 5.4
(adapted from Noden & Moss, 1994, p. 505; Noden & Vacca, 1994, pp.
93–94) are the following:

1. What descriptive details (or actions, if discussing English literature) create the feelings you have as you live through and talk through this text?
2. How is "sympathy" for the car TV created? Which words do you think
   are powerful in trying to convince readers of the car TV's merits? How
   strong will the effect of those words be in light of recent studies showing
   that the car phone has contributed to an increase in automobile accidents?
3. How do the emotions evoked in this text compare with the emotions you
   experienced in "How the Body Uses Food — The Great Breakdown"?

Metacognitive Responses

A third option for focussing discussion is the use of questions that elicit
metacognitive responses. Metacognitive questions require students to reflect
on process — on how they think as they read — thus promoting strategic
reading. Discussion of metacognitive questions encourages independent
learning. Like questions that focus on efferent responses, discussion questions
on reading strategies can be posed before, during, and after reading any chapter in a content area textbook. Suggested questions (adapted from Noden &
Moss, 1994, p. 505) include:

Pre-Reading Questions

What does the title suggest to you? What do the headings and subheadings
tell you about what the text is about? What do the pictures and "conversation bubbles" tell you about the text?

Questions during Reading

What sections of this chapter did you read quickly? Slowly? Skip altogether?
Why? What parts did you reread in order to better understand them? What
reading problems did you encounter? How did you solve them?

Post-Reading Questions

What other ideas or concepts would you have included in the book if you had
been the author? What was the most important thing in the content of the
chapter for you? Why?

Box 5.4
Driver's TV

It's hard to believe that when car radios were introduced 60 years ago, law-makers considered them dangerously distracting and banned them in many parts of the country. Well, if you're just getting used to car phones, you'd better sit down, because the car TV is just around the corner.

Driving and watching television at the same time is not outlandish nor dangerous, according to Jay Schiffman, an electrical engineer and consultant in Ferndale, Michigan, who conceived the idea 15 years ago. Schiffman was then designing Heads Up Display (HUD) systems for military aircraft. Those are the systems (now in some cars) that project navigational and other information into space ahead of the vehicle so that the operator never has to look down at the control panel.

The car TV operates on the same principle. A mini projector attached to the car's ceiling projects the image through a combining mirror to a point just above where the horizon meets the road. The combining mirror is a specially ground lens that reflects a "virtual image." This image appears to float above the road, about 15 feet [4.5 metres] in front of the car.

It would seem that watching "L.A. Law" and traffic simultaneously at 55 miles an hour [100 km/h] might be a problem. Not so, says Schiffman. "We've tested 300 drivers over 300,000 miles [480 000 km] without so much as a scratched fender."

"A person operates in terms of survival," Schiffman continued. "Five hundred thousand years ago, if a human ancestor was picking berries and noticed a shadow or change in light indicating a tiger approaching, he'd stop what he was doing and see about it. We're imprinted with the instinct to protect ourselves. If I was watching TV and the car in front of me slammed on the brakes, I'd know which was more important.

"The general consensus holds that it's not safe, but that's based on uninformed opinions. Years of research have proven it safe. In fact, it's much less distracting than a car phone."

Source: From *More Future Stuff*, by Malcolm Abrams and Harriet Bernstein, 1991, New York: Viking Penguin, p. 33. Copyright © 1991 by Malcolm Abrams and Harriet Bernstein. Illustrations copyright © 1991 by Viking Penguin. Used by permission of Viking Penguin, a division of Penguin Books USA Inc.

Shared Inquiry Responses

The fourth category of questions in the discussion framework centres on shared inquiry. Shared inquiry "uses efferent responses to encourage interpretation" (Noden & Moss, 1994, p. 505). Central to discussion is the asking of questions that engage students with the text and promote interpretation. These questions are neither generic nor factual; rather, they evoke multiple answers and interpretations from the text. Again, subjects like English, art, and social studies best lend themselves to the use of this interpretive model. Examples (based on Noden & Moss, 1994; Plecha, 1992) include the following questions on the text "The Profile of Africa" (see Box 5.5). As is readily seen, the opportunities for interdisciplinary transactions in discussion (social studies, art, science, mathematics, English, domestic science) are many.

1. Why are several "colours" listed in the poem?
2. Why is skin compared to a fabric? a flag? a map? How does this help us to think about skin in a new way?
3. What does the reference to planes, curves, and structures bring to mind?
4. Why is there reference to a mosaic?
5. Why does the author switch from using "we" in the first half of the poem to using "my" in the last part? How does this switch affect you?
6. Translate your understandings/impressions of this poem into a piece of artwork.

Box 5.5
The Profile of Africa

We wear our skin like a fine fabric
we people of colour
brown black tan coffee coffee cream ebony
beautiful, strong, exotic in profile
flowering lips
silhouette obsidian planes, curves, structure
like a many-shaded mosaic
we wear our skin like a flag
we share our colour like a blanket
we cast our skin like a shadow
we wear our skin like a map
chart my beginning by my colour
chart my beginning by my profile
read the map of my heritage in
my face
my skin
the dark flash of eye
the profile of Africa.

Source: "The Profile of Africa," by Maxine Tynes. Reprinted by permission of the author.

Transfer Responses

Transfer questions are application questions that relate to ideas in new contexts. Using the selection "*from* Vietnam Perspective" in Box 5.6, think of two or three questions to be used for discussion purposes. Two transfer questions are provided for you.

1. In what other recent wars has a similar degree of censorship been exercised?
2. What specific reasons besides "national security" were given for the censorship in these more recent wars?

Academic Knowledge Responses

Academic knowledge questions, as part of discussion, require students to make links among subject areas — from one topic in one subject area to related topics in other subject areas (Barton, 1995). These types of questions encourage the kinds of interdisciplinary transactions discussed earlier.

In the next two texts, note the possibility of moving from reading about a group, a country, or a group of countries, to a more personal stance — a

---

Box 5.6
***from* Vietnam Perspective**

Television reporting of warfare began to take shape in Korea, but its immense potential was first demonstrated in Vietnam. The U.S. administration — and probably every other government — was surprised by the profoundly adverse impact on national morale of uncensored war films being shown in the country's living rooms. Other military powers learned the lesson. The Russians have permitted only minimal and heavily censored TV coverage of the war in Afghanistan. Britain strictly controlled the television cameras during the Falklands campaign. And when the Americans and their allies invaded Grenada, the TV crews were kept on a tight rein. We can take it for granted, I believe, that the U.S. administration will never again give TV networks the freedom they enjoyed — and, it can be argued, frequently abused — in Vietnam. Henceforth whenever American forces are officially at war, the TV camera crews, like the print journalists and radio broadcasters, will undoubtedly be subjected to a degree of control or censorship on the grounds of national security — and rightly so.

Source: From *Wars Without End*, by Eric Downton. Reprinted by permission of Stoddart Publishing Co. Ltd.

viewpoint from within a group, race, or nation. This helps to see another aspect of transaction: the transaction between a complex social viewpoint and a personal viewpoint. In discussion, these stances will be evident. This ebb and flow between individual and group is what holds or sustains a discussion.

Using "I Grew Up" by Lenore Keeshig-Tobias (see Box 5.7) from an English literature course, and the segment from "Native Peoples and Resources" (see Box 5.8) from a social studies course, the following discussion questions are examples of academic knowledge questions. These examples will help illustrate the type of interdisciplinary transactions that can be made in discussion in social studies classrooms.

1. What is the difference between the term "reserve" (as used in the poem) and the "regions" Native societies once inhabited and presently inhabit (as shown on the map "Canada's Native Peoples")?
2. What is the difference between living through "forests" and "woods" in the poem and making sense of the map "Canada's Native Peoples" in the social studies text?
3. What is the difference in how the author of the poem "identifies" with her Native race and the Native peoples' attitude toward the term "Indian" and "Eskimo" discussed in the social studies text?
4. Estimate the percentage of land in Canada inhabited by each different Native group. Discuss reasons for the larger or smaller territorial differences.
5. Using the scale (given in kilometres), calculate the approximate size of the land tracts inhabited by each Native group. What made the calculation easy? difficult?

Life Knowledge Responses

Life knowledge questions require discussion participants to relate knowledge of academic subject matter to their own experiences and observations.

Using the selections from a geometry unit for Grade 9 mathematics (see Box 5.9), respond first to the questions in the excerpt and then to the following questions in a small-group discussion.

For Reflection 5.3

What interdisciplinary transactions were encouraged during talk/discussion in any one content area when you were in high school?

Box 5.7
I Grew Up

i grew up on the reserve
thinking it was the most
beautiful place in the world

i grew up thinking
"i'm never going
to leave this place"

i was a child
a child who would
lie under trees

back and forth
sweeping it seemed
the clouds into great piles

watching the wind's rhythms
sway leafy boughs
back and forth

and rocking me as
i snuggled in the grass
like a bug basking in the sun

i grew up on the reserve
thinking it was the most
beautiful place in the world

i grew up thinking
"i'm never going
to leave this place"

i was a child
a child who ran
wild rhythms

through the fields
the streams
the bush

eating berries
cupping cool water
to my wild stained mouth

and hiding in the
tree tops with
my friends

we used to laugh at teachers
and tourists who referred to
our bush as "forests" or "woods"

"forests" or "woods"
were places of
fairytale text

were places where people
especially children, got lost
where wild beasts roamed

our bush was where we played
and where the rabbits squirrels
foxes deer and the bear lived

i grew up thinking
"i'm never going
to leave this place"

i grew up on the reserve
thinking it was the most
beautiful place in the world

Source: "I Grew Up," by Lenore Keeshig-Tobias. Reprinted by permission of
the author.

Box 5.8
Native Peoples and Resources

NATIVE PEOPLES AND RESOURCES

Native peoples lived in what is now Canada for thousands of years before Europeans first arrived. Contacts made before Columbus' voyages, such as visits by Norsemen, had little effect on the Native peoples' way of life. When Columbus sighted and later explored the Caribbean islands, he thought he had reached the East Indies. For this reason he called the Natives "Indians", and the name stuck. Indeed, it is the term used in Canada's revised *Constitution Act, 1982*.

In Canada, the word "Indian" has a legal definition, given in the *Indian Act* of 1876. Canadians who have been registered as Indians by the federal

government are known as *status Indians*.

The Native peoples of the far North were first called Eskimos by Algonquin Indians, their "neighbours" to the south, but they dislike that name and never use it. They call themselves Inuit. The Inuit of the western Arctic use the name Inuvialuit, and those of northern Québec-Labrador, Innu.

The way the Native peoples of Canada adapted to their environment and used natural resources to provide the necessities of life varied greatly from region to region. The culture and technology developed in each region depended mainly on the climate and the kind of resources available. Early Native societies in Canada may be classified according to the regions they inhabited: Pacific Coast, Plateau, Plains, Subarctic, Arctic, and Eastern Woodlands (Figure 3.1).

PACIFIC COAST
The Pacific coastal area was rich in sea resources. The Indians of the Pacific coast region ate mostly fish (herring, smelt, halibut, and salmon) and sea mammals (whales, seals, sea lions, porpoises, and sea otter) (Figures 2.1 and 3.1). Of these foods, salmon was the most important. During the *spawning* runs, the Indians speared and netted large numbers of salmon. When they caught more salmon than they could eat at one time, they cured the extra fish by smoking or sun-drying to preserve them for later use.

The dense rain forest of the Pacific coast provided wood and bark for building shelters, carving dugout canoes, and making many household utensils such as boxes, baskets, bowls, and dishes. The Pacific Coast Natives became expert carvers as the intricate

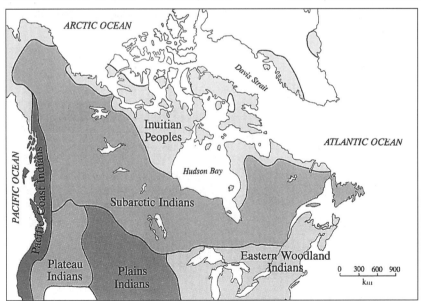

Figure 3.1 *Canada's Native Peoples*

Source: From *This Land Is Ours: A New Geography of Canada*, by Kreuger, Corder, and Koegler 1991, Toronto: Harcourt Brace Canada, p. 87.

Box 5.9
Geometry

Benoit is a jewellery designer. He started designing as a hobby, but soon realized that he could market his talent since his jewellery was so popular. Now he supplies several gift stores and street vendors with unique earrings.

In making his original designs, Benoit uses his knowledge of geometry. He relies on the "layout" skills he learned from night-school courses to draw **squares, rectangles, circles,** and other geometric shapes.

After doing part-time business for three years, Benoit decided that he had enough customers to make jewellery-making his full-time career.

Benoit attends seminars and courses on the latest technology in art production to learn faster and less expensive techniques. Recently he has considered extending his expertise by studying other areas of design.

• What shapes do you recognize in Benoit's designs? How might you construct them on paper?

• What other areas of design would use skills in geometry?

• Suggest some other occupations where geometric constructions are important, and explain how they may be used.

Source: From *Math Plus 9,* by C. Ballheim, M. Cheverie, C. Danbrook, F. Leddy, T. Romiens, A. Sands, and M. Warren, 1994, Toronto: Harcourt Brace Canada, pp. 348–49.

1. What geometric forms might be used to construct different kinds of kites?
2. What geometric designs are used in machines? quilts? buildings? toys? stained-glass windows? kaleidoscopes? floor tiles? coins? diamonds? furniture?
3. What computer programs are able to perform geometric constructions? What are their strengths? their limitations?

Discussion can play a part in developing higher-level thinking skills, such as making generalizations, questioning, reacting critically, and elaborating. As textbooks, trade books, and students' own compositions are used across the curriculum, students need to engage in aesthetic, rhetorical, metacognitive, and efferent responses at the interpretative level, the level of shared inquiry, as well as in transfer responses, academic knowledge responses, and life knowledge responses. Multiple types of questions need to be allowed to co-exist and complement each other in any discussion. But are there alternatives to using questions in a discussion?

Alternatives to Questions

A teacher's alternatives to asking questions to promote post-reading discussion are listed below (Dillon, 1984). In these discussions teachers and students would be expected to take a number of different stances.

1. Make a factual or declarative statement to start the discussion.
2. Make a reflective statement on a contribution made by a student.
3. Describe a student's assessment of something or his/her state of mind.
4. Encourage a student to elaborate.
5. Invite a student to ask a question.
6. Encourage students to ask each other questions.
7. Maintain a deliberate silence to promote reflection among the participants and to allow for "self-initiators" to step in.

To keep a discussion from "ping-ponging" between the teacher and individual students, teachers should refrain from responding to every comment or response a student makes (Alvermann, Dillon, & O'Brien, 1987). A teacher might also turn to a student and ask for his or her response to another student's comment/response.

Alternatives to Whole-Class Discussions

Alternatives to or building blocks for whole-group discussion include one-on-one transactions, dyads (pairs), triads, and peer-led discussion groups in clusters of five or six students. All of these alternatives "enhance the teacher's and students' sense of being partners in a caring community in which they carry out their work together. . . . Their talk is that of equals" (Lindfors, 1994, p. 188). Peer-led discussion groups are not without problems, however. Cohen's (1994) study showed that even if the teacher is absent from the discussion group, equitable relations are not always possible because students bring to the discussion different ways of thinking, talking, and acting because of peer status, gender, class, race, and/or ethnicity. Though relations are not always equitable, the type of collaboration that exists in discussion allows the hearing of voices that might otherwise remain mute.

Small-group events may be spontaneous or planned; membership may be determined by students and/or teachers; tasks/projects may be long- or short-term; and teacher presence may be frequent or limited. On occasion, groups may transact with members of other groups or classes or via the Internet with schools in other countries.

Diversity in the Classroom and in Discourse (Talk)

Each classroom consists of a community of learners (Barnitz, 1994). The community of learners in classrooms today is much more diverse — linguistically, ethnically, and socio-economically — than in the past. Discourse, the heart of any community, connects learners, who each bring to the discussion their own patterns of discourse, their diverse languages, their rich cultural backgrounds, and their unique talents, abilities (Barnitz, 1994), and learning styles. "A teacher's positive attitude toward each student's **diversity** supports the student in further learning" (Barnitz, 1994, p. 586).

Authentic literacy events occur when teachers are aware of the cultural diversity in discourse (interactional patterns) in their classrooms and of the strengths that such diversity brings (Jackson, 1993–94). For example, natural talk (authentic talk) is recommended during literacy activities for culturally diverse learners for whom talk is natural in contexts other than the classroom (Barnitz, 1994). But oral, collaborative literacy lessons may not be suitable for some groups — Native children or children of Japanese descent, for example — whose discourse rules differ (who can talk and when), for whom talk tends to be reserved for respected elders, or who tend not to set themselves apart from their group. Some students will not respond to questions where the answer is known (i.e., factual questions) because such questions are not asked in their communities. In terms of **learning style**, students from some cultures prefer working alone rather than collaboratively in groups (Schifini, 1996). Although the research on learning styles is inconclusive, some educators hold that learning can be enhanced by matching methods of instruction (oral, visual, for example) with students' sensory preferences (modalities such as auditory, visual, kinesthetic, or tactile) or learning styles (an individual's accustomed way of learning). The concept of learning style is somewhat broader than modality and may include emotional elements (e.g., motivation), sociological elements (learning alone or with others), and psychological elements (impulsive/reflective behaviours). Thus, students who learn better by engaging in talk with others would benefit from discussions (Malicky, 1994).

The six basic principles of instruction (Barnitz, 1994) for using authentic talk for the development of literacy in multilingual and multicultural classrooms are:

1. Encourage authentic discourse to build communities in classrooms — thought discourse, fact discourse, sharing discourse, and fun discourse (Enright & McCloskey, 1988).
2. Use authentic texts from students' cultural and language background — cross-cultural literature, menus from ethnic restaurants, health-care brochures, and newspapers — as they "fit" topics in the content areas.
3. Use strategies that require talk as part of the reading-writing process. Some of these are reciprocal teaching, the process approach to writing, and other collaborative/co-operative learning strategies. Sapon-Shevin and Schniedewind (1993) state that **co-operative learning** "entails learning to respect others' differences and to interact successfully with people from different racial, ethnic, religious and socio-economic groups whose skills are widely divergent. Co-operative learning is about becoming an advocate for heterogeneity in all aspects of our lives, not just skilled and comfortable with differences. Teaching students to learn and work cooperatively in schools prepares them for a multi-cultural society in which we live and work with people" (p. 62).
4. Incorporate cross-cultural schemata (content and structure) into literacy instruction — background knowledge that might influence comprehension, writing styles, and text forms from other cultures.
5. Encourage cross-age interaction in the classroom and the larger community — cross-age tutoring (discussed in detail later in the chapter) and involving parents of different cultures in the literacy program.

6. Assess literacy with authentic tasks and texts — texts that reflect students' interests and background knowledge — and acknowledge diversity/variation in interpretation.

Discussion in which students from diverse backgrounds and with different abilities participate promotes respect for their contributions.

Teaching to Diversity in the Classroom

Teachers can create a classroom climate that encourages favourable intercultural transactions among peers by using common strategies such as active listening, conflict resolution, and established procedures to discuss controversial topics (Jackson, 1993–94).

Seven specific strategies that should be important components of a culturally responsive pedagogy (elaborated by Jackson, 1993–94) can be used across subject areas and grades.

1. *Build trust between teachers and students.* An emphasis on the cognitive aspects of teaching often comes at the expense of affective aspects. Beyond the suggestions made to encourage students to share their aesthetic (and personal) transactions in discussion, trusting relationships must be built. Jackson (1993–94) proposes that instruction include learning names of students; pronouncing the names correctly; researching the names' origins and meanings and the family's country of origin or ethnic background; and then sharing that information.
2. *Become culturally literate.* Teachers need to become bicultural or multicultural in their thinking by learning about students' languages, learning and interactional styles, and value systems. Jackson (1993–94) points out that it is usually minority groups rather than the dominant group that have to become bicultural. Such procedures as "kid watching" (observation) in nonschool settings (community churches, discussions with community leaders, and home visits) permit teachers to learn about cultural diversity and to draw on and incorporate into the classroom the community resources (Jackson, 1993–94; Delpit, 1988).
3. *Build a collection of instructional strategies to provide a better match between instructional styles and different learning styles.* Students from non-European backgrounds have culturally specific learning styles that differ from those of the middle class and the Eurocentric perspective. In particular, these students may process information in nonlinear ways, value group association rather than individual competitiveness, and may be less nonverbal and more physically active. Thus co-operative/collaborative

learning experiences may be more suited to their learning styles. As well, teachers need to lay the groundwork for thinking processes that underlie the study of particular subject areas. Therefore making explicit thinking processes by **modelling** them (e.g., using a think-aloud) is necessary for diverse students to master a subject area.

4. *Use higher-order questions.* These types of questions encourage analysis, synthesis, and evaluative thinking; convey to students that their input as learners is valued; and "allow students to see themselves as knowledge producers rather than consumers" (Jackson, 1993–94, p. 301).

5. *Provide feedback that is concrete, specific, and directed toward academic learning.* Such quality feedback is provided in three ways: by highlighting the positive features of students' work; by focussing specific comments on academic quality; and by telling students how to correct their mistakes and how to improve the quality of their work.

6. *Analyze instructional materials.* This point is developed in Chapter 12, where Jackson's (1993–94) criteria for assessing instructional materials for culturally sensitive content are outlined.

7. *Establish positive relationships with families.* Teachers need to interact with the families of students and generate familial support by seeking communication early in the year to discuss students' interests, strengths, and weaknesses; to talk about the students' academic goals; and to invite the students' primary caregivers to visit the classroom and to contribute to the educational program in such content areas as social studies and career development.

Context for Classroom Discussion

"Context includes all the factors that affect classroom events" (Alvermann, Dillon, & O'Brien, 1987, p. 14). These factors include: instructional objectives, the physical space, the format of the discussion, the classroom climate (allowing for risk-taking or not), participants' perspectives (e.g., multicultural differences, and students' perceptions that it is easier to learn content from teachers than from textbooks), interpersonal relationships, expectations for the discussion, amount of teacher talk (discussed earlier), and the role of the content area textbook in discussions. This section elaborates on two of these factors: (1) the use of the textbook or the written composition, and (2) the physical setting.

Rather than treat high-school reading, writing, and viewing assignments as "private affairs" to be handled in isolation for homework or as work to be taught at home by a frustrated parent, teachers can use the textbook, film, or composition as the focal point for classroom discussion. Reading, writing, and viewing thus become integral parts of classroom activity rather than "outside activities" (Alvermann et al., 1987, p. 20).

The use of classroom space sends clear messages to students about the teacher's role in the discussion process. To organize a classroom for maximum student involvement through discussion, the following arrangements are suggested (Alvermann et al., 1987, p. 22):

1. seating students in circles rather than rows, or in a horseshoe arrangement with the teacher positioned at the open end of the horseshoe;
2. seating groups of students at round tables in a semicircle around the teacher's desk; and
3. seating students on opposite sides of the room but facing each other (especially for subject mastery discussion purposes).

Successful discussants know how to read the context, predict it, and shape it (Alvermann et al., 1987, p. 23). However, the reading, predicting, and shaping of the context may be more difficult for students from different cultural backgrounds.

Effective Discussions

"Leading an effective discussion can be one of the most difficult tasks of teaching" (Barton, 1995, p. 346). To increase your chances for success as an effective facilitator, several specific techniques are suggested (Barton, 1995): (1) teach strategies for effective listening, (2) include all students, and (3) use appropriate instructional language. This section elaborates on each of these techniques.

Teach Strategies for Effective Listening

While it is important to teach students how to carry on a discussion (you will recall our earlier mention of "holding a discussion," the difficulty of sustaining a discussion and of carrying on/holding ourselves through a "lived experience" of the discussion), it is just as important to teach students how to listen effectively to others. Speaking and listening are interrelated processes in the "give and take" of using oral language. Good speakers make connections between their listeners and their topic by speaking in a manner that will be understood by listeners. Most students, however, are ineffective listeners (Jalongo, 1991); and research shows that practice alone will not improve listening efficiency levels (Hunsaker, 1990).

Three strategies for enhancing students' listening abilities (Brent & Anderson, 1993, p. 123; Barton, 1995) are described below.

1. *Model good listening.* Active listening involves physical and cognitive behaviours that are evident in one-to-one situations and in discussions of small or large groups. These behaviours need to be modelled by the teacher. Among physical behaviours are leaning forward, nodding, making eye contact, facing the speaker, shaking one's head, reacting with laughter when appropriate, and giving others time to express themselves (turn-taking). Besides the nonverbal signals, appropriate verbal signals might include "I understand" or "I don't understand," feedback that helps carry the discussion. Cognitive behaviours that demonstrate active processing include making pertinent reflective comments, asking relevant questions, setting purposes or goals for listening, and getting students mentally prepared for the discussion in a variety of ways (e.g., bringing to bear prior knowledge). As part of modelling effective discussion patterns, teachers need to step back when students are in conversation to encourage student-to-student engagement.

2. *Provide specific listening instruction.* Teachers need to teach students specific skills such as predicting and anticipating what they might hear, identifying main ideas and supporting details, making inferences, using critical analysis, language appreciation, formulating questions, making mental associations, summarizing, and note-taking. Teachers also instruct students in making personal and **critical responses**. Teaching students to be selective in choosing listening strategies from their wide repertoire is also important. As part of this learning/teaching process, teachers need to:

   • identify a needed listening skill or strategy as they observe students;
   • teach a mini-lesson in listening, integrating it with other lessons;
   • supervise students' practice of the skill in new listening situations, allowing them to assess their own effectiveness; and
   • review listening skills and strategies periodically. (Brent & Anderson, 1993)

3. *Offer a variety of opportunities/situations to practise effective listening.* Settings might include large- and small-group discussions, sessions of reading aloud to students, presentations to the class by students, writing

---

For Reflection 5.4

What memories do you have of the listening environment and the types of instruction to improve listening that were provided in the content area classroom when you were in secondary school?

workshops (where students meet to plan, share, and revise their work), and co-operative groups (where students work on assignments and projects). Teachers must also practise modelling listening strategies with students if they are involved in any of these settings.

Include All Students

Teachers need to create a risk-taking environment in which the contributions of all students are valued. All students should understand that their lived experience of a discussion is important. (This is the value of the aesthetic stance.) A collaborative rather than an evaluative approach (Barton, 1995) is important, as is sincere feedback to students.

There are three specific ways to ensure participation by all students (Barton, 1995). First, enable the making of personal connections by asking students to share what they already know about the topic or what they have already experienced in terms of the concepts being discussed. What associations do they bring? What reactions do they have to some of the new ideas found in their readings? Student interpretations/responses to complex ideas discussed will be as diverse as the student population itself because values, viewpoints, myths, and traditions differ for various ethnic/cultural groups. Additionally, as mentioned earlier, there will be variations in the way students from diverse cultures listen, speak, feel, and communicate in the discussion.

Second, provide support for the reluctant speakers, the students who might otherwise remain silent throughout the discussion. Encourage them to use their new language. In private conversations outside the classroom, find out reasons for a student's nonparticipation. These conversations in themselves may raise students' comfort levels. Three good ideas (Barton, 1995, p. 348) for involving reluctant speakers are:

1. use group brainstorming sessions;
2. give them extra preparation time; and
3. provide nontalk options such as short, ungraded assignments.

In these ways, ensure that "non-speakers are not necessarily non-participants" (Barton, 1995, p. 348).

A third way to ensure participation of all students is to provide special support to ESL students by simplifying the instructional language used, checking frequently for understanding and misunderstanding, and supporting students' use of their first language along with English. Because receptive language outpaces productive language, many of these students comprehend well and are capable thinkers in the discussion context. Finally, a clear and explicit instructional goal is critical.

Use Appropriate Instructional Language

Establishing an interesting topic, generating a series of discussion questions (treated earlier in this chapter), defining new vocabulary, and using techniques such as graphic organizers or semantic webs all provide a structure for an effective discussion. At this point a few words need to be said on defining concept-related terms and on using some form of organizer. As will be discussed in Chapter 6, when an efferent stance is being taken, unfamiliar terms need to be defined to ensure that the content of the subject is being learned. These words need to be linked to other related concepts, and to aesthetic responses. Interdisciplinary connections also need to be made orally. Graphic organizers (see Chapter 7) not only help to record and integrate student contributions, but enable students to remember what was said, especially when a great deal of information is presented in the discussion (Barton, 1995).

Evaluating Discussions Informally

Conducting discussions without reflecting on or evaluating activities is unlikely to lead to improvement in classroom talk. Based on content area classroom observations, two holistic approaches to evaluating discussion are provided (Alvermann et al., 1987). These procedures permit teachers "to see what bugs need to be worked out" (Alvermann et al., 1987, p. 57) in classroom or small-group discussions. They enable teachers to see, for example, if the level of questions needs to be changed or if the pattern of transactions needs to be altered (Alvermann & Hayes, 1989; Fielding & Pearson, 1994). Generally, the decision as to which evaluation procedure to use is made by the teacher in the early stages of planning a discussion.

Bipolar Evaluation

The first evaluation procedure, the *bipolar evaluation*, spells out categories of activities a teacher may or may not want to employ during discussion (some activities will change depending on the instructional purpose for holding a discussion). Each category is divided into bipolar parts separated by a broken line. When teachers are evaluating, they need to look at all the bipolar components within each category to ascertain where the classroom discussion under evaluation fits in the range between two extreme poles. If there is a fit, mark with an X, either at the extremes or somewhere along the continuum. See Box 5.10 for the categories.

Box 5.10
Bipolar Evaluation

Category: Use of Written Material

Focus: How the textbook and other written materials are used relative to the discussion.

DIRECT USE -------------------- INDIRECT USE

Material in the text is used to verify a point or refute an argument.	Information in the text is mentioned in passing.
Questions are asked from the text and answers are read or paraphrased from the text.	The text is referred to but is not consulted.

Category: Pacing

Focus: How the discussion leader attempts to regulate the tempo of the discussion or establish some sort of rhythm in the interaction among the discussants.

VARIABLE ----------------------- STAGNANT

A variety of questions are used to tap existing knowledge.	Questions and answers are restricted to one type of information (e.g., factual recall).
Questions are rephrased for clarification.	Questions are repeated with no attempt to clarify.
A variety of tonal and verbal patterns are used to ask/answer questions or state an opinion.	A monotonic, patterned rhythm is used in asking/answering questions.

Category: Control

Focus: How the discussion leader attempts to maintain a dominant position in deciding the course of a discussion.

TIGHT CONTROL ---------------- LOOSE CONTROL

Content to be covered is carefully preselected.	Only the general topic is preselected.
Deviations from selected content are not tolerated.	Discussants are permitted to stray from the topic.
The amount of material to be covered is preplanned.	The amount of material varies according to the circumstances.

(continued)

(continued)

Category: Sustaining

Focus: How the discussion leader tries to maintain a discussion along a planned course.

NURTURE ---------------------- *NATURE*

Questions requiring critical thinking are asked to foster a variety of reactions/judgements.	Factual level questions are used to monitor who did or did not read an assignment.
Physical props, visuals, or other verbal devices are used to clarify concepts.	Little use is made of props or examples to clarify concepts.
A variety of reinforcement techniques are used to reward students for acceptable responses.	Students' responses are evaluated in a standard way but with an unclear intent (e.g., "okay" to reinforce or mark time).

Category: Sense of Audience

Focus: How sensitive a speaker is to his/her listeners.

OTHER-CONSCIOUS ------------ *SELF-CENTRED*

Teacher attempts to balance student participation.	Teacher directs attention to a favoured group.
Risk-taking atmosphere encourages participation without fear of rejection.	Students are unlikely to take risks because they perceive the teacher as an evaluator.
Students respond to other students and value their peers' comments.	Students participate to obtain teacher approval.

Source: From *Using Discussion to Promote Reading Comprehension,* by D. Alvermann, D. Dillon, and D. O'Brien, 1987, Newark, DE: International Reading Association, pp. 58–61. By permission of Donna Alvermann and the International Reading Association. All rights reserved.

The evaluation task using the bipolar procedure is not complete without making a profile based on the interaction patterns with students (see example in Box 5.11). In the left-hand column under *Current Activities,* list the components actually used in each category. In the right-hand column under *Possible Activities to Try,* write down activities you would like to try. Some categories and activities may be more desirable for specific discussion purposes. For example, you might wish to improve the "sustainability" of the discussion among students, as described in Box 5.11.

Box 5.11
Sample Profile for Bipolar Evaluation

Current Activities	Possible Activities to Try
SUSTAINING	SUSTAINING
I tend to respond to every question asked and I do that in a somewhat evaluative tone by saying "good answer," or "good comment."	I need to allow more student participation, especially more student-to-student dialogue, by avoiding the ping-ponging of answers to me, and I need to use a larger variety of feedback forms and elaborating probes.

Without singling out any students, teachers can discuss the bipolar chart with a student group as a means to improving discussions.

Evaluation of Discussion Activities

The second evaluation procedure, the *evaluation of discussion activities*, focusses on three discussion activities rather than on opposite poles within each category (see Box 5.12). For each discussion activity, the purpose is explicitly set, the problems that inhibit critical reading and thinking are studied, and suggestions for improvement are made. This procedure is most useful for analyzing discussion activities and patterns that occur after assigned content area reading. It permits teachers to develop profiles of personal effectiveness in conducting discussions for specific purposes.

A teacher might consider videotaping discussions and then analyzing with students both the tape and the transcription to see "what happened during the discussion, how and why student/teacher interactions proceeded as they did, and what changes might be suggested to facilitate more effective discussion in the future" (Alvermann et al., 1987, p. 43).

Collaborative vs. Co-operative Learning

While the term **collaborative learning** has not been emphasized thus far, we have earlier mentioned some of the positive outcomes of students' discussions (which were also called collaborative talk or conversations). It was stated that

Box 5.12
Evaluation of Discussion Activities

ACTIVITY 1:

The teacher assigns a content area reading and follows up in discussion based on a series of questions and answers.

Purpose. Two different purposes for the activity are possible: (a) monitoring the understanding of a reading, and (b) providing a review of material by summarizing the important information.

Problems. If question-and-answer sessions predominate in the sessions, there may be too much emphasis on testing rather than teaching critical thought and response. Additionally, there may be a problem with the type of questions asked.

Solutions. Replace question-and-answer sessions with discussions in which students do much more talking (see suggestions earlier in the chapter.)

ACTIVITY 2:

The teacher gives guidance (as opposed to interference) and refocusses the discussion as needed.

Purpose. Refocussing is intended to maintain the direction of the discussion without damping enthusiasm or spontaneity.

Problems. If refocussing produces rigid attention to particular aspects of the topic or segments of text, spontaneity may be curbed and students may suspect that the teacher is not interested in their comments and experiences.

Solutions. Introduce new questions and offer comments that encourage critical thought on the topic, while setting aside some time for digression from the topic. If discussions are perceived as truly open discussions, there will be little resentment when teachers refocus the student talk (Alvermann et al., 1987).

ACTIVITY 3:

The teacher prepares questions designed to elicit a variety of responses during discussion.

Purpose. In order that students orally explore a topic in depth, the teacher must develop questions that help them move to certain cognitive levels when thinking about what they have read (a number of multilevel questions have been suggested earlier in this chapter).

(continued)

(continued)

Problems. Student responses match the cognitive level of teacher-generated questions only about 50 percent of the time (Dillon, 1982), with many of the other responses falling below the expected cognitive level. Problems also occur when students are not given enough time to articulate answers, when direction is not given as to where to find the answers, and when too many questions turn the discussion into a recitation.

Solutions. Content area discussion can be improved by decreasing the number of questions asked (provided there is sufficient think-time) and advising students where to look for answers (e.g., in the text, from their own experience, in other disciplines or subject areas).

Source: Adapted from *Using Discussion to Promote Reading Comprehension*, by D. Alvermann, D. Dillon, and D. O'Brien, 1987, Newark, DE: International Reading Association, pp. 62–65. Reprinted by permission of Donna Alvermann and the International Reading Association.

personal construction of meaning results from transacting with peers in the process of negotiating a "group" meaning; positive student attitudes toward the collaborative process and toward learning also result (Watson, Baardman, Straw, & Sadowy, 1992). It is necessary to reassert here the link between collaboration as co-labouring, and "holding" and "carrying on" a discussion: working together is a way of holding together a topic, or carrying the topic along as it is opened up to exploration, inquiry, and understanding. Other benefits of collaboration (Leal, 1993) include the following:

1. When students themselves serve as catalysts for a discussion topic, the purposes for learning are both personal and authentic.
2. Peer collaboration and peer tutoring are enabled through problem solving, the presentation of other perspectives, and clarification and explanation.
3. Opportunities exist for "exploratory talk" with a real audience (that is, talking without having the answers in polished form).
4. Students have opportunities to take ownership of the learning process.

As well, colloborative activities provide opportunities for culturally and linguistically diverse and for special students (gifted, remedial) to contribute. Some confusion of terms that exists in educational circles now needs to be clarified. A review in *The Teaching Professor* (1995) states that while the terms "co-operative learning" and "collaborative learning" are often used interchangeably, they are really two different kinds of group learning experiences. Collaborative and co-operative learning are similar in that "both define learning through joint intellectual effort" (p. 134) in learning communities that can range from pairs to groups of up to six students. The remainder of this section elaborates on the distinctions between collaborative and co-operative learning as they are identified in the aforementioned review.

Co-operative learning, originating in basic education, "is a system of team learning that structures group-work in such a way that it promotes both academic and social outcomes" (*The Teaching Professor*, 1995, p. 135). The role of the teacher is very important in (1) managing classroom experiences through the use of practical instructional strategies, and (2) assessing the social and academic goals of the activities conducted by groups. Students are graded individually (that is, they are individually held accountable for outcomes), but all group activities are set up in such a way that students learn that "two heads are better than one."

Collaborative learning originates in the social constructivist perspective, in which "students learn complex processes through active engagement in holistic, meaning-centered endeavors" (p. 136). In the Vygotskian tradition, knowledge is socially constructed: "One interacts with other people in order to solve problems or grapple with concepts that one is incapable of solving or dealing with independently" (Baloche & Platt, 1993, p. 265). The authority of the teacher is challenged as students are encouraged to question and to behave as equal individuals in all conversations and discussions. Interdisciplinary contexts for dialogue are very important in collaborative learning. "Bringing heterogeneous groups of students studying different fields together is a way of recognizing that knowledge is a social artifact that requires us to re-examine the premises of all our education" (*The Teaching Professor*, 1995, p. 138). The idea of a community of learners is expanded to mean that while everything is individually defined, there is a collective vision. According to the author of the reviewed book (Brody, 1995), co-operative and collaborative learning need to join forces rather than stand in opposition to each other.

May (1993, p. 369) distinguishes between co-operative and collaborative learning arrangements even more clearly. He defines *co-operative learning arrangements* as shared activities in which students offer support to each other during task completion. Co-operation, rather than competition, is emphasized as students actively participate in a supportive environment (often the groups are self-chosen) that de-emphasizes individual accountability while emphasizing group accountability. Co-operative activities are seen as product-oriented.

May (1993) defines *collaborative learning arrangements* as activities and events that demand shared understanding. The students involved in the collaborative group likely have different information, a wide range of ideas, beliefs, values, and diverse opinions and attitudes that need to be shared, debated, and integrated to complete a task. Meaning is therefore negotiated, and discussion continues until a consensus is reached; the conclusion reached

For Reflection 5.5

What types of collaborative learning tasks did you engage in at the secondary-school level? What kinds of co-operative learning tasks? In what ways were they different?

is thus a "shared" one. In a collaborative learning arrangement the negotiation process is more important than the eventual product or outcome.

If some basic elements of co-operative learning groups are used in the process of discussion, difficulties that could be experienced are minimized (for example, two or three students dominating or arguments ensuing).

The five basic elements of a co-operative learning model (Johnson, Johnson, & Holubec, 1991; Johnson & Johnson, 1993; Kletzien & Baloche, 1994) are listed below:

1. *Positive Interdependence.* Students need to understand that they must work together to develop meaning, and that mutual benefits will accrue. Teachers need to increase this awareness by making explicit learning goals, clarifying roles, providing tasks that enhance "team" identity, and assigning resources (Johnson & Johnson, 1993).

2. *Face-to-Face Interaction.* Keeping the groups small and heterogeneous provides greater opportunity (and responsibility) for discussion and for verbal exchange among students. "Heterogeneity is the key — not just heterogeneity by ability, but heterogeneity by gender, social status, ethnic or economic background, learning styles, and content preferences" (Baloche & Platt, 1993, p. 266). "Acceptance of diversity . . . and building community across differences" (Sapon-Shevin & Schniedewind, 1993, p. 63) are important in this context. Further, "well-structured cooperative learning lessons are often multi-level and multi-disciplinary, calling for the 'gifts' of a variety of students" (p. 63).

3. *Individual Accountability.* Students need to come prepared for discussion; they need to contribute, to make an effort to understand the work of the group, and then to apply what has been learned in the group. Accountability is heightened by the use of index cards (such as the ones presented earlier) describing each person's involvement. Every-pupil-response activities (EPR) can also be used to encourage students to participate in discussions (Gaskins, Satlow, Hyson, Osterlag, & Six, 1994). EPR activities require brief written responses to the text read, whether in the form of answers to questions, Ogle's (1986) KWL activity (see Chapter 7), or brief explanations of concepts, problems, or issues. In English literature classes, students can write less structured responses in

anticipation of (and later in response to) the discussion of texts read. Eventually, student writing can incorporate the "text of the talk," that is, the ideas and language of their peers (Knoeller, 1993, 1994). Collaboration follows the completion of an EPR.

4. *Interpersonal Skills.* Teachers should identify and directly teach skills (interpersonal and small-group) needed for productive discussion (see earlier in this chapter for a simulation). Techniques such as Inside-Outside Circle (Kagan, 1992) and films that illustrate good collaborative/co-operative skills are also useful.

5. *Group Processing.* Students should be asked to reflect on, talk, and write about their work in constructing meaning as a group. In this process students evaluate their task completion, their goal accomplishment, and their efforts at establishing good working relationships. Such metacognitive sharing by students allows for generalizing thinking strategies in similar activities, and expands everyone's repertoire of strategies. "Talk about talk," or metadiscourse, also enables students to analyze through talk how they will proceed in their talk (Calfee, Dunlap, & Wat, 1994). The teacher, too, needs to assess each student's contribution, to make certain that students are reflecting on their working relationships. He or she must also work to improve the quality of co-operation/collaboration through organizing, structuring, and monitoring.

Peer Collaboration and Peer Tutoring

The current popularity of co-operative and collaborative activities and the presence of diverse learners in regular classrooms have renewed interest in **peer** and **cross-age tutoring**. In peer tutoring, students of the same age or grade teach (tutor) each other. In cross-age tutoring, older students in higher grades teach younger students in lower grades. "Currently, peer and cross-age tutoring are in vogue as applications of one of the central principles of collaboration: students in control of their own learning" (Rekrut, 1994, p. 356). Many collaborative activities, especially those requiring students to work in pairs, are essentially tutor and tutee relationships. Peer or cross-age discussion pairs or groups offer students opportunities to take turns teaching each other. A student may be assisted by another student in obtaining meaning, and in turn may provide an explanation or help solve a problem for another student.

Research on co-operative/collaborative learning has shown that working with a partner or partners increases motivation, promotes positive attitudes, and results in higher achievement. Research in peer tutoring has focussed on such subject areas as reading in the secondary school, elementary mathematics, high school physics, secondary composition, health practices among teenagers, second-language acquisition, and computer literacy. Peer and cross-age tutoring have been shown to have affective benefits as well, such as improvement of self-esteem and reinforcement of altruism and empathy.

The following guidelines, based on research insights, for cross-age or peer tutoring programs in the content areas are adapted from Rekrut (1994, p. 360–61).

1. Students of any age can be either a tutor or a tutee. Cross-age tutors should be at least in fifth grade, teaching students younger than themselves. Cross-age tutors from high school can tutor intermediate or middle-school students, provided there is an age gap of at least two years. Peer tutors in the same grade can tutor each other.
2. Peer and cross-age tutors are usually high achievers, but less accomplished students can also provide a valuable service; for example, low-achieving Grade 12 students can teach normal-achieving junior high students.
3. Same-sex partners work best in all tutoring situations. If such pairings are not possible, older girls should be chosen to tutor younger boys.
4. All tutors require training. The focus should be on interpersonal relationships, content, and management skills. Tutoring programs with guidebooks outlining tutor training activities include those by Bohning (1982), Johnson (1977), and Berliner and Casanova (1986).
5. Peer and cross-age tutoring can be used to attain cognitive and affective results. These include content knowledge and strategy or process learning, as well as self-esteem, self-confidence, co-operation, and sharing.

Summary

When students talk, they transact with the text and with one another; they jointly determine interpretations, and they respond aesthetically and efferently. Talk is one way of thinking one's way into the content. Learning is enhanced when talk involves a true discussion of topics. Comments are made and questions are raised by students rather than teachers. Student-to-student

---

For Reflection 5.6

What types of peer tutoring activities do you recall from secondary school? How effective did you find these to be?

and student–teacher dialogue in multiple transactions is a mainstay of discussion. Modelling for students how to hold a discussion consists of simulations, including role-playing of discussion types and behaviours. Questions, the foundation of many discussions, might require aesthetic responses, efferent responses, rhetorical responses, metacognitive responses, shared inquiry responses, transfer responses, academic knowledge responses, or life knowledge responses. Statements, comments, reflections, elaborations, encouragement, and critical silences are all important alternatives to questions in sustaining a discussion.

Because classrooms now consist of learners who are diverse linguistically, culturally, and ethnically, it is important to practise the basic principles and strategies for authentic talk in our classrooms. Some of these include active listening, accessing literacy with authentic tasks, and involving members of the community.

Specific techniques for facilitating a discussion include teaching strategies for good listening, including all students in discussions, and using appropriate instructional language. Reflecting on and evaluating the process of discussion can be done by using observer guideline cards or one of two holistic evaluation procedures: the bipolar evaluation (with categories of activities divided into bipolar parts) or the evaluation of discussion activities (which allows teachers to develop profiles of effectiveness by using different discussion activities).

Discussion, when defined as collaborative talk, opens up topics for exploration and negotiated understandings. Co-operative and collaborative learning, coming from different traditions, provide two different kinds of group learning experiences. Both are useful for different purposes and are powerful in the content area classroom. Collaborative/co-operative activities in the content area classroom include peer and cross-age tutoring, in which students take turns teaching each other.

Questions for Further Reflection

1. Read the text in Box 5.13 and formulate for discussion purposes *one question in each of the following categories of responses*: aesthetic, efferent, rhetorical, metacognitive, shared inquiry, transfer, academic knowledge, and life knowledge. The following sample question is provided for you: "How could this text be seen as a way to open up a discussion in social studies about how we define 'family'? 'marriage'?"

2. Hold a group discussion with your peers, with one individual taking the role of teacher. Analyze and evaluate the discussion according to the following criteria:

Box 5.13
Get Outta My Life

Vancouver-based Western Pro Imaging Labs recently launched a new service for divorced people called Divorce X that allows them to digitally "cut out" their often despised ex-spouses from family photos and replace them with backgrounds that make it look like the spouse was never there.

According to company president Keith Guelpha, it is even possible to manipulate the photo so that an ex-spouse can be replaced with the current spouse in a favourite photo. The technology behind the service is nothing new or earth shattering — just a good colour scanner, some high-end image editing software and the ability to output to photographic paper, photographic film or colour laser devices.

Guelpha says his technicians scan the photo into the computer, use digital image editing tools to "cut out" the offending spouse and then recreate the background where he or she would have been using elements of the existing background to create the new one. In order to do a professional job, Guelpha says the service takes two or three weeks and costs between $100 and $150 per photo.

Customers do, however, receive photographic negatives of the new photo so that they may have as many copies of it made as they like at any standard commercial photo-finishing outlet.

Despite the insistence by Guelpha and others that they do their utmost to ensure the technology does not get misused, the increasing use of digital imaging software to "polish" photos could soon render meaningless the old adage that "the camera doesn't lie."

Source: From "Get Outta My Life," by Geof Wheelwright. Reprinted by permission of the author.

---

    a. student–student dialogues
    b. modelling by teacher of desired behaviour in talking and listening
    c. changing roles of teacher and students
    d. depth of ideas/content discussed
    e. balance of questions vs. reflective comments to move the discussion forward
    f. variety of transactions (types of questions used) and interdisciplinary connections
    g. attention to diversity in culture and language

3. When do you think talk about "content" or process is helpful? Before reading, writing, or viewing? during? after? Explain your answer.
4. How can conversation and discussion be incorporated into your content area specialization?

Key Terms

Collaborative learning
Constructivist model
Co-operative learning
Critical responses
Cross-age tutoring
Discussion
Diversity
Learning style
Literature circles

Metalinguistic awareness
Modelling
Negotiate meaning
Oracy
Peer tutoring
Recitations
Simulation
Social contexts

CHAPTER SIX

Reading and Writing to Enhance Vocabulary Development

Questions to Consider for this Chapter

1. How can content area teachers generate excitement about learning words?

2. What is involved in knowing the meaning of a word?

3. What difficulties do you associate with learning vocabulary in the content areas?

4. In what ways did you increase your vocabulary knowledge in the different content areas in secondary school?

5. What specific instructional strategies/approaches do teachers use to build and extend vocabulary? How can aesthetic as well as efferent transactions be encouraged through such instructional strategies?

6. How can interdisciplinary transactions help a reader to move from an aesthetic to an efferent response and vice versa?

Overview

This chapter begins by examining efferent and aesthetic responses to vocabulary in the content areas and how such responses can be generated; it demonstrates how a lack of knowledge of vocabulary hinders an efferent and/or aesthetic reading of texts. It then elaborates on why it is inappropriate to ask students "Do you know this word?" and why acquiring full conceptual meaning of vocabulary in content areas is important to prevent difficulties in understanding and to promote content literacy across the disciplines. A section of the chapter discusses the main ways to foster the acquisition of word meanings through incidental learning and through instruction. Instruction includes teaching vocabulary directly, relating words to experience and to previous word knowledge, encouraging the use of context, and teaching morphological components and etymological analyses. The chapter concludes with a five-step strategy to develop and refine students' vocabulary knowledge. Some of these steps are carried out before reading, others during reading, and some following reading. Within each of these steps, suggestions are outlined for the use of specific strategies.

Aesthetic and Efferent Understanding of Words

As stated earlier, affective response can be the starting point for aesthetic or efferent responses and aesthetic response can be a step toward an efferent response. Content literacy involves aesthetic and efferent understanding of words or larger units of text. Expressed in another way, content literacy involves "hot" cognitions (aesthetic understandings) and/or "cold" cognitions (efferent understandings). Paris and Winograd (1990) have expanded the scope of metacognition to include not only knowledge of cognitive states (**"cold" cognition**) but also the affective aspects of thinking (**"hot" cognition**). Too often in the past, it was thought that only efferent understanding of text was important in content literacy. Efferent understanding of technical, scientific, and literary vocabulary is, of course, very important in the comprehension of subject area text. However, as stated earlier, to reach an aesthetic understanding of the vocabulary in the text, learners also must respond and transact with the words from personal experience, emotional awareness, a range of feelings, as well as from a range of knowledge and prior **conceptual understanding**. (This range of knowledge, associations, reflections, and emotions can include understandings of the words across disciplines [the interdisciplinary transactions discussed in Chapter 4]). For example, a word like "pollution" can involve a "cold" cognition when we understand it as a descriptor in science for the fouling of ecosystems large or small. This is a distanced

---

For Reflection 6.1

In light of your experience, which of the following series of words are "hot" and which are "cold": astonish, surprise, astound, and flabbergast, or odour, fragrance, aroma, and smell? What kinds of understanding were emphasized when you learned words in the different subject areas at school?

way of using "pollution." When "pollution" is used to mean drinking too much and suffering the consequences, it is used as a way to show what is *lived through* by the person. This is a "hot" response because of the emotional associations of abusing (literally, poisoning) our bodies in this way.

Building an Interest in Words

For aesthetic and efferent understanding of vocabulary to occur, teachers need to model an interest in words and to instil in students a love of language and language play. They also need to place value on the aesthetic response to words. "The single most significant factor in improving vocabulary is the excitement about words which teachers generate" (Manzo and Sherk, 1971–72). Teachers can achieve these aims by:

1. Making vocabulary learning an integral part of classroom life, not just the "objective" before a chapter is to be read or a lesson conducted on a topic. A teacher can create an excitement about learning words by interjecting word play and incidentally addressing new vocabulary throughout a subject area lesson. In this way "teachers foster initiative in vocabulary acquisition and encourage learning outside the classroom" (Richek, 1988, p. 263).
2. Demonstrating their own efferent and aesthetic understanding and use of vocabulary when teaching or responding to students' writing.
3. Building on the understanding of vocabulary specific to a content area in the context of integrated interdisciplinary reading and writing activities.
4. Exhibiting enthusiasm in discussions and conversation about specific vocabulary in content area texts.
5. Providing a nonthreatening classroom atmosphere and a variety of activities in which students are stimulated to use the subject area vocabulary.
6. Providing real and vicarious experiences to help promote vocabulary growth: films, labs, field trips, dramatizations, and books rich with photographs and charts.
7. Encouraging wide reading.
8. Teaching effective vocabulary learning strategies that students can gradually incorporate in vocabulary learning.

For Reflection 6.2
Think about how you personally learn new words now and how you acquired new vocabulary in the different subject areas at school.

Content Vocabulary

Gauthier (1990) points out that middle school (Grades 4 to 8) is the point at which students are introduced to the language or vocabulary of a content area. This occurs at the same time that students are required to make the transition from mainly narrative (a predominantly aesthetic stance) to mainly expository (traditionally a predominantly efferent stance) text (Tierney & Lapp, 1979). At this point, students are also required to make the transition from learning to read and learning to write (i.e., acquiring skill/strategy-based activities to learn to read) to reading-to-learn and writing-to-learn. These reading-to-learn and writing-to-learn strategies will help students read and write content area materials through middle/junior high school, through senior high school, and into postsecondary education.

Efferent and aesthetic strategies need to be taught to facilitate students' development of the language (vocabulary) of different subject areas. One of the major objectives of any content area learning is teaching students to understand the concepts related to the subjects and to remember the **referents**, or labels, that represent these concepts so that they can speak about and write the language of the discipline. Specific vocabulary is part of the language of different academic disciplines such as mathematics, science, English, and drama. Thus, learning the vocabulary of a content area becomes a central part of learning the content (Curry, 1989) and becoming a member of a **disciplinary club**. While much of this vocabulary will have to be retained after the reading, viewing, or listening (an efferent stance), that does not preclude aesthetic involvement with the words during reading, viewing, or listening or a switching of stances as one reads or listens. Technical words and symbols peculiar to a discipline (e.g., "centimetre" or "+"), common words that take on specialized meaning in the specific content area (e.g., "bank" or "fault"), and words with multiple meanings in different contexts (e.g., "revolution") need to be acquired so that students can understand the concepts in each subject area and be able to talk, read, and write about these concepts. Otherwise, students will struggle with insufficient vocabulary knowledge and present teachers with some "daffy definitions" based on their prior knowledge. Some examples follow (from *Calgary Herald*, Feb. 24, 1996, pp. 3–5):

> *Equator:* A menagerie lion running around the Earth through Africa.
> *Litre:* A nest of young puppies.
> *Magnet:* Something you find crawling all over a dead cat.
> *Momentum:* What you give a person when they are going away.

The *Calgary Herald* (March 2, 1996, p. B-4) also provided several examples of "unintentionally funny medical remedies" assembled from the test papers of junior high, senior high, and university students. The following demonstrate confusion in vocabulary use:

> Before giving a blood transfusion, find out if the blood is affirmative or negative.

> For drowning: Climb on top of the person and move up and down to make artificial perspiration.

Although the relationship between vocabulary (which reflects students' understanding of concepts since words are labels for concepts) and reading comprehension is strong, the knowledge of vocabulary in a discipline does not necessarily assure a high degree of comprehension in that subject. The relationship is much more complex. In the content areas, students need many opportunities to learn the vocabulary of the discipline by listening to it and by using it in talk, in writing, and when reading in a variety of contexts. They need to understand the different meanings words have across disciplines. For example, "solution" has a different meaning in science than it does in mathematics.

As mentioned earlier, many concepts that students encounter in their learning are not part of their experiential background. (For example, most Canadian students are unlikely to know the word "favela." This is the Portuguese word for "slum" but what is known as a "slum" in a Canadian city does not begin to parallel the "favelas" of São Paulo, Brazil. Portuguese-born students, however, would have a much more complete understanding of the word. Such concepts often lack concrete referents and are thus more difficult to learn. Additionally, students need many opportunities to learn how words are related to one another conceptually since concepts are linked by common elements or relationships to form networks of concepts (schemata). Networks of concepts will also reveal differences in meaning of the same word across disciplines. Conceptual, rather than definitional, understanding is the aim of vocabulary learning in the content areas.

Exercise 6.1
Text Comprehension

Read the following text silently and then reflect on your thinking as you read. Note in particular how knowledge or lack of knowledge of vocabulary helps or hinders an efferent and/or aesthetic reading of the text, and how it affects your involvement with the text and your comprehension of the content.

> Temple of Hera at Samos. The peripteral plan in such Ionic temples is embellished by doubling the surrounding colonnade, creating

a dipteral plan. This plan is also characteristically Ionic in the deep pronaos and closed cella (Gardner, 1959).

If you have no background knowledge about "Ionic temples," how do you make sense of this text? What is your reaction when you do not know the vocabulary of a discipline (in this case architecture)?

You might begin with a known word. If you know that Hera is the name of a Greek goddess, you can infer that this temple was erected in Greece in her honour. You can then make a second inference that an Ionic temple was built for religious purposes during an ancient period of Greek history. Another possible inference is that "Ionic" is a descriptor for the architecture of this temple.

You might also recognize "colonnade." I do, because I remember being in a shopping mall called a "colonnade" in a large Canadian city. When I live through the memory of that mall, I see a large space for walking. I can add a prediction that an Ionic temple includes a large space for walking.

Inferencing and predicting may help to move me forward in the understanding of this text, but the words "peripteral" and "dipteral" are unknown to me. I recognize "peri-" as a prefix in words such as "perimeter" and "perambulate." By association I can predict that "peripteral" refers to a space at the outer edge of the temple. The other word, "dipteral," begins with a prefix that is fairly common. I know a few words that begin with "di-": "digress," "dilate," "dilute," "diptych," "divide." In these words the prefix "di" refers to "widening" or simply "two." A "dipteral plan" could mean a plan that provides for a space widened into two parts. I still do not know, however, the difference between "peripteral" and "dipteral" in an efferent sense.

You may have noticed that while I have attempted to draw on a wide variety of knowledge, an aesthetic response to this passage is impossible at this point. However, I have been able to make an aesthetic response to a single word, "colonnade." This raises the question of how we really do *know* words. In the example, I have made small inferential moves toward understanding new words but I cannot reach an efferent understanding of this text without using strategies for extending my knowledge of these words.

What Does It Mean to Know a Word?

What it means to know a word is a question researchers have tried to answer for many years (Baumann & Kameenui, 1991). The answer to this question is beginning to emerge. In general, learners refine their knowledge of word meaning as they increase in age and experience.

Vocabulary knowledge refers to four different vocabularies in two categories: expressive (i.e., speaking and writing) and receptive (i.e., reading and listening) (Kameenui, Dixon, & Carnine, 1987). *Expressive vocabulary* requires the production of a specific label for a known meaning (for example, "honey — a sweet substance produced by bees from nectar"). *Receptive vocabulary* requires the association of a meaning with a label. Receptive use of words is somewhat less demanding as partial knowledge can provide the required gist of meaning in a text (Scott & Nagy, 1994). Knowledge of a word is seen in terms of the extent or degree of knowledge a person has of the possible meanings of the word. Word meaning is not a static entity; it has a fluid quality, with additional characteristics and attributes taken on as the learner has more and more experiences with each particular word (Simpson, 1987). Thus, word meanings are learned on a continuum, not as discrete entities. Eventually, many possible meanings can be at play at the same time — for example, in a reading, as you read in my attempt to make sense of the passage on Ionic temples — but some meanings will dominate the reading of a text because of prior experiences/prior knowledge of the words or the stance taken.

Several models have been proposed to describe the levels of word knowledge through which a learner progresses. Three of these will be described here as a backdrop for the rest of the chapter.

Models of Word Meanings

The first model of word meaning comes from a landmark study by David Russell (1954), whose answer to the question "How do you know a word?" was that you accumulate a height, breadth, and depth of word meanings. According to Russell, *height* refers to the range of words (quantity, volume) a person knows to some varying degree. For example, it includes all the words people understand when they read them (or hear them but cannot read them) or the words they can use in their own writing. *Breadth* includes the multiple meanings of each word in a variety of contexts that a person has accumulated. This type of word knowledge is particularly important in the content areas where words that have a "common" meaning in everyday discourse take on a specialized or technical meaning — for example, words such as "crust" or "fault." As a further example, one can be said to have a breadth of meaning for the word "shot" if one understands its meaning in each of the following sentences:

1. He was injured by a shot from a rifle.
2. He was given a cholera shot.
3. He declared that someone took a cheap shot at him.
4. He took a shot of whisky before he gave his answer.
5. He took a shot at the answer.
6. He shot the Canadian Rockies on his last trip.

For Reflection 6.3
Describe the nature of the interdisciplinary transactions that you have experienced with vocabulary in specific content areas.

---

7. He was out by a long shot.
8. What a shot in the arm that grade on the last assignment was for him.

Depth of word meaning refers to the increasing precision or nuance acquired in word meanings. For example, "illness," "ailment," "disease," "sickness," and "poor health" are all synonyms but there are differences among word series such as astonish, surprise, astound, and flabbergast, or odour, fragrance, aroma, and smell.

When a learner has knowledge of a range of words (height), knows multiple word meanings (breadth), and can evoke nuances and precise differences among words (depth), aesthetic and efferent responses as well as interdisciplinary transactions are much richer.

The second model of word meaning is Dale's (1965) conception of the continuum concept of vocabulary development. He purports that we learn words in four stages or degrees of cognition: (1) "I've never seen the word," (2) "I've heard of it, but I don't know what it means," (3) "I recognize it in context or I can associate it with something," and (4) "I know one or several meanings of the word, so I think I know it well." An example of this movement on a continuum of vocabulary development can be seen in the passage about Ionic temples. I knew several meanings for "Hera" and "temple" and I recognized "Ionic," "peripteral," and "dipteral" in context or could associate them with other words. To arrive at meanings for these last three words, I have to move from the third stage to the fourth stage in Dale's (1965) model.

In the third model, Dixon and Jenkins (1984) and Kameenui et al. (1987) also depict a continuum of word knowledge from (1) full concept knowledge to (2) partial concept knowledge to (3) verbal association knowledge. I reach *full concept knowledge* when I recognize examples of the targeted word and discriminate them from similar examples of other concepts. Such knowledge involves the rich understanding of a word. *Partial knowledge* is defined as possession of the set of critical features or the set of variable features of concepts, but not both. Critical features are features common to all examples of a concept, such as the tails, four legs, etc., common to all breeds of dogs. Variable features, then, are the differentiating features that distinguish one example of a concept from another, for example, the features of a Corgi that make it different from another type of dog. *Verbal association knowledge* reveals a lack of conceptual understanding but an ability to match the word label to its definition. Using the Dixon and Jenkins model in the case of "Ionic," "peripteral," and "dipteral," I had to move from verbal association knowledge to partial concept knowledge and finally to full concept knowledge. I cannot "take away" meaning in the sense that Rosenblatt (1989) describes as efferent until I can define what "Ionic" and "peripteral" and "dipteral" mean.

So, if I ask myself, "How do I know the word 'peripteral'?" I can answer that I know the prefix but not the root of the word. Knowing the prefix, I can begin to make predictions and extend my schema for the concept of an Ionic temple, but I still cannot define "peripteral" or use the word in my own writing. Likewise, I know the prefix for "dipteral" but I cannot define the word or use it in a piece of writing.

One does not either know or not know a word. Thus, for teachers, "Do you know this word?" is not a legitimate question because "No, I don't know this word" and "Yes, I know this word" are not possible answers. The more appropriate question is "How do you know this word?" Students can offer responses such as "I can pronounce it, but I don't know what it means" or "I looked it up once and have a sense of what it means" or "I can understand what it means when I read it but I can't define it, nor can I use it in my own writing." As Blachowicz and Lee (1991, p. 190) state: "Knowing a word is not an all-or-nothing proposition."

How Models and Theories of Word Knowledge Inform Content Area Instruction

The models described above suggest that if students are to succeed in a content area, they must acquire full conceptual meaning of the subject's vocabulary. There are two ways in which vocabulary knowledge appears to be related to reading comprehension and knowledge of content (Anderson & Freebody, 1981, 1985). One is the *instrumentalist hypothesis*, which suggests that reading comprehension depends partly on quick access to word meanings via associational links. Vocabulary instruction based on this model emphasizes **automaticity** of word meaning, usually through rote learning of words and knowledge of definitions and synonyms, as well as repeated and meaningful use in a variety of contexts. Automaticity involves the fluent processing of information, making cognitive energy available for other tasks, such as comprehension breakdowns.

On the other hand, the *knowledge hypothesis* suggests that **conceptual knowledge** of vocabulary is the link to strong reading comprehension. Thus, as mentioned earlier, in the content areas vocabulary instruction would seem to be more effective if it presents words and concepts in relational categories and networks. See Figure 6.1.

Figure 6.1

Semantic Web Related to Sculpture

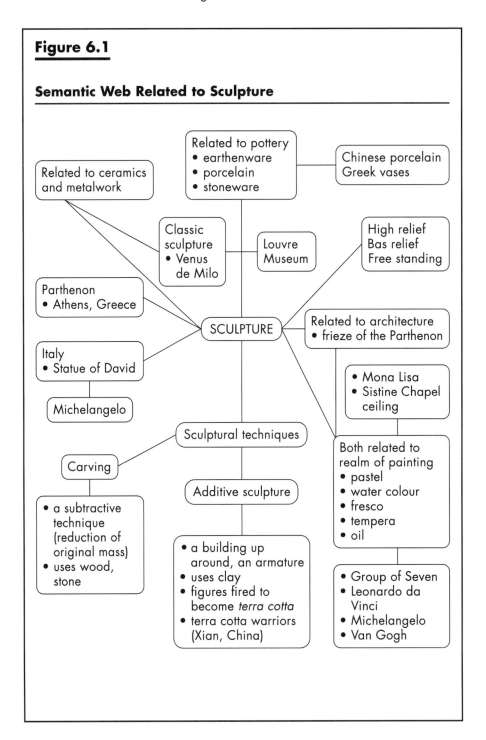

Activities such as graphic organizers and semantic word maps help to depict spatially the relationships among words and concepts and are further enhanced by collaborative work in small groups. A teacher might proceed in the following way:

1. Establish with students a major concept or core being discussed and name it on the board/overhead and draw an oval around it.
2. The learners think of words, ideas, and concepts to describe the topic. These responses are written on the board/overhead and boxes put around them. Then the boxes are linked with arrows to the main concept. Learners might write phrases on the arrows to indicate relationships between the main concept and the boxed words.
3. Learners might then provide more examples of the topic under each box and write these in ovals using arrows to connect to the main topic. The networks should include the range of knowledge associated with the words that remain after the study of the vocabulary, and the range of feelings and personal experiences evoked by individuals in the group.

The lack of success of vocabulary training programs in improving reading comprehension in the content areas may be the result of giving too much attention to rote learning and too little to constructing relationships among words (Blachowicz, 1985). The deeper the level of processing (i.e., the constructing of conceptual relationships) (Craik & Lockhart, 1972), the stronger the chances the student will learn the word's meaning and retain it (Blachowicz, 1985). As stated earlier, one usually thinks of (word) meaning as linked to the purpose for reading the text (e.g., mastering content), that the meaning of the words is predetermined, that meaning is given in the word itself, or meaning is provided in the sentence. In an efferent reading of text, this is indeed the case.

Before instructional approaches are presented the following points about learning content area vocabulary (Nelson-Herber, 1986) will be helpful to junior and senior high-school teachers.

1. Students do not automatically transfer reading skills and strategies from elementary school because higher-level texts contain heavy concept and vocabulary loads and deal with unfamiliar topics.
2. Rewriting difficult text materials to students' reading levels will not result in comprehension because the difficult words and complex sentences are essential to understanding the content and therefore must be taught, not changed or deleted.
3. Students will not be able to understand their textbooks just by reading them independently because such texts are designed for teaching vocab-

ulary, concepts, facts, relationships, and values that are beyond the current knowledge and experience of students.

Instructional Approaches to Vocabulary Improvement

Problems in vocabulary acquisition are an inherent part of the content areas themselves. The technical vocabulary of the content areas is a problem because it is unfamiliar, multisyllabic, and must often be learned in relation to other concept clusters of unfamiliar, multisyllabic words. For example, Nelson-Herber shows that the meaning of *economics* cannot be understood without knowing the meanings of *investment, production, employment, consumption,* and *equilibrium.* Technical vocabulary is rarely if ever used outside the classroom. Thus the opportunities to read, speak, write, and listen to content area vocabulary to refine and reinforce it are limited. As Nelson-Herber asks, when was the last time you encountered the word *rhombus* outside the classroom? (Nelson-Herber, 1986).

In subject area textbooks, students are faced with heavy vocabulary (concept) loads. A number of "new" words appear in rapid succession, making the text dense in content. Some of the words are highly technical or specialized vocabulary unique to each individual subject area (Curry, 1989), for example, *cochlea* and *cytoplasm* (science) or *numerator* and *improper fraction* (mathematics). Other disciplines may use familiar words in unfamiliar ways, for example, *fault* and *bank* (in science). Still other words take on different meanings in different content areas, for example, *operation* (in mathematics, social studies, and health) or *revolution* and *division* (in the sciences, social studies, and mathematics). These words provide opportunities for interdisciplinary transactions. At the same time, an efferent reading will require a grasp of appropriate meaning within the context of the specific subject area, meaning that can be taken away after the reading.

Also problematic in the acquisition of vocabulary is the use of figurative language. For example, when writers speak of the steppes in Russia they often refer to them as the breadbasket of the country. Picture students reading a sentence such as: Russia's steppes, the breadbasket of the country, also fill the breadbaskets of Eastern Europe. Would students understand the first reference to breadbasket to mean a region that supplies much grain? How would they understand breadbaskets in that sentence? As the stomach (for which breadbasket can be the slang expression) or as the container in which bread is commonly placed on tables at meal time? Such meanings would be part of an efferent reading of the text. It is important to remember that at times interdisciplinary transactions could obfuscate the intended meaning of a word in a particular subject area unless discussion of meanings was invited in the classroom.

Graves (1987) writes that there is little vocabulary instruction at the secondary level. Yet, as mentioned earlier, the technical vocabulary of a content area textbook goes beyond what junior and senior high-school students have experienced. When reading efferently, how can they "visualize" what they have never seen before, and how can they understand what they have never experienced? Because some terms and their meanings are encountered for the first time in the content area lesson/chapter, we turn our attention to instructional approaches to vocabulary learning in the content area classroom.

There are two main ways to improve the learning of word meanings in the content areas: incidental and instructional. In incidental learning students pick up words relevant to certain subject areas by hearing the words from others; using them in discussion with teachers, parents, and each other; watching television; listening to radio and CDs; and reading for recreation. Their personal transactions in these contexts can build word knowledge. Some of the best ways to learn vocabulary are based on the ways people naturally develop their language abilities (Lehr, 1984). Vast numbers of words are best learned through wide exposure to texts and through experiences (Lehr, 1984). The difficulty, of course, is that it is not always possible to have experiences with the concepts in many of the content areas (English language arts is an exception) and thus to be able to make associations with these words. Instructional approaches include teaching vocabulary directly, relating words to experience and world knowledge, teaching morphological components and etymological analyses, and using contextual information. The aim is to strike a balance between direct instruction and incidental learning.

Direct Teaching of Vocabulary

Because the number of words to be learned in a content area is so large, only a small fraction of vocabulary can be taught directly. The techniques used for direct instruction in vocabulary need to be selected carefully. Further, the instruction must be extensive (up to twenty minutes of instruction per word), frequent (up to 24 exposures), and multifaceted (dealing with the words in a variety of contexts, in and outside the classroom) (Marzano & Marzano, 1988). A strong emphasis should also be placed on grouping words in semantic categories to foster a deeper understanding of words and to include personal experiences and associations. The use of such direct instruction methods as the word list, involving the memorization of dictionary meanings, has been shown to be least effective; yet it is still the most widely used technique for vocabulary development.

Marzano and Marzano (1988) point out that even the most ambitious direct instructional program could not possibly cover all words students encounter in reading; therefore, wide reading and language-rich activities must play a critical role in vocabulary instruction. Several principles are set out to guide direct vocabulary instruction (based on Blachowicz, 1986; Blachowicz & Lee, 1991; Marzano & Marzano, 1988; Carr & Wixson, 1986; Armstrong, 1994; Rosenblatt, 1989).

1. Concentrate on words that are important to a given content area — ones that have a high yield in knowledge of a particular topic or of general knowledge. Focus on usable vocabulary (for reading, listening, or writing, and for retaining word knowledge long term).
2. Since word knowledge is learned and stored in many different ways (mental, **kinesthetic**, **olfactory**, taste, semantic, and/or linguistic associations), include many ways of knowing a word.
3. Use activities that stress active learner involvement, such as discussion (see Chapter 5), student application of meaning in writing (see Chapter 8), and maps and advance organizers (see this chapter). Create opportunities for students to use the new vocabulary in pre- and post-reading discussions. Research has shown that there is a critical link between discussion and the amount of vocabulary learning that occurs (Barron & Melnick, 1973; Stahl & Vancil, 1986). For example, it is the discussion that contributes the most to vocabulary in a semantic mapping activity. Encountering the new words in texts to be read is insufficient for learning and retaining these words.
4. Provide for transfer of the direct instruction strategies to the learning of new words. Practice in word learning tools can lead to independent use of the strategies taught for vocabulary acquisition and extension/elaboration. Teach students to "learn how to learn the meanings of words," to be strategic readers who have control over vocabulary learning. Teach them how to engage in initial selection of terms to be defined and learned so that they become independent learners.
5. Establish a conceptual base or schema (a rich semantic network) for vocabulary learning. New words can then be linked to these frameworks or structures via attributes, categories, examples, and personal associations. According to research, such teaching fosters a deep interdisciplinary understanding of words and develops comprehensive word knowledge, particularly in high-school learning disabled (LD) social studies students (Anders, Bos, & Filip, 1984). In other words, develop students' breadth of word knowledge.
6. Provide repeated exposure to the new words, and motivate students to maintain interest in the new words.
7. Make sure students know how to use the dictionary, thesaurus, and other resources for word study.
8. Assist students in relating/associating the new words learned to their previous experiences and learnings, in core subjects such as English, social studies, science, and mathematics, and in other subjects such as the fine arts.

9. Use reinspection of context and semantic manipulation of words to flesh out knowledge of words and to encourage word use in the post-reading discussion.
10. Use the vocabulary in an integrated way (seeing, hearing, reading, and writing the terms) and, if possible, in response activities that have the students use the words in artistic, dramatic, or aesthetic ways (see Box 6.1).

Content area teachers need to be aware of which teaching/learning strategies incorporate the above principles. For example, when using a structured overview (see this chapter), students relate new vocabulary to previous experiences and learning, develop elaborated word knowledge (breadth), and are actively involved in meaning construction, but they do not learn a strategy for acquiring new vocabulary.

Relating Words to Experience and World Knowledge

Students can increase their knowledge of content vocabulary by being involved in activities that promote awareness of words in their various environments outside their classrooms (Richek, 1988). Teachers should use methods that show students how the vocabulary in their content areas is related to their everyday lives and to their knowledge of the world (Richek, 1988) (e.g., meanings of proper names or the names of automobiles). Such activities can be used to expand students' vocabulary by teaching meanings of more sophisticated concepts (e.g., words such as "mercurial," "nuclear," "byte," and words derived from Latin).

Teaching Morphological Components and Etymological Analyses

Research with secondary-school students (Graves & Hammond, 1980) has shown that activities involving the study of a word's origins and structure can contribute to vocabulary development. **Morphology** is the study of how words are structured and formed, including derivation, inflection, and the formation of compounds. For example, the word "biology" comes from the Greek *bios* (= life) and *logos* (= knowledge) and means the study of living things. **Etymology** is the study of a word's origins and development since its earliest recorded occurrence in the language. It also traces the transmission of a word from one language to another. For example, "denim" comes from "serge de Nîmes" (see Box 7.2). A word may be analyzed into its component parts (i.e., morphologically) or traced to a common ancestral form.

Learning how words have changed over time helps students remember words. For example, the word "flabbergast" once meant to embarrass or confound and is derived from the roots "flabby" and "aghast." Now "flabbergast" means to astonish or surprise. The study of the components of words enables

Box 6.1
Using Vocabulary in an Integrated Way

To learn the vocabulary in a unit, a Grade 10 science teacher recently asked students to prepare, in pairs, an oral presentation based on a written report as well as an artistic visual (e.g., a poster) of the key vocabulary in the unit. Chris and Anya were assigned the names, characteristics, and functions of three types of muscle cells. Each pair discussed and read the words, wrote a report, and then prepared an oral presentation based on the vocabulary important for learning the content.

For their presentation, Chris and Anya chose to do a skit, in which a news anchor interviews a research correspondent. Their presentation went like this:

Anya: We interrupt your regularly scheduled program to bring you a special report on muscle cells. Chris, are you there?

Chris: Thank you Anya. Although you may think muscle cells are not interesting, they are the essence of life. [A short introduction follows on muscle cells].

Anya: Tell us more, Chris.

Chris: Well, there are three types of muscle cells: smooth, skeletal, and cardiac . . . [he goes on to describe the smooth cells].

Anya: Quite interesting, Chris.

Chris: Why, thank you Anya. So what do you know about skeletal muscle cells?

Anya: Well, I know they are also called striped or striated. I learned that in high-school biology. These cells are . . . [she goes on to describe them briefly].

Chris: Thanks Anya. If you remember that much from high-school biology, I think I've just been fired [laughs]! But let me talk about the third and final type of muscle cell, that is, the cardiac muscle cell . . . [he goes on to describe these briefly and concludes by saying] Smooth, skeletal, and cardiac muscle cells are all responsible for the movement of an organism . . . [He turns back to Anya] . . . Back to you Anya. Anya? Anya! [Only to discover she has drifted off to sleep and he adds] Okay, just shut off the cameras.

The visuals consisted of two items: a labelled poster of the three muscle cells and a cooked chicken wing (with the muscle exposed for classmates to view as it was passed around in a plastic bag).

us to derive the meaning of root words. When words are used over a period of years, they gradually change in meaning and in form.

Using Contextual Information

Since effective methods of direct vocabulary instruction are limited by the time required to teach the meaning of even a small number of new words, wide reading should be encouraged as a vehicle for learning new vocabulary. Research with secondary students has shown that during this wide reading incidental learning of words occurs *from context*. Material such as another word, a phrase, a sentence, or a paragraph that surrounds a word and reveals its meaning becomes one of the major determinants of vocabulary growth (Nagy, Hermann, Anderson, & Pearson, 1984; Hermann, Anderson, Pearson, & Nagy, 1987; Nagy, Hermann, & Anderson, 1985). Teachers should model how to determine the meanings of words from naturally occurring context. Use of context clues enables the student to focus the reading transaction on the appropriate meaning from a number of possible meanings that may be at play during the reading. Konopak (1988), in a review of current research on contextual information in textbooks, lists the characteristics of "considerate" (rich, explicit) contexts. These are:

1. The closer the relevant context is to the unknown word, the easier will the reader find the information.
2. The clearer the connection between the context and the word, the better will the reader be able to infer the connection.
3. The more detailed the context, the better will the reader obtain a precise meaning of the word.
4. The more complete the context, the better will the reader be able to obtain a full understanding of the new word.
5. The more important the unknown word is to understanding the meaning of the passage, the more attempt will the reader make to figure out its meaning.
6. The stronger the reader's prior knowledge of the topic, the more familiar will the content be to the reader.

Assuming that the context is explicit and complete, the following types of clues can help students learn the meaning of subject area vocabulary: **semantic, syntactic, typographical,** or **pictorial/graphic clues.** Some of these may overlap.

Semantic Clues: These types of clues enable readers to grasp the meanings of words in text. They are:

1. *Definition or explanation*: The context explicitly defines the new word either through the use of signals such as the verb *to be* (*is, are*) or the

word "means," or through the use of commas surrounding an appositive phrase. For example: *The species is the smallest natural group of animals or plants.* Definitions must relate to the reader's experience or use vocabulary that is known to the reader for aesthetic and efferent transactions to occur.

2. *Restatement*: The context uses different words to say the same thing and signals these words by the use of *that is, or,* or *in other words*. For example: *The cell wall is fully permeable to water and gases. That is, it allows gases and water to "pass through" it in either direction.*

3. *Comparison or contrast*: The context likens the unknown word to something else that is known through the use of signal words that compare or contrast. Two examples follow: *The outer layer of cells on a stem forms a skin (like our skin) and is called the epidermis. Excretion, the elimination of body wastes, should not be confused with egestion, or the removal of undigested food from the intestine.*

4. *Synonyms and antonyms*: The context offers a word that has a similar or opposite meaning to the unknown word. For example: *Vascular bundles, sometimes called veins, are made up of vessels and sieve tubes.*

5. *Figures of speech*: The context provides appropriate similes or metaphors that elucidate the meaning of the word. For example: *Root hairs are tiny, finger-like outgrowths from the cells of the epidermis.*

6. *Summary statements*: The context provides a concise summary description of the meaning of the word. For example: *Students who are interested in intellectual inquiry and research are curious and creative thinkers. They are said to be inquisitive.*

7. *Inferences*: The context provides clues that help the reader to infer the meanings of unfamiliar words. For example: *Obvious signs of irritability in living organisms are the movements made by animals as a result of noise, being touched, or in response to the heat of the sun.*

8. *Tone or mood*: The context provides subjective clues and triggers associations that help define an unknown word. For example: *The dreary day was made even more dismal by the droning rain that pounded on the drenched rooftops and the dark window panes.*

9. *Examples*: The context provides examples that assist in defining the unknown word. For instance: *Robins are an example of a species.*

10. *Groupings*: The context presents other words in the same category or class of meaning. For example: *Tissue, such as bone, cartilage, nerve, or muscle, is made up of hundreds of cells having nearly identical structures.*

Syntactic Clues: The context may indicate some clue to meaning by virtue of the new word's grammatical form or placement. In the English language, certain grammatical forms fit only in certain places, and the word order may reduce the possibilities of meaning that the new word can hold. For example, in the sentence *Tissue, such as bone, cartilage, nerve, or muscle, is made* *up of hundreds of cells having nearly identical structures,* "such as" signals a listing of examples and the placement of "identical" before "structures" signals a descriptive word or adjective.

Typographical Clues: These give visual clues for determining the meanings of words, and include quotation marks, parentheses, italics, boldface type, use of capital letters, and definitional/explanatory footnotes. The text below demonstrates the use of some of these clues.

```
Seedlings are excellent material to use in irritability (sensitiv-
ity) experiments because their growing roots respond readily to such
stimuli as light, moisture, and gravity. Such "growth movements" (in
which the direction of growth is related to the direction of a stim-
ulus) are called tropisms.
```

Pictorial and Graphic Clues: The use of illustrations, pictures, charts, graphs, diagrams, maps, and tables can lend clarity to vocabulary found in the content areas and lead to the learning of new words and concepts.

Students' failure to use context clues effectively is caused by several factors: inadequate modelling and instruction by the teacher, weak inferencing abilities, low reading abilities, lack of sufficient prior knowledge of the topic (Hafner, 1967), and failure of some textbook authors to provide contexts with sufficient clues for learning the meaning of words.

Nontechnical narrative or expository text such as that found in English or the language arts usually provides sufficient clues in a rich context so that readers can use the contextual information to understand the meanings of words. However, adequate contextual information can be lacking in content area subjects, where knowledge of the precise meanings of words may be critical to the learning of the content. In such texts we say that the context provided is "inconsiderate" (severely limited) for learning the meanings of new words (Konopak, 1988).

The sections that follow provide specific instructional strategies for developing students' vocabulary through extension and refinement and using the methods described in previous sections (direct teaching of vocabulary, using context, and associating words with previous experiences and word knowledge).

Developing Content Vocabulary by Fostering Extension and Refinement

Most vocabulary exercises both extend and refine vocabulary. Extension addresses the breadth and height of meaning whereas refinement refers to height and depth of meaning. Blachowicz (1986) outlines a five-step strategy for developing new vocabulary before, during, and after reading and suggests appropriate instructional activities to carry out these steps.

Steps 1 and 2: Before Reading

Before reading, two steps focus on activating students' knowledge and relating it to the topic to be studied. Both steps require the student to be metacognitive by asking a question at each step. Let us see how we can use the five-step strategy to learn the words *osmosis* and *transpiration* as part of a word study in a section of a unit on "Growing Plants" (see Box 6.2). In each instance, one activity will be demonstrated; other activities suitable for each step will be provided in the appendices at the end of this chapter. While the stance taken in these five steps is predominantly efferent, it is clear that aesthetic elements will enter into the meaning making and that both efferent and aesthetic dimensions will be evident. Some interdisciplinary connections will also be made at this stage.

Step 1: A student's first strategic step is to ask, "What do I already know about the words *osmosis* and *transpiration*?" Teachers need to teach students using various activities such as brainstorming, knowledge ratings, and word sorts to make them aware of their prior knowledge. (Brainstorming is described below; the other activities are discussed in Appendix I.)

Using the brainstorming technique, the teacher asks students to give all the ideas they associate with the two words. As the students provide their ideas (see the points made in discussion below), the teacher writes them down. Next, students and teacher review the list and check off the most important ideas. The ideas could be categorized into efferent, aesthetic, and interdisciplinary (see Box 6.3). This activity could also be done in smaller groups who then compare their checked items.

Step 2: A student's second strategic question is, "In previewing this text, how are the words related to each other and to the topic and structure of the selection?" You'll note that the question directs students to an efferent reading. Through such activities as concept ladders, graphic organizers, semantic maps, semantic feature analyses, predict-o-grams, and capsule vocabulary activities, students see that words are parts of meaningful networks. The teacher guides the students in making a semantic map of the ideas they checked off. A semantic pre-reading map of the brainstormed words is provided in Figure 6.2; other activities appear in Appendix II.

A discussion following the creation of a semantic pre-reading word map ensures that the connections among the words and related words generated in the discussion are added to the map. For example, the before-reading discussion provided below may add the following points on *osmosis* and *transpiration*:

Box 6.2
Growing Plants — Inner Actions

Part 2: Which Way?

The surface of a root hair is a membrane through which water passes. Water moves from each of these cells through the membranes to other cells in the plant. This means that water must be able to move out of cells as well as into them. What makes water move in any particular direction through cell membranes? Try this and see.

YOU WILL NEED

- two containers
- water
- salt
- plants from which pieces may be removed

WHAT TO DO

1. Put some water into container A and a concentrated salt solution into container B.
2. Into each container place several plant pieces such as a 5 mm thick carrot slice, a fern frond, a lettuce leaf or a geranium leaf. Be sure to place the same kind of things into each container as shown in the drawings.
3. Observe and compare the plant pieces in the containers after 20 or 30 minutes and again after 1 or 2 hours. Also compare them with the plants from which they were removed.
4. Which plant pieces remained crisp or became even firmer? Which ones lost firmness and became spongy or limp?
5. In which direction do you think water moved in container A? in container B?

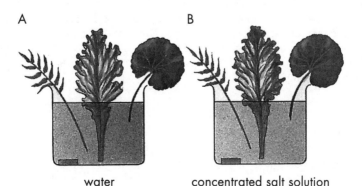

A   B

water   concentrated salt solution

(continued)

(continued)

In container A, the movement of water was into plant cells. In container B, the water moved out of the plant cells and into the salt solution. This shows that water can move into or out of plant cells. Such water movement is called *osmosis*. What determines the direction in which the water will move? Water moves through cell membranes from areas where water is more concentrated to areas where water is less concentrated. What does this mean? You already know a lot about dilute and concentrated solutions. You know how the amount of solute in a certain amount of solution determines how dilute or concentrated the solution is. Now, think about a solution in this way:

Water (the solvent) and any solute dissolved in it are made of tiny particles.

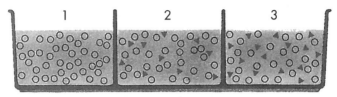

⊙ water particle   ▲ salt particle

In compartment 1 in the diagram, all of the particles are water particles. In compartment 2, the water is less concentrated because there are some particles of solute mixed in with it. In compartment 3, there are many particles of the solute mixed in, so that the concentration of the water particles is even lower than in compartment 2. Predict what would happen if the walls between these liquids were cell membranes. Would water move through the cell membranes? For how long?

Look again at the observations that you made when you put the pieces of plants into containers A and B. Think about the liquids involved and see how they compare with the liquids in compartments 1, 2, and 3 of the diagram above.

In container A, the water inside the plant cells had dissolved substances in it such as minerals, which plants need. The water in container A that the plant pieces were put into did not have these dissolved substances in it. Water moved from the container into the plant cells, as it would move from compartment 1 to compartment 2 in the diagram.

* * *

Part 5: Exit

Water reaches the leaves of a plant, where it is needed for the food-making process called photosynthesis. Extra water is released from the leaves into the air. It is easy to collect some of this water.

(continued)

(continued)

YOU WILL NEED

- a geranium or other plant with large leaves
- a plastic bag
- tape

WHAT TO DO

Cover one of the leaves of the plant with a plastic bag and tape it so that no air can enter or leave. Leave the plant in the sunlight or under a bright lamp for at least half an hour. Look closely at the inside surface of the bag. What do you see?

Transpiration is the term used for the movement of water out of the plant through the leaves.

Try these!

1. A leaf has been likened to a wet towel on a clothesline.
    a. What conditions help a towel to dry?
    b. Suggest what you could do to find out if these conditions would also increase the transpiration rate of a plant.
    c. What ways can you think of to make any drying effect of transpiration less of a threat to plants?
    d. What beneficial effect might transpiration have on plants on a hot day?
2. Would plants be threatened by water loss from transpiration in the space biosphere?
3. In the space biosphere, the plant's water supply would have to be maintained. How would you retrieve the water lost by plants through transpiration?

(continued)

(continued)

4. Neil and Marie are farmers. They plant a field of corn with 50 000 kernels. The minimum germination rate for sweet corn (Canada #1 Seed) is 90%. Suppose that two-thirds of the germinated seeds grow into mature corn plants. One corn plant gives off about 200 L of water by transpiration while it is growing.
   a. How much water would all of the corn plants together lose through transpiration during one growing season?
   b. What soil type would you consider to be the best for growing corn? Why?
5. Are there any areas in Canada where water loss from transpiration might cause problems for farmers? What can they do about it?

Source: From *Science Plus: Technology and Society 8*, 1990, Toronto: Harcourt Brace Canada, pp. 383–84, 385.

Box 6.3
Brainstorming Activity

Efferent

OSMOSIS	TRANSPIRATION
water ✓	photosynthesis ✓
breathing	perspiration
air	respiration ✓
evaporation	dry weather
interaction ✓	high humidity
root hairs ✓	oxygen ✓
absorption ✓	carbon dioxide ✓
cell membranes ✓	leaves ✓
experiments	sunlight ✓
nutrients ✓	
enters ✓	
moves out ✓	

Aesthetic

OSMOSIS	TRANSPIRATION
water	materialization/
air	becoming
evaporation	perspiration
hockey	dry weather
	high humidity
	leaves

Interdisciplinary

perspiration/respiration (physical education)
oxygen (physical education)
breathing (physical education)
interaction (statistics)

experiments (social studies)
high humidity (social studies)
dry weather (social studies)
nutrients (health)

Figure 6.2

The Pre-Reading Word Map

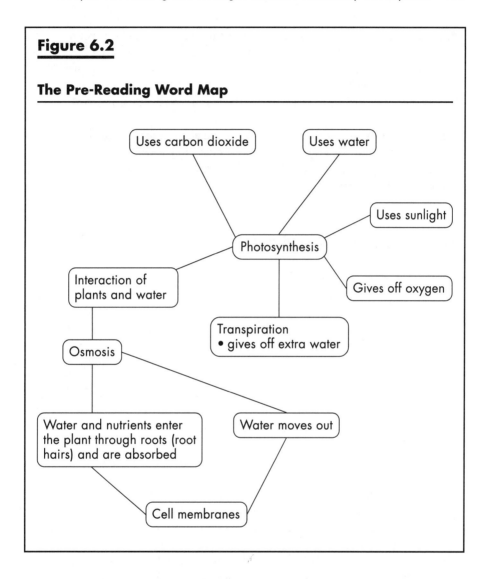

1. We learned earlier that cell walls are permeable (gases and water can pass in or out). I can add gases to the map.
2. My mother says she learned the game of hockey by osmosis — the televised hockey games are always on at our house and understanding eventually seeped in through so much exposure, she says.
3. I remember doing some experiments to show how plants absorb water through their root hairs. We used different solutions, some with salt in them.
4. *To transpire* is to happen, to occur, to materialize, to become. Could this be a different meaning of *transpiration*?

5. What about everything we studied in the unit previous to this one — on solutions — like the concentrations of solutions? Doesn't that have something to do with how quickly solutions pass through membranes? What about "solutes"?

6. How does photosynthesis fit in with osmosis and transpiration?

After the before-reading discussion, all of the above ideas might be added to the conceptual map in Figure 6.2. You'll note that some associations across the disciplines were made, despite a specific focus provided by the teacher by asking the strategic question.

Step 3: During Reading

Blachowicz's (1986) third step in her five-step strategy is part of the plan for vocabulary acquisition during reading. Students need to be taught how to use the context in which they encounter words to gain meanings of words. In an efferent transaction, the aim would be to take away these particular meanings after the reading.

Step 3: A student's third strategic step is to ask, "How can I figure out the meanings by using the words around the target word?" This step should help resolve questions raised in the first two steps. A variety of instructional activities are needed for students to gain the "full" meanings of words. Many students may have only partial meanings of some words as a result of the pre-reading activities.

The suggestions for context instruction need to go beyond introducing students to the different kinds of context clues (described earlier in the chapter) and instructing them to identify them as they read or to use them in determining word meanings. Strategies to glean meaning from context need to be modelled by the teacher, practised by students under teacher guidance, and then applied independently by students in the content areas. A *metacognitive approach for using context* (Blachowicz & Zabroske, 1990) to gain word meaning is described here. The other approaches are found in Appendix III.

The metacognitive instructional program consists of three components. The first component involves teaching students why and when to use context in reading. Awareness needs to be developed of both the contributions to and the limitations of context in gaining word meaning. Using preselected examples with varying degrees of context, verbalize through a think-aloud the processes used, the choices of clues, and the confusions, in an attempt to gain word meanings for a number of preselected words. A teacher might use the examples provided in the earlier section on semantic, syntactic, and typographical clues to conduct the think-aloud.

The second component in the metacognitive approach for using context clues involves using an inductive approach, rather than presenting students with a prescriptive list of types of context clues. Familiarize students (through a think-aloud) with clues that may be supplied by the context. A think-aloud might have the following elements as needed:

> Context can clue you to — what a word is (what it's like); what a word isn't (what it's different from); what it looks like; something about its location or setting; something about what it's used for; what kind of thing or action it is; how something is done; a general topic or idea related to the word; other words related to the word; and so forth. (Blachowicz & Zabroske, 1990, p. 506)

The following is an excerpt from Box 6.3:

> In container A, the movement of water was into plant cells. In container B, the water moved out of the plant cells and into the salt solution. This shows that water can move into or out of plant cells. Such water movement is called *osmosis*. What determines the direction in which the water will move? Water moves through cell membranes from areas where water is more concentrated to areas where water is less concentrated. What does this mean? You already know a lot about dilute and concentrated solutions. You know how the amount of solute in a certain amount of solution determines how dilute or concentrated the solution is. Now, think about a solution in this way:
>
> Water (the solvent) and any solute dissolved in it are made of tiny particles.

The following is what a think-aloud to determine the meaning of *osmosis* would sound like using the elements from the excerpt:

```
In this case, the context tells you what the word is, what it
means. The definition/explanation says "such water movement [mean-
ing the movement of water into plant cells and water moved out
of plant cells and into the salt solution] is called osmosis."
It doesn't tell you how this word is different from other simi-
lar words. The text doesn't tell you anything about the word's
location or setting, or what it's used for here. But it does tell
you what kind of action it is or how something happens: "Water
moves through cell membranes from areas where water is more con-
centrated to areas where water is less concentrated." That water
would be the salt solution. The text also tells you about a topic
or idea related to osmosis and that is dilute and concentrated
solutions — solutes and solutions. These words are in the second
last sentence of the paragraph. These words might be the other
words this word is related to — solutes and solutions and, yes,
solvent (the term for water). It's in the next sentence.
```

The third component in the metacognitive approach for using context clues is to teach students working in teams how to look for and use context clues. Students need to be directed to:

Look — before, at, after the word.
Reason — connect what you know with what the author tells you.
Predict — a possible meaning.
Resolve or redo — decide whether you know enough about the word's meaning, whether you should try the context again, or whether you need to consult a reference, the teacher, or a peer.

Students will be directed to get the meaning of *transpiration* from context and expected to work independently. The teacher would guide them as follows:

```
That's an easy one. Looking "before the word" under "What To Do,"
there is a hint that there would be moisture on the inside of the
plastic bag. Experience with  owers delivered, plants covered
before a frost, and the moisture on window panes from plants next
to windows would support that premise. Looking "at the word"
itself, transpiration, suggests breathing, letting off gases and
moisture. Looking "after the word" gives you the definition — that
transpiration means the movement of water out of the plant through
its leaves. The word is is used to signal a definition.
    As for reasoning, some of that reasoning was already done when
looking at the text before the word — because you'd connect what
you already know with what the author told you. In fact at that
point, you'd predict what transpiration meant — to let out mois-
ture. Resolve or redo? In this case, the decision is easy. No need
to try to read the context again or consult anyone as you already
know the word's meaning. You would, however, want to consult fur-
ther if you wanted to differentiate transpiration from respira-
tion or perspiration (in animals).
```

In all three components (each introduced in stages), the teacher must first model the processes. Later, the teacher must guide the students through some textbook passages in order to find the clues and explain how they are used in the context. The teacher can incidentally name the clues (e.g., "it's defined, restated"; "you make an inference"; "there's a comparison to another word") as he or she verbalizes. Finally, the students would act as teachers in leading the lessons and independently explain how they used context to acquire meaning. Writing can also be used in the contextual learning process (Blachowicz & Zabroske, 1990). When context is not found to be helpful in defining/explaining certain words or concepts, students can rewrite sections of the context to provide better clues. These rewritten versions can be filed and used for future students who will read the same textbooks (Blachowicz & Zabroske, 1990).

Steps 4 and 5: After Reading

The defining, refining, and reformulating of word meanings usually occur in activities and discussions after the reading of an assigned passage or chapter. This coincides with Blachowicz's (1986) final two steps in her five-step strategy for long-term acquisition of new words.

Step 4: Students need to learn how to define and refine word meanings and their underlying concepts. Students at this point ask, "How can I use what I have read to confirm or clarify my initial ideas about the meanings of the words?" Instructional strategies would include post-reading word maps, post-graphic organizers, and post-reading capsule vocabulary. After reading, students would add to their maps or graphic organizers, based on information gleaned from the reading. Initially, these activities might be done with teacher guidance.

Figure 6.3 provides an example of a post-reading word map on osmosis and transpiration.

A post-reading mapping might also be made of the interdisciplinary transactions that occurred as a result of the reading. Figure 6.4 provides examples of possible transactions across the subject areas.

Step 5: To extend new vocabulary knowledge through application, students should ask themselves, "To make the word mine, how must I read it and use it?" The student must use the word in a variety of language contexts and modes such as reading, speaking, writing, viewing, and listening. Application really occurs in the many and varied natural situations in and out of the classroom. Take a word like "culture," for example. What does "culture" mean when you place it in the context of biology if you want to show how to "grow a culture" or in the context of history if you are thinking of the "Native culture in North America"? In the context of natural science, you might focus on the culture of the environment as an aspect of the natural world (e.g., natural habitat of wild animals, like bears). As we have discussed in Chapter 4, many interdisciplinary transactions are possible: this is so with a word like "culture." Read the poem below and see how many meanings of "culture" you can evoke. Say some aloud; write the others down.

When is a bear more than a bear?

If you were
a bear's biographer,
studying a single species
in a single place,
you might find out the height,
weight, diet, and nocturnal habits
of this bear —
and wrap up your report.

Figure 6.3

The Post-Reading Word Map

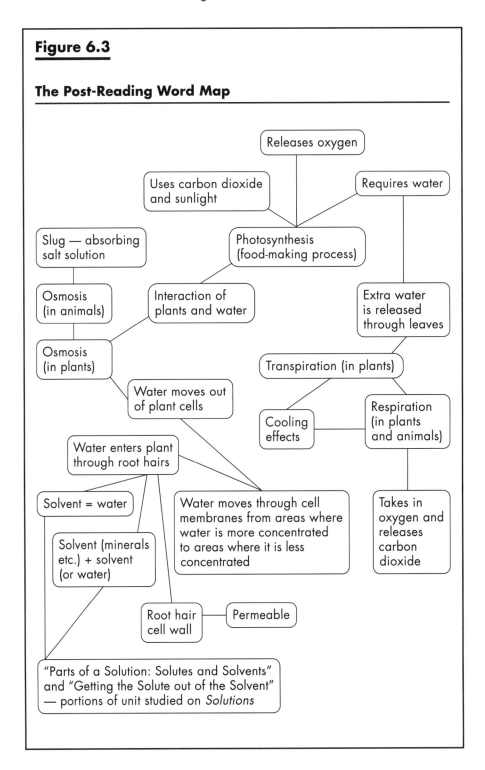

Figure 6.4

Post-Reading Word Map: Interdisciplinary Transactions in "Growing Plants"

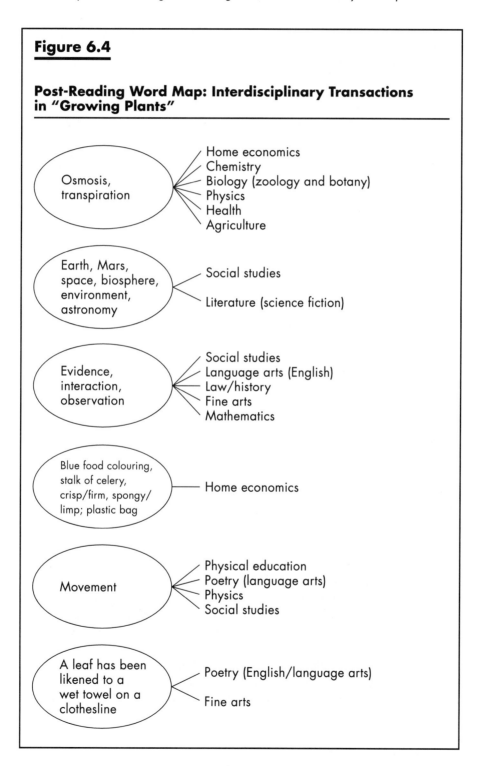

Osmosis, transpiration	Home economics Chemistry Biology (zoology and botany) Physics Health Agriculture
Earth, Mars, space, biosphere, environment, astronomy	Social studies Literature (science fiction)
Evidence, interaction, observation	Social studies Language arts (English) Law/history Fine arts Mathematics
Blue food colouring, stalk of celery, crisp/firm, spongy/limp; plastic bag	Home economics
Movement	Physical education Poetry (language arts) Physics Social studies
A leaf has been likened to a wet towel on a clothesline	Poetry (English/language arts) Fine arts

But step back a bit
and think of *genus* bear
as a creature of the world —
and the meaning of "bear"
deepens.
You have questions
about habitat, predators, climate,
population, trees.
Your classmates think of other
topics bears bring up —
lumberjacks,
honey, pawprints.
Someone reports on
bears in cave art.
You wonder,
Do coyotes attack bears?
You write for the ingredients in
gummy bears but
fail to reproduce them at home.
You ask whether bats
can live in the same caves as bears.
You take home a book about the
Plains people and
find yourself wondering,
Were bears part
of Native American culture?
Are there any buffalo left?
You write in your journal
that you would be
a different kind of cowboy.

Source: From Significant Issues in Reading brochure, in *Heath Literacy: Where Worlds Open Worlds.* Copyright © 1995 by D.C. Heath & Company. Reprinted by permission of Houghton Mifflin Company. All rights reserved.

Rosenblatt (1980) once asked the question, "What facts does this poem teach you?" to counter those teachers who teach poetry solely from an efferent stance. Rosenblatt argued further for more aesthetic reading in all subject areas. The poem "When is a bear more than a bear?" exemplifies how the meaning of the word "bear" is enhanced if aesthetic as well as efferent transactions are emphasized in the literacy process.

When I read about the bear in the poem, I move from efferent meanings of "bear" to aesthetic meanings. In a sense I am like the poet: I create a world of language to live in and to live through as I continue to read. I create a kind of poem out of a reading of the poem. I can do this by focussing on individual words that call up both an efferent and an aesthetic response.

The word "nocturnal" can make me think of dark nights, Halloween, dark spaces, caves, bats, spiders' webs, or fear. I might think of ghosts, spirits, vampires, or beings who can live only in darkness. This is an aesthetic response to the word.

When I come to "genus" I notice it is italicized. I may recognize genus as a biological term for classification at the same time as noting that it is made to stand out because of the typographical difference.

A change of stance may occur when I come to the word "predator" because it may connect with "nocturnal." I move back and forth in my reading stance from the "cold" cognitions associated with "bear" as "genus" to the "hot" cognitions of "bear" as "nocturnal" and "predator." When I confront the "bear" in relation to the concept of "culture," the poet's questions throw open the whole concept of culture. These questions break open my "lived through" prior understanding of what culture means. When I live through this kind of questioning, I am doing the kind of reading Rosenblatt describes as aesthetic. I may begin to see that living through the making of meaning is as important to the development of literacy as the efferent ways of reading that ensure carrying away meaning.

Summary

Literacy in the content areas involves aesthetic as well as efferent understanding of words. To make meaning, learners must transact with and respond to vocabulary from personal experience and feelings as well as from a conceptual understanding of the words in texts; conceptual understandings can come from several different disciplines. The most important factor in expanding students' vocabularies is the excitement that teachers generate about words. They can do this by demonstrating their own efferent and aesthetic understandings of words, exhibiting excitement about specific vocabulary, encouraging wide reading, and promoting growth through talk, reading, writing, and dramatizations.

To know a word is to know *degrees* of possible meanings of words. As readers assume efferent and aesthetic stances, they are constantly refining their knowledge of word meanings. Teachers can assist students in the content areas in acquiring and fine-tuning meanings by presenting and discussing words and concepts in relational categories and networks that incorporate the range of students' feelings and personal associations. Technical and specialized vocabulary in each subject area is often unfamiliar to students and must be learned in concept clusters of both familiar and new words. The two main ways to improve content vocabulary are through incidental learning and through instruction. Instruction includes:

1. direct teaching of vocabulary that follows sound instructional principles, one of which is creating opportunities for students to use the vocabulary in talk and writing before and after reading;
2. relating words to experience and to already accumulated knowledge across the disciplines;
3. studying the morphology and etymology of words; and
4. teaching students how to use context clues and encouraging them to do so independently.

The five-step strategy is a useful plan for developing vocabulary before, during, and after reading. Within these five steps, several strategies for encouraging a predominantly efferent stance can be used: brainstorming, knowledge ratings, word sorts, semantic networks or maps, graphic organizers, semantic feature analyses, predict-o-grams, capsule vocabulary, the vocabulary self-collection strategy, the concept of definition, and the metacognitive approach for using context. Some of these strategies are outlined in the appendices to this chapter.

Questions for Further Reflection

1. In small groups, read the list of words below, first taking an aesthetic stance, then an efferent stance. Have each person in the group demonstrate his or her transaction with these words by thinking aloud to show efferent and aesthetic understandings of these words for teaching purposes.

celestial bodies	operation	permutation
interest	gain and loss	transformations
rounding	precision	notation
symmetry	prism	proportions

2. From which subject area were the majority of these words drawn? What interdisciplinary connections did you make in your reading of the words?
3. How would your approach to teaching vocabulary in the various subject areas differ from the approach used when you went to junior and senior high school? What would you do differently in the subject area in which you have the most specialization?
4. From experience, what instructional strategies can you add to those provided in the chapter that would effectively develop and/or expand students' word knowledge? Next modify or alter these strategies to take efferent and aesthetic responses to words into account. Finally, modify them to include interdisciplinary transactions.

5. How can a teacher use discussion to move students into the discourse conventions and vocabulary of different disciplines?

Key Terms

Anticipation guide
Automaticity
"Cold" cognition
Conceptual knowledge
Conceptual understanding
Disciplinary club
Etymology
"Hot" cognition
Kinesthetic

Morphology
Olfactory
Pictorial/graphic clues
Pre-reading plan (PReP)
Referents
Semantic clues
Syntactic clues
Typographical clues

Appendix I

Knowledge Ratings

The use of a **pre-reading plan** (Langer, 1981, p. 154), or **PReP**, or an **anticipation guide** (Readence, Baldwin, & Bean, 1981) can help teachers to make learners aware of their prior knowledge of vocabulary. These activities are generally referred to as knowledge ratings.

PreP has three phases:

1. asking learners to brainstorm for their initial associations (words and images) with a concept or topic — e.g., what they associate with the idea of a *myth* or *life in the desert* or *wolves*;
2. asking learners for their reflections on those initial associations — for example, why they associate myths with ancient civilizations, or why they associate wolves with northern countries;
3. asking learners to verbalize associations that have been elaborated or changed during discussion — e.g., myths are stories that endure into the present, and the same myths can be found in different "cultures"; wolves hunt in packs and are an endangered species.

An anticipation guide is a series of statements that enable learners to make predictions or take stands about concepts or ideas they are about to encounter during reading or viewing or through discussion. Procedurally, a teacher (and, if possible, a learner, when he or she is constructing an anticipation guide for other learners) needs to follow these steps:

1. Analyze the text in question in order to determine some major ideas/concepts that will resonate with most learners.
2. Put these ideas/concepts into short, clear declarative statements. The statements should be emotive for the reader and in some way stimulate the learners' reflections on the world they are familiar with. The statements must be concrete.
3. The statements are then put into a format so that the learner is able to anticipate the text's content and locate the learner's expectations through prediction.
4. The teacher and learner should discuss the predictions and anticipations before engaging with the text. This reinforces the learner's expectations about the text.
5. The text is then engaged with.
6. Compare and contrast the learner's predictions with the author's intended meaning.

Word Sorts

Word sorts (Gillet & Kita, 1979) can be open or closed. In the open word sort, no category or criterion is known in advance of the sorting, and thus divergent and inductive reasoning is favoured. The learner must be able to give reasons for grouping words into categories. Here is an example of a list of words that can be arranged in a number of different groupings:

cells	skeletal
striated	smooth
cardiac	organism
bone	cartilage
nerve	epidermis
muscles	tissue

A closed word sort helps learners to think about words critically by requiring them to classify terms in relation to more inclusive concepts. Most of the words in the list given above, for example, can be classified under two types: "Kinds of Cells" and "Kinds of Tissue." In this case the two types are given to learners before sorting to enable them to think about the classification to which the words belong and to reinforce concept development.

Appendix II

Graphic Organizers

A graphic organizer enables learners to see vocabulary in relation to a concept. The vocabulary is shown as a textual structure, which helps learners to anchor concepts by seeing relationships among the ideas. Figure A6.1 is an example of a graphic organizer for the texts in Chapter 1 concerning cardiovascular fitness and aerobic exercise:

Semantic Feature Analysis

This strategy is an effective way to reinforce learning of the vocabulary related to concepts. Essential vocabulary is built into a grid, in which major features, characteristics, or concepts are listed on the left-hand side and the vocabulary related to these is listed across the top of the grid. Individually or in co-operative groups, learners may review and discuss the vocabulary, and then check off the appropriate cell in the grid to indicate which words are related

Figure A6.1

Graphic Organizers

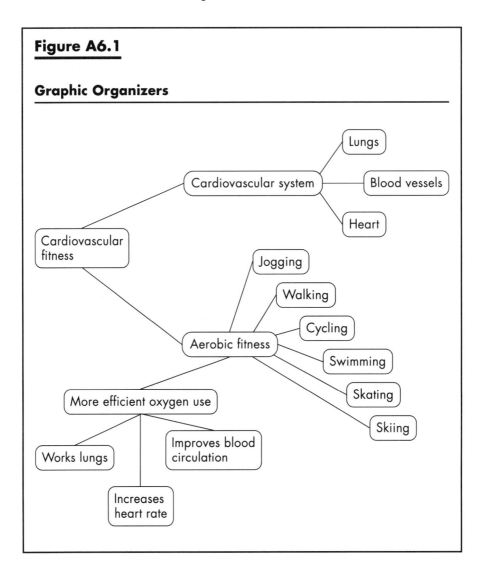

to which concepts. Figure A6.2 depicts a semantic feature analysis for the concept "cardiovascular fitness" (see Chapter 1).

Predict-o-Grams

Instead of using semantic maps to organize the brainstormed words, students might be asked to predict where vocabulary fits into the structure of a passage and chart it on the basis of their predictions (Blachowicz, 1986). If the piece is a narrative, the story grammar of a narrative might be used in the

Figure A6.2

Semantic Feature Analysis of Cardiovascular Fitness

	SYSTEM	EXERCISE	OXYGEN	ENDURANCE	GLYCOGEN	OXYGEN DEBT	LACTIC ACID
CARDIOVASCULAR	✓						
AEROBIC		✓	✓	✓			

charting process. Students would be expected to predict how the author would use the words in the narrative. They might also be asked to describe the setting, characters, or feelings based on the vocabulary. Vocabulary such as *combine*, *lobotomy*, *psychiatric*, *football*, *McMurphy*, *rebel*, *Ratched*, *medication*, *neurosis*, and *freedom*, drawn from Ken Kesey's (1962) *One Flew Over the Cuckoo's Nest*, might be charted in this way (see Figure A6.3). Try the activity by predicting where the words fit.

Similarly, the teacher might draw out the text structures and key vocabulary of specific expository texts to be read (see Chapter 2). Students, using their prior knowledge of the topic, would predict which words fit in certain categories. In using expository text, some text in the form of subtitles or full sentences would assist students in their predictions based on structure. Read the selection on Canada in Exercise 12.2 and assess whether the following words fit as shown in Figure A6.4: *immigrants*, *Confederation*, *Industrial Revolution*, *farms*, *villages*, *working conditions*, *inventions*, *machinery*, *cities*, *factories*, *farmers*, and *problems*.

Capsule Vocabulary

In this activity four modes of learning new vocabulary — listening, speaking, writing, and reading — are used collaboratively by students (Crist, 1975). Here's how it works:

Figure A6.3

Predict-o-Gram for *One Flew Over the Cuckoo's Nest*

THE SETTING

THE GOAL OR
PROBLEM (CONFLICT)   THE RESOLUTION

THE CHARACTERS

THE ACTIONS/
EVENTS   OTHER

---

1. Present students with a series of words on a topic in a content area. For example, in the subject of economics, let's say that you, the teacher, choose the words *investment, production, employment, consumption,* and *equilibrium.* To begin with, you define each of the words in relation to the topic and provide examples of the correct use of these words in sentences and passages.

Figure A6.4

Predict-o-Gram

EARLY DEVELOPMENT (BEFORE CONFEDERATION)	BIRTH OF A NATION	RESULTS OF EXPANSION (AFTER CONFEDERATION)
farms	Confederation (1867)	working conditions
immigrants	Industrial Revolution	(poor)
farmers	factories	problems
villages	cities	
	machinery	
	inventions	
	immigrants	

2. Students pair off to discuss the topic for five minutes using the designated vocabulary. While one student discusses the words, the other records the number of words used in the talk-aloud. Student roles are then switched.
3. Each student writes a summary of the topic using the series of terms. The students then exchange and read each other's compositions.

Each vocabulary lesson should focus on clusters of related words and activities that *expand* vocabulary, *refine* vocabulary, and require students to *apply* their newly acquired knowledge of vocabulary in reading, writing, and speaking so as to gain control over a concept cluster of vocabulary (Nelson-Herber, 1986).

Appendix III

Vocabulary Self-Collection Strategy (VSS)

Rapp-Haggard Ruddell (1986, 1992) proposes the vocabulary self-collection strategy (VSS) to make students aware of and to improve their learning strategies for defining words in their natural contexts. VSS uses lists of words chosen by students and emphasizes the personal experiences and word knowledge that students bring to text.

The main purpose of the activity is to locate vocabulary that will assist students in learning the content. Student participation is maximized by dividing the class into teams of several members (two to five) so that students work collaboratively. The steps for using VSS are:

1. Divide the class into student teams to nominate/identify a word or concept. The teacher also identifies one word.
2. The teacher writes the words on the chalkboard. Individual members of the team:
   a. read the sentence/paragraph in which the word is located, thus providing the context in which the word appears;
   b. explain what the word means based on the contextual information; and
   c. provide reasons for why the word was chosen for study.
   (The above process should first be modelled by the teacher with his or her nominated word.)
3. Invite class members to contribute information to each definition in group discussion. Where possible, encourage students to relate the meanings to personal experience and previous learning and to consult references for words whose meanings are unclear from the context.

4. Record the words and their meanings in vocabulary notebooks or personal journals. Students and teachers, as a group, may choose to reduce the number of words to be recorded, or individual students may wish to record additional words in their personal logs/notebooks.
5. Follow-up extension activities to clarify and refine the concepts and study activities may be based on the vocabulary lists.

With its emphasis on student choice in vocabulary study and student experience, in conjunction with its use of contextual information, VSS stimulates enthusiasm for word study and develops active, independent word learners (Rapp-Haggard, 1986; Rapp-Haggard Ruddell, 1992).

Concept of Definition (CD)

Concept of definition (CD) (Schwartz, 1988; Schwartz & Raphael, 1985) is a general structure or word map that exhibits the hierarchical pattern of a concept and its relationships to other concepts in the content areas and is based on semantic networks (Pearson & Johnson, 1978). Similar in content and structure to other mapping procedures, CD is distinguished by its focus on development of independence in learning (i.e., development of learning-to-learn strategies). Concept of definition goes beyond defining words from context by providing a framework for organizing conceptual relationships. According to schema theory, concepts (schemata) in our minds are organized in conceptual hierarchies according to class, example, and attribute (i.e., these relationships are based on our experiences and prior knowledge). The more superordinate concepts (e.g., "holidays") subsume the subordinate concepts (e.g., "religious holidays") in a class or category. Each class contains examples (e.g., Christmas, Yom Kippur, Ramadan) of the concepts in that category, each possessing similar or different attributes. CD is most useful with nouns. (See Figure A6.5.)

In the centre of the map students write the concept to be learned. Around the centre node, students write the word that best describes the category into which the target concept fits, several examples of the concept, and, if possible, three related but different concepts associated with the target concept. Finally, the students describe properties of the target concept. In each instance students are guided by prompts, such as "What is it?" "What are some examples?" and "What are some properties?"

By internalizing the general structure of CD, students can then engage in metacognitive reasoning by (1) examining their present word knowledge in terms of the components they know and don't know, and (2) selecting and monitoring strategies (i.e., use of context or morphological clues) needed to

Figure A6.5

Generic CD Maps

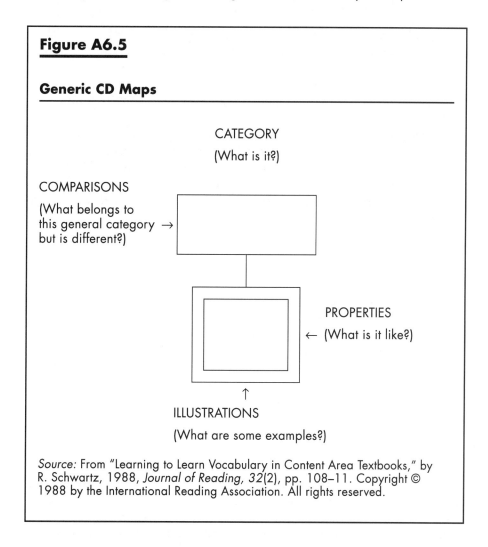

CATEGORY

(What is it?)

COMPARISONS

(What belongs to
this general category →
but is different?)

PROPERTIES

← (What is it like?)

↑

ILLUSTRATIONS

(What are some examples?)

complete the rest of the information on the concept map or to differentiate the concept from other concepts.

Teacher modelling of the CD map should precede students' independent use of authentic content area texts. Feedback and practice should be provided under teacher supervision as students gradually assume more and more responsibility for their learning. Eventually students can construct their own CDs as they encounter concepts in their textbooks. Modelling of CD instruction can follow this suggested sequence:

1. Demonstrate the purpose of a CD map by relating it to memory organization and the use of such structures in comprehension.

2. Introduce the structure of a CD map using a familiar concept such as *bicycle*, guiding students' construction of the map and using the three prompts that define a concept ("What is it?" "What are some examples?" and "What are some properties?").

3. Walk students through several CD maps, using vocabulary from a content area.

4. Encourage students to use the CD maps independently to guide their drawing of meanings of concepts from content area textbooks as they read. Whenever students encounter passages where only partial meaning (for completion of the CD map) can be drawn from context, encourage them to use background knowledge, their peers, and other resources to complete the maps.

Use of Context Clues

A suggestion that can be adapted to content areas by extending the use of context clues to composition and co-operative learning is also presented (Tipton, 1991). Once students can demonstrate that they recognize and use various context clues (definition, synonym, and comparison), the content area teacher should select and write a series of words on a topic on the chalkboard or a wall chart, one word per student. These words are displayed for a day or a week (as long as needed). As part of the lesson, students choose one of the words and check it off. As a first step, each student defines the chosen word — using context (based on a particular clue such as example, contrast, synonym), the dictionary, or background knowledge — and then writes a sentence or paragraph in which the word is used. As a second step, when the composition is complete, students work in pairs. They exchange papers and, based on context clues used in their compositions, tell each other what each of the two vocabulary words means. Discussion is encouraged in these pairs. In this second step, the teacher continues to circulate to answer questions, check meanings, and provide assistance. As a final step, students retrieve their papers, on which they write the word (and its meaning) that was learned in the peer exchange, giving them a total of two new words.

CHAPTER SEVEN

Enhancing Content Comprehension and Metacomprehension

Questions to Consider for this Chapter

1. How do you conceptualize reading for comprehension? for metacognition? How does your understanding reflect the current thinking of practitioners and theorists?

2. Which of the following words do you think best describes what happens when you comprehend a new concept or text: "grasp," "embrace," or "overview"? How does your choice reflect what you understand about "comprehension"?

3. Which of the following words best defines the prefix "meta-" as it occurs in the word "metacomprehension": over? behind? changed? above? higher? How does your choice reflect what you understand about "metacomprehension"?

4. How would you compare a transaction with a printed text and a transaction with a visual text in the content areas?

5. Describe comprehension and metacomprehension of a visual text.

6. How can you embed the teaching of text comprehension into the viewing, reading, discussion, and writing of texts?

7. List three reasons why a repertoire of strategies for efferent reading is useful in all content areas.

8. What are the merits of using literature-based materials (e.g., novels, magazines) or films in a content area?

9. What do you think are the essential components of a program to improve content comprehension?

Overview

The chapter begins by discussing what is known about comprehension and metacomprehension (thinking about one's understanding). A visual text from biology is then used to illustrate how comprehension and metacomprehension occur first during an aesthetic response and then during an efferent response. Understanding of the concept of DNA using visual text is illustrated in more than one content area.

Using six different texts, we next demonstrate how teachers can encourage both efferent and aesthetic responses and interdisciplinary transactions while embedding the teaching of comprehension strategies into readings and discussions. Texts are drawn from social studies, mathematics, geography, the English language arts, and biology. The chapter concludes with a brief summary of the main components of an instructional program to improve comprehension and metacomprehension.

Comprehension in Reading and Writing

As shown in Chapter 2, reading and writing are complex processes made up of linguistic, cognitive, affective, and associational **reservoirs**. Our understanding of reading and writing emerge from our life experience, not just from our school knowledge. Our "reservoirs" for understanding what is read and what is written about are renewable; the reservoirs are constantly being regenerated from life experience and school experience.

Readers and writers can open up these reservoirs by attending to the stance they take as they live through their reading/writing about a text. In other words, comprehension of a text read/written depends on which position or stance is taken and how readers/writers focus their attention before, during, and after reading/writing. In addition, an ability to monitor changes in the position or stance taken for reading/writing should be developed by the readers and writers.

Although reading and writing are not exactly the same processes, each is a kind of composing process (Anderson, 1990; Tierney & Shanahan, 1991). They are also sociolinguistic processes (Harste, Woodward, & Burke, 1984) that draw on personal, cultural, and contextual interpretations of reality. Readers/writers engage in a strategic recursive processing that requires constructive thinking (Flower 1994; Scardamalia & Bereiter, 1986). In Pearson's (1993, p. 502) words, the reader (or writer) is a "builder," filtering the text through a personal reservoir of knowledge and revising text meaning as needed. When carried out as interrelated processes, reading and writing act together as transactional composing processes (Rosenblatt, 1989). Understanding what occurs during the composing process in reading supports our understanding of the composing process during writing, and vice versa. In a sense, then, we write our readings of a text just as we read our writings of a text: when we compose or construct a comprehension of the text, we are reading in somewhat the same way we compose a text we are writing.

Writers place themselves on the flip side of the reading process: instead of trying to make sense of the marks on paper, they try to make marks on paper that have the potential to make sense to another reader, who may also become a writer in response to the writing. To create text that has this potential, writers learn to engage in reading and reading their writing. They learn how to change their role from reader to writer and then back again: they use reading comprehension strategies in the midst of using writing strategies to create readable text.

Active, self-regulated readers and writers energetically take on "the problem of making sense" of their reading and writing. They can analyze and make meaning to fit their own background experiences and knowledge as well as that of their readers. When learning goals are set and strategies used to reach these goals (Santa, 1992, p. 246), readers grasp what it means to comprehend.

When readers are learning to integrate new knowledge with prior knowledge and experience they are engaged in **comprehension**. The following example of the comprehension process describes a transaction with visual text.

Transacting with a Visual Text: An Aesthetic Beginning for Comprehension

Rosenblatt's (1989) concept of transaction can be applied to reading and writing about texts other than literary texts. While transactions with literary texts can work in rich and often unpredictable ways, as we discovered with the poetic and prose texts presented in Chapters 3 and 4, a reader can also transact with visual text in the content areas in surprising and rewarding ways. Figure 7.1 contains an example of a visual text with which one of the other authors of this book transacted by taking an aesthetic stance even though the image was not intentionally produced as a piece of art.

As she prepared herself to read aesthetically, to "live through" this text, she also took the position that to read in this way and to write about the living through is a way of comprehending the text in relation to her past and present experience and knowledge of the content. She also took the attitude that this text is a world to which she must continually return.

Figure 7.1

Visual Text of DNA

Source: From *Biology: Teacher's Edition,* by E.J. Kormondy and B.E. Essenfeld, 1984, Menlo Park, CA: Addison-Wesley Publishing Company. Copyright © 1984 by Addison-Wesley Publishing Company. Reprinted by permission.

As I begin to read this visual text I am aware that in the past I have read visual texts similar to this in many different contexts: several times in a Content Area Reading course with student teachers from different disciplines and a few times in workshops with practising teachers. In addition, a coloured visual text similar to this black and white one was also read many times with Visual Arts students to elicit from them names, descriptions, and explanations for the shapes and composition that make up this textual world. These past experiences of reading are already in transaction with this present reading: living through now means also living through a memory montage of prior reading experiences. There is one important difference at play in this reading, however. This time I am deliberately paying attention to and writing about this reading. I am deliberately putting into play my awareness of the metacomprehension strategies I use during the reading, and I am articulating those strategies as I write about what I live through during the reading. I have never written about a reading of this text before.

I notice as I begin to write about this reading that there is a sense of comfort as my eyes follow the tight arrangement of "rails" and "ties" from the bottom to the centre of the page. As I write this sentence I become aware of the **analogy** that has started to grow in my mind: that the marks that make up the world of this visual text as a whole are like a twisted railroad. This analogizing contributes to a growing sense of understanding because the image of a railroad, even though it is twisted, provides structure, a "big picture." The analogy acts like a map because, as with a map, the structure of shaded "ties" and "rails" provides me as a reader with a sense of ordered space. I notice as I write about the creation of this analogy that there is a sense of *living* comfortably within this visual space: as I begin to feel more comfortable with the analogy, I begin to feel more comfortable with *questioning* the unknown details of the structure of this visual composition. Just as I begin to feel comfortable, however, I note that the experience of beginning to give names to the arrangement of "ties" and "rails" is something other than comfortable; the initial experience of ordered space offers a degree of pleasure as well as a strong sense of satisfaction with the predictability of the design of this text. Comfort and pleasure and satisfaction are at play as I gather in and try to name each sign of neatness and stability.

However, as I continue to read this visual text upward, I also experience a sense that the entire apparatus is oating, that it is not still but moving, that this neat and orderly arrangement is not altogether stable or predictable, that within this order there is the possibility of sudden change, perhaps even of disorder. At first, I experience a moment of panic. The thought of *predicting* the possibility of disorder seems to have the effect of enhancing the comfort of order. Rather than working against each other, the experience of order and the apprehension of disorder make the reading of the text more challenging, more interesting, more puzzling, and more exciting.

I realize as I continue to read that I don't know what is going to happen with this text. Reading this text has become something of a mystery. As I reread, as I glance back to the top of the visual text and read across and down again, I notice the way that the "ties," shown as differently shaded halves of connectors, are not at all predictable. The orderliness I first thought to be a dominant feature of this visual text is broken by unpredictable combinations: there is no predictable sequence at all!

In one loop, for example, one "tie" is composed of a dark half at the top and a light half at the bottom. The next two "ties" are reversed. The "ties" do not line up and match on one side in a predictable way, nor do they match with each other in a predictable sequence.

The loop above and to the left contains a different sequence of "ties," and then another combination, and so on. So I begin to see that within the apparent orderliness of this twisted railroad, there is indeed unpredictability. I now cannot even count on my comfortable analogy of a railroad; the sense of safety derived from the predictability of that analogy is beginning to break down!

I am beginning to experience puzzlement, a sense that "reading" this text is not all comfortable. Still, I note that the sense of order has not altogether disappeared; rather, there seems to be something of a tension, even a struggle between order and disorder, between the possibility of order and the probability of disorder. I do not feel safe, but I do feel excited because I do not know what is coming next. I experience being in a state of knowing and not knowing at the same time. In one moment a sense of order is being jostled by a sense of impending disorder.

When I follow to the right at the top of the text — the "rails" and "ties" that make the twisted railroad — I am thrown into a state of *questioning*: there is a sudden wrenching apart of the once-orderly though somewhat unpredictable "railroad." The bands I have been calling "rails" suddenly separate altogether and the "ties" begin to break up. They break apart not just from the band to which they were attached but also from each other. The "ties" are no longer "tied." Suddenly I have no way to name what is happening. "Ties" oat away and become two pieces, taking with each piece a section of the once comfortably ordered railroad holding everything together. Half-sections oat off and away up into the right corner. The world of this visual text is coming apart: every part is marked by separation; the "railroad" is splitting and breaking. Here in the middle of the world of this visual text everything is coming apart, every part is marked by separation: there is nothing but splitting and breakage. The twisted railroad seems barely able to contain itself in some kind of order. In the lower-right-hand corner there is more separation, but in this corner there is only a hint of the splitting of connectors. Now I can predict as I read this part of the visual text that if I could extend the image beyond the visual world presented to me in this composition, the "ties" and "rails" would be reconnecting, that there would be at least a tentative order taking place once again. I am aware that at this point of living through a reading of this text, I am engaging in *prediction*. The prediction of the possibility of order restores once again, if only for a moment, a sense of comfort.

So now, what can I begin to make of this experience of living through this unnamed, unworded visual text? How can I begin to make sense of this world of separation co-existing with order? This unpredictability living side by side with stability? How do I live through and with this apparent ambiguity?

One way to begin to make sense would be to follow up on an elaboration of my analogy. I have given two names to this visual illustration: "twisted" and "railroad." I have named the parts of the railroad "rails" and "ties." Since I have already experienced similar texts before, I have been using analogies many times over as a way to construct meaning about this visual text. Here, however, I have gathered together names in written form. With the presence of this written form in front of my eyes, I can summon up a holistic picture in my mind and then define the parts that make up this picture. I analogize to create a *visual image* of a visual image, but the image I create through analogy is drawn from my prior knowledge and experience, from what I already know. When I write about the process of building an analogy, I find a way to begin building a comprehension of this text, and I give myself a form to which I may further respond and, further, for which I may build metacomprehension strategies. The writing transacts with the reading and helps me to work my way from what I know toward a comprehension of the unknown.

Metacomprehension

As readers learn to actively and consistently apply and use strategies to achieve the integration of the earlier transaction, they are engaged in **metacomprehension**. They are aware of their own cognitive processes and have the ability to regulate or control them. They understand their thinking and feeling processes, and they think about and come to an understanding of how to fit their background knowledge and experience with the texts they are reading and writing. At the same time, they learn how the texts that are read and writ-

---

For Reflection 7.1

What do you understand by the term *comprehension* now? How do you comprehend a visual text in a content area?

ten can change their renewable reservoirs of knowledge and experience. Pearson (1993) uses the metaphor of the reader as "fixer" (p. 503) or problem solver who applies a repertoire of strategies metacognitively (and flexibly) to repair any comprehension failures that occur. Metacognitive processing can be conscious or automatic.

To comprehend means to grasp and to actively and consistently embrace the structure and content of a text together with an understanding of the structure and content of our own lived experience and reservoir of knowledge. Moreover, to comprehend in a content area means being able to accomplish reading and writing tasks involving new texts in a discipline and being able to overcome the difficulties encountered in reading and writing about new knowledge and experience. In short, metacomprehension means knowing how to help oneself as a reader/writer when challenged with reading/writing about new content knowledge. A comprehension strategy is "a kind of knowledge that readers use to help themselves construct meaning in preparation for reading" (Aulls, 1992, p. 232). This definition can apply to writing processes in that comprehension strategies are also invaluable in preparing for writing and for performing a writing task.

Metacomprehension, therefore, means that readers/writers are aware of how they use, alter, and adjust a repertoire of comprehension strategies during reading and writing processes. Successful reading and writing in the content area occur when requisite skills are at an automatic level, freeing cognitive energy for metacognitive endeavours. Metacomprehension means that learners experience a sense of being over, yet also behind, perhaps even being above and looking down on their own cognitive and affective processes, watching them, monitoring and changing them while they are engaged in playing their comprehension strategies into a reading or writing task. In a sense, comprehension and metacomprehension processes transact with each other during the performance of reading and writing activities. Readers stop reading to write a note, and writers stop writing to read a paragraph, knowing that the one will act upon and affect the other to help either to make sense of what they are reading or to make their writing more readable. This is why reading-to-learn and writing-to-learn activities should "occur daily in every part of the curriculum" (Santa, 1992, p. 248) and not be left to the language arts and English teacher.

Choosing a stance for reading is important for our comprehension of the world of possible meanings in the text being read. Likewise, choosing a stance

For Reflection 7.2
Using your memory of school experiences, recount how you came to understand a concept or a text in one of the content areas. How was the "meta-level" involved?

for writing makes all the difference in whether the world created with our words is meaningful to others.

The next section provides an example of metacomprehension by continuing the description of a transaction with visual text.

Building Metacomprehension Strategies: Combining an Efferent Reading with an Aesthetic Reading

Our colleague has examined a visual text of DNA several times in the past. She informed us that when she first began reading the visual text shown in Figure 7.1 she knew nothing about the concept that the text serves to illustrate. She understands more now than when she first began to examine this text because each time she read it she did more research on the concept. She continued to read the visual text from an aesthetic stance in order to make connections between what she found in her research and what she had already come to know through reading the visual text (that is, what she took away from the reading). She shares her comprehension and metacomprehension strategies below.

The analogy of "ties" and "rails" in the twisted railroad has emerged over time. When this text is examined by other readers, other analogies surface: for example, a roller coaster, a necklace, a spiral staircase, or a twisted ladder. My analogy helps me to think of ways to describe the relationships of parts in this visual world. Can you think of another analogy for this image?

The words that can be used to elaborate on these analogies are limited and limiting. They are descriptive but they do not explain what I need to know to comprehend the topic in some depth. I need to learn the vocabulary for the concept for which this visual text is an illustration. I need to know how these parts are named and used in the content area for which the illustration is designed. To achieve greater comprehension I must read other texts, both written and visual, some of them so difficult and complex that I must take an efferent stance. I must concentrate solely on what I can take away from my reading. Rereading the visual image aesthetically will continue to serve as a link between the new understanding I glean and the prior knowledge I have gathered over time, but I must shift stances for a time to achieve a deeper comprehension of the topic. To do this I must move beyond the visual text and seek to add to my comprehension of the visual text by adding transactions with other texts. We can call these additional transactions with other texts *transactional intertextuality*.

I will be adding to my awareness of comprehension processes (metacomprehension) by reading, researching, and writing about other texts because I will be able to track the differences in reading and writing strategies. As I read, I write about *what* I read and *how* I read the texts differently. To construct a bridge between my aesthetic reading of the visual text and an efferent reading, I take time to expand on and question the analogy of the "twisted railroad." If I question the comparison of the visual image to a "railroad," I can see that this word does not fully describe what I am seeing; I can begin to understand that I need other words, a new vocabulary, to achieve a greater depth of comprehension.

I can begin to see as I question my analogy and explore other analogies that this is no ordinary railroad because the "ties" and "rails" twist and untwist like the tracks of the roller coaster. This image does not exactly fit the image of a railroad.

If you see the image as a "zipper," you might also see that the ties or connectors are like the teeth and the cloth of a zipper that is opened at one point and closed at another. In the visual world of this text the ties or connectors can be seen to act like a zipper, yet the polarity of open and closed states still does not fully explain the apparent chaos of some aspects of this image. This arrangement suggests the teeth in a zipper but this analogy still does not explain what the different shades of grey mean. The connectedness and disconnectedness of this visual world is not just a matter of order and disorder in an abstract way; this world is made up of bonds that break from time to time.

We might ask several questions at this point: Is this bonding and unbonding purposeful? If there is a purpose, what might that purpose or function be? To answer, we can tentatively return to our analogy of the zipper: a zipper closes to hold two parts together, and it opens when these parts need to be separated. We know already that opening and closing, making a bond and breaking a bond, are equally important in the operation of a zipper.

Have you been able to deduce what this image illustrates? Can you make a prediction? If you know or remember something from your high-school biology courses, you might be able to make an intelligent guess at this point. This visual text is an illustration of DNA.

When I consult a biology textbook for information on DNA, I find that DNA stands for deoxyribonucleic acid. I am told that DNA is a complex molecule found in the nucleus of the cell. An analogy is offered to me: this molecule containing DNA is "a reference library because it stores a wealth of information that can be used when needed" (Poole, Pilkey, & Johnson, 1992, p. 14). Like a book, DNA can be read again and again, and, like a reference book, it cannot be removed from the library. DNA can also be copied but the information is "copyrighted" since, "under normal circumstances, only the cells of the same organism can reproduce it" (p. 14).

DNA is composed of two strands and is often referred to as a "double helix." Two molecular chains are wound around each other to form a double chain. Here my analogy of the ties and rails forming a twisted railroad proves to have been helpful in building prior understanding of the structure of DNA. The scientific word for the subunits that make up these two strands is *nucleotides*.

What can we make of the connectors in the visual image we have just explored? Why do they sometimes appear to hold the double helix together and sometimes break apart? To answer these questions we must examine the nucleotides more closely. Each of these is composed of three molecules: a sugar, a phosphate, and a nitrogenous base. Further, DNA has four nitrogenous bases: cytosine (C), thymine (T), adenine (A), and guanine (G).

Returning to the scientific text concerning DNA, I find that every **A** base is linked to a **T** base, and every **G** base is linked to a **C** base. When the bases separate, they do so only to reconnect with the same bases in a complementary chain alongside the original chain. The two chains form a DNA molecule, but the chains are complementary so that they form a spiral ladder or ribbon, or what scientists call the *double helix*. The bonding, separating, and rebonding is called *replication*. I see now that the visual text I have analogized as a twisted railroad is an illustration of the process of replication of DNA. Living through the visual text without words and names has helped me to build a picture of the structure and behaviour of DNA before learning the scientific vocabulary. The transaction between prior knowledge and experience is itself a kind of double helix, since multitudes of connections and combinations are possible as we work to construct relationships between our knowledge and our experience.

In summary, metacomprehension can be viewed as a construct distinct from comprehension, made up of two interdependent components — awareness of and control over comprehension. Both comprehension and metacomprehension processes transact with each other during reading, writing, listening, and viewing. By using a visual text, we have gained some insight into these transactions, taking first an aesthetic and then an efferent stance.

Broadening the Concept of Transaction: Interdisciplinary Transactions

One content area that was opened up in our aesthetic and efferent reading of the DNA text is visual art, in particular, the requirements for creating an illustration. Living through a reading of this visual text without a verbal text — without names for the parts — has called on our ability to analogize, that is, to create another visual world from which to draw prior knowledge. When we analogize, a pattern is created, the pattern is named, and then analysis of the known pattern begins. Illustration as an art form often uses recognizable patterns, an order or structure, that communicates to many different readers. Illustrations in magazines and newspapers usually draw on popular knowledge and common experience, unlike a piece of art such as an abstract expressionist painting, which may be so unique with regard to composition that no pattern or structure is recognizable. Another opening into visual art as a content area is the use of colour as part of the visual composition. Still another topic is the concept of composition in the creation of visual text. Our co-author did not pursue these topics as visual art concepts, but certainly they could be explored as content area topics to be researched, read about, and written about, particularly in relation to the art of illustration.

The other content area that is opened up by reading this visual text from both an aesthetic and an efferent stance is biology. The complexity of the topic of DNA has been suggested. This topic could also be explored in relation to social studies. Examples are racial differences, gender differences, physical similarities and differences within families, social conflicts related to perceived differences between races, and racial conflict as a cause of war. Links can also be made to other areas such as law (the use of DNA samples in court cases); medicine and genetic engineering; and cancer and HIV research.

Without much difficulty it can be seen that an interdisciplinary unit involving illustration as an art form, DNA as an important biological concept, and gender and racial differences as a social studies topic could provide the basis for a collaboration between a number of education practitioners. The unit could begin with this visual text as a reference point for any number of topics across these content areas.

Building Comprehension and Metacomprehension through Strategic Interdisciplinary Transactions

The six texts discussed in this section were given to teachers at Mount Royal Junior High School in Calgary, Alberta, during a workshop on reading as a transactional process. The teachers (representing a variety of subject area specializations) were asked to work in collaboration to describe what they lived through as they read these texts, and then to switch stances to read the same texts efferently. The participants in the workshop were then asked to identify the content areas to which each text could be related.

For Reflection 7.3
Recount a secondary-school experience in which, when you were trying to understand a visual text, interdisciplinary links in one subject area were made to other subject areas.

To assist the participants in the workshop a list of strategies believed to be useful with these texts was provided. All of these strategies can be used at a subconscious or conscious level. Although teachers need to focus on the metacognitive aspects of each of these techniques (Miholic, 1994), several strategies already fit well into the metacognitive realm, for example, KWL, think-alouds, and response journals. As mentioned earlier, embedding comprehension strategy instruction into text reading and text discussion — a type of "situated cognition" (Brown, Collins, & Duguid, 1989) — results in strategy learning as a secondary outcome in learning content (Fielding & Pearson, 1994). A strategic reader selects from a repertoire of strategies and uses them with flexibility — that is, the reader discards and re-selects to maximize comprehension.

Strategies for Efferent Reading

1. **Anticipation Guide** — a set of statements about a topic being studied to which students respond before reading; designed to provoke discussion and even disagreement. (See Chapter 6 for an extended description of this procedure.)
2. **Autobiographic Writing** — a form of writing that allows students to recall (usually before reading texts) information relevant to texts, especially to make personal connections and to evoke feelings and images. (See Chapter 8.)
3. **Charting or Semantic Mapping** — a strategy that helps students to summarize and visualize the interrelationships among key ideas. (See Chapter 6 for more on charting/mapping.)
4. **Co-operative Learning** — small-group activities in which students share what they know and what they are learning, and discuss the topic being studied. (See Chapter 5.)
5. **Exit/Admit Slips** — an anonymous writing activity in which comments are written on cards and collected at the very beginning or end of class as admit/exit tickets. The purpose is to have learners react to (summarize, synthesize, comment on difficulties they experienced, evaluate, or project) class materials or processes. Prompt questions could be: (a) "What's confusing you about . . . ?" (b) "What problems did you have with the text assignment?" or (c) "What did you like (dislike) about . . . ?"

6. **Focussed Writing** (Crowhurst, 1989) — writing designed to extend or reformulate knowledge in content areas through the use of (a) "What if . . ." questions: "What if there were no gravity?" (physics); (b) "I am . . ." statements: "I am volcanic rock" (science); or (c) imaginative writings such as poems and dialogues.

7. **Graphic Organizers** — a diagram, chart, or graph showing the relationships among concepts and terms within the text to be read. Learner-generated organizers include word webs, semantic maps, tree graphs, and other key visuals. These strategies are particularly useful for second-language students in the content areas ([Early, 1989). (See Chapter 6.)

8. **Guided Writing Activity** — a five-step process including brainstorming, listing student ideas, writing on the topic using the student ideas already generated, reviewing the writing after reading an assigned text, and following up with a multiple-choice and/or essay exam on the text's key ideas. (See Chapter 8.)

9. **KWL** (Ogle, 1986) — a framework for learners that is based on three components: (a) recalling what is *k*nown through brainstorming ideas and categorizing them, (b) determining what students *w*ant to learn by encouraging them to wonder about the topic in the form of shared questions, and (c) identifying what is *l*earned after reading by responding to their questions.

10. **Oral Retellings or Verbal Reporting** — activities in which learners put into their own words what they have just been reading and report aloud for others to hear and question and discuss.

11. **Prediction Activities** — a strategy in which learners generate some form of prediction in advance of reading, or are given the opportunity to read visuals, title, headings, subheadings, or a short segment of the text, and, based on this limited information, predict what they expect to read in the passage.

12. **Previewing** — helps learners analyze the task at hand and enables them to make plans for engaging with the text by asking: (a) "What kind of text is this?" (b) "What is my primary goal or purpose?" (c) "Should I try to remember details or read for the main ideas only?" (d) "How much time will I devote to the reading assignment?" (e) "What do I already know about the topic and what do I need to know?" Previewing and questioning require active participation. Procedurally, the process is as follows: (1) Read the title. Then convert the title into a question. (2) Read the introduction, and any summary, or questions about the text. What seem to be the author's intentions? (3) Read the heads and subheads if the text is factual. Convert these titles into questions. (4) Read any special print that would indicate a need to be attentive to the text. Ask, "Why are certain words, phrases, or sentences different from the text body?" (5) Study visual materials such as pictures, maps, or diagrams. Ask, "What do the graphics tell me about the chapter's content?"

13. **Questioning** — a process in which students generate questions about a topic *before* reading (that is, questions that can take the students into the topic), create questions about the text *during* reading (to take students through the content), and add questions that arise *after* reading (to take them *beyond* the reading). (See Chapter 5.)

14. **RAP** — engages the student in *r*eading text, *a*sking questions about material read, and *p*araphrasing what has been read. (See Chapter 8 for more on paraphrasing.)

15. **Reading Guides** — enhance the processing of text and promote higher levels of thinking. Guides are designed to stimulate thinking before, during, and after text encounters. They focus attention on information and ideas and must be text appropriate. Reading guides follow this general format: (a) Read the material and decide what information is to be emphasized. (b) Determine how much assistance learners require to process information at a meaningful level. (c) Try to make the guide as imaginative as possible so that it will be used enthusiastically and appropriately. (d) Ask learners to be prepared to respond with evidence from the text and prior knowledge. (See Chapter 8.)

16. **Response Journal** — a book in which the reader responds to text on a regular basis using a double-entry format, and comments on difficulties encountered during reading. (See Chapter 8.)

17. **Split-Page Notetaking** — a strategy in which the student establishes the purpose of reading the text, previews the text, then decides on the important concepts and supporting information. The student records the important concepts in a column on the left side of a page, then enters supporting information in the space on the right side of the page, leaving extra space for new entries. The student can study the notes by covering the right column and using the left-hand entries as recall prompts, and vice versa. (See Chapter 8 for an extended presentation.)

18. **Summarizing** — condensing information and ideas; involves deleting redundancies and categorizing information. (See Chapter 8.)

19. **Text Previews** — involve using a short passage to help learners approach a text. Procedurally, learners begin with a series of short statements and one or more questions that spark interest, provide a link between a familiar topic and the text topic, and encourage learners to actively reflect upon the theme; provide a synopsis of the text materials that includes key elements in the text structure; and define several key terms within the context of the preview passage. In a preview for pre-reading instruction, use the following procedure: (a) Tell the learners you are going to introduce the upcoming selection. (b) Read the first few sentences of the preview. (c) Give learners two or three minutes to discuss the question(s). (d) Read the remainder of the preview. (e) Have learners begin reading the target text immediately after you complete the preview.

For Reflection 7.4
Which of the strategies for efferent reading do you recall using in the content areas in high school? Did you find them useful? Why or why not?

20. **Think-Aloud** — the verbal reporting of thought processes as one reads; the reporter tells how he or she is processing the text being read as it is being read. (See Chapters 1–4, 6, and 7.)
21. **Vocabulary Development through Contextual Analysis** — identifying and questioning the meanings of words by using context. (See Chapter 6.)
22. **Word Scavenger Hunt** — an activity in which the teacher selects vocabulary words from a text being studied; students are divided into teams of four, and the rules for the hunt are clearly explained; students are instructed to bring in objects and/or pictures to match the words on an agreed-upon date; secrecy is maintained (or at least attempted); varying points are allotted for each match, and the team with the most points wins.
23. **Wordless Picture Books** — books with visual text but no written text; especially useful with ESL students and to help students to write a story, script, or text to accompany the visual text.

Text 1: Social Studies

The first text offered to the teacher-participants in the workshop was written by a student (Donna Phung) and is therefore autobiographical in nature. A portion of the text is reproduced in Box 7.1.

When asked to take an aesthetic reading stance with this text, the participants described an array of emotions and thoughts in transaction with each other. One reader thought of a student in her class whom she knew to have arrived in Canada as a "boat person." This teacher found that an aesthetic reading of this text allowed her to see this Vietnamese student in a new light: she saw for the first time how difficult, how sorrowful, how lonely her student must have been and perhaps still is with members of her family left behind and out of touch. Another reader experienced a deep sense of empathy with the children separated from their fathers. This reader was astonished and angry at the lack of help and care offered to these people: he had not realized how alone and rejected the "boat people" were until he read this text.

An effective way to promote an aesthetic response might be the use of focussed writing using a stem such as "I am now a boat person. . . ." As the workshop participants worked their way through an efferent reading they could see that journal responses would provide interesting discussion mate-

---

Box 7.1
Alone on the Ocean

My escape from Vietnam was the most dangerous and most difficult experience of my life.

At dawn on October 14, 1978, my mother, brother, cousin, and I left Vietnam, each of us carrying a small bag of clothes and another bag of dry food and water. We gathered together at the place where we had registered with the government and waited for the bus to the port. I was surprised by the number of people who were also waiting to leave.

The people were all excited when the buses came. We packed ourselves on the bus because we were afraid to be left behind. Our bus started to go, followed by my father, uncle, and cousin on motorcycles. Our hearts were all as heavy as the overloaded bus. When we arrived at an unknown port in a small village, we were met by some officers who called our names and studied our faces, matching them with the pictures on their lists before they allowed us on board.

That was the moment when I felt very concerned about leaving my father. I swallowed my tears and kept my eyes shut. My heart was crying bitterly inside as if hundreds of blades were cutting it.

Then my father said to me and my brother, "You have to listen to your mother and take care of each other. Do not complain about any hardships because the most bitter of the bitter you suffer will make you into the best people." I was as heavy as a stone when I heard these words.

Suddenly, I heard our names being called and we kissed each other good-bye. We dragged ourselves on the boat with heavy footsteps. We started our adventure on a small boat only 60 feet long; it carried 230 people. Our baggage and food were thrown into the cabin, and the women and children were forced to jump down into the cargo hold. It was all in darkness and we could just sit on the floor with bent knees. Soon the hold was filled with people packed in like sardines.

Source: From "Alone in the Ocean," by Donna Phung, in 1991, *New Canadian Voices,* Toronto: Wall & Emerson Inc. Reprinted by permission of Wall & Emerson Inc.

rials related to social studies, language arts, health, geography, and history. The genre of autobiography can be studied in language arts with this text representing a contemporary form of autobiography. Further research can be carried out in relation to a number of interdisciplinary topics: differences between North American and Asian cultures; language as a way of defining oneself and one's culture; the isolating effect of language difference; the effect on the human body of prolonged food and water deprivation; the effects of war; the problems encountered by immigrants to Canada; autobiography as a portrait of power inequalities within a culture; the geography of southeast Asia; and the history of Vietnam.

The teachers involved in this workshop could imagine planning guided writing and careful research across all of the content areas named above. They saw that they could teach students something about "how to comprehend in a discussion" by using the title to make predictions, and that significant questions could be asked that could lead to discussion, research, and individual written responses. They agreed that reading and writing activities across a number of disciplines could be undertaken if the activities were planned carefully. Some of the questions that can be generated as starting points for writing and research activities are:

1. What is the effect on this child of being separated from her father?
2. What reasons can you give for this family leaving Vietnam?
3. What are the health risks and dangers when too many people are crowded into a small space for a long period of time?
4. What is the effect of being deprived of water for a long period of time?
5. Why were other travellers unable or unwilling to help these people?
6. What is the effect of not having enough to eat?
7. What is life like in a concentration camp?
8. What difficulties are experienced when you cannot speak a language?
9. What benefits do we enjoy in Canada that other people in the world do not experience?
10. What can be done about economic inequality?

Text 2: Mathematics

The second text offered to the teachers in the workshop was a mathematics text. The beginning portion of the text is shown in Box 7.2.

After taking an aesthetic reading stance with this text related to decimals, a mathematics teacher in one group commented that there was a decided lack of relevance to learners' experience. Though an attempt had been made in the text to link the content on decimals to the denim jeans worn by many teens, and the approach was historically correct and interesting, the content concerning denim jeans did not relate at all with the lived experience of the young teenager. The teachers acknowledged that this text could be used for an opening into the study of the history of denim and jeans, and that the text also could be opened into topics related to social studies as well as language arts. They suggested that vocabulary preview and study through a graphic organizer would be necessary for effective efferent comprehension since the intro-

Box 7.2
Decimals

1.4 DECIMALS

Chances are you own a pair of denim jeans. You may or may not wear them to school.

To make denim, cotton fibres are spun into thread, then tightly woven into cloth. Denim is the most durable cotton fabric available. Originally, it came from Nimes, in the south of France, on ships worked by Genoese sailors. The fabric was called "serge de Nimes", which is where the word *denim* comes from. The word *jeans* is from "Genoese".

The diameter of a thread is so small that we use decimals to talk about it. The diameter of one cotton thread used for denim is about 0.55 mm, or fifty-five hundredths of a millimetre.

As you move to the right in a place-value chart, the place value is one tenth of the previous place. Ten is one tenth of a hundred, a unit is one tenth of ten, a tenth is one tenth of a unit, and so on.

12

If 100 cotton threads are woven side by side into denim, how wide is the piece of fabric so far?

Understand the Problem

What do you know that can help solve the problem?
There are 100 cotton threads side by side.
Each thread is 0.55 mm in diameter.
Denim is tightly woven.

Plan How to Solve It

You can solve this problem by multiplying the width of one thread by 100.

Carry Out the Plan

$0.55 \times 100 = 55$

The fabric is 55 mm wide.

Look Back

Since each thread is about half a millimetre in diameter, and $\frac{1}{2}$ of 100 is 50, 55 mm is reasonable for 100 threads. You also can say the fabric is 5.5 cm wide, since 55 mm is 5.5 cm.

LET'S DISCUSS

1. Here are the widths of several fibres. Order the widths from least to greatest. Explain how you decided on the order.

Fibre	Width
Silk	0.014 mm
Fine wool	0.040 mm
Coarse wool	0.177 mm
Linen	0.025 mm
Cotton	0.016 mm

2. What is the width of each fibre in words?

CHECK YOUR UNDERSTANDING

3. Use the facts in Question 1.
a) How much wider are fine wool fibres than silk fibres?
b) How much wider are coarse wool fibres than fine wool.

13

Source: From Math Plus 8, by C. Ballheim, M. Cheverie, C. Danbrook, F. Leddy, T. Romiens, A. Sands, and M. Warren, 1995, Toronto: Harcourt Brace Canada, pp. 12–13.

> **For Reflection 7.5**
> Which strategies would you have recommended for teaching learners to understand the content of the text "Decimals"? Justify your choice.

duction contains geographical names and words that are likely to be unknown to many North American teens.

Text 3: Geography or Science

The third text includes a number of illustrations and requires comprehension of both verbal and visual texts. A short segment of the text is presented in Box 7.3.

After an aesthetic reading of this text, teachers strongly suggested the need for colour in the illustrations. They reported experiencing a strong degree of frustration with the text, described the expository prose as "dry," and recommended that the text be personalized (possibly through the use of magazine and newspaper articles and trade books) so that the text would be more accessible to readers. Some autobiographical writing to recall experiencing climates in areas one has previously lived in might promote aesthetic response. An important strategy that needs to be embedded in the teaching/learning context of this text is the integration of printed text with the illustrations. One way this could be demonstrated is through a teacher thinkaloud. The group of teachers collaborating on this text saw openings for interdisciplinary reading/writing activities in social studies, language arts, mathematics, and science.

Text 4: English Language Arts

The fourth text is a poem entitled "Sweet," which is accompanied by an illustration. See Box 7.4.

The workshop participants reading this poem from an aesthetic stance experienced a range of thoughts and feelings: they noticed the gaps and spaces between lines and words and phrases and found that these caused them to hesitate, and then anticipate. The hesitation and anticipation reminded them of actually playing basketball, took them back in their memories of the actions associated with planning a move and executing a play. This was a source of pleasure, and at the end of the poem there was an experience of relief at the moment of success. The poem seemed to present in its form a simula-

Box 7.3
Climate

CLIMATE

This part of Chapter Two tells more about the climate of Canada and its influence on vegetation and soil. So far we have been focusing on Canada's physiographic regions, but Canada can also be divided into other natural regions, according to climate, vegetation, and soil.

WEATHER AND CLIMATE

Weather consists of the temperature, *precipitation*, wind, cloud cover, and humidity for any given time in any given place. The day-to-day weather in all parts of Canada is very changeable. The weather in a particular place on a certain date may also vary greatly from year to year. In Canada a weather record is broken somewhere almost every day.

Canada's weather is recorded daily at a number of weather stations across the country. These stations use special equipment to make accurate records of a number of factors that relate to weather.

Every weather station in Canada keeps temperature-measuring instruments in a Stevenson screen. It is a vented white box supported above the ground on posts. Within the box are two horizontal thermometers that record current temperature, as well as the highest and lowest temperatures reached since the last reading. The liquid in the thermometer tube moves small metal markers; the markers remain at the highest and lowest temperatures. A magnet is used to move the markers back each time a weather person records the temperatures. There are also two vertical thermometers inside the box; these are used to record the amount of moisture in the air.

Wind vanes and anemometers show wind direction and wind force. The wind vane has a pointer and a fin to show the direction the wind is blowing from. The anemometer has rotating

cups to show the wind force.

The sunshine recorder is a glass sphere that concentrates the sunlight to a small point on a cardboard chart. The concentrated sunlight burns holes into the chart.

Small amounts of rain cannot be measured accurately without a rain gauge. The hole into which the rainwater flows is one-tenth the size of the

large opening at the top of the gauge. A graduated tube of the same diameter as the small hole extends down inside the container.

On a windy day in winter, weather persons find it hard to decide whether snow has fallen from a cloud or has blown up from the ground nearby. Snow gauges are designed to measure only the snow that has actually fallen.

At a Weather Station

A Stevenson screen

Wind vane and anemometer

Snow gauge

Inside a Stevenson screen

Rain gauge

Sunshine recorder

Source: From *This Land of Ours: A New Geography of Canada,* by Krueger, Corder, and Koegler, 1991, Toronto: Harcourt Brace Canada, p. 51.

Box 7.4
Sweet.

Sweet.
by Arnold Adoff

You are at the line. You take a deep breath.
                     You take a deep breath.

You know: a free throw
                 is really
          a free throw:
                 no hands in your face;
                 no race   down
                              the court;

                 no block,
                 no clock.

This is the place to score. This is the time to pour   it in,
          and beat those nasty bad guys   on the   other   team,
                                            once   and   for   all.

This is the time to win this game.

You bounce the ball once, and wish   for all the luck
                                    you know   don't need.
You shoot,   and the ball
             flies
             and arcs   and speeds   down   through
                        the hoop   to meet the net.

You get   your point; your score; your wish.   Swish.
                                                   Sweet.

Source: From *Sports Pages,* by Arnold Adoff, 1986. Text copyright © 1986 by Arnold Adoff. Used by permission of Harper Collins Publishers.

tion of the actions required to make a "free throw" and that awareness lived through during their readings of the poem was a distinct source of pleasure.

To enable effective comprehension from an efferent standpoint, the teacher-readers saw a need to understand vocabulary such as "the line," "free throw," and "block." One teacher suggested that a KWL strategy would be useful in helping those who do not know the game of basketball to learn something about the rules and plays; another teacher suggested that a graphic organizer would help learners to grasp the idea of the game. One teacher saw oral retellings as a useful strategy that could lead learners into writing their own "game poems."

This poem acts as a transactional link between language arts, physical education, and health, and the illustration accompanying the poem allows for the possibility of engaging in reading and writing about and creating illustrations in a visual arts class.

Text 5: Biology

The fifth text links math, science, social studies, and language arts. The text, entitled "How Small Is Small" (see Box 7.5), appears in a science textbook and aroused reactions of repulsion as well as interest. Further visualizing activities might be encouraged to bring personal experiences to the reading. Discussion might ensue about why we are fascinated by very small or very large things and why the microscope and the telescope are two of our most ingenious inventions.

The KWL was suggested as a useful strategy for building comprehension of this passage, and vocabulary study was also seen as a necessary strategy. Reviewing measurement vocabulary would be beneficial for mathematics comprehension, as would investigating the meaning of the word "bacterium" to better comprehend the biological concept of the cell.

Text 6: Language Arts or Social Studies

The last text, "Boys at War," aroused the strongest reaction of all the texts read during this workshop. The text is given in Box 7.6.

The workshop participants responded to this text with anger, disbelief, fear, amazement, surprise, and concern. They found themselves drawn to the photograph and to repeated aesthetic reading of the visual image in relation to the written text. They wondered about the journalist shooting the photograph and writing the story. What were his motives? Did he get to know the boys in the photograph? What happened to the boys after this? Why are these boys going to war? Where are their families? What will happen to them? How

Box 7.5
How Small Is Small?

How Small Is Small?

Plant and animal cells are small. But just how small are they? When you want to describe the size of anything, you measure it and use some convenient unit (such as metres, centimetres, or millimetres) to express the size.

What unit would be most convenient to measure the size of something viewed under a microscope? Normally you have no difficulty seeing something the size of 0.1 mm (about the thickness of a hair) without a microscope. If you had a microscope that magnifies 100X, what would you be able to see with it? Did you calculate 0.001 mm or one-thousandth of a millimetre? This unit is called a **micrometre** (μm). The Greek letter "μ" means "micro."

Think of it this way: Divide 1 m (about the height of a doorknob above the floor) into 1000 parts and each part is 1 mm (about the thickness of a dime). Divide 1 mm into 1000 parts and each part is 1 μm. Under 100X power, a micrometre looks about the thickness of a hair. A micrometre is a convenient unit to use to express the size of small things like cells.

Try This

One type of cell is 2 μm wide. How many of these cells would it take to cover a distance of 1 mm?

A Staggering Size Fact

One bacterium is a single cell. In a 1-cm³ space (smaller than a sugar cube), there could be 1 000 000 000 000 (one trillion) bacteria. More than 250 000 bacteria could fit on the period at the end of this sentence.

Compare and Be Amazed!

You know how big a flea is. Suppose you enlarge a picture of a flea so that its foreleg is as big as in (b). A liver cell from your body enlarged to the same degree would be the size shown in (a).

(a) human liver cell   (b) foreleg of a flea

Source: From *Science Plus 9*, by Morrison (Author-in-chief), 1994, Toronto: Harcourt Brace Canada, pp. 237–38.

can we prevent this? Have we played a part in causing these boys to die at such a young age? Questioning was a good strategy to enhance aesthetic response.

In taking an efferent stance, the participants saw that before even reading this text, learners can have a challenging discussion about the title, and that "Boys at War" can become an anticipation guide for research and discussion into a host of related topics. These teachers saw opportunities for planning a number of co-operative/collaborative learning activities involving

Box 7.6
Boys at War

One day I was out in Managua shooting some street pictures when a journalist friend of mine, who was based there, told me of an unusual opportunity. A friend of his had just called to say that there was going to be a funeral service at the home of a young man who had been killed in action. They were planning to march his coffin through the streets to the cemetery. "It's going to be sombre," he said, "but if you want to document how the war here hits home, you might want to be there."

We drove to a private home in Managua. It was a nice home. Dozens of students, many wearing their school uniforms, were gathered to pay their last respects. Someone took out a military flag, which features a soldier with a gun raised over his head and the words "Long Live the Revolution." They draped it over the coffin. Several young boys, including his four brothers, lifted the coffin onto their shoulders and marched through the streets. I followed them all the way to the cemetery.

Cevasco Aviles Velasquez, the son of a prominent doctor, and a student in Managua, was the young man in the coffin. He was nineteen years old. He hadn't waited to be called up for military service. Instead, he had felt it was his civic duty to join the Sandinista Army and he did. He had been in the army two months when he was killed.

(continued)

(continued)

The funeral was strange for me personally because I was the only photographer, American or otherwise, who was there. It was also very odd to be there because it wasn't a "news" event; it was a private funeral.

My presence was awkward because it was obvious that I was an American. I felt very self-conscious in that this young man had died in a battle with the contras, which my country supported. I didn't really fear retaliation but I still felt guilty, like a voyeur, taking photographs at a funeral. Something has to be sacred, I thought to myself. Yet I had made eye contact with the parents, I had made eye contact with the students. In a gesturing manner looking down at my camera and up into their eyes, I would dip my chin as I opened my eyes wide, gesturing, Okay? You understand? And their response would usually be to tighten their bottom lip, bob their head up and down very slowly, and blink as if to say, Yes, it's okay. No words were ever exchanged, but I had asked for permission and they had granted it.

Cevasco Aviles Velasquez was buried in a crypt. They took the crypt lid off to reveal a hole in the ground. There was just enough space to drop the coffin down with ropes. I was within the crowd of young people who were reaching over to touch the coffins. Some cried, said their last good-byes, and dropped flowers into the crypt.

At one moment I found myself on the edge of the crypt looking down, and directly across from me — four feet [1.2 m] from me, on the other side, so close that I could just about reach out and tap them on the shoulder — were his four brothers, who had all sort of crowded at the edge of the crypt to look down as the coffin was being lowered. One was crying, one or two of the others were staring blankly, sort of glancing down, one was sobbing.

When I saw those boys crying, I have to admit, the human part of me felt out of place. I felt awkward, but the journalist side of me said, Why am I here? I'm here to document this war and its effects, cause and effect. Symbolically, the four brothers said it all. Anybody could identify with them. They were not in military uniform, they were just regular kids. It could be any town, anywhere in the world.

I turned off the camera's motor drive, advanced the film manually, very quietly, and raised the camera. I don't even remember focusing. And I snapped just one frame.

I have to say, having shot a million frames, some of which have been very difficult, nothing was as hard to shoot as that frame. I always want to be a human being first and a journalist second. If I had had any less eye contact or less feeling of approval, I could not have done it.

One element that I think added to the power of that image is that the four were all brothers and all close to fighting age themselves. They may have been looking down at their own future.

Source: "Boys at War," by Michael Williamson. From "Teenage Soldiers, Adult War," in Rosen and McSharry (Eds.), 1991, *Icarus I*, New York: Rosen Publishing Group.

For Reflection 7.6
What did you live through when you read this segment of "Boys at War"? What did you take away from this reading? What interdisciplinary connections did you make?

reading and writing but also photography as a medium of communication. They could see how collecting photographs of war can provide a very different but enriching way to understand the human suffering of war. They could also see the possibility of having their own learners give oral retellings of what they found memorable and meaningful in their readings of these texts. They saw how a unit on war could connect Central American history and geography and the art of photography and photojournalism as a career with issues such as the role of the media in our society and the causes of war in Central America. The participants saw that the three disciplines — language arts, social studies, and fine arts — could be related in a single unit of study, and that, with careful planning, a powerful unit involving all three disciplines could begin with this text.

An Instructional Program to Improve Comprehension

In summary, an instructional program that will improve comprehension and metacomprehension includes the following components (based partly on Fielding & Pearson, 1994), which should complement one another in the classroom:

1. Devoting ample time to the reading of a variety of literature-based printed and visual texts. Reading increases knowledge of concepts and content and promotes aesthetic and efferent reading.
2. Improving knowledge and use of comprehension and metacomprehension strategies through teacher-directed instruction. Explicit instruction includes teacher modelling and explanation of the strategy; guided practice with gradual release of responsibility to the students; independent practice plus feedback; and application in multiple reading situations. Such instruction enables learners to internalize the strategies for aesthetic and efferent reading.
3. Providing opportunities for peer and collaborative learning in reading-to-learn, viewing-to-learn, and writing-to-learn activities.

4. Providing opportunities for talk/discussion with the teacher and with peers about responses to text. Such discussions change teacher–student interaction patterns, allow the possibility of multiple interpretations and reactions, and embed strategy instruction in the discussion of texts.
5. Inviting interdisciplinary learning by promoting transactions across the traditional content area specializations.

Summary

Reading can be seen as a constructive process in which the reader is as important as the text in the meaning-making process. The reader is a "builder" (when comprehending) and a "fixer" (when being a metacognitive problem solver) and is part of a community of learners negotiating meaning with the author, peers, and teacher (for example, in a discussion group). In transaction with text, a reader may take an aesthetic response to begin the comprehension of content area text. Living through the text allows the reader to comprehend a text based on past experiences, associations, feelings, and previous content knowledge. An efferent stance allows the reader to focus on mastering the content and to become aware of strategies (such as context clues, questions, or predictions) being used. During aesthetic and efferent reading a number of opportunities occur for interdisciplinary transactions. To enhance comprehension, teachers can involve students in reading texts aesthetically and efferently and assist them in making interdisciplinary transactions. During the reading and discussion of texts, teachers and students can embed strategy teaching and learning in what is called "situated cognition." A strong instructional program to improve comprehension of content includes (1) the provision of ample time for reading, viewing, and writing; (2) instruction in comprehension and metacomprehension strategies; (3) provision for peer and collaborative learning; (4) opportunities for talk and discussion about content, text understanding, and different responses to text; and (5) provision for interdisciplinary learning.

Questions for Further Reflection

1. Describe how you "grasp concepts" as you read through (live through) a difficult scientific text? Describe briefly what you are "grasping."
2. Describe your reading transactions with a sonnet. How is the poem similar to or different from scientific text?

3. Describe how you "overtake" a new concept as you begin to understand a text you are reading. What are you "overtaking"?
4. Describe the changes you experience as you successfully complete a piece of writing about a text that you have read. What has changed?

Key Terms

Analogy	Metacomprehension
Comprehension	Reservoirs

CHAPTER EIGHT

The Role of Writing in Developing Content Literacy

Questions to Consider for this Chapter

1. How is writing a transactive activity?

2. What types of reading do you do during a writing activity?

3. What types of positive writing activities do you recall from your experiences in content area classrooms?

4. How and when do you "write your reading"?

5. What do you think are content area teachers' responsibilities with respect to writing?

6. What are some writing activities that improve the comprehension of material read, heard, or viewed and that can be used in a subject area?

7. What are some writing-to-learn activities using journals? How can students be helped to make interdisciplinary connections when writing journals?

8. How does the computer lend itself to the process approach to writing?

9. What types of writing formats need to be taught in the content areas? Why? What skills need to be taught for students to be able to successfully write these formats? How should these skills be taught?

10. How can writing in the content areas be evaluated?

Overview

This chapter describes the transactive nature of writing, by which the author transacts with personal, social, and cultural factors as well as with the text itself and with other writers. The chapter helps you understand how writers are the first readers of their texts, and how they are also readers with the eyes of a potential audience. One section of the chapter describes how writing has traditionally been used in the secondary school; both negative and positive uses are presented. Responsibilities of teachers in using writing-to-learn activities and in teaching students to write the content of their disciplines are then listed. Several activities are provided for writing to enhance comprehension of content, for using journals as writing-to-learn vehicles, for encouraging the use of computers for content area writing, and for learning to write the formats common across subjects in the curriculum. Aesthetic, efferent, and/or interdisciplinary transactions are encouraged in each of the activities. The chapter concludes with several suggestions for assessing writing in the content areas.

The Writing–Speaking Relationship

Further to the discussion in Chapter 1 on oral and written language development, it should be noted that there are subtle and complex similarities and differences between speaking and writing (Rafoth, 1994). Writing (and reading) requires knowing "the print code" (for example, the sound–symbol relationship), the features that have only a very rough correspondence to vocal features used in speaking (and listening), which is the critical difference between oral and written language. Writing does, however, have oral qualities such as voice and rhythm. This enables readers to use their knowledge of oral language to process printed text. Both oral language and writing use context to communicate to their audiences. Speakers and writers communicate differently, depending on the understandings of their listeners and readers.

Research on the differences between written and oral language (Chafe & Danielewicz, 1987; Halliday, 1987; Horowitz, 1991) has focussed on a variety of oral and written **discourse types** (dinner talk, lectures, textbooks, academic papers, for example) and found that differences exist in vocabulary, structure, global or overall organization (macrostructure), and cohesion (Horowitz, 1994). For example, word choice in written language can be reflected on and edited, whereas in oral language (informal talk, especially) vocabulary is selected quickly and references may be more implicit. However, with the advent of modern technology (e-mail, for instance), written language may acquire more speechlike attributes (Horowitz, 1994).

The Role of Speech in Writing

Vygotsky's (1962) research suggests that speech has a role in writing growth because internalized speech forms the basis for thinking and, in turn, for writing. This implies that students who draw on their "inner speech" during **free writing** and in discussing their writing with teacher and peers become better writers (Rafoth, 1994). The composing process is fostered by free writing, reading aloud, and talking about what one is attempting to put into writing (Rafoth, 1994). Thus, speaking supports writing; that is, talk supports the process of learning to write, and talk and discussion support students' composition activities. As stated in Chapter 2, a sociocognitive perspective of writing views writing, like speaking, as a social act that is shaped by culture and by individual and social factors (Flower, 1994; Nystrand, 1986a; Rosenblatt, 1989). Speakers co-construct meaning as they interact with each other; writers converse with their readers to this same end. As in oracy, students develop their literacy (reading and writing) in different genres and modes of discourse (Gambell, 1989). Learning to write includes anticipating one's audience, as meaning resides in the transaction shared by writers and readers — in the dialogue between readers and writers (Nystrand, 1986a; Rosenblatt, 1989). Conversations and conferences with peers and teachers thus are important in the writing process.

Writing as a Transaction

As stated earlier, writing is a transactive activity. According to Rosenblatt (1989) the author/writer, in the process of writing, transacts with personal, social, and cultural factors as well as with the text being written. Like the reader, the writer needs some focus. Focus has two elements: (1) the reason for writing, and (2) the awareness of potential readers (the audience) for whom the text is written. The writer needs to adopt a stance (purpose) that falls somewhere on the efferent–aesthetic continuum. Alternately, writers often integrate efferent and aesthetic stances in varied proportions as they write. Audience awareness (anticipating an audience's needs) improves an author's writing. Audiences in school can include peers, the teacher, younger students, parents, or members of the community.

Writers need to begin with a strong linguistic and experiential base. To be successful as a writer, one needs a knowledge of language structure (syntax or grammar), content concepts, and the related vocabulary, as well as appropriate writing conventions (mechanics and formats that can frame the writing). The topics of one's writing need not always be personal but they must engage the writer's (and the readers') prior knowledge, interest, need, or curiosity. Rosenblatt (1989) also writes that "live ideas" (those worth writing about) grow out of activities, discussions, or problems. The discussion activities mentioned in the chapter on talk (Chapter 5) are thus particularly useful for enhancing writing. When writing is viewed as a social rather than a solitary act, writers also transact with others — peers, parents, or teachers.

When writers and readers transact, they can generate, extend, and refine meaning. In the process approach to writing, there are many opportunities for students to read and discuss each other's text, since text is the medium of communication among readers (Rosenblatt, 1978). Discussing to "negotiate the writer–reader conversation" (Sperling, 1996, p. 67) supports and enhances writing. Rosenblatt (1989) states that all of the writer's drafts, and their final products, must be viewed as only stopping points in what is actually a journey. Even a finished piece of writing is not an end; it is a means to undertake more journeys and more compositions (pp. 171–72).

The difference between reading-one's-writing and writing-one's-reading will now be elaborated.

Reading-One's-Writing

Rosenblatt (1989) describes two kinds of reading that occur during writing: **reading-one's-writing** for revision purposes and reading-one's-writing as if one was the potential reader (the audience). Since all writers are the first readers of the texts they write, reading one's writing is part of the composing process and leads to revision *during* the writing process. In this reading, the writer tests vocabulary choices, sentence structure, the flow of text, and the content (ideas). This type of reading moves forward the purpose for writing, whether the purpose is efferent or aesthetic. In this type of reading, the writer is transacting with the text being written. In certain kinds of writing (e.g., diaries and journals) this may be the only reading going on as one writes purely for oneself.

As well, writers read texts as potential transactions. The reading of one's text then is done through the eyes of potential readers (the audience). To read one's own composition like a potential reader is a sophisticated activity that requires the writer to take into account potential readers' prior knowledge, experience, and linguistic ability. In reading the composed text through a reader's eyes, the writer reads to ascertain the meaning others may make of the text, and how the meaning fits the writer's own purpose. Therefore, the selection of a stance is critical: is the stance predominantly efferent or aesthetic, or does it allow for the integration of stances throughout the reading?

Writing-One's-Reading

Writing one's own reading occurs when a reader describes, responds to, or interprets something read or viewed. (The reader could, of course, "speak" instead of write about a transaction with text — the text may not necessarily be a printed page.) In this writing (or speaking), a new text is produced. Also, the "reader-turned-writer" (Rosenblatt, 1989, p. 169) explains the meaning he or she got out of the text. The reader-turned-writer once again chooses a stance. With the expanded notion of text (anything read, heard, or viewed) that is used in this book, writing one's own listening or viewing is possible when the viewer-or-listener-turned-writer explains a transaction with a text (a picture, a visual, a film, a piece of music, a mountain, or lake scene). Several examples of **"writing-one's-reading"** have already been provided in Chapters 3 and 4. Another example follows. It is a description of the meaning one of the authors of this book generated to make sense out of the DNA text shown in Chapter 7.

Setting out to write about this DNA text proved to be difficult until I decided to take an efferent stance to carry away meaning from the original longer piece. Taking this stance led to a decision to construct meaning from the smaller parts of the text, the words or terms used to describe DNA.

The central words selected were: deoxyribonucleic acid, nitrogenous base, nucleotides, cytosine, thymine, adenine, guanine, replication. Throughout my search to construct meaning, however, one question persisted: What is essential to understand about DNA?

Dictionary meanings for the terms named above proved unsatisfactory: they lacked detail and were unrelated to each other. The meanings I found in a biology textbook were helpful, but another text proved to be more useful: *The Double Helix* by James D. Watson, co-discoverer of DNA. Scanning, skimming, and searching the book for meanings, and reviewing diagrams were helpful, but reconstructing a holistic and visual concept of the helix was essential to the process of comprehension. Here is what happened as I searched for meanings for the words.

A copy of a letter written by Watson provided a list of characteristics about DNA. I listed these characteristics on paper in my own words: first, the basic structure of DNA is helical; second, the inner core of the helix is a horizontal structure like the steps in a ladder or staircase, and is composed of bases with hydrogen bonds; third, the two outside strands are vertical structures composed of sugar and phosphate; fourth, the helical structures are not identical but are complementary; fifth, the thymine base always connects with the adenine base, and the cytosine base always connects with the guanine base; sixth, replication occurs when the outside strands and inner steps separate and create their own new helical structures.

Summarizing these characteristics in my own words helped me to gradually rebuild a visual picture of DNA: the vertical outside sugar-phosphate strands are joined by the horizontal hydrogen-bonded bases as "steps" to form a spiral staircase. Analogizing by building an image of the unknown from the known continues to work well as a strategy to get a whole picture of the concept. I still do not understand why sugar and phosphate

> **For Reflection 8.1**
> What opportunities for "writing-your-reading" do you recall from secondary school? Besides the specific content knowledge gained (the efferent stance), what did the writing include?

must be joined to make up the outside strands, nor do I understand why the four bases are always relentlessly paired in the same way, but I have a firmer grasp of how DNA looks and what happens when replication occurs.

The construction of meaning about the text seemed to emerge as a transactional process: the meanings of individual terms or words were questioned and reviewed, but the question of how the parts acted in relation to the whole kept coming up throughout this questioning of individual words. The process was one of relating parts to the whole and whole to parts until a clearer and stronger understanding of DNA had been rebuilt and I could describe the structure in my own words.

In wonderment I re ect that this very movement of relearning the concept of DNA is akin to the movement of the replication of DNA: the parts and whole move in relationship together, separate, rejoin, rebuild, and grow more solidly into a reconstruction of the concept. DNA is, as Watson (1951) described it, "beautiful" (p. 120) and "too pretty not to be true" (p. 134). It is the structure of life itself.

Traditional Writing in the Secondary Content Areas

Brown, Phillips, and Stephens (1993) trace some traditional ways of using writing in the schools. Most frequently the focus on writing has been on the product rather than the process with little or no instruction provided for students on how to complete their written work. Without helping students work through the writing process (pre-writing, drafting, revising, editing, and final drafting), teachers would simply grade the finished product and assign grades. Products were often first-draft efforts.

The two most common types of writing in the subject areas at the secondary-school level have been nontransactive writing activities: writing for assessment/evaluation purposes and writing for mechanical or noncomposing purposes (Applebee, 1981, 1984). The main purpose of writing activities used for evaluation is to reveal to teachers what students know or do not know. Students "write their own studying/learning" in these activities, which

For Reflection 8.2
Which of the writing activities described thus far do you recall doing in the content areas when you were in secondary school?

include essay exams, short-answer (one or two sentences) exercises, and fill-in-the-blank tests. Mechanical or noncomposing writing activities consist of multiple-choice activities or tests, taking notes from dictation, and copying text from the overhead projector or chalkboard. Most of the "thinking through writing" has been done by the activity composer, leaving for students only the mechanical task of copying. No real transaction occurs in such writing activities.

In the past, well-meaning teachers may also have misused or abused writing in four ways (Brown, Phillips, & Stephens, 1993). First, writing may have been assigned as punishment — for example, forcing the students to write "I will not talk in class" 100 times on the chalkboard, or asking them to write an essay on their problematic behaviour. Such writing is a form of discipline or a tool for classroom management; it is not a content learning activity.

A second misuse of writing is to ask the student to copy passages from a dictionary or encyclopedia — sending the message that not only is writing a punishment, it is boring too. At other times, students may be asked to recopy their own compositions in order to provide a neat final draft.

A third misuse of writing is to ask students to write in a subject area without providing guidance, instruction, or models for the writing process. An example would be to give directions such as "Write a report on any topic you would like in this science unit" without teaching the writing process and the specific subject area skills required to complete the assignment. The writing skills that students learn in their English language arts classes will provide students with the skills for handling the mechanics (punctuation, capitalization, spelling) to compose, but they will not provide them with the knowledge of text structures, the logic of a particular discipline, or the vocabulary peculiar to each subject area. Each discipline has unique writing demands, and teachers need to adapt writing requirements to the content, structures, and processes of their discipline.

The fourth and perhaps most common abuse of writing is to create formulas for students to follow to the exclusion of a more open-ended approach. Fixed (and highly structured) formats are set out for students to follow when writing. The five-paragraph theme is one type of formula writing in which high-school students are asked to present the thesis (purpose) in the first paragraph, develop or explore it in the next three paragraphs, and summarize in the last paragraph. Another example is the formula for a "position paper": students are asked to write a paragraph explaining, for example, "Why you think gambling should or should not be used as a form of fundraising by governments." Students state their position and then provide supporting evidence. The fixed formats of formula writing can stifle the creative composing process. Fixed formats also tend to portray writing and thinking as linear processes.

Traditional writing instruction in the content areas, however, has produced three positive types of writing strategies. One of these falls in the category of informational, factual, or technical writing and requires the taking of an efferent stance. In strictly factual writing, students make notes based on material read, record their experiences (e.g., laboratory or scientific observations), report on events (e.g., news stories), summarize longer texts, or carry out generalization or classification activities. These activities allow students to get involved actively in learning content and to use such processes as analyzing, summarizing, and paraphrasing. For these activities, students need to be taught information-gathering and report-writing skills.

Another category of writing in the content areas is learning to write the discourse forms of the content area. In mathematics, it may mean learning how to write using an explanation pattern, to write a story problem, or to integrate the explanation pattern with diagrams when writing. In the English language arts, it may mean learning how to write poems, stories, essays, and plays. In social studies, it may mean learning to write historical sketches, editorials, commentaries, and book and film reviews. In science, it may mean writing scientific observations and technical or laboratory reports, or devising directions for experiments. In each of these, critical observation, imaginative writing, and technical skills are necessary, as is knowledge of the content. In this type of predominantly efferent writing, writers need to integrate aesthetic and efferent stances, as appropriate. Guided instruction by the teacher and the use of the process approach to writing will help the student compose a better-quality product in this category of writing.

The third category of writing activities in the content areas consists of using composing activities with the aim of self-discovery and learning. In these "writing-to-learn" activities, writing is used as a tool for learning. These writing activities require thinking about and sorting through the content of a subject area to inquire, discover, recall, organize, classify, analyze, connect (synthesize), and/or evaluate. Both efferent and aesthetic transactions occur in this type of writing. Such activities frequently accompany reading and serve to enhance comprehension. Included in this category are note-making, learning logs, and response journals. The aim is to make sense of what has been heard, viewed, or read on the topic in the subject area in light of one's previous knowledge and experience. Through the writing, students are adding to and sharpening their knowledge.

The three positive categories of traditional writing strategies provide many opportunities for readers to "write their own reading."

For Reflection 8.3
Which of these positive writing activities did you experience in your secondary classroom? How did you feel about these writing activities?

Responsibilities of Content Area Teachers Teaching Writing

To ensure that students have positive types of writing experiences in the content area, teachers need to:

1. acknowledge that writing is a tool that helps students learn the content and how to "write the content";
2. encourage students to adopt a writing stance (purpose) on the aesthetic–efferent continuum and to make interdisciplinary connections across the traditional content areas;
3. have students use activities for writing-to-learn content without undue focus on learning the mechanics and conventions of writing;
4. encourage students to "write-their-reading"; and
5. teach students "how to write" the content (structures, formats, logic, and vocabulary) of their disciplines by implementing writing activities as part of content area instruction and by providing instructional guidance in how to write the content of their subject area.

Because "the demands of and needs for writing instruction are unique to each discipline" (Brown, Phillips, & Stephens, 1993, p. 48), content area teachers need to implement three basic instruction techniques to improve students' writing (Brown et al., 1993):

1. Expose students to samples of the type of writing you wish them to complete. Have students read a number of these samples.
2. Using an overhead, point out features of each type of writing (e.g., a lab report, a report of a scientific phenomenon, a position paper, a biography, a story, or a "writing of one's reading"). Focus on organizational pattern, style of writing, and vocabulary, each of which places special demands on the reader and the writer.
3. Use the process approach to enhance the writing transaction in the content areas.

The next section elaborates on the process approach to transactional writing.

A Transactional Approach to Process Writing

There are five components to the writing process, each of which requires an instructional commitment from teachers and a "practice" commitment from students (Atwell, 1987). The five components, which provide the scaffolding for the composing process, are: pre-writing or creating; drafting; revising; editing/proofreading or evaluating; and post-writing or publishing. These are not linear, but recursive, activities in which the writer can move backward or forward at any stage of the process. For example, a writer can move back to creating at the proofreading stage or forward to evaluating at the drafting stage.

Pre-writing. Teachers should begin by providing an environment that is supportive to writing, by recognizing the value of content area writing, and by using writing to explore content as an important facet of the subject area curriculum. Students need assistance in defining the parameters of a topic, discovering what they know about a topic through "free writing," choosing a stance, gathering information on the topic, organizing ideas, generalizing ideas, and deciding on the most relevant information for a particular audience. At this creating stage, pre-writing can be more of a mental or an oral activity rather than an "on-paper" activity.

Drafting. In drafting, students translate their ideas into a rough draft, writing down the words, sentences, and paragraphs in an unpolished form. Students may draft and re-draft a piece of writing several times to focus or shape it, holding to a particular stance (efferent or aesthetic) or integrating the two.

Revising. When revising, the writer transacts with his or her text by being its first reader. As mentioned earlier, vocabulary selection, sentence structure, fluency, and ideas are reconsidered, modified, discarded, or rearranged in an attempt to "polish" the writing. This reading is usually done on a unit-by-unit basis (as words, sentences, or paragraphs are written) rather than just at the completion of a whole text. The writer also transacts with the text as its potential reading — reacting to the meaning an audience may get out of the composition and choosing to revise accordingly. During revision, sharing the piece with peers and/or the teacher provides suggestions for further revision. As in speaking, the responses of others to students' writing is critical in the learning process.

Editing or Proofreading. In editing, the focus is on the form and mechanics of writing — spelling, grammar, and punctuation — rather than on meaning or content.

Post-writing. In publishing, or post-writing, the student's writing "goes public." Audiences include the teacher, peers, parents, students in other grades, the school newspaper or newsletter, or the outside community (politicians, businesses, agencies, and organizations). It is important to note that several drafts may be required to create a finished product.

Using Writing Activities to Enhance the Reading of Content

Reading and writing activities have been included throughout this book as balanced parts of the transactional process that support each other in enhancing learning. As stated earlier, by providing reading and writing activities in the subject areas, teachers provide opportunities for students to increase their understanding of content. Each of the subject areas (disciplines) has specialized vocabularies, writing styles, genres, and conventions. As described in other chapters, teachers who provide opportunities for talk and discussion, reading, writing, art, and drama increase students' chances of acquiring the ideas and principles of the content areas.

Through writing-to-learn activities, one can also learn the content of a discipline. Writing-to-learn activities encourage students to explore and think about ideas in a subject, and to clarify their thinking and increase their depth of understanding of the content of a discipline. It has been said that if ideas have already been thought out, what need is there to write except to report ideas? In writing-to-learn activities students use such processes as analyzing, paraphrasing, summarizing, synthesizing, responding, and evaluating.

In this section, some practical ideas for writing-to-learn are presented with a view to using writing as a way of thinking about and sorting one's way through the ideas in any given topic in an effort to increase the comprehension of content (Crowhurst, 1989). These activities need to be practised by students under teacher guidance.

For Reflection 8.4

Before reading about the types of instruction that can enhance learning through writing, recall one instructional activity provided by your content area teachers that involved you in writing-to-learn.

Brain Racing

A type of brainstorming (Brown et al., 1993, p. 204), brain racing is a pre-writing or creating activity that requires students to develop ideas, thoughts, feelings, and interdisciplinary connections on a broad topic (e.g., a war between Canada and the United States). Students quickly generate a written list of ideas. They then reflect on, review, and edit their listings. Then they select one item from their own list and do a second brain racing. Next students generate at least five questions based on what they want to learn about the topic. Finally, they speculate about and write answers to the questions. In sum, they recall, question, and speculate (RQS). The students then read the chapter/selection (or listen to a presentation) and compare what they have written with what they learned through reading or listening. Students can elaborate on or modify their final answers or write a paragraph on the topic.

Brain Writing

A variation of brainstorming, brain writing is a pre-writing activity that activates prior knowledge, personal associations, and interdisciplinary connections or requires students to predict depending on the purpose set (Brown et al., 1993). Students generate ideas individually (as above) and then in small groups, which provide the context for interaction among and reaction from participants. The process for brain writing is as follows:

1. Divide the class into small groups of three to five students.
2. Have the students respond with any ideas, feelings, or associations they have about the topic they will be reading about.
3. Have students exchange papers and read each other's writing until all the ideas are discussed.
4. Have students make a master list for each group to be shared with the whole class. Students can also ask questions about the ideas provided by each group.
5. A master list can be generated from the contributions of all the small groups to be used by students as a guide for reading and note-taking.

Questioning

Questions can be developed to guide students as they read content area texts, allowing for meaningful transactions during reading. Higher-order questions can be generated by students and teachers. Students can reflect on them during reading, and answer them in writing during or after the reading.

Cubing

Cubing (Brown et al., 1993, p. 205) can be a pre-reading and pre-writing activity as well as a post-reading activity. As a pre-writing activity it helps the student to quickly explore a topic. Once a student chooses a topic, he or she writes for three to five minutes on each dimension in the cube (see Figure 8.1). It provides the students with six springboards for writing: describe it; compare it; associate it; analyze it; apply it; argue for or against it. The student may choose to write a paragraph on one or two items in the cube. Some of the springboards provide opportunities to take an aesthetic stance in the

Figure 8.1

Cubing

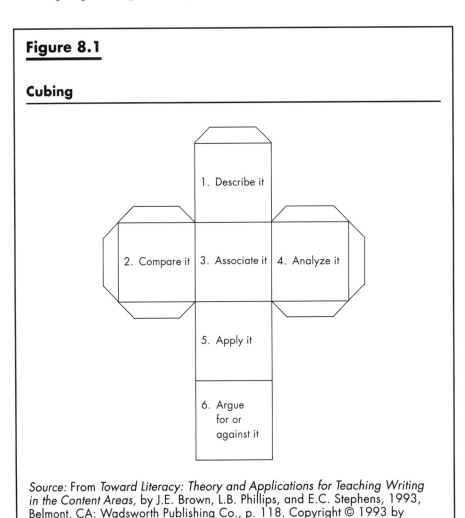

Source: From *Toward Literacy: Theory and Applications for Teaching Writing in the Content Areas*, by J.E. Brown, L.B. Phillips, and E.C. Stephens, 1993, Belmont, CA: Wadsworth Publishing Co., p. 118. Copyright © 1993 by Wadsworth Publishing Co.

writing. As a post-writing activity, students can add to each dimension on the cube the information learned when reading content selections.

Autobiographical Writing

As a pre-writing and pre-reading activity, autobiographical writing (Hamann, Schultz, Smith, & White, 1991) is a means of helping readers link content with personal experience by evoking personal connections, associations, feelings, images, and ideas with the content material to be read or written. This is a way of encouraging aesthetic and interdisciplinary transactions through writing. Personal dilemmas may be posed in relation to the content to be read. Students are asked to write for several minutes about their own experiences of such dilemmas.

Guided Writing/Reading Procedure

This procedure (Konopek, Martin, & Martin, 1987; Smith & Bean, 1980) engages students in cycles of reading and writing. Prior to reading, the class quickly brainstorms ideas about the topic they will be reading. The ideas are then grouped into categories. Each student selects an idea about which to write individually and chooses a stance for the writing. The students then read the selection and add to their original ideas through writing. Students then reread the selection and revise their writing based on the second reading.

A Transactional Approach to Using Journals in Writing-to-Learn

Journal writing is one of the most common writing-to-learn activities in the content areas.

Types of Journal Writing in the Content Areas

Journal writing is a form of free writing that allows students "to be introspective about themselves as learners and about the ideas, concepts, and principles of the content they are learning and experiencing" (Brown et al., 1993, p. 62). Thus, by keeping a journal students are able to reflect on the content of a subject. Such writing is often self-motivated, giving students "the opportunity to explore and interact with subject matter and to make it part of their world"

For Reflection 8.5
Reflect on the types of journal writing activities you engaged in as a student in secondary school. To what extent was an aesthetic approach encouraged as a way to enhance content learning through reflection in journals?

(p. 62). Journal writing adds a measure of personal learning in the subject areas as it gives students opportunities to experience aesthetic, efferent, and interdisciplinary transactions and to describe them by "writing their reading."

In free writing, students write down ideas quickly without concern for grammar or spelling. It is useful as a process of discovery and exploration of the concepts in a discipline (Elbow, 1973). Although free writing does not necessarily lead to improvement in writing skills in the content areas, it does use writing as a vehicle for learning content. Free writing in journals is probably most useful in the English language arts classrooms.

In other disciplines, journal writing might be more prescribed. In **structured** or **prompted journal writing** the teacher gives directions or asks questions in order to prompt the students' learning. Different prompts can encourage efferent, aesthetic, and interdisciplinary writing transactions.

Content area teachers, too, can benefit from keeping a journal. By responding to their own assignments, they can be informed about how students will respond to the work assigned. Teachers can also reflect on their teaching activities — addressing items such as classroom interactions, students' responses to content and activities, or the pace of a lesson.

While the different types of journals described below are all useful in content learning, it is important that teachers, when using journals, specify the type of journal students should use so that they are not penalized for using the wrong kind.

Dialogue Journals

Dialogue journals (using free writing) are talks on paper or transactions between teacher and students or between a pair of students (Gordon, 1993). In this conversation, students share their knowledge of content as well as their questions, reactions, and insights on the subject. They explore what they know and what they are having difficulty with. They have opportunities to learn content and language and writing skills from teachers or from their writing partners. Writing in journals is also one of the few good ways to get students to be metacognitive (Miholic, 1994; Gordon & Hunsberger, 1991; Gordon & MacInnis, 1993). The samples from university students' journals in Chapter 1 are examples of free writing in dialogue journals.

If students are having difficulties using a free-writing format, teachers can use a series of open-ended questions (adapted from Proett & Gill, 1986) to prompt them:

What did I learn?
What confused me?
What questions do I have?
What connections can I make? (Here interdisciplinary connections should also be encouraged.)

The teacher should use this type of journal writing to make instructional decisions, rather than for evaluation purposes.

Prompted or Response Journals

In more structured journal writing, students can reflect on what they know and do not know by responding to specific questions posed by the teachers. At the same time, teachers gain insights into students' understanding of specific concepts in the content areas. Teachers can see how students "work their way" to understanding as they explain concepts by writing in their own words. For example, after reading about decimals in a mathematics textbook and hearing the teacher's oral explanation, students might be asked to respond to a number of prompts, including the following:

1. Write what you would say to another student to describe *area*.
2. How would you explain to another student the difference between area, perimeter, and volume?
3. What do you know about decimals?
4. Which is larger: 0.8 or 0.92? Why?
5. In what other subjects have you used these mathematical concepts? How?

When responding in journals, teachers can comment, question, assure, suggest, encourage, or even reteach with succinct explanations. For example, "Remember, Jill, that 0.8 is the same as 0.80. Now which is larger?"

In science, misconceptions can be altered through "conversations" in prompted or response dialogue journals. In the study of the earth's revolution around the sun, for example, students could be asked: "Why is the temperature warmer on earth in the summer than the winter?" Many students will erroneously reply that it is warmer because the earth is closer to the sun, thus revealing their original misconception. After reading texts that explain the phenomenon, and through discussions with teacher and peers, students can use journal writing as a means to restructure their knowledge and to bring about conceptual change.

Personal Reaction Journals

Personal reaction journals (Brown et al., 1993) are often used by proponents of the reader response approach in English language arts classes. In personal reaction journal writing, students are asked to react to the affective as well as cognitive aspects of learning in a content area. Intertextual and interdisciplinary connections are encouraged in these responses. Students can also respond to how they are learning, which provides opportunities for metacognitive development. When discussing and exploring their feelings about content and methods of instruction, students provide teachers with insights into "learning how they learn" and anything else of interest to the students in the study of a subject area. Students might volunteer information in open-ended entries through free writing or they may be asked specific questions such as:

> Why do you have difficulty in mathematics?
> What makes mathematics easier for you?
> What do you like about math?
> What don't you like about learning mathematics?

Sample responses to such prompts (all drawn from Gordon & MacInnis, 1993) include:

> When you talk and ask questions I don't even have time to think because people have already told the answer.

> What could help me is if you could just go a little slower.

> You teach so that I understand. At my old school, they never repeated anything.

> You are teaching too much stuff and I'm getting confused.

> I don't have anywhere quiet at home to do my homework.

Students also have opportunities to share problems in learning, especially if the journal is not perceived as an evaluative tool. For example:

> I am pretty sure I understand about whole numbers, but decimals, I'm a bit confused about them. I understand about place-value. I don't understand about the base-ten system.

Students can also share discoveries and insights such as applications to and connections with other subject areas:

> Mathematics is everywhere. I use it in all my science courses, French classes (we wrote equations) and even in music.

Project Journals

Project journals (Brown et al., 1993) allow students to keep an ongoing record of their progress when working on individual or small-group projects. Entries might include notes on the planning, organizing, and implementing of the project for the purpose of reflection and decision making.

Guidelines for Using Journals

Content area students need to understand the purpose and value of journal writing. Several guidelines (adapted from Brown et al., 1993, pp. 67–68; Anderson, 1993) are offered for teachers to follow if journals are to play a positive role in students' learning:

1. Develop a rationale for journal writing by outlining for students the purpose, objectives, and justification for using journals.
2. Decide on the type of journal writing students should do and how journals will be used (how often entries will be made by students and read and responded to by teachers or peers).
3. Help students enter into the **writing–learning relationship** by showing them how journals will heighten their understanding of the concepts in a subject area.
4. Model the type and process of writing you expect in the journal by sharing successful sample entries and examining why the writing is effective. Demonstrate "the reflection, synthesis, evaluation and experimentation" expected (Anderson, 1993, p. 304) and the aesthetic, efferent, and interdisciplinary transactions that are possible.
5. Implement regular journal writing as part of the curriculum so that students develop the habit of writing.
6. Establish and discuss with the students the evaluation procedures that will be used so that they receive helpful feedback on their entries.

Evaluating Journal Entries

In the private communication of journal writing, a communicative bond develops in the transaction between the teacher and student (or student and

---

For Reflection 8.6
What guidelines were you given for journal writing in secondary school? How useful were these guidelines?

student). Since the journal is the "hot-line" between a teacher and student (Gordon & MacInnis, 1993), students feel comfortable in taking risks and in sharing their strengths and weaknesses in a content area. They do this only if the teacher makes it clear that the journal is not an evaluative tool. Teachers' comments need to be positive, sincere, and regular, not evaluative or judgemental. Teachers' comments on the entries should question, prompt, or reteach so that "stretching of thinking" occurs.

Some content area teachers allot a certain percentage (e.g., ten percent) of the final grade in a subject area to journal writing, acknowledging students' growth in understanding and willingness to take risks and to expand their thinking. Other teachers use a pass/fail or credit/no credit system based on criteria established with the students.

The Perils of Journal Writing

One of the major problems with journal writing is overuse, especially if all content area teachers have a journal requirement (Brown et al., 1993; Anderson, 1993). It is prudent to check with other content area teachers to ensure that students keep journals only in some selected courses (Anderson, 1993). A second problem is the grading of journals (Anderson, 1993) and the criteria used to evaluate them. Anderson suggests that students should have a role in deciding on the worth/weight of the journal activity in relation to the rest of the grades assigned in a course. Using established criteria (rubrics), students might play a role in evaluating their journals so that they can develop a greater awareness of the weaknesses and strengths of their reflections. A number of useful rubrics are presented in Chapter 11.

Using Computers to Enhance Content Writing Transactions

With the increased use of technology in schools, computers are now widely available in classrooms (and in students' own homes) for use in content area writing. Word processing software lets students store and retrieve information, compose their drafts, and fine-tune their writing by editing and revising. Computers can be used to quickly record fragmented or disconnected ideas, to organize and review ideas, and to rearrange chunks of text. Word processing software may also include a spell checker, a style checker (to correct awkward phrases and faults in grammar and punctuation), and a thesaurus. A clean printed copy of the text can be produced, even after multiple revisions. Proofreading of the final draft can be done from a printed copy as

---

For Reflection 8.7
Recall the role computers/word processors played in your secondary-school writing activities and describe the role they play now in your postsecondary studies.

---

even spell checkers will not correct all grammar and punctuation errors (for example, using it's for its). Software programs are also available that allow students to turn their papers into "publishable" work, enabling students to headline items, format columns, insert graphics, and polish their work in a type of desk-top publishing endeavour.

Computers can also be used as tools for learning content through writing. As Brown et al. (1993) state, "Students using the computer . . . pay more attention to the development of ideas and generate more material. Using a computer increases the quantity and quality of ideas, promotes fluency, and makes critical thinking more of a focus for students" (p. 290).

The following springboard activities (based on Brown et al., 1993) allow teachers and students to use the computer to improve writing in any content area. Teachers can modify any of the following or add to the list.

Free Writing. The teacher can prepare a list of topics within a unit of study (e.g., "invertebrates"), across the whole subject area (e.g., science), or across disciplines (e.g., language arts, social studies, and drama). Students can be asked to free write on the topic, print out a copy, circle any specific subtopics or ideas they wish to explore further, and then return to the computer to outline details under the subtopic chosen.

Questioning. Using the journalistic questions of who, what, where, when, why, and how, students can keep files of questions on computer to use in writing assignments. For example, a list of questions on invertebrates kept digitally might include: how did invertebrates evolve? and what are some examples of invertebrates? The questions can be called up, applied to a new topic, and answers typed in to use as the basis for a paper in a particular subject area or across disciplines.

Graphic Organizers. At the beginning of a topic of study, students can use the computer to prepare a graphic organizer. As they read on and study about the topic they can expand the organizer.

Footnotes and Reference Lists. Software programs can facilitate the recording of sources from which students draw ideas. Note-taking programs such as Endnote help in compiling bibliographies. Programs like Endnote even have options for bibliographic style (e.g., APA or MLA style).

Electronic Media and Library Research. If classrooms are interconnected via computer networks (in-house or world-wide [for example, Internet]), students should be shown how they can access and use these resources. Entire encyclopedias, for example, are available on CD-ROM and students can do much of their initial research by accessing them. (See "Note-Taking from CD-ROMs" below.)

Collaborative Writing. When students feel that their drafts could benefit from peer input, they can send their draft to a classmate (either a hard copy or an electronic copy). Some computer programs allow a peer editor to make suggestions on screen (which might show up shaded or underlined) without destroying the original text.

Learning to Write Different Types of Genres in the Content Areas

Written discourse is different for each discipline (Faigley, 1986). Students, therefore, must become familiar with the conventions of writing in a particular subject area (Sperling, 1996). There are, however, four types of writing that are common across the curriculum: report writing, exposition, argumentation, and narration (Singer & Donlan, 1989). (See Table 8.1.)

Report Writing

Writing a research report (or term paper) is a common writing assignment in the content area classroom. It is also "one of the most complex of academic tasks" (Alvermann & Phelps, 1994, p. 226). To write a report, students need to selectively collect information, summarize, organize, and paraphrase to communicate it in a draft, and then in final form, to others. When writing the report, the writer must choose which expository structures to use and must adopt a formal, academic tone. At the same time, the writer must learn the mechanics of quoting and crediting sources (documentation). In report writing, the writer adopts a predominantly efferent stance.

Gathering and Organizing Information for the Report

Students need instruction in how to use the various research resources at their disposal, such as library catalogues, books, magazines, encyclopedias, videotapes, audiotapes, electronic networks, and CD-ROMs.

Note-Taking from CD-ROMs. CD-ROMs are becoming more common in schools and in students' homes. Once a student has located information on the topic of the report, he or she can use an "electronic type of note-taking" by selecting (highlighting) on screen any phrases, sentences, or paragraphs to be printed. Students should be instructed to write this mate-

Table 8.1

Characteristics of Four Basic Writing Types

WRITING TYPE	PURPOSE	WHAT IS REQUIRED OF THE STUDENT	SAMPLE ASSIGNMENT
Reporting	Organize and relay information	Gather information and organize it according to questions or other directions	1. Answers to study questions 2. Answers to essay questions 3. Library research
Exposition	Explain	Interpret, analyze, and react to information	1. Solve a problem 2. Tell how to do something
Narration	Entertain	Retell fictional events in chronological order; use dialogue	1. Anecdotes 2. Vignettes 3. Short stories
Argumentation	Persuade	Defend a point of view by supplying only the evidence that supports it	1. Taking a stand on a current event 2. Attacking an individual 3. Defending a political belief

Source: From *Reading and Learning from Text,* by H. Singer and D. Donlan, 1989, Hillsdale, NJ: Erlbaum, p. 289.

rial in their own words and to acknowledge their sources when quoting someone else's material.

Note-Taking from Library Sources. Students need to be taught how to record information from a variety of sources, or they resort to verbatim copying of material on their topic or using photocopied key passages without paraphrasing. Three methods of note-taking (on which teacher-directed lessons should be provided) are data collection (or reference cards), the directed note-taking activity, and, as previously mentioned, computer note-taking.

Note-taking on reference cards can be taught as follows.

Using 3 × 5 index cards, students locate and record important words and facts on their topic, as well as direct quotations (see Box 8.1). For the teacher-directed lesson, each student should be asked to complete two cards, each on

---

Box 8.1
Reference Card

Reference Card

Topic: _____   Student's Name: _____

Words: _____

Facts/Ideas: 1. _____
(Paraphrased)
2. _____

3. _____

4. _____

5. _____

Quotations with page numbers: _____

_____

_____

NOTE: Students should provide complete biographical data for their sources, including author's name, title of book or article, volume and number of journal, publisher, date of publication, and page numbers. These data can be written on the back of the reference card.

Source: Reprinted by permission of Marilyn Rocco. Kenmore — Town of Tonawanda School District, Kenmore, NY.

---

the same topic. Students then assemble as a class or in small groups and sort the cards according to categories of information. The teacher then assists with paraphrasing, summarizing, reflecting on, clarifying, and rearranging ideas as preparation for the writing of a group report.

After the group report writing practice, students are assigned a research topic, collect their own information on index cards, and meet individually with the teacher before beginning to write a draft copy of the report.

The directed note-taking activity (Spires & Stone, 1989) involves a split-page method of taking notes (Palmatier, 1973) and the use of self-questioning, both of which require teacher-directed instruction.

To use the split-page note-taking method, students should work through the following steps under teacher guidance:

1. Fold an $8\frac{1}{2} \times 11$ sheet of paper so that the left-hand column is A and the right-hand column is B. (Table 8.2 has been developed on the basis of a text entitled "Factors of Production.")
2. Make notes in the right-hand column, recording both primary and secondary ideas.
3. Reread the notes to determine the major concept. Then write the concept in the left-hand column directly opposite the more detailed information in the right-hand column.
4. If the notes in the right-hand column are unclear or lack detail, refer back to the source. Add needed information (use the back of the paper if necessary).
5. Use the split page as a studying aid by folding it so that only the left-hand column is visible. Recall and review information in the right-hand column as required.

To monitor levels of involvement when using the split-page technique, students can ask themselves questions before, during, and after the note-taking. Examples of questions relating to affective and cognitive domains include:

Before taking notes (during planning)
Do I feel motivated?
Am I interested in this topic?
If I am not too interested, how can I become interested?
What is my specific purpose for reading this article/watching this video?

While taking notes (for monitoring)
Am I understanding what I read or hear?
Am I differentiating between main ideas and supportive details?
What strategies do I use if comprehension failure occurs?

After taking notes (evaluating)
Did I attain my purpose?
Were satisfactory levels of concentration, motivation, and comprehension maintained? (Spires & Stone, 1989, p. 37)

Two important skills are needed for students to collect the information for note-taking for a research report. They are paraphrasing and summarizing. Singer and Donlan (1989) present a three-step method to teach students to *paraphrase*. The steps incorporate semantic and syntactic paraphrasing.

Table 8.2

Split-Page Note-Taking

Topic: Factors of Production
Based on: Chapter 1, *Contemporary Business Education*, by Applebaum, Beckman, Boone, & Kurtz (1990)

Definition of factors of production	• inputs required for businesses to operate effectively
Four types of factors	• natural resources, labour, capital, and entrepreneurship
1. Natural resources	• everything that can be used from natural environment, e.g., land, forests, mineral deposits
2. Labour	• everyone who works for a business or a company, e.g., president, sales rep.
3. Capital	• funds to run the business (investments, profits, etc.)
4. Entrepreneurship	• the taking of risks to set up and operate a business. Entrepreneur is the risk-taker in a *private-enterprise system* (see notes on private enterprise in a mixed economy.)

Source: Based on "Factors of Production," in *Contemporary Canadian Business*, Third edition, by Steven H. Appelbaum, 1990, Toronto: Holt, Rinehart and Winston of Canada, p. 13. Copyright © 1987, 1985, 1982 CBS College Publishing. Copyright © 1979, 1976 The Dryden Press. Copyright © 1990, 1987, 1984 Holt, Rinehart and Winston of Canada, Limited. All rights reserved. Reprinted by permission of Harcourt Brace & Company, Canada, Limited.

Semantic paraphrasing means using synonyms to reword a sentence; for example, "The way your body produces energy is similar to the way a car gets its energy" could be changed to "There is a similarity between the manner in which your body makes energy and the way an automobile obtains power." Syntactic paraphrasing involves changing the word order of a sentence; for example, the earlier example could be changed to "The way a car gets its energy is similar to the way your body produces energy." The three steps are outlined in more detail in Table 8.3.

Table 8.3

Steps in Teaching How to Paraphrase

Step 1: Present the original passage from the textbook with its paraphrase. Have students discuss the language differences.

TEXT*

For millennia deafness was considered so catastrophic that few ventured to ease its burdens. Isolation in a kind of permanent solitary confinement was deemed inevitable; a deaf person, even in the midst of urban hub-bub, was considered as unreachable as a fairytale princess locked in a tower.

PARAPHRASE

Deafness was seen to be such a tragedy for thousands of years that little was done to lessen its ordeal. Permanent solitude and inaccessibility were accepted states for the deaf.

Step 2: Use a series of questions to help students paraphrase short passages from a text.

The first attempts to educate deaf children came in the sixteenth century. As late as 1749 the French Academy of Sciences appointed a commission to determine whether deaf people were "capable of reasoning."

TEXT HINTS

1. Does the language of the first sentence require a semantic or a syntactic change?
2. What phrases can be substituted for "appointed a commission to determine" and "capable of reasoning"?

(continued)

(continued)

Step 3: Introduce longer passages, reducing the number of hints each time.

TEXT #1*

Lately, though, the deaf community has begun to speak for itself. To the surprise and bewilderment of outsiders, its message is utterly contrary to the wisdom of centuries: Deaf people, far from groaning under a heavy yoke, are not handicapped at all. Deafness is not a disability. Instead, many deaf people now proclaim, they are a subculture like any other. They are simply a linguistic minority (speaking American Sign Language) and are no more in need of a cure for their condition than are Haitians or Hispanics.

TEXT #2*

The embrace of what looks indisputably like hardship is what, in particular, strikes the hearing world as perverse, and deaf leaders have learned to brace themselves for the inevitable question. "No!" Roslyn Rosen says, by shaking her head vehemently, she *wouldn't* prefer to be able to hear. Rosen, the president of the National Association of the Deaf, is deaf, the daughter of deaf parents, and the mother of deaf children. "I'm happy with who I am," she says through an interpreter, "and I don't want to be 'fixed.' Would an Italian-American rather be a WASP? In our society everyone agrees that whites have an easier time than blacks. But do you think a black person would undergo operations to become white?"

TEXT HINTS

1. What is a synonym for "contrary"?
2. What words can be substituted for expressions such as "wisdom of centuries" and "groaning under the weights of a heavy yoke"?
3. Can "subculture" and "linguistic minority" be used interchangeably in your paraphrase?

*From "Deafness as Culture," by E. Dolnick, in Jon Terpening , 1989, *Insights: Cultures*, Toronto: Harcourt Brace Canada, pp. 27–36.

Source: Adapted from *Reading and Learning from Text*, by H. Singer and D. Donlan, 1989, Hillsdale, NJ: Erlbaum, pp. 263–64.

Three steps (Hidi & Anderson, 1986) are necessary to write a *summary*:

1. Delete the unimportant information (words, phrases, sentences).
2. Condense the remaining information by combining information or constructing superordinate (general) terms for information that can be grouped or labelled more concisely (e.g., "factors of production" for natural resources, labour, capital, and entrepreneurship). (It may be necessary to identify or construct topic sentences at this point.)
3. Convert the information into writing.

The three-step summary process is shown below using the first two paragraphs of a feature on Louis Braille (Poole, Pilkey, & Johnson, 1992).

```
The Braille system of writing for the blind, which uses patterns
of raised dots on paper to represent letters, was not invented
by a scientist or an educator. It was invented by a fifteen-year-
old boy who was himself blind.
    Louis Braille was born in a small town in France in 1809. His
father, Simon Braille, was a leather worker who made harnesses
and saddles. While playing in his father's workshop when he was
three, Louis accidentally stabbed himself in the eye with an awl
(a long, sharp tool used for punching holes in leather). His eye
became infected, and the infection spread to the other eye.
Because there was no way to treat such an infection in 1812, Louis
soon lost his sight forever.
```

Steps 1 & 2 (Deleting and condensing):

```
Braille system, writing for the blind, patterns of dots for let-
ters, invented by 15-year-old Braille, born 1809 in France.
Playing in father's workshop, stabbed self in one eye, awl, infec-
tion spread to other eye, lost sight.
```

Step 3 (Converting above into writing):

```
The Braille system of writing for the blind consists of a pat-
tern of dots to represent letters. It was invented by a 15-year-
old blind boy, Louis Braille, who was born in France in 1809. When
playing in his father's workshop he stabbed himself in the eye
with an awl. The infection spread to his other eye and he lost
his sight.
```

Writing the Research Report

As stated earlier, information, once gathered, needs to be organized so that it can be used in the written report. Cards containing similar information should be grouped and appropriately incorporated into paragraphs for a report. Decisions need to be made on paragraph type (see Table 8.4) and organizational patterns (e.g., chronological, problem-solution, cause-effect, as described in Chapter 12) to use. After paragraphs have been written for each set of cards, a decision needs to be made on the type of organization or the number of organizational patterns that can be used within the overall structure of the whole text. Transitional sentences and paragraphs will be required, as will an introduction and a summary (or conclusion). Care needs to be taken that report writing does not become "writing according to a formula." Students should read drafts of each others' reports for some critical evaluation and provide suggestions for shaping, editing, and polishing before a final copy is presented to the teacher.

This section concludes with a brief description of the three other types of writing that students are likely to encounter in the content areas.

Exposition

Exposition, or expository writing, is "objective" writing that explains an idea, a philosophy, a process, a point of view, or a work of art or literature. In this type of writing the writer must interpret, analyze, and/or react to the topic at hand. An efferent stance predominates, although aesthetic elements are possible — that is, exposition is not just reporting the information. When organizing one's explanation, the writer generally needs to include an introduction, a body, and a conclusion. An example of exposition is shown in Box 8.2.

Argumentation

Argumentation is more subjective than exposition. An aesthetic stance predominates. The aim of the writer is to persuade the audience about an ideology or a cause, to take a stand on an important issue, or to attack or defend someone by using logic and/or persuasion. Crowhurst (1990) reports that while students' argumentative writing improves as they progress from elementary to secondary school, most of their argumentation lacks organization, structure, and appropriate language. An example of argumentation is provided in Box 8.3.

Narration

When writing narration, the author presents a series of events in chronological order. Dialogue is often included. Besides short stories, narration may

Table 8.4

Paragraph Types

PARAGRAPH TYPE AND PURPOSE	EXAMPLE	SIGNAL OR TRANSITION WORDS	TEACHING STRATEGY
1. *Introductory* Overview, establish purpose (sometimes written in narrative style).	"In this chapter we will explain three ideas."	*This chapter describes; Let's examine; Here we will study* . . . (questions)	State major points of section or chapter.
2. *Narrative* (who, what, where, when, how) Tell a story, integrate ideas and feelings in concrete situations, form visual images.	"John is going through three steps now."	The scene is	Answer *wh* questions.
3. *Descriptive* Set the scene, visualize.	"Picture this scene . . ."	*describe; imagine; picture*	Draw a picture or diagram.
4. *Definitional* (may overlap with expository) Clarifies meaning of word, phrase, or clause.	"Rubella is a virus."	*called; for example; means; that is* (aids: parentheses, comparison or contrast, synonym, appositional phrase)	1. Tell what something is or means. 2. What is something like? 3. What is another word for?

(continued)

(continued)

PARAGRAPH TYPE AND PURPOSE	EXAMPLE	SIGNAL OR TRANSITION WORDS	TEACHING STRATEGY
5. *Expository or Explanatory* Explain and inform.	Steps in process; chronology; directions; relate cause–effect; problem–solution; question–answer	*first, next, after, then, to make, to do, since, because*	1. Outline steps or events. 2. Answer question on cause for effect or solution for problem or answer to question.
6. *Summary and Conclusion* Restate essential ideas.	"To summarize the two main points covered: (1) _____ and (2) _____."	*thus; to briefly review; consequently; hence; you can see; in summary; to conclude we found . . . ; from the evidence; therefore, as a result . . .*	State major points of section or chapter.
7. *Transitional* (hybrids, mixture of two or more types) Relate what proceeded to what follows (may be in question form).	"Now that we have covered our first two points, let's go on to our third point."	*Now we shall consider . . . ; What do these reports tell us?; however; on the other hand; yet; meanwhile; although; conversely; nevertheless; otherwise*	Separate preceding from forward-pointing ideas

Source: From *Reading and Learning from Text*, in H. Singer and D. Donlan, 1989, Hillsdale, NJ: Erlbaum, 298–99.

Box 8.2
Exposition — An Example

Technology and Ecology

Technology has become the primary means by which humans interact with the Earth-home. An outcome of artifice guided by human beliefs and purposes, technology makes visible the deep beliefs that consciously and subconsciously motivate society. Through it the people/planet relationship is made explicit. Hence the importance of a critical appraisal of technology, of its effects on the world and of the extent to which its various forms are appropriate.

Technology, the Big T, has been variously defined. All agree that it is more than hardware, more than machines, tools, material instruments. An inclusive definition of T is *a reproducible and publicly communicable way of doing things.* The key word "communicable" shifts T into the world of ideas, language, beliefs, culture — which explains why T-transfer from industrialized to non-industrialized nations is difficult until, either directly by acceptance or indirectly by acculturation, the receiving populations adopt Western values, beliefs, perceptions. To benefit from our technology, they must first believe what we believe and want what we want. According to a recent Mercedes-Benz advertisement: "Technology is only opportunity knowing — the secret is to open the right doors." To be effective, T must be directed to the right openings, the right visions, such as owner pride and smooth high speeds in the Mercedes model M-B 300.

An essential part of T consists, therefore, of cultural ideas, especially the values and goals espoused by influential people — in our society by business people. Their materialist philosophy provides the inspiration and encouragement for industry's material production. The built environment, steadily expanding, is the visible expression of T's cultural authority, influence and growth. Progress is T, and T is progress.

Source: From *Home Place: Essays on Ecology,* by Stan Rowe, 1990, Edmonton: NeWest Publishers Ltd. Reprinted by permission of the author.

---

include anecdotes, jokes, tall tales, or vignettes. Narrative writing requires predominantly an aesthetic stance. Box 8.4 provides an example of narration.

Evaluating Content Area Writing

When writing is defined as a social transaction, writing competence is seen to be situational (Greenberg, 1994). That is, writing competence varies across tasks, topics, and different groups. The best way to assess writing ability is to

Box 8.3
Argumentation — An Example

The time has come for native people to make our own decisions. We need to have self-government. I have no illusions that it will be smooth sailing — there will be trial and error and further struggle. And if that means crawling before we can stand up and walk, so be it. We'll have to learn through experience.

While we're learning, we have a lot to teach and give to the world — a holistic philosophy, a way of living with the earth, not disposing of it. It is critical that we all learn from the elders that an individual is not more important than a forest; we know that we're here to live on and with the earth, not to subdue it.

The wheels are in motion for a revival, for change in the way native people are taking their place in Canada. I can see that we're equipped, we have the tools to do the work. We have an enormous number of smart, talented, moral Indian people. It's thrilling to be a part of this movement.

Someday, when I'm an elder, I'll tell the children the stories: about the bush, about the hard times, about the renaissance, and especially about the importance of knowing your place in your nation.

Source: Excerpted from "Growing Up Native," by Carol Geddes, 1990, in *Homemaker's Magazine* (25) 7. Reprinted by permission of the author.

Box 8.4
Narration — An Example

As soon as she arrived she went straight to the kitchen to see if the monkey was there. It was: What a relief! She wouldn't have liked to admit that her mother had been right. *Monkeys at a birthday?* her mother had sneered. *Get away with you, believing any nonsense you're told.* She was cross, but not because of the monkey, the girl thought; it's just because of the party.

"I don't like you going," she told her. "It's a rich people's party."

"Rich people go to Heaven too," said the girl who studied religion at school.

"Get away with Heaven," said the mother. "The problem with you, young lady, is that you like to fart higher than your ass."

The girl didn't approve of the way her mother spoke.

Source: From *The Stolen Party*, by Liliana Heker. Copyright © 1982 by Liliana Heker. Translation copyright © 1985 by Alberto Manguel. Reprinted by permission of Westwood Creative Artists Ltd.

obtain writing samples from students. Since content and clarity rather than mechanics (capitalization, spelling, punctuation, handwriting, format) are the prime focus of writing instruction in the subject areas, emphasis in evaluating writing should be on the *process* rather than on the *product* itself. Evaluation should be seen as a method of helping students to improve the quality of their work and their knowledge of the content. This is **formative evaluation** on first and subsequent drafts of pieces produced by students. Evaluation of finished products or final (polished) drafts is **summative evaluation**. Both types of feedback (discussed in Chapter 11) are required in content area writing.

Approaches for Evaluating Writing in the Content Areas

Portfolio Assessment

The contents of portfolios include samples of students' writing. Content area teachers often work in co-operation with the English teacher in a "common," across-the-subject-areas portfolio for each student. (**Portfolio assessment** is described in detail in Chapter 11.) There are several other approaches to evaluation of writing in the content areas: holistic evaluation, analytic scoring, and primary trait scoring (Sperling, 1994).

Holistic Evaluation

Holistic evaluation involves a "quick response" to a student's piece of writing because it is based on the total impression using a general list of features (minimally described). A scoring guide, or rubric, is used (see examples of rubrics in Chapter 11) listing all the elements of a composition at different levels of competence. Raters (teacher and students) assess on the basis of immediate impressions, with little analysis, with the purpose of ranking one piece of writing against another. The emphasis is on content rather than mechanics. Teachers need to take some class time to teach students how to evaluate papers consistently and with accuracy. Through the use of rubrics, students also acquire a knowledge of expectations held for each level of achievement and hence gain control over their own learning.

Analytic Scoring

Analytic scoring uses rubrics to give a detailed assessment of writing features. Each feature may be rated as low, average, or high in quality. Analytic scoring provides a score point value for each of the elements or skills being assessed.

Primary Trait Scoring

Like analytic rubrics, primary trait rubrics are detailed; however, they emphasize only a selected element of a writing assignment or focus on writing features characteristic of a particular type of discourse (for example, autobiography). For example: The students in a mathematics class have been asked to write a story problem that requires knowledge of a particular concept (e.g., the speed of light) in order to find the solution. The purpose of the evaluation of the story problems then is only to ascertain whether the writing of the story problem excludes the particular concept. An example of primary trait scoring in an English class would be to assess if students had successfully adhered to the format and style of writing an autobiography.

Evaluation Scales

Evaluation scales are the most frequently used evaluation device in the content areas, particularly for primary trait and analytic scoring. They are especially valuable to English, social studies, and science teachers. Points (marks) are assigned for each component in a composition (see Box 8.5 for a scale for expos-

---

Box 8.5
Sample Evaluation Scale

Name: _____   Date: _____

Title of Assignment: _____

CATEGORIES	POSSIBLE POINTS	EARNED POINTS
Content (ideas, principles, interdisciplinary connections)	65	
Vocabulary (specialized, general)	15	
Structure (organization, coherence)	10	
Mechanics (spelling, grammar, punctuation)	10	

Areas of strength:
Areas for improvement:
Specific comments on "how" to improve these areas:

Source: Based on *Toward Literacy: Theory and Applications for Teaching Writing in the Content Areas*, by J.E. Brown, L.B. Phillips, and E.C. Stephens, 1993, Belmont, CA: Wadsworth Publishing Co., p. 145. Reprinted by permission of Wadsworth Publishing Co.

itory writing). The emphasis, or weighting, in scoring will vary. In the example in Box 8.5, the largest portion of points (i.e., 65 percent) is earmarked for the content of the paper (the demonstrated mastery of ideas and principles). Another portion is allocated for the use of specialized vocabulary. The remaining marks are allocated for form, mechanics, and organization (or structure) of the ideas. For each category, students are shown the marks they earned out of the maximum possible. Provision is also made for teacher comments on areas of strength and weakness and any additional comments that would assist the student in improving his or her future expository compositions.

Guidelines for Self-Evaluation in Content Area Writing

Self-evaluation is an important ingredient in portfolio assessment (see also Chapter 11). It is also a helpful device for improving the quality of one's compositions on the basis of guidelines that are known to both student and teacher. An evaluation checklist for students and teachers should be provided to students as they write so that they can "check" their work before they hand it in (see Box 8.6 for an example).

Box 8.6
Evaluation Checklist for Student and Teacher

STUDENT CHECKLIST FOR EVALUATION
1. What was your purpose in writing this paper?
2. Do you feel that you accomplished your purpose? Why or why not?
3. Who is your audience?
4. Is your word choice appropriate for your audience?
5. Did you organize and develop your ideas fully?

TEACHER CHECKLIST FOR EVALUATION
1. The purpose is clear.
2. The paper is appropriate for its audience.
3. The ideas are clear.
4. The ideas are well developed.
5. The paper demonstrates a mastery of content concepts.
6. The paper is well organized.
7. The paper uses appropriate diction.
8. There are no significant mechanical problems.

Source: From *Toward Literacy: Theory and Applications for Teaching Writing in the Content Areas*, by J.E. Brown, L.B. Phillips, and E.C. Stephens, 1993, Belmont, CA: Wadsworth Publishing Co., p. 145. Copyright © 1993 by Wadsworth Publishing Co.

Summary

Writing, like speaking, is a social transaction shaped by culture and social and individual purposes. Writing is fostered by talk, reading aloud, and reading about what one wants to write. Conferencing, discussion, and collaborative activities thus become important in the writing process in the content area classroom.

Two types of reading occur during writing: (1) readers, as first readers of their texts, read during and after reading to shape and focus the writing (the writer as reader is transacting with text); and (2) writers read texts through the eyes of a potential audience (the writer as reader transacts with potential readers).

The two most common types of writing in the secondary classrooms are nontransactive actions. Writing is used for assessment/evaluation and for noncomposing purposes (such as multiple-choice activities, note-taking from dictation, or copying). Traditionally, writing in the classrooms has been misused (i.e., using writing as a form of punishment). More positive types of writing in the content areas are undertaken for efferent purposes. These are: (1) technical or informational writing in a subject area, (2) writing to learn the discourse forms of a discipline, and (3) writing-to-learn activities. Opportunities exist, particularly in writing-to-learn activities, to "write-one's-reading," that is, to describe the meaning generated and the stances taken when making sense out of subject area content. One of the responsibilities of content area teachers is to encourage students to write their reading to enhance the learning of content. Another responsibility is to teach students how to write the content of their discipline using a process approach to enhance writing transactions. Reading and writing activities such as brain racing, questioning, cubing, and autobiographical writing can be used to evoke aesthetic, efferent, and interdisciplinary transactions. Journal writing allows for reflection and can provide opportunities for "writing-one's-reading" as well as for more structured types of responses. Modern technology, particularly computers, are a powerful means to enhance content area writing through free writing, questioning, **collaborative writing**, and the use of software programs to address spelling and bibliographic concerns.

Another content area specialist's responsibility is to teach students to write the discourse of each discipline, including report writing, exposition, argumentation, and narration. Finally, content area teachers need to evaluate, and to invite student self-evaluation of, processes and products in the content areas through the use of holistic methods, analytic and primary trait scoring, and portfolio assessment. Students' writing competence will vary across topics and tasks.

Questions for Further Reflection

1. Taking an aesthetic stance, write about the Oklahoma bombing. Then write about the same topic from an efferent stance. "Read-your-writing" two different ways.
2. Read the text in Box 8.7 and then "write-your-reading." What aesthetic and efferent transactions occurred? What interdisciplinary transactions were evoked?

Box 8.7
Food Irradiation

The foods we eat may have bacterial infections or animal infestations. These could cause the food to spoil, make us sick, or even cause death. More than one-quarter of the world's food production goes to waste because it is destroyed by bacteria, insects, or rodents. Because of the need to avoid food spoilage and protect human health, the food industry and government scientists are continually searching for effective methods of preserving food while keeping it wholesome for us to eat.

Food irradiation is the most recently developed method for food preservation. Salting and drying are methods which are more than one thousand years old, while pickling and freezing have been in use for about 175 years.

Food irradiation is a non-chemical process which preserves food, making it longer-lasting and safer to eat. Many foods can be irradiated without significant change in taste or nutritional value. Irradiation has several beneficial effects. First, it kills the micro-organisms that normally cause food to spoil. Second, irradiation kills micro-organisms and parasites that can cause human illness. Third, irradiation can slow the ripening process of certain fruits and vegetables, and can prevent the sprouting of root vegetables like potatoes and onions.

HOW IS FOOD IRRADIATED?

Food is irradiated in a way that is similar to the way luggage is X-rayed at airports. Food is passed through a thick-walled chamber on a conveyer belt. The chamber contains a source of radiation. The ionizing radiation (gamma rays) from the radioactive source passes through the food, destroying insects, bacteria, and other micro-organisms. Because of the nature of radiation, the food does not have to be removed from its crates or boxes to be treated. Food irradiation does not make the food, or the consumer, radioactive!

(continued)

(continued)

Food irradiation is often done using cobalt-60, an artificial isotope which also has many medical and industrial uses. Cobalt-60 has also made its mark in agriculture. Radiation from this isotope can change the genetic structure of plants and hence their behavior. Two examples of this are faster growing rates and increased crop yields. For some crops, a faster growing rate allows more than one crop to be produced per growing season. In addition, some cereal crops have been found not only to mature faster, but also to produce higher yields after bombardments with radiation.

Source: From *Chemicals in Action*, by T.R. Donovan, M.C. Poole, & D.J. Yack, 1995, Toronto: Holt, Rinehart & Winston of Canada, pp. 426–27.

3. Plan a collaborative writing activity for your content area students.
4. What is your reaction to using computers for content area writing?
5. What two types of journal writing activities would you see as essential in your subject area specialization? Why? How would you incorporate them into your curriculum?
6. What kinds of writing activities do you see as essential in your content area specialization? Why?
7. How would you evaluate writing in your content area? Would you evaluate journal writing if you expected students to do it? Why or why not?

Key Terms

Collaborative writing
Discourse types
Formative evaluation
Free writing
Portfolio assessment

Reading-one's-writing
Structured/prompted journal writing
Summative evaluation
Writing–learning relationship
Writing-one's-reading

CHAPTER NINE

Strategic Learning for Life: Learning to Learn

Questions to Consider for this Chapter

1. What does it mean to become content and/or process literate in your content area? What knowledge, skills, and attributes are required?

2. What knowledge base, learning skills, and inquiry attributes do you think a learner needs to become a strategic reader and a purposeful author in your content area?

3. How would you describe your own present levels of content knowledge, learning skills, and disciplinary attributes as a strategic learner in your content area?

4. What learning strengths do you have in your content area? Across other content areas?

5. How might you strengthen your knowledge, skills, and attributes in your content area? Across other content areas?

Overview

Time awareness dominates our existence. In lived time a minute passed cannot be banked for use tomorrow, nor can a minute be borrowed from yesterday to be used today. Understanding time is important if teachers and learners are to make the best use of each instructional and/or study minute. We know structured institutional learning is governed by time — by schedules, clocks, and calendars. Yet we also know that people learn in different ways, at different rates, for different purposes, and produce different results.

This chapter is dedicated to framing learning strategies for teachers and learners so that they consciously make the best use of their available time.

Learning to become a learner for life involves an awareness of, and teaches the skills to utilize, time and task. Successful learners know when to structure time for specific learning, know how to note what needs to be remembered, and know how to study strategically to prepare for formal and informal assessments. Time and task understanding is a significant factor in a person's successful learning for life.

It has never been possible to learn everything in a subject area. And with ever-increasing explosions in information and knowledge, the likelihood of ever knowing everything in a subject area seems more remote. Therefore, learners, with the help of their teachers, must understand what they need to learn in order to control the proliferation of information they will be expected to know and use. By focussing on the knowledge, skills, and attributes required to fulfil solid learning goals, to take useful notes, to study smart, and to take tests efficiently, learners can learn how to prepare themselves for living and working in the twenty-first century.

Concepts Central to Understanding Learning for Life

1. Learning is a time-framed, recursive, and lifelong engagement.
2. Learning to learn happens in a complex inquiry relationship involving the learner, others, and the world.
3. Learning to learn requires the ability to strategically read context-specific, reflective, and representative texts generated by others.
4. Likewise, learning to learn requires the ability to strategically write context-specific, reflective, and representative texts for others.
5. The knowledge, skills, and attributes associated with learning for life can be shown through the learners' accomplishments.

Reading as the Primary Tool for Learning for Life

To begin a chapter on learning for life requires full recognition of the connections between a learner's ability to read well and his or her ability to be strategically engaged with a task at hand. As Monahan and Hinson (1988) remind us,

Learning is response. . . . People are not blank, absorbent tablets. Instead, a person responds by hunting through his mind for knowledge and understanding he already has to see how he can make the old meaning connect to the new. . . . Of course, as no two people have identical temperaments, perceptions and life experiences, the way one sees, hears, touches, smells, and tastes his world will lead him to a unique point of view and interpretation of the world. [And] . . . Learning is recursive. When one connects a new idea to something familiar in order to make meaning, he may have to go back and verify it, or else connect the idea to something different and rethink. (p. 5)

So, the reading process as described here, and as defined in Chapters 1 and 3 of this textbook, requires a clear recognition from content area teachers that a learner's ability to learn for life depends on a significant pedagogic relationship between a teacher, a learner, and the disciplinary learning task at hand. This teaching/learning/context relationship involves teachers and learners coming together over a commitment to the following:

1. Establishing an authentic learning context such that prior knowledge and background from a learner's life world is advanced.
2. Reading task texts (print, electronic, or visual) so that learners become strategic inquirers into the ideas embedded in a content area.
3. Responding to task texts so that learners generate reflexive, responsive, organized, shared, and reshaped responses.
4. Extending the task text by appropriately advancing a form of demonstrated accomplishment connected to but beyond the initial text encountered.

It is this understanding of reading the world as if it were an intentionally authored text that helps students appreciate the possibilities of learning for life in a content area. The motivating question is, How does a learner, with a teacher, frame time strategically to enable the encountering, experiencing, and engagement with societal/cultural texts that in turn frame real and/or imagined relationships to the world?

For Reflection 9.1

Quickly reread Chapters 1 and 3. Form conversation groups (maximum of four learners) and discuss the following terms: content area literacy, text, reading-to-learn and learning to read, aesthetic reading, efferent reading.

A Little Philosophy Study for Becoming a Learner for Life

There will be a time when you believe everything is finished.
That will be the beginning.

Louis L'Amour

This textbook establishes, especially in Chapters 1 and 3, a particular stance regarding reading. Reading for success in secondary schools or in postsecondary institutions rests on a readiness to learn how to think about and control one's reading with respect to the task at hand, the process strategies involved, and how understanding will be demonstrated. The following section differs in tone from the rest of this chapter and from previous chapters. The difference is due to an attempt to convince the reader of this text of the pedagogic importance of being ready to understand how natural it is to learn to learn.

Readiness to learn in a content area requires a willingness and a commitment by learners to want to engage in learning. Competence, confidence, and desire go together. However, the common reality is that most people find themselves in certain situations where they lack competence, confidence, or desire. That is why learners, at some point, need teachers. It is possible for a teacher to pique a learner's natural interest in the world. It is possible for a teacher to raise the level of a learner's knowledge, skills, and attributes. It is possible for a teacher to motivate a learner to encounter different learning contexts in ways that are purposeful and meaningful. Good teachers possess basic knowledge, skills, and attributes that enable them to read and write the world. Good learners/teachers have a repertoire of learning strategies.

A learner and a teacher must come together to act, interact, and transact strategically with texts, others, and the world. Thus, learners and teachers explore, map, and journey together. But it is the teacher who has been this way before. And what is the philosophic ground for the possibility of studying the world as a pedagogic site to be read efferently and aesthetically? It is simply an awareness that:

1. Learners (and teachers as learners) are naturally *tantalized* by the world, and so teachers must teach from texts to which learners are drawn.
2. Learners naturally seek ways to make sense of the world and beyond in order to show their demonstrated competencies. Teachers must allow learners to show what they already know, what they can already do, and ultimately what they have newly learned.

3. The world is encoded in, through, and by the *texts* that learners and teachers encounter and, indeed, construct through engagements with the world, and so teachers must show learners that the ability to read texts transfers into an ability to read the world.

4. To *tease* meaning out of constructed texts requires the strategic knowledge, skills, and attributes of a consciously learning learner, and so teachers must establish learning environments that lead learners to understand the complex relationships between **task awareness**, **strategy awareness**, and **performance awareness**.

5. If these are conditions for learning, then learners show they are *learners for life* by reading and authoring efferent and aesthetic texts, and so teachers must structure learning environments with ample opportunities for reading–writing connections.

6. Ultimately, there are learning *strategies* available to learners that teachers can teach, and so learners must be prepared to accept a teacher's instruction in order to become strategic learners for life.

To illuminate these points, a little more philosophy:

First, learning to learn is a giving over to an awareness of the world as a contextualized tantalization of learning possibilities. The word *tantalize* comes from the Greek myth of Tantalus, the King of Phrygia. Tantalus was often a guest at the gods' table, but he revealed the gods' secrets to mortals. The gods condemned him to stand, naked, up to his chin in water. Whenever he lowered his head to drink, the water retreated. Whenever he reached for fruit-laden branches overhead, they receded. As learners already deeply immersed in the world, is it not part of our natural desire that our reach exceed our grasp? Are we not already in a condition whereby we learn from our errors in judgement? So how is it possible to have before you learners who have seemingly given up on learning about themselves or the world? A cheap response is they have been taught to. But there does exist an array of tantalizing experiences a reach away.

Second, embedded in tantalizing learning environments are the tools that enable learners to be strategic about how to achieve a desired goal. Another Greek tale will illuminate! There was an office in ancient Greece called the

---

For Reflection 9.2

Take a moment to recall an experience in which you tried for something you felt was unattainable. If you eventually reached your goal, what did you learn about yourself? If you didn't attain your goal, what did you learn about yourself? Share your story with others.

For Reflection 9.3

With respect to learning a concept in your content area, briefly describe, in outline form, a strategic learning/teaching plan. How would specific learning tactics or skills be part of your strategic learning/teaching plan? Be prepared to discuss your plan with your peers.

"Strategus." This office housed a commander-in-chief, or chief magistrate. The strategus was responsible for a "strategy," which was a government or province given to his command. To strategize was to direct large community operations. A strategy differed from a "tactic" in that a tactic was seen as a mechanical movement of bodies, whereas a strategy was a learning/teaching plan that utilized tactics. A strategy, then, was a complex, artful design for a multitude of manoeuvres. It was a conscious plan designed to solve problems. Unlike the contemporary understanding of strategy as an "arming" of learners with tactics — as if learning were a military exercise — the true root of the word shows that learning is a strategic enterprise, not a tactical operation.

Third, once there is a readiness to be tantalized by a wonderfully mysterious world, and an understanding about why one needs to be strategic in achieving a desired learning goal, learning to learn also requires an understanding of the word "tease." In the contemporary world, teasing has become associated with the notion of worry or irritation. But teasing is also an ancient word. It is originally associated with the art of weaving. A tool called a teasel was used to separate fibres in preparation for spinning. This teasel technology mimicked plants like Fuller's teasel or wild teasel, which have prickles for flowers. The weaver's teasel was used to comb out rough fibres before spinning as well as to dress cloth after weaving. Dressed cloth was teased to raise the nap. A learner must live in the world as a teasel seeking to utilize strategies, technologies, or tools to tease out the text(ures) of the world.

Fourth, the focus for learning to learn should not only be on a learner. Learning is about learning something — content. And in most cases content is embedded in text — especially the content area text. The word "text" has been used from the beginning of this textbook. In this chapter — contextually — the meaning of the word "text" flows from the Old English word *textus*. Text understood in this way is a tissue, a web, or markings of any kind — signs, signatures, tracings, leavings, indeed any fibrous material. A text is not only the wording, the structure, or the rhetorical arrangement of words into sentence units. A text is an intentionally composed, tissued embodiment of the possibilities and actualities of human thought and action. Texts may be pictures without words, words without pictures, sights and sounds, collages, paintings, music videos, computer graphics, graffiti, designer coffee cups, T-shirts, bumper stickers, marks on paper, on the Earth, in the sky and underground, novels, of course, and film, television, banners, cards, and anonymous notes — even content area textbooks. Understood in this way, a text does not exclude learners, nor does it isolate them as only consumers. Rather, learners are part of life's textual transactions created when readers/authors, words/images, and texts meet. Learning to learn is about being ready to strategically tease out meaning making by reading and authoring text(ure)s.

This little "philosophy session" has served to establish how exciting and natural it is to read and write the world efferently and aesthetically as a learner. Learners are born into the tantalizing enjoyment of learning something new so that grasp and reach, expectation and attainment, do connect — if only momentarily. It is this feeling of "getting it" that leads to more learning — and thus a purposeful learning for life. New concepts, skills, ideas, or even the discovery of previous learning made anew when used in a different situation, are all exciting. What reluctant learners must see and experience is how successfully motivated learners engage with a learning task. There is much to be taught while in the service of learning. This positioning regarding learning then must include the pragmatics of successful teaching. To reach the condition of being a self-motivated learner, reluctant learners need a teacher, to be taught strategy systems, in order to successfully complete specific tasks. The pedagogic demand, however, remains. The goal of strategic teaching is to move learners from being externally motivated and reward-dependent, to becoming internally motivated, autonomous, self-rewarding participants in their own learning and in that of others.

To review:

1. Learners are tantalized by the essence of learning — to reach beyond this for that.
2. Learners must know that there are strategies of attainment available.
3. Learners need to use strategies to tease out and make meaning, which, in turn, leads the learner on to increasing depth, sophistication, and efficiency.
4. Learners need to know that the world is a textual space. Texts are transactional reflections and representations of the world. Learners must strategically learn to read and author texts in order to have a meaningful place in the world.
5. Teachers need to be participants in a learner's learning.

For Reflection 9.4

Think about why you want to teach learners in your content area. Write a 50-word philosophy statement, to be read by others not in your content area, stating the essence of your desire to teach in your content area. Be prepared to share your response.

The Need for Strategic Awareness

Time teaches all things.

Aeschylus

Teachers must teach learners to be strategic, that is, teach learners to control their own learning. Learners must know when and how as well as why they should utilize learning strategies. In this textbook many strategies have been offered to prepare learners to face content (before reading), to guide learning of content (during reading), and to build upon content (after reading). All learning strategies as such must provide for a gradual increase in a learner's ability to do something. Only in this way will learners be able to discipline themselves as learners for life.

A large part of this learning process is the philosophical and pragmatic awareness that it is a teacher who invites a learner to believe learning strategies are essential for reading and writing texts. So this chapter emphasizes the awareness of learning strategically. Without an awareness of a larger strategic picture, a learner may accept the teaching of strategies for learning, but then fail to utilize them. Learning for life as a strategic learner is about transferring learning skills between contexts and tasks. Strategic learning is certainly about learning in a specific situation. For example, many well-defined **note-taking** systems are available to learners. But a system itself doesn't guarantee that learners will use it well or, even if the system is used well, that it will suit the needs of a specific learner. There is no magic in the tactic of note-taking. The magic is in the learner's awareness that as a learning strategy note-taking is needed because it is connected to a larger picture of success. Teachers must directly teach and model the use of strategies for learning in order for learners to know when to use them. Effective instruction is the teaching of knowing what a strategy is, why it will work in this or that case, how it should be used properly, and, most importantly, when it should be used.

A common challenge for learners at the secondary level is to organize learning activities, such as identifying, selecting, and using appropriate task strategies, while being metacognitively aware. Being metacognitive involves the ability to think about and control one's own learning (Baker & Brown,

---

For Reflection 9.5

What have you noticed about successful learners when they encounter an unfamiliar text or task? Do you feel that successful learners are strategic learners? What does "strategic" mean to you in this context?

For Reflection 9.6

When you read, do you underline, or take notes, or fold back pages, or photocopy text sections, or electronically scan text and then produce notes on the computer? If you do, then you already know about making task awareness, strategy awareness, and performance awareness decisions. Explain how you learned to do this.

1984; Brown, 1980). Essential to this notion of control is a learner's awareness of (1) task awareness, (2) strategy awareness, and (3) performance awareness (Reynolds, Wade, Trathen, & Lapan, 1989). And what is common about each form of metacognition, beyond the fact that they are deeply integrated and recursive, is the word "awareness."

Why teach awareness? Simply, it is the bottom line for learning for life. Only by knowing what to do, how best to do it, when to do it, and why it should be done, as well as by knowing if it has made a difference with the task at hand, will learners be empowered to name themselves as successful learners for life.

To review:

1. Learners must understand the world as a space riddled with tantalizing, teasing textual expressions, representations, and reflections that are intentionally authored and, therefore, require purposeful reading and study.
2. Learners must understand that there are strategies available to enhance their abilities to read, study, and, thus, write texts.
3. Learners must be aware that teachers can offer strategies in order to increase learning transfer across different contexts.
4. Learners need to learn to value what they are being taught and what they teach themselves and eventually will teach others.

Then,

1. Teachers must govern their professional expectations in accordance with a learner's present needs and future desires.
2. Teachers must have the knowledge, skills, and attributes associated with a discipline (content) and must act as passionate disciples of the content they know well.
3. Teachers must know how and when to bring learners to a metacognitive awareness of the learning process.

And finally, assuming both learners and teachers come together over a learning task, both must:

For Reflection 9.7
How will you raise learner awareness of task, strategy, and performance metacognitions in your content area? Formulate a strategic plan. Be prepared to share it with your peers.

---

1. Come to an understanding of the specific task awareness.
2. Agree on how best to engage the task through strategy awareness.
3. Know that learning to learn is grounded in knowing when to extend the learning into action via performance awareness.

Learning-for-Life Strategies

This chapter honours a strategic approach to learning that is both attitudinal and procedural. Obviously, attitude has been stressed so far. Procedurally, the strategies to be advanced incorporate *schemata* research (the mechanism by which people access what they know and match it to the information in a text) and *metacognition* research (including self-knowledge and self-regulation of task knowledge). This chapter now moves directly to an awareness of some of the learning requirements for encountering content area instruction in the contemporary world. As a learner for life, learners need to be aware of: (1) **goal-setting**, (2) note-taking, (3) studying smart, and (4) **test-taking**.

Goal-Setting

Life is busy. In fact, there are those who claim that living at the end of the twentieth century has become hyper-real. Almost every aspect of living in the world is time-driven or time-motivated. In order to be successful as a lifelong learner, one must be aware that planning ahead is required. Learners must be presented with an awareness of the importance of controlling time through goal-setting.

The key steps in controlling one's time in order to set and obtain goals are:

1. Set a concrete, pragmatic goal.
2. Establish a time/action plan to accomplish the goal.
3. Implement and execute the plan.
4. Understand the value of feedback with respect to the process of attaining the goal.

This goal-setting process seems simple enough. However, while goal-setting and time management seem to be on everyone's agenda, few do it well. Why? Most people fail to plan carefully because they misunderstand what goal-setting is. Goals are motivators for accomplishing what needs to be done in a specific time frame. To establish a goal and to meet it within a specific time period is very important because it establishes a successful pattern. Therefore, make sure that time is available to devote to the goal. Time must be managed carefully. If this is possible, achieving the goal should provide a learner with more time. As well, the goal must be worthwhile and authentic. It must be a learner's goal and not one imposed by others.

To use effective goal-setting, learners must provide a positive, concrete direction for their energies, and obtain feedback on how well they are progressing/learning. Therefore, a goal itself should:

1. emphasize what a learner is doing and de-emphasize the outcome of the event;
2. be measurable and very specific;
3. be realistic and challenging;
4. be stated positively;
5. be framed at different levels — for example, short-term (daily), intermediate (weekly-monthly), or long-term (yearly or over several years); and
6. be made explicit — that is, be written down.

With more to do in our lives and seemingly less time to do it, goal-setting seems to be a required strategy for the twenty-first century.

Most people go to bed each night with the goal of getting up each morning. We are goal-setting creatures. We set goals each and every day. It is a human strength. Teachers must model a positive, active goal-setting strategy for content area learners.

To review:

1. In the late twentieth century, time management and goal-setting are more important than ever.
2. As goal-setting and goal-attaining creatures, learners naturally use the laws of cause and effect. If the cause is missing, misidentified, or misguided, then the effect is reduced. Goal-setting requires being conscious about the

---

For Reflection 9.8

Try to write a positive, concrete goal for yourself. Then outline a time/action plan with a feedback mechanism to show how you would know if the goal was attained.

task at hand. Specific actions are required, with progress monitored, and persistence rewarded. Can teachers teach that? Will you?

3. Teachers should model and teach goal-setting.

Note-Taking

If this textbook is being used in a class, and if you are a student in that class, are you taking notes from a content area textbook or from a class lecture/presentation? If you are, you may be alone. Very few students seem to take advantage of taking notes.

In 1983, Carol Carrier reviewed the extensive research on note-taking and concluded that students who take notes learn more than those who simply listen in class. Carrier indicates that note-takers seem to be more active as learners. They get closer to the content. They select, interpret, and connect information. And when students review their notes systematically they seem to do better on examinations than those who do not. In 1988, Kiewra and Frank found that note-takers who took their own notes, those who took notes using a skeletal format, and those who followed detailed notes performed similarly on an examination. And students who studied detailed notes scored higher on factual recall tests when given a chance to review. Kiewra and Frank claim that notes serve as a record of lectures for future reference. The problem is that most students record less than half the important elements of a lecture/class presentation. However, until the texts of all lessons and classes are made fully available to students — and that may happen with voice-activated computing techniques — note-taking still has some advantages. Remember that audiotaping a lecture is often impractical, and listening to it again too time-consuming.

Carrier (1988) claims that note-taking will be successful if teachers take time in the first class to frame note-taking as an expectation. Then teachers must provide information about how to take notes. Remember that even a slow speaker can speak at 100 words per minute; a note-taker can record only 20 words a minute. Effective structured talking and listening, then, is at the core of good note-taking. And using a systematic, strategic approach to note-taking enhances a learner's ability to take and then review notes.

For Reflection 9.9

Did you take notes as a learner in your content area? If yes, why? If no, why not? Do you think that note-taking has much value in your content area?

One prominent method of note-taking is the **Cornell note-taking system** as developed by Pauk (1988). To prepare for note-taking using this method, learners should use a large, loose-leaf paper notebook, using only one side for note-taking, and draw a retrieval format (for example, a note-taking column and a recall or review column).

Before note-taking in class, learners must develop a mind-set for active listening, and should:

1. Test themselves with previous lecture materials;
2. Skim any relevant set-up or pre-reading materials; and
3. Make sure they are physically and mentally alert (for example, eating if necessary).

During the class and while note-taking, learners should take the following steps:

1. Listen for clues to the content structure and the information the speaker deems important.
2. Pay attention to the speaker's physical, oral, and visual clues to indicate important points.
3. Try to resist distractions or mental wandering during note-taking.
4. Be consistent in note-taking form and in the use of abbreviations.
5. Skip a line on note-taking paper to show a break in thought.
6. If inconsistencies in the notes are discovered, attempt to correct them as soon as possible.
7. Label, tag, or colour-code points that are important.
8. If possible, ask questions for clarification.

After the class, the note-takers should do the following:

1. Attempt to clear up any questions by asking the speaker or audience peers.
2. Read the notes taken and make them more legible if necessary. Fill in missing points or correct misunderstandings.
3. Edit the notes for clarity, label all the main points, add details from memory, and highlight important points.
4. Use the recall or recovery column and summarize as a response to the notes taken.
5. Cover the note-taking column and study from the recovery or recall column summary. Test yourself immediately after the summary has been written.
6. Periodically review the notes and the summary and test yourself.

Some helpful formats for recording notes are provided in Box 9.1. (The directed note-taking activity was discussed in Chapter 8.)

Box 9.1
Sample Note-Taking Formats

Edit & summarize notes here	Text notes recorded here	Reflections, ideas, and relevant questions here

Edit & summarize notes here	Text notes recorded here
Reflections, ideas, and relevant questions here	

If content area teachers want to enhance their learners' note-taking skills, they can provide an overview of the lecture using an advanced organizer, graph, map, or chart. Tag important ideas, points, or headings and make them explicit (visually or orally). Pace is important — a teacher can talk faster than students can write. Take pauses. Check for comprehension. Ask questions. Ask for a response from the audience. Use a chalkboard or overhead projector to reinforce important or difficult points. If the content lends itself, create and distribute a skeletal outline. Link current work to previous and future topics. Review the content at the conclusion of the class. Besides class note-taking, teachers often ask learners to take notes from texts. This can take the form of summaries, questions, paraphrasing, or précis writing.

One way to help students develop note-taking skills is the guided lecture procedure (GLP), devised by Kelly and Holmes (1979). The steps are:

1. Before the class starts, the teacher writes the class objectives/goals (maximum of three or four) on the chalkboard or overhead projector. New terminology, if any, is also defined.
2. Learners set up a notebook and copy this information into their notes. This locates a class purpose, sets expectations, and begins the process of note-taking.
3. The teacher begins and speaks for 30 minutes. Learners actively listen without taking notes.
4. The teacher stops. The learners have five to ten minutes to write down everything they feel was important in the teacher's talk. Learners are encouraged to categorize and relate ideas in terms of time/space, cause-effect, problem-solution, comparison-contrast, or definition-example.
5. Learners then form groups of three or four. Each learning group is asked to talk about the lesson and reorganize notes accordingly. If a group needs help, they consult the teacher.
6. As a homework assignment, learners reflect on individual and revised notes.
7. In the next class learners are asked to write from memory a piece of text covering the main points of the teacher's talk, drawing their own conclusions. This procedure helps learners develop higher-order skills and long-term memory.

Pauk (1978) once asked, "Why take notes?" His answer: because we forget. Half of the material read or heard in class is soon forgotten. A systematic approach to note-taking based on active listening and direct teaching helps provide learners with skills for needed recall.

Studying Smart

Whether to satisfy curiosity, to prepare for an event, to fulfil a formal research request, or to complete an assigned task, learners must be able to engage in appropriate forms of study. Learners must be able to understand and engage in a complex set of inquiry and study activities (Baker and Brown, 1984;

For Reflection 9.10

Try a guided lecture procedure using content from your discipline. Try the procedure with learners from a different content area. What do you think you might learn about your presentation effectiveness, your audience's note-taking abilities, and how your audience might do if tested on the material covered?

Brown, 1980). When learners show they know what to study, how to study, and when to study, they are study smart. Such learners know where to find and how to use appropriately the various processes associated with three aspects of the concept of study: study skills, study strategies, and study systems.

Devine (1991), in a chapter entitled "Studying: Skills, Strategies, and Systems," outlines three aspects of the concept of study:

> The term *study skills* has come to embrace a wide variety of competencies associated with academic learning, from taking lecture notes to writing a library research paper. . . . A smaller number of these skills may be better viewed as *study strategies* that directly promote comprehension, retention in memory, and the ability to demonstrate learning. . . . Teachers and researchers have sometimes combined two or more of these specific strategies as *study systems* on the grounds that related strategies when used together somehow become more effective. . . . All three — study skills, study strategies, and study systems — are bound by a common goal; each is intended to assist students to learn on their own. They are suggested as aids for independent learning, for student use rather than teacher use. (p. 743)

Many of these skills, strategies, and systems have been outlined in previous chapters of this book.

A good study system is often the result of a learner's use of specific skills and strategies. Such use is the result of being study smart. Using a good study system is also evidence that learners understand that it is relatively difficult to move through life without some strategic learning systems in place; for example, being able to define, preview, note-take, outline, or summarize. However, people seldom recognize the detailed operations of strategies they use. To teach learners to be study smart begins with helping them develop the metacognitive awareness that will enable them to be more successful and to become increasingly independent learners.

There are many textbooks, handbooks, and guidebooks available to promote study skills, strategies, and systems that offer ways for learners to become independent inquirers (for example, see Bragstad & Stumpf, 1987; Devine, 1987; Graham & Robinson, 1984; Kahn, 1984; Palmer & Pope, 1984). Although several of these publications are concerned with research and theory, most focus on the procedural aspects of using study skills and strategies and suggest ways that teachers may develop these in students.

Devine categorizes the existing research on study skills. Specific strategies include the following:

- Previewing, overviewing, or surveying
- Questioning
- Underlining, underscoring, or highlighting
- Note-taking

- Outlining, traditional and free-form; and recent variations such as mapping, graphing, networking, array-outlining, and pyramid outlines
- Summarizing

Some of these strategies are discussed in Chapters 6 and 7.

Devine (1991) lists the following study systems that have been mentioned prominently in the research literature:

- SQ3R (Robinson, 1970) — Survey, Question, Read, Recite, and Review
- PQRST (Staton, 1954) — Preview, Question, Read, State, and Test
- Triple S Technique (Farquhar, Krumboltz, & Wrenn, 1960) — Scan, Search, Summarize
- OARWET (Norman & Norman, 1968) — Overview, Achieve, Write, Evaluate, Test
- OK5R (Pauk, 1974) — Overview, Key Idea, Read, Record, Recite, Review, Reflect
- PQ4R (Thomas & Robinson, 1972) — Preview, Question, Read, Reflect, Recite, Review
- S4R (Stetson, 1981) — Survey, Read, Recite, Record, Review
- PQ5R (Graham and Robinson, 1984) — Preview Question, Read, Record, Recite, Review, Reflect
- ERICA (Stewart-Dore, 1982) — Effective Reading in Content Areas involving preparing for reading, thinking through information, extracting and organizing information, and translating information
- SRUN (Bailey, 1988) — Survey, Read, Underline, and Take Notes
- HEART (Santeusanio, 1988) — How much do I know about this topic? Establish a purpose for study? Ask questions as study? Record answers? Test self?
- PORPE (Simpson et al., 1988) — Predict, Organize, Rehearse, Practice, and Evaluate
- PSRT (Simons, 1989) — Prepare, Structure, Read, and Think

If you are hooked up to the Internet, the Virginia Polytechnic Institute and State University, University Counseling Center, maintains a web site entitled "Study Skills Self-Help Information" (http://www.ucc.vt.edu). There are many similar web sites at other learning institutions across North America, including the University of Toronto (http://www.campuslife.utoronto.ca/Handbook/learning/studyskills.html) or the University of North Carolina (http://www.unc.edu/depts/ucc/TenTraps.html).

This section on studying smart has been written to show what is presently available in terms of research and practices for study skills, study strategies, and study systems. In an attempt to be consistent with the belief that learners learn by doing, you have the opportunity to engage in a study of what will work for you in your content area. No learner can do this work for you and make you the kind of teacher you aspire to be.

> **For Reflection 9.11**
> Have you used any of the study systems listed on page 293? Under what circumstances did you learn them? Class participants should select a system that they feel would work with their content areas. Investigate that system. Be prepared to present your findings to the rest of the class.

Test-Taking

Academic testing is similar to most of the tests one faces over a lifetime. Most testing establishes individual and group standards of performance, provides critical feedback, and ultimately shows the measure of successful learning. And, as in life, successful academic test-taking is linked to the understanding of how much of one's learning is attitudinal. As such, this chapter begins with the issue of testing anxiety before moving on to strategies for the successful taking of **essay tests**, **problem-solving tests**, and **objective tests** (**multiple-choice**, **true-false**, and **matching**).

Tests are a specific measure of what students have learned. Tests also measure a student's ability to take tests. If tests are deeply connected to testable material, a learner needs to know the material — the disciplinary content. In addition, there are skills a learner can acquire to overcome anxieties about test-taking. (See also Chapter 11.)

Test anxiety is that feeling of distress, anguish, or agitation we experience before and often during a testing situation. Although anxiety can keep people mentally and physically alert, it can also be disabling. Learners may experience increased heart rates, muscle spasms, or excessive perspiration. They may experience an inability to act, make decisions, or express themselves. In a testing situation, a learner may have difficulty reading or understanding the questions, organizing thoughts, or even remembering previously learned material.

Anxiety can result from any number of factors: lack of preparation, inadequate time management, lack of goal-setting, poor study strategies, inadequate note-taking, or lack of opportunities to practise with content. Adequate preparation seems to be a significant factor in reducing test anxiety.

> **For Reflection 9.12**
> Have you ever felt anxiety while studying for a test? This is called "anticipatory anxiety." Have you ever felt anxious while writing a test? This is called "situational anxiety." What did you do to overcome these feelings of anxiety?

Strategies for Successful Test-Taking

Strategies for successful test-taking fall into three categories: preparing for a test, taking the test, and analyzing a returned test.

1. There are two elements to consider when preparing learners for a test. The first element involves the issue of test anxiety. If teachers have learners experiencing test anxiety, then they need to help those learners better prepare themselves for a testing situation. In addition to presenting the material in interesting and informative ways, stressing note-taking and regular and participatory reviewing, and teaching a study system, a teacher can also teach stress reduction management techniques such as deep breathing exercises, muscle relaxing exercises, or using guided imagery.

   The second element to consider in general test preparation involves familiarizing learners with the testing context and the test content. Teachers must teach learners to do the following:

   - Ask questions about the test beforehand.
   - Review, individually and in groups, key concepts, issues, or problems deemed testable.
   - Review any previous tests from a test file bank, if available.
   - Use memory skill games and self-testing to refamiliarize oneself with course materials.
   - Try compare or contrast arrangements with testable concepts, ideas, or problems.
   - Try to apply testable principles, or theories, or solve practice problems and predict possible outcomes.
   - Review the work to be done to prepare for the test and establish a review schedule.
   - Establish learning goals as soon as possible after the test date is assigned.
   - Read unread materials and review previously read materials.
   - Integrate notes, texts, and information into summary sheets using diagramming, charting, outlining, categorizing in tables, or writing out concise summaries.

   If the test is problem-driven, then set up problems to be solved. If the test is an essay test, then draft writing attempts under time limitations. If you were making up the text, what would you ask? If possible, find other students to study with and use visuals to clarify difficult concepts and to add additional information to study notes.

2. Taking tests and doing well on tests requires a solid understanding of the subject content and sound test-taking skills, but equally important is a good test-taking attitude. That being so, a learner should follow these general rules:

- Be rested and arrive at the test site ready with the necessary materials.
- If possible, arrive at the test site early and choose a desirable seat.
- When the test is handed out, use the back of the test paper or a scrap of paper to jot down all the information that might be forgotten.
- Review the whole test before answering any one question and make sure the test is complete.
- Plan time wisely. Which questions have the most marks? Remember to allocate enough time at the end of the test time for review.
- Start with easier questions and move on to the harder ones. Face anything unfamiliar by reading closely and using the question's context as a lead, if possible. Read the question as it is. Avoid overanalyzing or oversimplifying the question. Accept the question as stated.

3. When analyzing a returned test, identify the reasons questions were answered incompletely or incorrectly. Check the level of response expectation in relation to your responses. Note where the test's primary focus was located; was the test primarily based on lectures, readings, assignments, or labs?

Test-taking is something many teachers fail to deal with in any extensive way with learners. They assume content reviews are sufficient preparation for testing, or that preparation is the responsibility of learners. Teachers must think of testing as one more opportunity to teach and treat the task of preparing for the test as a pedagogic experience for the learner.

Testing takes many forms. However, the three broad categories of tests that dominate academic work are the essay test, the problem-solving test, and the objective test. Each of these categories of testing has its own means of assessing strengths and weaknesses. Nevertheless, there are several test awareness issues common across the categories of testing. These common issues fall into the generic categories of preparing for the test, taking the test, and analyzing the results of the test.

Essay Tests

The essay test requires learners to respond in a structurally and functionally organized way that attempts to explain, describe, analyze, or narrate. Often an essay response combines one or more of these prose types. In responding in an essay form, the learners may do so in one of two ways: a long-answer or extended-response format, or a short-answer or limited-response format. If the response is long or extended, then the response is assessed for the learner's writing skills and ability to retrieve and organize ideas in a limited time period. If the response is short or limited, then the learner is assessed primarily on the content mastered.

In preparing for an essay test, the learner should attempt the following:

- Review the course syllabus and write down the course objectives stated or implied. Look for relationships between course topics and note if themes recur. Try to generate possible essay questions from the course outline.
- Review the course assignments, readings, texts, and notes. From those materials, try to determine what the major themes are and if they support or challenge the themes generated in the course outline. Modify and refine a generated themes list as more information is added. Create a sheet of relevant information from texts that support the themes being generated.
- Always look for relationships among topics. The generated themes list should invite active searching for information on possible topics in the time limits set for studying. Topics lead to themes, and themes are a primary focus of essay tests.

A procedure like PORPE (Simpson, 1986) is a specific aid to learners preparing to write essay tests. The steps of PORPE are:

1. Predict. Construct potential essay questions. Locate them in course readings, texts, materials, or lectures. Use the same words that would be used on a real essay test, such as explain, compare, or analyze.
2. Organize. Organize the information necessary to respond to the question. This can be done with charts, diagrams, lists, and so on.
3. Rehearsal. Over several days, memorize required content through retention exercises, recitation, and self-testing.
4. Practice. In detail, write out the answers to the predicted questions.
5. Evaluate. Judge the accuracy and completeness of the answers, and perhaps share the evaluation with a peer for critical feedback.

When taking the essay test, learners should do the following:

- Read all the test instructions and essay questions quickly once before beginning any response.
- Jot down response ideas on scratch paper as the questions are reviewed.
- Be aware of time constraints when plotting a response strategy. Make sure the time spent on a question is commensurate with the marks allocated.
- Always allow time for proofreading.
- Reread each essay question and underline key words and ideas, like *compare, define, justify, describe, relate,* or *explain*.
- Begin with the essay question that seems the easiest.
- Create a diagram or schematic (a blueprint-like drawing showing process or organization), a chart, or a graph that will hold information that facilitates a response.
- State a specific thesis statement as a direct response to each question asked.

- Provide both general and specific information in the response as required. Use examples, facts, illustrations, or details as required. Use the vocabulary of the content area.
- Try to leave spaces for additions to the response by writing on every other line and on only one side of the page. Write clearly and legibly. If a question is particularly difficult, brainstorm about it on scrap paper. Try to recall specific readings, lectures, or discussions on the topic and write these images/ideas down.
- At the end of the self-imposed time for a given question, move to the next. Partially answering all the questions required is better than fully answering only some. If time is running out, write a response plan in outline form. The instructor should take this attempt into consideration.
- Quickly reread the responses before time is called. Make any additions or deletions necessary for completeness or clarity. Check for mechanics (grammar, spelling, and punctuation) and style.

When essay tests are returned, the learners should read all comments and suggestions, not just the grade attached. Did most of the information the tester expected come from lectures, texts, outside readings, or course discussions? As well, the learners should try to determine the source of their errors. Was it misreading the question? Inadequate preparation? Anxiety? Writing skills? Lack of detail? Problems with thought patterns? Difficulty with style or correctness? This information can be used on the next essay test in this subject area.

Problem-Solving Tests

Problem-solving tests are designed for learners to show an understanding of and the ability to apply specific content concepts, organize theories in relation to each other, use specific formulas, and apply particular definitions, etc., in a method-solution format. By posing problems, the tester asks learners to show competence in a taught method of solution finding, critical thinking, or case study work.

In preparing for problem-solving tests, a learner begins by reviewing course notes and texts. Then learners should:

- list the major concepts and/or formulas covered before the test period;
- highlight those topics and problems that were emphasized in class; and
- prepare by solving problems, as many as possible.

Therefore, learners must also analyze all the problems presented in the course for key concepts, specific formulas, or governing rules and solution methods used. The learners should ask themselves, how is the problem presented — visually, in words, or numerically? Also, can the approach to the problem be simplified? In a narrative form, the learners should write a note beside each problem-solving step explaining their reasoning. As well, learners should practise working problems in random sequences in order to prevent themselves from settling into fixed solution patterns, and work within a time limit to simulate test conditions.

While taking the test, learners should jot down all the formulas, relationships, and definitions they remember. They should read the test instructions, then the questions, and then develop a plan. If anything leaps to mind, it should be noted beside the appropriate question. As well, learners should:

- Leave enough time for the higher-value questions and reserve time at the end for reviewing the work.
- Start with the easiest problems. For the more troublesome ones, the problems should be reread carefully.
- Mark key words. Identify givens and unknowns in their own words.
- Sketch a diagram to anticipate the form and characteristics of a solution.
- List the possible formulas that might be relevant to the solution. If no solution method seems evident, then write out an equation to express the relationship among all the givens and unknowns.
- For more difficult problems, think back to similar problems and design a simpler version of this problem that could be solved. Substitute simple numbers for unknowns to reduce the amount of abstract thinking required. Break the problem down into a series of smaller problems. Work each part, building up to a solution.
  - Also, it might help to guess at an answer and work backwards and check it. This will possibly suggest a problem-solving method.
  - If everything else fails, then leave the problem and come back to it later. There may be clues in other problems on the test.
- For all problems (easy or hard), once a solution method is chosen, follow it carefully.
- Check each step for consistency in notation.
- Document the work carefully and write legibly.
- Evaluate all the solutions. Check answers against the original problems to make sure they seem plausible.
- If time runs out, try to gain partial credit by setting up a problem plan even if it can't be carried through. This gives the teacher something to work with.

In analyzing a returned problem-solving test, the procedures are very similar to those used for the returned essay test. The learner should simply:

- Read all the grader's comments and suggestions.
- Locate the source of the test errors. Look for carelessness, misreading of questions, anxiety, poor time use, or problems not practised.
- Locate the source of the test problems by reviewing lectures, notes, labs, texts, or discussions. Then note any transformations in the problems from

a class or lab context to the test format. Again, this information may be useful for a later test.

For problem-solving tests it is important that learners use these general rules of test-taking to develop their own schema for problem-solving. This schema should include the following question organizers:

1. Do I understand the problem?

   - Have I read for what is given and what is being asked?
   - Have I checked for any word or phrase clues that I do not understand, and are there any hidden assumptions at work that contain information I need in order to proceed?

2. How will I solve the problem?

   - In making a plan I should consider making a diagram, simulating the problem, making a chart, using a formula, writing a number sentence, breaking the problem into its elemental parts, or guessing at an answer and testing it.

3. In carrying out the plan, have I asked myself the following:

   - Am I getting somewhere? Do I need to modify or revise the plan? Am I keeping track of what I am doing so that there is evidence of success or needed revision?

4. Was I successful?

   - Is my answer reasonable, and can I explain or defend the solution in terms of processes and results?

Objective Tests

Objective tests measure one's ability to remember facts and figures as well as relationships among items of information. Test-takers must prepare themselves to think at a high level of critical reasoning and be able to make fine discriminations to determine the best possible answer. The most common forms of objective testing are multiple-choice questions, true-false questions, and matching tests.

To do well on such tests, learners must be familiar with the content area material and know how to interpret the test-maker's intentions. A learner must be able to distinguish the differences and similarities among ideas, facts, theories, or other observations.

To prepare for objective tests, review the notes, texts, and readings, and list the major concepts that have been covered. Highlight topics that seem to dominate the course. Try to note why they are stressed. Think about the vocabulary of the course. Every field has its own disciplinary vocabulary. Create flash cards or memory games to remember the vocabulary. Treat the vocabulary as if you were learning a second language. Do as much comparison and contrast with course materials as possible. Set up charts, graphics, tables, and lists to test yourself. Seek precision in your materials. Set up 15–20-minute intensive review sessions. Set a timer and then put aside the materials and write out as much as you can recall.

When writing an objective test, begin by jotting down facts or details you are still trying to remember. Look the test over and make a plan. If information comes to your mind, jot it down. Read the instructions carefully. Look for time limits. Some objective tests still use right-minus-wrong formulas. Understand how the test will be graded. Begin with the section that is accorded the highest marks. Pace is important, so work quickly. Avoid over- or under-reading the question. Interpret objective test questions literally. To find key words in questions, look for responses to the What, Who, Where, When, Why, and How questions.

Multiple-Choice Tests. Multiple-choice questions make up the most common form of objective tests. These types of exams feature a question or statement (the stem), followed by three to five choices (distracters) from which the student must select the correct answer(s). The questions test memory of facts, details, procedures, and vocabulary as well as comprehension skills and problem-solving abilities. To face such a test, read the stem as if it were detached from everything else. Try to anticipate the phrase that would complete the request. Read each choice even if the first one seems to fit. There may be a better choice. Also, it may be helpful to read the stem and answer choices as if they were true-false statements. If the choice makes the completed statement false, cross it out. Be aware of words like *not*, *but*, and *except*. These words indicate a directionality and/or limit to the question. Words like *always*, *never*, and *only* must be read as if there are no exceptions. If two choices seem correct, then judge them against each other; usually the one with the more complete information is the correct answer. For some questions, more than one choice may be the correct answer.

True-False Questions. True-false tests have only two possible answers. Usually these tests focus on details. In order for a statement to be true, it must be so 100 percent of the time; every part of the question must be true. True-false questions often contain built-in distracters in selected use of phrases and words — words like *some*, *usually*, and *not frequently* usually indicate true statements. However, be careful to interpret each distracter as a specific single case. Part of the detailed reading required of answering true-false is in understanding the purposeful mismatching of details by the tester.

Matching Tests. In matching tests, the information is normally presented in two lists or columns, and learners must match an item from the first column to a corresponding item in the second. Matching tests are designed

---

For Reflection 9.13

There are many forms of evaluation and assessment (see Chapter 11 for the distinction between the two terms). What traditional forms of testing have you experienced as a learner? Which ones do you value as learning experiences? How did your teachers prepare you for testing? How will you prepare your learners for testing in your content area?

---

to assess learners' understandings of associations and relationships within a single topic. That being so, in matching tests there is usually:

- One match allowed per item — once an item is eliminated, it is not re-used.
- A common relationship to all included items. If one column contains item X, then the opposite column contains the relational and necessary complement. For example, one column names capital cities, the other provinces.

In summary, to be test-wise as a learner is to have a strategic plan for being prepared and ready to take a test. Test-wise learners know how to prepare for tests in terms of both content and process. Such learners are confident about their test knowledge, skills, and attributes. They can face the anxiety issues around testing. Teachers, however, must take testing seriously as an opportunity to teach learners about test-construction, test-taking, and post-test analysis. It is the content area teacher's responsibility to make testing a pedagogic opportunity for learners.

Summary

This chapter indicates that learners must be aware of what it takes to establish learner goals and realize what it means to become a strategic learner for life. Most simply, to be strategic, learners must be aware of the importance of goal-setting, note-taking, studying smart, and test-taking for academic success. This chapter is not a standard study skills one in that it does not specifically feature ways of arming learners with tactical learning skills, strategies, or systems. If anything this chapter seeks to reinforce the need to be grounded in an approach to learning that encourages and guides learners to becoming autonomous learners for life. This means learners must, for themselves, become aware of the study skills, strategies, and systems necessary to achieve their learning goals. Therefore, this chapter is referential. It requires learners to face one of life's fundamental lessons; it is really your learning journey, and what you make of it depends so much on your understanding of that ownership.

Questions for Further Reflection

1. Select a piece of text from your content area. Frame the piece as a note-taking exercise for those familiar with your content area, and as a testable text for those in other content areas.
2. Suppose an administrator were to ask you to write down your teaching goals for the first five years of your professional life. What would you submit in your professional strategic goal plan? (Does the idea of goal plans remind you of financial planning or corporate or government strategic planning? It might be interesting to bring in texts that show how common the vocabulary is across institutions.)
3. Recall the most stressful experience you have had with a testing situation. Write down words that evoke this experience. Exchange this reflection with a peer. Respond in writing to the other person's experience. Exchange your responses and talk about the experience. Specifically, discuss how that will inform what you will do when you are in a position to test others.

Key Terms

Cornell note-taking system
Essay tests
Goal-setting
Matching tests
Multiple-choice tests
Note-taking
Objective tests

Performance awareness
Problem-solving tests
Strategy awareness
Task awareness
Test anxiety
Test-taking
True-false tests

CHAPTER TEN

Media Literacy: Learning from Electronic Image-Texts

Questions to Consider for this Chapter

1. How do electronic image media construct reflections and representations of the world?

2. What meanings (implicit and/or explicit) are encoded in electronic image media and how are these meanings communicated?

3. What is the relationship between your personal values and those promoted by the electronic image media?

4. Whose agenda does today's electronic image media industry serve?

Overview

This chapter is about electronic image media literacy. Using theory and practice, the chapter demonstrates how to read image-texts from both an aesthetic and an efferent stance. The reader is invited to consider the contemporary context that frames the relationship between words and images. Then the chapter presents a frame to see the tension between the image-text's form and its meaning. Finally, the chapter advances a pedagogic perspective that enables readers, as learners and teachers, to read image-texts.

Concepts That Frame a Perspective on Media Literacy

In approaching the topic of electronic image media literacy (understood here as film and television), most people bring relatively unexamined perspectives.

To focus on the topic, a context is needed. Duncan et al. (1989) suggest eight concepts that frame a perspective on media literacy:

1. All media are constructions.
2. The media construct reality.
3. Audiences negotiate meaning in media.
4. Media have commercial implications.
5. Media contain ideological and value messages.
6. Media have social and political implications.
7. Form and content in media are closely related.
8. Each medium has a unique aesthetic form.

Media Literacy: In the Beginning . . .

> Seeing comes before words. . . . It is seeing which establishes our place in the surrounding world; we explain that world with words, but words can never undo the fact we are surrounded by it. (Berger, 1977)

> Media literacy is concerned with helping students develop an informed and critical understanding of the nature of mass media, the techniques used by them, and the impact of these techniques. More specifically, it is education that aims to increase students' understanding and enjoyment of how the media work, how they produce meaning, how they are organized, and how they construct reality. Media literacy also aims to provide students with the ability to create products. (Ontario, 1989)

The tension between images and words goes back to biblical times: "Thou shalt not make unto thee any graven image" (Exodus, 20:4). The Commandment seeks to ban visual images of the earthly or the heavenly. Images were deemed seductive, and capable of luring people away from religion. Moses confirmed writing as a way to honour and symbolize the experience of living in the world. Writing offered the desired distance necessary to provide convincing evidence of a heavenly, nonvisual supreme god. Writing was able to symbolically indicate the difference between here and there, this and that. Writing was portable and transferable. It was an ideal conveyance for associative meaning.

Human history — as the story of meaning-making beings attempting to catch glimpses of the "real" — shows that every aspect of our lives has been and is deeply affected by the tensions between the word (representations of the "real") and the image (reflections of the "real"). The word has the power to transcend. It elevates the mind's eye to imagine the possibilities otherwise grounded by our bodily existence. The image has the power to ground our elevated symbolic existence. It locates the body through direct, immediate, and touchable experiences.

What we — as readers and writers, speakers and viewers, thinkers and doers — must understand in this chapter on media literacy is that the tension between the word and the image is ever-present. Yet we must also understand that the word has been privileged, and a particular form of literacy has been valued. Since literacy has come to be associated with a certain fluidity and dexterity with words (reading and writing), our preference for words as a codified sign system privileges those who have mastered their use.

To understand electronic image media, we must emphasize the word–image tension. Only then does there exist a pedagogic opportunity to see electronic image media literacy as a valuable way to learn and to teach more about who we have been, are, and might become as human beings. In a pragmatic sense, this means that a learner needs a way of reading image-texts that is both aesthetic and efferent.

The Importance of Words in Relation to Images

Let's imagine that all modern systems of knowledge are the result of meaning-making frames that are, in turn, framed by a "metanarrative" or "grand discourse." A metanarrative or grand discourse is a story of mythic proportions encompassing everything that defines us as human beings. Philosophy, science, commerce, politics, art, education, religion, and every other human activity are all part of a story that has been authored with the intent of moving humankind toward perfection.

Over the past thirty years, the grand story has been called into question. The result is a postmodern condition, in which many little stories are emerging and competing — so many stories, in fact, that we have become overexposed to a babble of diverse and contradictory words and images.

A random flip across the television channels turns up hundreds of vivid images of others, real and imagined, living different lives. Gone is that modern sense of living within a coherent cultural direction. Perhaps this sense of loss explains our longing, in our current difficult times, to go back to a romanticized past or to project ourselves virtually into a utopian future. Walter Anderson, in *The Truth about Truth* (1995), writes:

> The postmodern condition . . . is a major transition in human history, a time of rebuilding all the foundations of civilization, and the world is going to be occupied with it for a long time to come. And, although it touches different people in different ways, it is happening to us all. We are all emerging from

our tribes, traditions, religions and world views into a global civilization that is overwhelmingly pluralistic. (p. 8)

Although being surrounded by competing societal truths is not new, the societal flux we are undergoing today is radically different in content and form from previous upheavals. For the first time in human history, society has become aware that reality is a socially constructed event. Whereas the answers to the big ever-present questions could once be found in a belief in God, and then a belief in ourselves as godlike, truth is now commonly understood as an "agreed arrangement," or it is "relative to the context," or it "knows no singularity, but rather there are multiple truths possible." Gone is the assuredness of questing after an unchanging ideal. Life's dynamic diversity is what now attracts and repels us.

This shift in awareness has been paralleled by a corresponding shift in our language sign system. Instead of seeking the truth of language in its rules, codes, and protocols, we now realize that language is a highly complex construction that involves mind, body, personal experience, community context, and the accumulated history of humanity. No longer is language-framed meaning making primarily understood as something to be uncovered or discovered. Meaning is now clearly understood in the context of a constructed event. Every human event is the result of both large and small constructions. Human events are intentional, authored, and in the service of the dominant historical perspective.

At one time a one-to-one correlation existed between the thing itself and the word or sign used to represent it. Communication was understandable if one was able to use the tools according to agreed on rules. Today, however, a split has developed between the object and the word. The meaning of a thing is now only understandable through its positioning within a deeply connected presence-absence of many other word-thing arrangements.

We once used words to fix our reflections/representations of reality. We needed words in order to make sense of the chaos we were born into. But what our naming did was to create the possibility that there was an absence to any basic reality. The possibility of not being true was as deeply embedded in the naming of the idea or an object as was our agreement to proceed as if there was a connected truthfulness. That possibility of the connection's being otherwise, false, remained ever-present. Now the possibilities for truth and falsehood are competing openly, and thus the connection between the image/word and a reality is open to interpretation and renegotiation.

At the end of the twentieth century, as words are increasingly disconnected and reconnected to meaning, the power of the image is emerging to rival that of the word. Images are seemingly becoming a privileged sign system.

To inquire into **electronic image-texts** means it is important to understand the following:

1. Knowledge and knowing are constructed by individuals and communities.
2. Reality is multidimensional and multiperspectival.
3. Truth is grounded in everyday experience.
4. Life is a textual expression and thinking an interpretive act.
5. Facts and values are inseparable.
6. Every human activity is value-laden.

Hlynka and Yeaman (1992) indicate that thinking and acting creatively with electronic image-texts in today's world requires:

1. a commitment to a plurality of perspectives, meanings, methods, values;
2. a search for and appreciation of double meanings and alternative interpretations, many of them ironic or unintended;
3. a critique or distrust of "big stories" meant to explain everything, including scientific theories, religious myths, and the accepted knowledge of professions;
4. a plurality of perspectives and ways of knowing, a recognition that there are multiple truths.

Finally, Hlynka and Yeaman (1992) indicate that with respect to electronic image-texts, learners must:

1. Consider concepts, ideas, and objects as texts. Textual meanings are open to interpretation.
2. Look for binary oppositions in those texts, for example, good/bad, progress/tradition, science/myth, love/hate, man/woman, and truth/fiction;
3. "Deconstruct" the text by showing how these oppositions are not necessarily true.

It is our pedagogic task to see these tensions at work in electronic media — to be aware of the social construction of images. The larger issue of content literacy is ever-present. To become literate in image-texts means acquiring the necessary knowledge, skills, and attributes that enable learners to control their relationships to words and images. This is an urgent requirement for learners moving into the twenty-first century.

The Importance of Being Image-Text Literate

From the "natural" beauty we ascribe to nature, to the "constructed" beauty of a building, to the "virtual" beauty of our visions for leaving this planet, there is abundant evidence to prove we privilege the sense of sight. It is imperative that learners be strategically grounded in methods of inquiry into a world that is very much a word-defined, yet visually-framed, space.

Media literacy is required to live with some sense of self-control in the twenty-first century. To be skilled as a learner "learning for life" requires being skilled at "reading, writing, seeing, hearing, and speaking" the world as a textual construction.

The Technical Difficulties of Understanding a Visual Technology

The difficulty with understanding and being skilled at image-text analysis is embedded in the original difficulty of understanding what an image is. Images are grounded in the principle of non-transparency. Images are not just reflections or representations of the world, they are also constructions in and of themselves.

Glasgow (1994) summarizes the need to understand this double-sided nature of images by writing

> Why should we spend time on visual literacy? First, our students need it. Since our goal is to educate them for the contemporary world and encourage them to make texts their own, we must provide them with the skills to interpret the content of visual images as well as print. By helping them learn how to decode . . . we can help them move away from the role of "passive receiver of the message to active unraveler." (p. 499)

So what would practical work with electronic image media look like? Glasgow (1994) suggests that one way to restore the tension between the word and the image to its original function as a means of making sense of the world is "to develop the critical skills needed to interpret texts, I suggest deconstruction . . . a way of reading against the text" (p. 495).

We need ways of seeing and reading such that every picture of the world (be it a novel, a scientific law, a sculpture, a photograph, or a movie) is a constructed text and invites interpretation. To refine upon the definition proposed in Chapter 1, a text is an inscribed piece of mark-making (word and/or

---

For Reflection 10.1

What, if anything, do you know about the term "deconstruction"? How do you think such a process could be applied to electronic images?

image) that is a product of authors, at a given point in time, in an intentional given form of discourse, that also takes its meanings from the interpretive gestures of individual readers using the grammatical, semantic, and cultural codes available to them. Any one text echoes other texts. This way of understanding text requires a reader to wonder what went before, what is happening during, and what might happen after engagement with the text. As well, the possibility exists of opening up what text is.

Image-texts are not neutral. What is seductive about the image is the realization that the desire it presents is based on what is absent but necessary; that it is as specific and exact as it is general and spacious; that it is as intentionally authored as it is intentionally read; and that it is as confined as it is seamless, polished as it is rough, and untouchable as it is consumable. The experience of being moved by an image-text is a consumable, and often pleasurable, moment that seemingly satisfies but, in its presentation and consumption, calls for yet another experience. So we return to the image again and again. As such, a desire to redo and re-experience is created. Thus, the multibillion-dollar media industry. A key element of seeing/reading the image-text is to break the text's seductive allure, to interpret the seamlessness, to be critical, to actively interact where passivity is asked for, to remain passive where hyperactivity is demanded. To engage in such activities is to be a seer/reader of image-texts and to be media literate.

Certainly, the image-text has borrowed from other forms of expression such as painting, photography, sculpture, dance, music, drama, and literature. However, the electronic image-text experience extends, honours, and privileges a visual orientation to the world. Therein lies the problem. The image-text's evocative transforming power blurs the link between what it is and what it can do. Wurzer and Silverman (1990), writing about electronic texts, state:

> Filming is the activity which renders into film what is not film. It is not the machines (projectors, cameras, and video-editors) which technologically produce film. Filming is the making different of that which is not film into that which is film. In its spacing, differencing, textualizing, filming is the production of films in a filmic language that has become text. (p. 185)

To see and interpret image-texts as constructed, storied pictures of life's sights and sounds means it is possible to understand each aspect of the image-story represented as surface statements regarding aspects of contemporary life. However, so much also depends on the deeper, often hidden, aspects of the story required but for the most part unseen and unheard.

An image-text is a *sight* to behold. As a visual product, an image-text is a showing and a revealing within a field of vision. We look and often we see ourselves in the image-text. This appeal is personal and is enhanced by the kinesthetic qualities (the size of the screen, the images, the surrounding dark-

---

For Reflection 10.2

Recall the last film you saw. Can you describe something about the film that was pleasurable to you, or disturbed you? What was it about the film's plot, characters, or cinematography that made the film a visual experience?

---

ness, the stereophonic sound, the reaction of others, and so on) of the visual experience. We experience (albeit vicariously) feelings, events, situations, and relations we may, or may never, encounter in our daily living.

An image-text offers itself as a *site* to be explored and, again as a product, presents itself as a place for numerous things to happen. In these spaces it is possible to existentially explore a wide range of human experiences. Image-text reflexively uses a picture of life to frame life as a picture. This process heightens awareness and encourages the consumer audience to think of film as a site where the ordinary may become extraordinary and the extraordinary becomes ordinary. Image-texts (and imagining) can be mapped from a specific perspective — historical, psychoanalytical, sociological, aesthetic, technological, and so on.

An image-text may also offer itself as a *cite* to be told. Many image-texts have become part of the contemporary social fabric, and their characterizations, actions, and themes are readily citable. For example, familiar lines from movies, television, or advertisements are overwhelmingly incorporated into our daily communications. Perhaps an image-text's particularity offers a generalization about life. Or a group of image-texts may focus on a particularity of life. In this sense image-texts are seen as a source for thematic analysis, illustrative criticism, or example.

The challenge is to read image-texts deeply through reflective articulation that interrupts our gaze:

> Film pulls us into the visible world: the one into which we are thrown at birth and which we all share. Painting does not do this; it interrogates the visible. Nor does photography — for all still photographs are about the past. Only movies pull us into the present and the visible, the visible which surrounds us all. Film doesn't have to say tree: it can show tree. It doesn't have to describe

---

For Reflection 10.3

Think about films or television shows you have seen recently. Think about these image-texts as sites to show possible human experiences. List, chart, or diagram the range of human experiences you have seen in these media.

For Reflection 10.4

On Sunday, February 23, 1997, the NBC television network presented the Academy Award–winning film *Schindler's List*. The film was presented uncut and without interruption. If you have not seen this film, it is about the Holocaust and a German businessman who saved the lives of about one thousand Jews from the atrocities of the concentration camps. Although the film has significance as a document about remarkable events in human history, do you think it should be shown in prime time with children watching? Discuss with classmates the importance and the problems of using images to make cultural, social, moral, commercial, or political points in your content area.

---

a crowd: it can be one. It doesn't have to find an adjective for mud; it can be up to the wheels in it. It doesn't have to analyze a face, it can approach one. It doesn't have to lament, it can show tears. . . . What is saved in the cinema when it achieves art is a spontaneous continuity with all mankind. . . . In the sky of the cinema people learn what they might have been and discover what belongs to them apart from their single lives. Its essential subject — in our century of disappearances — is the soul, to which it offers a global refuge. This I believe, is the key to its longing and its appeal. (Berger, 1977, p. 17)

Ways of Seeing Electronic Image-Texts

The first step in learning to see electronic media is to acknowledge that there are many ways to see. For example, scholars such as Lynch (1983), Berger (1977), and Cook (1985) suggest the following ways to study electronic image media:

The Micro Approach. This approach uses detailed evidence to frame a general statement about a work. The following review of the action film *Marked for Death* (1991) illustrates this approach. Starting with a meticulously detailed analysis of the protagonist's clothing, the reviewer satirically makes a larger point about the insanity of being "dressed to kill":

For Reflection 10.5

At this point it is worthwhile to reflect on how one might use film or television in a subject area discipline to enhance content literacy. Outline, orally or in writing, what image-texts (films or televison series or interactive CD-ROMs) you might use in your content area, and how their use would enhance content area literacy.

So, while maiming and killing several Mexicans, he'll wear: Black linen-cotton Versace matador jacket; dyed black Levi's 501s; black silk shirt, buttoned at the neck; gold Rolex. When it's time to pistol-whip a Jamaican crack dealer, Seagal changes into a black velvet jacket with two Oriental dragons stitched on the front and a tiger on the back. And for the climactic eye-gouging, back-breaking, impalement finale, the wardrobe includes a long black coat over a gray silk baseball jacket. Simply smashing. (*Edmonton Journal*, 1991.)

The Macro Approach. In this approach, a thematic statement about a film is made. That statement is subsequently supported by specific references to the film. In *The Godfather* the eternal struggle between good and evil reveals itself in Michael's choice to avenge the death of his father. This tension is supported by the film's light and dark motif. At the beginning of the film, Michael is often seen full-figured basking in natural sunlight. By the film's mid-point, especially during the hospital scene, close-up shots of Michael's face are bisected half in light and half in shadow. At film's end, Michael closes the door on Kay and the screen goes completely black.

The Thematic Approach. A film is often a site of recurring themes that offer universally applicable lessons. For example, the overriding theme of *The Corn Is Green*, *To Sir, with Love*, and *Why Shoot the Teacher?* is a teacher's desire to improve his or her students' lives while facing tremendous odds.

The Sociological Approach. If films reflect a collective dream reality, then both the sanctioned and the deviant behaviours of individuals and communities should be represented in the films. For example, *Three Days of the Condor* (1975), *Chinatown* (1974), and *Marathon Man* (1976) are all post-Watergate films that document a nation's distrust of an increasingly corrupt power structure.

The Psychoanalytical Approach. The psychology and psychiatry attributed to Freud, Jung, and Lacan are used to explicate relational events, to explain character motivation, and to analyze character behaviour in a film. Horror films, in particular, have become prime subjects for psychoanalytical study.

The Historical Approach. This approach may use three interconnected techniques. First, it is possible to analyze events that occurred in the year a film was made to see if they offer any thematic, cinematographic, and sociological-psychological insights. For example, many films made in the 1950s reflect Cold War phobias about the threat of Communism (for example, *Reefer Madness*). Second, some films offer historical insight by being "period pieces." These films attempt to authentically duplicate the time and space in which the story actually occurred (for example, *Ben Hur*). Third, a group of films may be explored via sampling across successive decades. This may reveal a historical progression (for example, studying the similarities and differences in how adult–adolescent conflicts are depicted in films from 1930, 1960, and 1990).

The Genre Approach. Most films can be approached as examples of a particular style or genre. The western, science-fiction, horror, detective, teen-pic, gangster, musical, and comedy are some recognized genres. For example, films in the action-adventure genre include the *Rambo* series, all the James Bond films, *Die Hard*, the *Indiana Jones* movies, the *Terminator* series, and so on.

The Auteur Approach. This approach is driven by the assumption that the final product is ultimately the responsibility of one person — the director. Viewing many movies by one director (such as Ford, Coppola, Spielberg, Truffaut, Peckinpah, Stone, or Hitchcock) reveals certain thematic preoccupations, recurring motifs, common incidents, and stylistic characteristics that are specific to that director's works.

There are many other ways of seeing (interpreting) electronic image media. Each method is rooted in its own assumptions and makes its own claims. As this brief outline of the approaches to viewing media demonstrates, interpretation is a pervasive human activity. This is an important point since in most learning institutions film, television, or media studies are not usually taught as a separate course of study; in most cases, media study is integrated into content area courses. But if every content area course is essentially a disciplinary way to interpret the world, then learners must understand how words and images interact within a discipline.

The Practical Work of Deconstruction

Now to the practical work of interpreting image-texts. Deconstruction is a significant way to inquire into image-texts. As educators, our responsibility is to offer a way for individuals and communities to have informed conversations and make collective decisions by helping create a visually literate student body. Ironically, the way into the image is to see the power of the word. At the heart of both the word and the image is the question of distance. We need to be rigorous in this understanding. The word reveals the world from a critical, distanced perspective. However, the image seeks to reduce distance; with limited distance, there is less possibility to be critical. So to read images as texts requires the selective use of strategies that we currently use with words. One such strategy is deconstruction.

Deconstruction is a way to understand how meaning is made in the contemporary world by reading the world's texts for both what is present and what that which is present refers to. Modernity, the presently named world construction, is a deceptive offering. In order to advance humanity's journey, we must, as individuals and as groups, engage in tasks that are rigorous, reasonable, and rational. It is language that enables us to be rigorous, reasonable, and rational. Yet a close look at the nature and structure of language opens up other possibilities. These possibilities — to speak and be otherwise — often delegitimize modernity's foundational tenets of rigour, reason, and rationality.

In North America, scholars such as Norris and Benjamin (1988), Ulmer (1985), and Culler (1981, 1982) have attempted to apply deconstruction through specific strategies that offer opportunities for a close reading of a text. However, the purpose of a deconstructive reading is not to determine the text's meaning; rather, it is to explore how the foundations on which the text rests undermine the seemingly apparent fixed meaning of the text itself. Deconstructing a text suggests that the text is susceptible to different, yet equally legitimate, interpretations. But a deconstructive analysis does not replace the interpretive process. Rather, it encloses interpretation within a more complex process of a double reading. Thus, a deconstructive analysis ensures that no "proper" or "correct" methodology can ever be formulated for all texts. In this sense, the interpreting process must consciously be understood as unique, open, and continuous.

A deconstructive reading revolves around three strategies. The first strategy itself consists of three movements: (1) The first movement is to "dramatize" how a specific dominant discourse replicates the binary opposition evident in Western intellectual history. Such oppositions could be white-black, good-evil, tradition-chaos, male-female, mind-body, reality-appearance, and so on. The first term in the dichotomy is usually privileged. The right-hand term is usually regarded as a complication, a negation, a disruption of the first term. (2) In the second movement the deconstructive intention is to "reverse" the opposition through arguments secured from the contextual surroundings supportive of the privileged term. This is an attempt to show the nonprivileged term is really the referent or determining term. This revelation begins the undermining of what was first understood as privileged. (3) The third movement involves an "overturning" of the privileged term, thus revealing that its repressive, exclusive boundaries could not exist without that which has been negated. For example, in the male-female dichotomy, male could be envisioned as a form of female and both polar elements (being singularly male or female) may be understood as different. Yet it is also possible to understand a united form of gender that has characteristics of both separate genders, as in the belief that some women may need to be behaviourally masculine to succeed in business, or that to be a male in the twenty-first century requires a new-age sensitivity toward others.

A second deconstruction strategy is to look for key words, central images, definitive moments, and definitive relations that frame the text's privileged term. These elements not only point to the dominant term, but also provide traces indicating the violence inherent in the dominant term's oppression of its opposition. Through careful teasing out of these traces, different lines or directions of inquiry become possible. For example, in the film *Dead Poets*

Society, the use of poetry is essential to character development, plot movement, and the thematic tensions of the film itself. By reading the poetry closely, much can be added to the study of the film.

A third deconstruction strategy is to pay close attention to the marginalized features of a text. These features often point to the text's dominant oppositional tension. In the margins there is often an identification of the exclusions on which hierarchies may depend and by which they might be disrupted. A concentration on the marginal is an identification of what in a text resists the identity established for it by other readings. For example, the film *Dead Poets Society* contains many images of the woods and hiding places within the woods. In exploring what appears to be a backgrounded feature of the film, there is the possibility of confirming or questioning the film's dominant thematic focus.

In summary, Boyd (1989) writes:

> In practice, deconstructive criticism involves the close rhetorical analysis of a text, not to determine its meaning, but rather to explore the ways in which it undermines any readily apparent meaning and necessarily renders itself susceptible to mutually incompatible, but equally legitimate interpretations. It replaces the interpretative quest for a single determinate meaning with . . . "the careful teasing out of warring forces of signification within the text itself." Or rather, instead of replacing the interpretative process, deconstructive analysis strategically encloses it within a more complex process of what Derrida calls "double reading," paradoxically acknowledging the legibility of a given text while simultaneously demonstrating the text's inevitable subversion of that legibility. (p. 146)

A worthwhile approach to media literacy must be an inquiry/research-based approach in which the analysis of cultural representations becomes the topic. When such an approach is used, the questions about the relationships between the production and reproduction, and the reflection and representation of power, emerge. When looking at what counts as power and how it is presented in image-texts becomes the inquiry focus, learners become operationally media literate.

For Reflection 10.6

Can you see the possibilities for a deconstructive approach as part of an interactive, integrative strategy for visual literacy in your content area? Which electronic image-texts (documentaries, feature films, television shows) would best lend themselves to using deconstruction to enhance visual literacy for content learning in your subject area?

Teaching and Learning with Deconstruction: A Visual Literacy Portfolio

A good way to inquire into image-texts is to use deconstruction as means of inquiry. And a way of structuring such an inquiry is to have learners establish and work through a visual literacy portfolio. What follows is a practical way of setting up a portfolio as a process and as a product.

The Set-up: Framing the Project

To set up a visual literacy portfolio a learner must accomplish a series of tasks. The texts being studied are moving images. Therefore, it is important to defend each selection. However, there is no need to over-frame the selection process. Let it be invitational and creative. And yes, a teacher still needs to be aware of the often complex issues of copyright as well as the ethical/moral text standards (explicit/implicit) set by the school and supporting communities. But remember, the magic of using moving images is that even the most humble of inquiry processes will lead to the larger issues embedded in most selections.

Ask learners to make a case for using each image-text that appears in their portfolios. See Box 10.1 for an example.

The quality and quantity of the image-texts studied depends greatly on the teacher's time/space arrangements, the learner's interests and abilities, and issues of curriculum. Teachers must make planning decisions regarding the depth and scope of a learner's inquiry into image-texts and how this will relate to their other teaching responsibilities.

The Inquiry Process and Procedures

Learners need to become engaged in a series of tasks around selected image-texts. Learners should focus on the image-texts they seek to inquire into. However, the issue of access must be addressed beforehand since what learners may wish to inquire into might be pragmatically unattainable. Learners inquiring into a continuously moving image-text that cannot be stopped, or freeze-framed, are going to have more difficulty in their inquiry than learners primarily using still image-texts. Also, having had previous experience with an image-text will make a difference to the learners' inquiry. Whether the images are to be used by individual learners or the inquiry project is to be made a group effort must also be discussed as the inquiry proceeds since these

Box 10.1
A Visual Literacy Portfolio

Making a Case for My Choice

Proposal sheet # _____

Name: _____

Date submitted: _____

A. SELECTION DATA

   1. Image source information. (Title, director, year, characters, running time, etc.)

   2. Image viewing information. (When was this text seen, where, with whom, and why?)

B. ATTRACTION STATEMENT

   1. What attracts me to this image-text is:

C. DESCRIPTION STATEMENT

   1. Briefly, the image-text story is:

   2. One specific affect (feeling) that is central to what I saw is:

D. PROPOSAL STATEMENT

   1. In terms of wondering about this image-text, one point of inquiry would be:

E. REVIEWER'S RESPONSE

Date: _____

Comments:

situations bring with them different possibilities. Considering all these factors, learners should provide a statement regarding the type of image-text they are inquiring into and whether it is moving, still, has been previously encountered, or is new, and if the inquiry will be an individual's project or the focus of group work. What follows is a way of proceeding with the image-text to set up the deconstructive approach.

The First Movement: To Describe

Learners are asked to begin literally with the concrete — the image-text at hand. They must be invited to see the image-text aesthetically. Jagodzinski (1995) offers six layers or dimensions for encountering the lived aesthetic experience of image-texts. These layers are not mutually exclusive and are deeply interrelated. For a learner they are useful organizers that frame the task of describing the image-text at hand. Jagodzinski's (1995) six layers are described as follows:

Line: The Lived Experience of Directionality. Movement is a defining human feature. Most of life's journeys consist of getting lost and finding a direction — directionality is often ambiguous, paradoxical. The images of the experiences of life's movements show a rhythmic criss-crossing journey between intentionality and happenstance. Describe moments/images in the text that show this movement between plan and chance.

Colour: The Lived Experience of Mood. Colour is the felt conversation between self, others, and the world. Human lives are riddled with colourful and colourless moments, images, and words. Colour, and/or the lack of colour, frames life's moods. Human personality is evoked, exposed colour. Describe a conversational moment in the text that colours the text.

Texture: The Lived Experience of Familiarity. Texture is the rough and smooth contact with the things of the world. The world is always in touch with us. We might be in or out of touch with it. The fibres of our existence are all interconnected. Going against the grain makes it rough for us, but going with the flow ensures smooth sailing. The texture of the new and the old surrounds us. We long to make a mark on the world before we lose touch. Describe a rough/smooth moment in the text's directionality/colour.

Size: The Lived Experience of Scale. We have a history of being attentive to the mega and/or the micro aspects of living in the world. We marvel at the gigantic and the miniature. Do we seek to be bigger than life? Who is larger than life? Are these small desires? Is privilege judged by size? The microscope and telescope are significant modern tools. Describe what is big/small about the text.

Mass: The Lived Experience of Gravity. We have a history of seeking both gravity (permanence) and lightness (move-ability). Tradition offers a common, locatable grounding. But that we could be otherwise beckons us.

We are no strangers to living between heaven and hell, good and evil. Such are our weighty concerns — to lighten the load. We gather in mass, as individuals, to celebrate our common differences. Describe what is large/small about the text.

Space: The Lived Experience of the Cosmos. We have a history as architectural builders and space destroyers. We unearth the earth to construct spaces for gatherings. We are architects of our selfhood. We colonize the unconscious spaces into recognizable formats. Yet we long to be returned to the expanses of the garden as a style of existence. We have sacred and profane spaces, spaces codified and lived, spaces public and private, spaces filled up and spaces left vacant. To know and name space is our desire, and cosmology our quest. Describe moments of creation/destruction in the text.

These aesthetic dimensions locate the affective experience of reading image-texts. By writing through rich description, a learner is taken out of the usual media inquiry questions: "Who is in the image? What is being said? How is it being said? Did you like it?" By using Jagodzinski's dimensions, a reader/viewer becomes conscious of the binary oppositions that (in)form every level of perception. The next step is the recognition that these oppositions are complementary more than they are dichotomous. To organize an aesthetic response, see Box 10.2.

The Second Movement: To Decode

The descriptive work (in images and in words) must provide an opportunity to show/tell what the dominating presence is in the image-text. Then the inquiry shifts to wondering about the privileged, dominating image(s) within the image-text itself. To decode an image-text, the focus is on imploding and/or exploding the image-text's rich descriptions. Both of these tasks get at the genealogy of an image — that is, the tracings, residue, and associations that let the image convey the multiple meaning(s) it does. Imploding and/or exploding involves locating a strong element of an image-text in the middle of a page. Using a listing or a visual graph/web/chart or some text/visual organizer, try to go into the image's elements to show its dependencies, or branch out from it to show its connectedness. Box 10.3 may be helpful.

The Third Movement: To Advance the Absent

Once the visual power of the image-text has been located for what it might be, then the work is to read against it so as to point to what is absent yet referentially present. A learner may use the principles of association and juxtaposition to map the terrain between what is present and what is absent. What gets revealed is the hierarchical, dichotomous nature of the image-text itself. The themes of the image-text, be they political, economic, spiritual, or

Box 10.2
A Visual Literacy Portfolio

Describing the Image-Text

Name: _____

Date submitted: _____

For each descriptor bin below record what you feel/think the image-text offers.

LINE:
The lived experience of directionality.

_____

_____

_____

COLOUR:
The lived experience of mood.

_____

_____

_____

TEXTURE:
The lived experience of familiarity.

_____

_____

_____

SIZE:
The lived experience of scale.

_____

_____

_____

(continued)

(continued)

MASS:

The lived experience of gravity.

_____

_____

_____

SPACE:

The lived experience of the cosmos.

_____

_____

_____

SUMMARY:

Provide a listing of what you think is strongly present in the image-text that corresponds to each dimension. Then, imagine the absence that complements each strong presence described.

LINE   COLOUR   TEXTURE   SIZE   MASS   SPACE

social, begin to appear. Drawing inferences about the ideologies of a given culture becomes possible. The underlying tensions of world-view attitudes, periods, classes, styles, and persuasions are laid bare. See Box 10.4.

The Fourth Movement: To Demonstrate Acquired Literacy

Once the mapping has been drawn out with some degree of rigour and depth, then a learner needs to play with the possibilities of "flipping" an image-text. A creative piece of work (written, visual, or performative) needs to be initiated and completed as a visual literacy project. A learner must propose a project that frames the tensions inherent in the image-text. The project

Box 10.3
A Sample Aesthetic Response (the Second Movement)

Madame Sousatzka, a 1988 film by John Schlesinger, has a strong theme of intentionality. What follows is an exploration of the word *intentionality*. All the word-link references are from *Funk and Wagnalls Standard College Dictionary* (1975). *Intention* is first located in the dictionary, leading the learner to pursue words in random association.

Intention: purpose, either ultimate or immediate; *intend*; goal; design; earnestly attentive.

Intend: hope; expect; to stretch; planned; proposed; results; *tend* to.

Tend: aptitude; disposition; inclination; watch over; protect; attend to; to be *tender*.

Tender: offer; give; *minister* to.

Minister: to act as servant or agent of another; to be *authorized*.

Authorized: empowered; to be commissioned; attentive to; *responsive* to.

Responsive: inclined; ready; in accord; reply; harmony; to be *answerable*.

Answerable: called upon; liable; *responsible*.

Responsibility: a duty; trust; obligation; answerable to, attentive to, ministering to a purposeful call in an *intentional* manner.

Each connector word shows that what constitutes intentionality is bound to the question of responsibility. Pedagogical intentions are a teacher's actions oriented toward a student with loving care, trustful hope, authorized ministering, and ultimately a sense of responsive responsibility. Teachers attempt to be aware of their intentions for a student and the power of their influence with respect to the student. Teaching is a ministering on the teacher's part, grounded in recognition of who the student is while balancing the hopes for who the student can become. Pedagogic intentionality is the way a student comes to understand who he or she is. In the student's seeing of self and other, there is often an authorizing influence evident on the student's part that effects, affects, and infects a teacher's intentions for the student. If the educative relationship between teachers and students is pedagogic, then students know that the teacher has their best interests at heart.

In *Madame Sousatzka* there are indications that a teacher's pedagogic orientation, just like that of a parent's, may occasionally become deflected by negative feelings and thoughts. But the film also shows that when a student is with a teacher, or a parent, the teacher and parent are called upon

(continued)

(continued)

to do something. Even if the actions of a teacher or a parent are confused by mixed motives, the moral tension between what they could and should, can and might do will not go away. This sense of doubting on a teacher's part, especially regarding their actions, will demand, at some point, a reflective consideration on those actions by the teacher.

If teachers' doubts encompass reflections about their actions being good for students, then the conditions are right for pedagogy itself to affect the teachers' understanding of their influence. Pedagogical doubting in a teacher's preparedness becomes a valuable and valued experience. This constructive opportunity to rebuild a weakened pedagogic relationship begins with the destruction of mixed-motive intentionality. Being pedagogically sensitive involves seizing the opportunity to recover one's understanding of what constitutes being intentional with learners and responsible for their learning.

Box 10.4
An Aesthetic Response (the Third Movement)

Dead Poets Society is more than a black and white portrayal of the tragic consequences of the struggle between conformity and nonconformity. Embedded in the film's images are the workings of a Western consciousness that manifests itself in a distanced, uninvolved, and ever-increasing level of abstraction applied to every aspect of life. Welton College features educationally privileged hierarchies, honoured discipline specializations, selective theoretical conceptualizations, and a respect for science. The boys of Welton are asked to live in the service of the ideas that will turn them into the managers of Western society. They are destined to control the knowledge and the technology that dominates the end of the twentieth century. To ensure that the influence and corresponding sense of responsibility is appropriate as the correct world vision of life, a criteria-based series of interactions grounded in input-output measurement are utilized. Appropriately then, observable performance is judged efficient and effective by testing, evaluation, and accountability. So in its language, in its looks, in its gestures, and in its actions, Welton privileges and legitimates images of a positivist discourse, a discourse grounded in a history conceptualized by Western society as an ideological quest for perfection. Welton's primary administrative, moral, and educational influence and responsibility is to act as that social-cultural-political institution perpetuating the exclusively sanctioned norms of a privileged ruling class of society.

(continued)

(continued)

John Keating enters and immediately opens the possibility for a different understanding of how people might speak and act together. Is Keating the embodiment of both a destructive and a constructive force? How does Keating go about speaking and acting in a way that deconstructs Welton's entrenched power structures? Keating exposes the primary texts (sounds and images) of Welton as selectively chosen narrative constructs. Welton's texts reveal themselves as interpretations of interpretations. Keating shows that it is the present that always contains the traces of what is absent. His deconstructive stance works to show the intimate regress and arbitrariness of the interpretation process. He attempts an attentive rereading of Welton's privileged texts in order to show what is problematic in Welton's well-intended educational practices. Keating may concede the space created and the freedom glimpsed may only be accessible for a moment, but he also knows that a lived experienced moment is all it takes to change a life's direction forever.

Perhaps the deconstructive point embodied in the film's portrayal of Keating as alternative, as different, is that in every discourse, and in some more than others, and in every way of acting, no matter how restrictive or open, there exists a certain embedded alterity or otherness. This otherness lives within, above, and beneath the discourse or practice that a society has chosen to honour. Eventually there is the possibility, the opportunity, that this otherness will be consciously felt, seen, heard, and given voice. This often sudden awareness happens when the privileged order becomes dissipated, cracked, or exploded under its own weight, or from attacks from the outside.

The lessons embedded in *Dead Poets Society* open up for discussion questions about the nature of pedagogical intentionality, influence, and responsibility. And in doing so the film requires a response on our part as we wonder about the very condition that makes teaching possible. This wondering goes to the heart and soul of the educative project. If the height of a teacher's responsibility is to wonder about the origin of what calls for a response, then the film's images are in the service of this directionality.

must summarize the tensions and show how the surface features of the image-text are reflections and representations of a cultural viewpoint concerning values. This project will show how the learner's metacognitive abilities have increased by showing a conscious movement through the deconstruction process, the self-knowledge acquired, and the awareness of the vulnerabilities of image seduction. See Box 10.5 for an example.

The Fifth Movement: To Assess the Portfolio Tasks

What follows is a way to create multiple rubrics that help assess work beyond such traditional forms as reports and essays. A key to assessing a visual liter-

Box 10.5
A Project Reflection Form: Checking for Understanding

Name: _____

Project Title (if applicable): _____

Date Submitted: _____

INSTRUCTIONS

In a narrative term, please indicate the tensions discovered in the drawing-out deconstructive process you engaged in with the image-text. Perhaps the following questions will help:

1. What are the specific elements/aspects of the image-text that seek to dominate the viewer/responder?

2. In a deconstructive sense, what oppositions or dependencies do the strong aspects/elements of the image-text evoke?

3. Where does your work need to go from here?

REVIEWER'S RESPONSE

acy project is to balance the tension between student, peer, community, and teacher assessment. In some combination, all of the participants can offer an assessment perspective. Still, it is the teacher who is ultimately responsible for the assessment arrangements. It is hoped that a teacher will invite multiple assessment perspectives. Worsnop (1996) suggests that all forms of expression should have certain things in common:

1. They should have content: ideas and details.
2. They should be organized in some way.
3. They should use (or not use) a form of **effective language**.
4. They should display (or fail to display) an author's **voice** and awareness of **audience**.
5. They should demonstrate a degree of **technical competence**.

These elements can be used to differentiate work that is exceptional from that which requires improvement. Once levels of performance have been indicated, an assessment rubric is created (see Box 10.6).

Summary

Image-texts are grounded in the ever-present tensions between words and images. However, using the assumption that every text is a constructed narrative event, it is possible to apply deconstruction as means of textual inquiry to image-texts. Interrupted and understood in this way, images invite viewers as readers to reflect on their experiences. In bringing interpretations about images into reflective articulation, there is an opportunity to make conversational the constructed significance of human experiences. Van Manen (1990) writes:

> Thoughtful reflection is itself an experience. Thoughtful reflection is an experience that gives significance to or perceives it in the experience upon which it reflects. So the significance that we attribute through thoughtful reflection to past experience leaves a living memory that is no less embodied knowledge than are the physical skills and habits we learn and acquire in a less reflective manner. However, this thought-engaged body knowledge of acting tactfully attaches a mindful, thinking quality to our ordinary awareness of our everyday actions and experiences. (p. 209)

To look at image-texts in a pedagogic way is to engage in a reflective inquiry practice. Learners' lives can be enhanced and enriched by reflexively inquiring into image-texts, which already surround them, in order to develop a new and better understanding of how they live in the world as individuals

Box 10.6
A Visual Literacy Portfolio

An Assessment Rubric

GOALS OF RUBRIC ASSESSMENT

Rubrics should be detailed enough to ensure reliability in a way that is helpful and diagnostic and yet generic enough to be useful for several kinds of student expression. There should also be room for negotiation concerning the emphasis or weighting to the parts of a rubric. Generally, a rubric may have several levels of demonstrable accomplishment but the three main levels are: (1) beyond expected range of performance, (2) within the expected range of performance, and (3) not yet within the expected range of performance. Finally, the rubric needs to use straightforward language that is useful for assessing, instructing, and reporting.

RUBRIC SAMPLER

What follows is an example of a holistic rubric that deals with the work as whole rather than in segmented detail. The rubric consists of a series of levels and associated descriptors. Specific to this example is consideration for the learner's personal feelings. This example could have been worked out by a teacher with learners.

A Rubric Example

LEVEL STANDARD	DESCRIPTION
Level 6	The learner provides SUPERIOR INTEGRATION of personal feelings with the image text that is BEYOND EXPECTATION. The response INSIGHTFULLY CITES the image-text. There is a SIGNIFICANT UNDERSTANDING of the image-text presented, and APPROPRIATE CONNECTIONS are made to other texts.
Level 5	The learner provides SIGNIFICANT CONNECTIONS between personal feelings and the image-text. The response APPROPRIATELY CITES the image-text. There is a CLEAR UNDERSTANDING of the image-text presented, as well as an ATTEMPT AT CONNECTIONS to other texts.
Level 4	The learner provides WITHIN EXPECTATION a GOOD EXPLORATION of personal feelings with the image-text. The response ATTEMPTS TO GROUND itself in the image-text. There is SOME UNDERSTANDING shown of the image-text, as well as an ATTEMPT TO MAKE CONNECTIONS to other texts.

(continued)

(continued)

Level 3   The learner SIMPLY RETELLS or PARAPHRASES a response to
           the image-text. The response SKIMS the image-text, and
           UNDERSTANDING IS QUESTIONABLE; as well there is LITTLE
           ATTEMPT to connect to other texts.
Level 2   The learner FAILS TO SHOW recognizable personal connec-
           tions to the image-text. The response is NOT GROUNDED in
           the image-text. UNDERSTANDING IS NOT EVIDENT. There
           has been NO ATTEMPT TO LOCATE OR CONNECT to other
           texts.
Level 1   The learner response is irrelevant, incomprehensible, or absent.

The above example is one of many possible rubrics. Learners/teachers can
construct rubrics by setting up levels of accomplishment and then agreeing
on what is strong about the work at hand, what needs improving, and where
to go from there. Rubrics can be set up to deal with time use, controlling
ideas, organization, use of voice, presentation of ideas, and so on.

---

and as group members. Therefore, this chapter attempted to establish
that deconstruction is an important and fruitful way to learn about images
and to become media literate. In order to deconstruct image-texts, it is
important:

- To know that the contemporary world contains both word-texts and
  image-texts, and that these two forms of texts are both complementary and
  antagonistic.
- To understand the inquiry skills associated with deconstruction, which
  emerged as a way to inquire into word-texts but is now also applicable to
  image-texts; and
- To have the necessary attributes associated with becoming and being a
  reader of worldly texts in order to know the truth about living in a textual
  (word-image) world.

There is much to be taught to learners through specific content areas by using
a deconstructive approach to image-texts.

Questions for Further Reflection

1. What is it about images that is so seductive? Are most people visually
   literate?

2. In what ways could you enhance your learning abilities to understand visual literacy?
3. How might you integrate visual literacy into your content area?

Key Terms

Audience

Effective language

Electronic image-texts

Technical competence

Voice

PART THREE

Assessing and Evaluating in the Content Areas

CHAPTER ELEVEN

Assessing and Evaluating Students' Content Literacy

Questions to Consider for this Chapter

1. What types of assessment did you experience in secondary school? How are these traditions changing?

2. What is your understanding of the difference between the terms *assessment* and *evaluation*?

3. What characteristics do you think of when you read such terms as *performance assessment, authentic assessment*, and *portfolio assessment*?

4. What new directions in assessment have you recently discovered?

5. How can you assess a student's (a) aesthetic response in reading or writing, (b) interdisciplinary transactions, and (c) reading awareness?

Overview

This chapter discusses the meaning of the term *assessment*, distinguishes between assessment and evaluation, and moves on to consider the paradigm shift (change) that is occurring in the field of assessment.

The terms **alternative assessment, authentic assessment, performance assessment, traditional assessment**, and **performance standards** are then clarified. Guidelines for linking assessment to instruction are provided, and criteria for judging the quality of alternative assessments are discussed. Portfolio, as one form of an alternative assessment, is explicated. Underlying principles for portfolio assessment are outlined, and suggestions and examples are given for the construction and use of portfolios in the content area classroom. New directions in assessment such as co-operative assessment, panel assessment, and computerized assessment are then highlighted. The chapter concludes by presenting several practical techniques for alternative assessment. These include assessing reader response (aesthetic and efferent) in the content areas, assessing the monitoring of one's own comprehension, assessing writing in the content areas, assessing interdisciplinary transactions, and assessing reading awareness.

Defining Assessment

In Chapter 1, content literacy was defined as the ability to talk, read, and write about the discipline and to use reading, writing, and talking to learn still more about the content area. Literacy activities were then viewed as ways to maximize the learning of content. Affective dimensions were not separated from cognitive dimensions. Aesthetic reading and writing were viewed as a point of entry into efferent transactions with text. Aesthetic transactions were seen as opening surprising ways of connecting knowledge (subject matter) with lived experience. In addition, it was emphasized that a text can be understood as a world of surprising possibilities that can be explored by many routes: by shifting back and forth between aesthetic and efferent stances, a reader can understand the text more deeply. How do we then assess whether students have become content literate? What methods can be used to assess cognitive and affective dimensions? Aesthetic and efferent transactions? Before these questions can be answered, we need to examine what "assessment" means.

Shanahan (1994) and Harris and Hodges (1995) point out that the term **assessment** is often used interchangeably with terms like *testing, measurement,* and *evaluation.* Some writers define assessment as the process of gathering information on students' learning strengths and weaknesses. Other writers go further to refer to the judgements (interpretations) made after data have been collected. Shanahan (1994, p. 93) brings some clarity to the confusion by outlining the subtle differences in terms. These are:

Assessment is an umbrella term that includes the processes of testing and measurement, the use of observations, surveys, and self-reports to collect information on students' learning. Thus, assessment includes quantified results (e.g., test scores) and qualitative descriptions (e.g., think-alouds revealing students' understandings).

Testing and **measurement** are systematic procedures (e.g., test instruments) designed to provide numbers for quantifying or scaling test results.

Evaluation includes procedures for interpreting information based on goals, standards, or rules. Evaluation also connotes an assessment that is more comprehensive; that is, it extends from students to instructional programs and whole educational systems. According to Harris and Hodges (1995), assessment forms the basis for evaluation, but not the reverse.

For Reflection 11.1
How would you define assessment? How has your definition changed since you read this section?

Several authorities (Maeroff, 1991; Wiggins, 1989) also point out that the intended meaning of assessment is "to sit with" a learner and to strive to find out whether a student's responses to tasks being completed "really mean what they seem to mean" (Maeroff, 1991, p. 276). Maeroff quotes Wiggins to elaborate: "Does a correct answer mask thoughtless recall? Does a wrong answer obscure thoughtful understanding? We can know for sure only by asking further questions, by seeking explanation or substantiation, by requesting a self-assessment, or by soliciting the student's response to the assessment" (p. 276).

"Sitting with" a student is much like the notion of "living through" an experience (described in the chapters on reading and writing and talking in the content areas) as opposed to the traditional method of testing with the teacher "sitting above" the student. "Sitting with" a student "in assessment" can therefore be viewed as a transaction: the student is transacting with texts and tasks; the student is also transacting with the teacher or with a peer. It can readily be seen that traditional, standardized forms of assessment have moved away from such a definition of assessment. These traditional tests do not reflect our present knowledge of reading and writing as transactive processes or of learning as a constructive activity. With the current **paradigm shift** toward "alternative" assessments, the move is back to the original intent of the term *assessment* in the way students are assessed. Since testing is only one form of assessment, we are moving away from a *testing* culture and back to an *assessment* culture (Wolf, Bixby, Glenn, & Gardner, 1991; Hebert, 1992). Thus, "we are at a crossroads in assessment" (Valencia, Hiebert, & Afflerbach, 1994).

Reforms in Assessment

Traditional Achievement Tests

Traditional standardized tests that measure achievement (usually of the multiple-choice variety discussed in Chapter 9) provide very limited information on which to base instruction. Standardized, commercially available tests are often used to test groups of students in whole school districts for comparative purposes in subjects such as English language arts (particularly reading and writing), mathematics, science, and social studies. Administration, scoring, and interpretation of results is standardized in all settings. Such tests are usually norm-referenced; that is, each student's score is compared with a norm group or population that is representative of a province, state, or entire nation. In the comparisons made, each raw score is first converted to a "derived score" such as a standard score, age- or grade-equivalent score, or percentile rank. These scores are defined as follows (O'Donnell, 1994):

1. *Standard scores* involve the transformation of an individual's raw scores in the norm group into scores that fall under a normal curve distribution. For example, "How far is Pradeep's score from the mean in terms of the standard deviation of the distribution?"
2. *Percentile ranks* show the proportion of students in the norming group who received raw scores that were lower or higher than a particular score. For example, if Pradeep has a percentile rank of 38, he has scored as well as or better than 38 percent of the norming sample but lower than 62 percent of that group.
3. *Age- and grade-equivalent scores* are obtained by computing the average raw score of students in a particular age group or a given grade level.

Another major category of traditional achievements tests is criterion-referenced tests,. *Criterion-referenced*, or *domain-referenced*, tests as defined by O'Donnell (1994) focus on the degrees to which skills and knowledge have been mastered in a specific content area. A comparison is made not with other students but with how much a student has learned in relation to specific objectives that enable him or her to reach stated goals. Criterion scores are selected in advance. For example, successful mastery can be defined as getting 80 percent of the test items correct on each chemistry test.

Standardized norm-referenced tests give only a rough estimate of a student's ability and provide little information for instructional purposes in the content area classroom.

Teacher observation as a form of authentic assessment provides a better indication of students' needs in content literacy. However, such authentic assessment does not replace all aspects of standardized tests. Nonetheless, it can be argued (Birrell & Ross, 1996) that standardized testing and authentic assessments, while different, are complementary methods. As standardized testing will likely remain a deeply ingrained element in the public school system for some time (Birrell & Ross, 1996), teachers need to use both methods in combination to make informed decisions about students' growth. Teachers also need to recognize that the degree to which "traditional" assessment and the newer trends in assessment can be implemented across the curriculum will vary according to disciplinary traditions. The new assessment approaches are more suited to some disciplines than others.

The body of research on the effectiveness of alternative assessments (such as authentic assessment and performance-based assessments) is small, but growing steadily. However, research on traditional testing shows that standardized tests can have negative impacts on program quality (and, in turn, student learning). For example, the pressure for accountability forces educators to prepare students to perform well on tests by providing skill instruction in the formats found on tests; in addition, the curriculum becomes narrowed to emphasize basic skills rather than higher-level thinking (Herman, 1992). Nevertheless, despite these criticisms, standardized tests are still used frequently. Efforts should be made to improve the tests themselves, to avoid misuse and misinterpretation of standardized test results, and to place these scores in the broader context of authentic assessments (Pikulski, 1990).

Alternative Approaches to Assessment

Alternative methods of assessment employ procedures other than standardized tests to achieve "direct, 'authentic' assessment of student performance on important learning tasks" (Warther et al. as cited in Harris & Hodges, 1995, pp. 7–8). One type of alternative assessment is authentic assessment, which reflects "the actual learning and instructional activities of the classroom and out-of-school worlds" (Harris & Hodges, 1995, citing Hiebert, Valencia, & Afflerbach, 1994). Constructive, integrated, holistic, and authentic approaches to teaching, learning, and assessment are more meaningful and effective (Bembridge, 1994; Jongsma & Farr, 1993) than methods that break down knowledge into discrete pieces and test them separately (as is the behaviourist tradition of reductionism on which standardized tests are based).

Alternative forms of assessment have emerged to reflect a shift from describing student performance in terms of "norms" and "products" to defining it in terms of standards (what students should know and do) (Jongsma & Farr, 1993). These include portfolio assessment, hands-on experiments, computer testing and/or simulations, video and audio evaluations, interactive and dynamic assessment, classroom-based assessments (tasks completed while participating in daily learning at school), and performance-based assessment (on-demand tasks that require responses similar to those in instructional

---

For Reflection 11.2

Think about how you were assessed by your teacher (or peers) in each of the subject areas when you were in secondary school. What system- or province-wide assessments do you recall? What were your reactions to these various forms of assessment?

situations). Additionally, system- and nation-wide testing programs are moving in directions that reflect the curriculum and blend various alternative forms of assessment with the more traditional approaches.

Authentic and Performance Assessments

At this point, to avoid confusion, it is necessary to review in detail the meanings of two widely used forms of assessment: authentic and performance. Each type of assessment encompasses a wide range of different formats and procedures. These definitions are based on Hiebert, Valencia, and Afflerbach (1994) and Harris and Hodges (1995).

Authentic assessment (the term preferred to "alternative" assessment) refers to the assessment of different kinds of abilities in contexts that are likely to be encountered in the real world of the classroom and in the world outside school. In authentic assessment the learners' experience is allowed to be in transaction with prior subject matter knowledge. Higher-level abilities form the basis of such assessments.

Some classroom-based assessments are more "authentic" than others (Hiebert et al., 1994; Meyer, 1992). For example, assessment of writing is more authentic when students write several drafts on a topic in science until they submit the final draft for assessment purposes. Let us illustrate by using an example from the "real world." If asked to deliver a eulogy to a favourite aunt, one would not be expected to draft it under standardized test conditions. Further, one would have choice of content (topic) for the eulogy, the amount of time spent on it, and the pace at which it was written and redrafted. In other words, the locus of control, a significant criterion for the authenticity of a writing task, would be with the learner (Meyer, 1992). That does not mean that authentic assessments are not also performance assessments but in authentic assessments much of the artificial structure of "testing" has been removed.

The term "**informed**" rather than informal assessment has been proposed to describe "the process by which knowledgeable teachers should have meaningful goals for instruction and clear purposes for assessment, use a variety of strategies to observe selectively and systematically, and document their students' performances in meaningful learning activities across diverse contexts and over time" (Wolf, 1993, pp. 518–19). The features of informed assessment have become characteristics of authentic assessment. These are:

1. *Knowledgeable teachers*: Teacher-based assessment requires knowledge about curriculum, teaching, developmental theory, and the place in learning of language, culture, and social context. This knowledge must then be applied to set goals for learning and to explicate performance standards and benchmarks for assessing student progress.

2. *Systematic observation*: As students read, write, talk (discuss), work on projects, and solve problems, teachers can learn about students' strengths and weaknesses.
3. *Systematic documentation*: Documentation and records consisting of student portfolios (collections of students' work and students' reflections) and classroom portfolios (teacher's notes on each class as a whole, checklists, or profiles of the class) enable students and teachers to evaluate learning.
4. *Multiple methods*: Many different "windows" on student learning are needed because each provides a more complete picture of each student. Cognitive, affective, and social processes should be assessed. Assessment should be seen as "a series of conversations" (Johnston, 1995) and as a learning transaction.
5. *Diverse contexts*: Students perform differently across different texts, tasks, and settings even if the content being tested is similar. Thus students need to be assessed across a number of diverse contexts. For example, a student may be more competent in writing an expository text than writing a poem or a story.
6. *Ongoing assessment over time*: Because of the continuous and dynamic nature of learning itself, student and class performances need to be viewed on a number of occasions so that patterns in performance can be discerned.
7. *Meaningful learning activities*: Rich and valuable insights into the range of talents and insights possessed by students can only be gleaned if the curriculum consists of authentic learning tasks. "It is difficult to fashion a silk purse assessment out of a sow's ear curriculum" (Shulman as cited in Wolf, 1993, p. 521).

Performance assessment involves on-demand tasks performed by students to show their level of knowledge (e.g., performing science experiments; reading a long passage and responding to it rather than selecting from multiple-choice answers). Some tasks require several days to complete. However, most tasks are conducted in fairly standardized testlike contexts.

The use of performance assessments has increased because "they provide information about students' ability to analyze and apply information — their ability to think" (Marzano, 1994, p. 44). In other words, on-demand performance tasks measure higher-level thinking skills by assessing students' performance on complex learning tasks (e.g., the students' ability to solve a problem). "The tasks include essays, demonstrations, computer simulations, performance events, portfolios of their work, and open-ended questions and problems" (Guskey, 1994, p. 51). Often these tasks are authentic and "directly related to real-world problems" (p. 51). They also provide students with explicit guidelines about what teachers expect students to learn.

Performance assessments are often used in **outcome-based education** (OBE), which aims for certain outcomes or proficiencies that are usually assessed within the context of performance tasks.

Performance-based assessment has gained ground because educators have acknowledged that learning is complex and that diverse methods are needed to assess such learning. Traditional assessments test recognition and recall of information. Performance-based assessments are an integral part of the instruction and "the distinction between instruction and assessment [becomes] 'seamless'" (Guskey, 1994, p. 51). Some educators see performance-based assessments (if they are authentic) as driving instructional improvements (McLaughlin, 1991; Guskey, 1994). In performance-based assessments, achievement can be measured on any performance tasks in the subject areas — mathematics, science (Schnitzer, 1993), social studies, English, art, drama, or vocational education.

Performance tasks require a lot of time to administer. Additionally, professional development opportunities are often required to adapt one's instructional practices to the demands of authentic, performance-based assessments (designing them and allocating the time to administer them).

In most present-day classrooms, both authentic and performance assessments are common.

Alternative assessment, authentic assessment, and performance assessment have become the educational buzzwords of the 1990s. The decade has seen a move toward more *formative assessment* of student progress — that is, the use of collected data to assist in the improvement of performance through self-evaluation. This type of assessment, as evidenced in the use of portfolio, is a shift away from the more traditional *summative assessment*, which emphasized scores on standardized tests (Valeri-Gold, Olson, & Deming, 1991–92, p. 298).

Examples of Alternative Assessments

Across the continent, educators are concerned with ensuring that students learn more than just basic skills; that they learn such skills as solving problems, working collaboratively, and synthesizing knowledge across disciplines (O'Neil, 1992). Therefore, new directions in testing include authentic and performance assessments, individual tasks, as well as **portfolios** or multidimensional profiles of students' processes, work-in-progress, and final products. These types of assessments are part of a continuous process that is tied directly to teaching. "This kind of assessment does not drive the curriculum; it grows out of the curriculum and is part and parcel of curriculum" (Maeroff, 1991, p. 274) because "the assessment task is part of instruction" (p. 275). Assessment, then, is actually embedded in instruction. This point connects with the view of assessment as a transaction between teacher, learner, subject matter, and text: all are involved in the transaction of learning. This view of assessment is compared to a philosophy extant in the performing arts (drama, music, art, and studio arts), in athletics, in vocational education, and in medical schools. It is only now making inroads into the academic subjects.

Examples of this type of assessment include asking students to write essays or stories rather than answer questions about the conventions of writing; or having students perform science experiments rather than asking them questions about experiments. Many of these types of assessments take time (teachers' and students'), are labour-intensive, and hence are expensive to administer. Many lack any kind of standardization, a concern for administrators and policy-makers. In authentic assessment, emphasis is on a student's individual progress from point A to point B. Yet students, parents, and the general public often want to know whether students' progress is in line with that of their peers.

Other informal (rather than standardized or formal) methods of alternative assessment, some of them less authentic than others in the context of the classroom, include observation of students, interviews, anecdotal records, checklists, inventories, conferences with students, teacher-made tests, and **self-assessments** by students of their own work through reflective activities (such as journals, for example), as well as assessments by peers. Many of these items can be incorporated into student portfolios to provide information about both the process a learner goes through and the products of learning.

Assessing Content Literacy

Assessing students' ability to read, write, or discuss the content of the disciplines can be referred to as *content literacy assessment*. Until recently there have been no substantive advances in content literacy assessment at the secondary level of schooling. Content area teachers, however, need to modify or "reshape" traditional assessments of students' understanding of content area concepts by using reading, writing, discussions, and student presentations as part of the assessment process (Moje & Handy, 1995).

In the content areas, a balance between performance and authentic assessments is needed. Teachers must identify the purpose of assessment carefully to determine whether performance or authentic assessment is appropriate (Meyer, 1992). Many performance assessments in the classroom are not authentic, but authentic assessments are always performance assessments because they require students to demonstrate their performance, although in more natural situations. Authenticity is multidimensional (Meyer, 1992). Authentic assessment can be authentic in several aspects: locus of control (for example, who has control in determining topic, time spent, and pace?); stimuli (what directions/guidance are provided?); task and task complexity;

For Reflection 11.3
What types of authentic assessments do you recall from secondary-school content areas? What performance-based assessments were you given? Which performance-based assessments do you feel were most authentic? Why?

---

resources that can be accessed; motivation; conditions under which the task is completed; spontaneity; criteria for the assessment; standards; and consequences of doing well or not. Standardized assessment works on assumptions about progress and learning as a linear process, whereas performance and authentic assessments attempt to account for differences in learning styles, interest, innovation, and cognitive and affective understanding.

Guidelines for Linking Assessment to Instruction

Educators should make assessment a part of their instruction to make each more effective (Winograd, Paris, & Bridge, 1991; Maeroff, 1991). This section outlines some guidelines for developing and improving authentic assessments in education (Winograd, 1994; Winograd, Paris, & Bridge, 1991, pp. 110–11; Jamentz, 1994, pp. 56–57).

1. *Clarify goals of instruction.* What is the theoretical orientation in the curriculum? What are the goals for instruction? Does instruction direct assessment? What measures fit in with the vision of the curriculum in place? In other words, what do you want to measure?
2. *Clarify purposes of assessment.* What are the purposes for testing? To diagnose student needs? To choose appropriate materials? To report progress? To rank students? To determine standards? To decide on promotion or nonpromotion? To provide accountability? What assessment tools are appropriate for each purpose? Who are the potential audiences for the assessment results? Students? Teachers? Parents? Administrators? Politicians and legislators?
3. *Use multiple measures.* Which variety of meaningful assessment measures are needed to assemble portraits (rather than snapshots) of students' abilities in each subject area? The questions are: How should information be gathered on students? How should assessment approaches and tasks be selected and/or developed? Should one use a portfolio that contains infor-

mal records, observations, checklists, samples of students' work, self-evaluations, and results on performance tests? How much teacher and student time will be required to collect, organize, and interpret multiple-measure results? What time and support will be provided by administration to implement these types of assessments?

4. *Set performance standards.* What forms/criteria for interpreting students' performance will be used in place of the traditional standards and measures (such as grade equivalents and percentiles)? Are rubrics (guidelines that describe student work in the content areas) available or will they have to be developed? How will the standards (rubrics) be made known to students so they can use them to improve their learning? (Rubrics are discussed later in the chapter.)

5. *Interpret results and monitor student learning to inform instruction.* Is interpretation within the same theoretical framework that undergirds instruction? That is, would interpreting the results of assessment only from a traditional framework be problematic if a whole language philosophy undergirded instruction? What do results say about the instructional goals? Are the goals being met? What can students do and what do they still need to learn? What techniques need to be used to improve learning in light of the results?

6. *Improve teachers' capacity to use assessment to improve instruction.* How will teachers learn to translate standards into instructional plans? How will their capacity to analyze students' work be improved? Will they have opportunities during the day to collaborate with other teachers to plan for increasing the alignment between meaningful instruction and meaningful assessment?

7. *Teach students how to use assessment to improve their learning.* How will students be taught to become skilled at using information from assessments to improve their learning? How will performance standards be translated and communicated so that they are meaningful to students? What opportunities will be provided for practising self-assessment? Will self-assessment be modelled for students? Will students be able to review their performance on previous tasks/tests? What questions will be asked to encourage students to reflect on their performance? How can students be encouraged to compare their work against a rubric (a standard) to determine what is needed to reach a standard of excellence? What kind of feedback will be provided on their work (general or specific) and on their assessments of their own work?

8. *Establish management methods.* Will alternative assessments (performance and/or authentic) replace traditional assessments or complement them? What balance will be maintained between the different types of assessments? How will alternative assessments become more manageable and

---

For Reflection 11.4
Which of the guidelines for linking assessment to instruction would be the most difficult to implement in the content areas? Why?

---

less time-consuming? What time and support will be given by administration for collaboration with other teachers?

Authentic Content as Part of Authentic Assessment

Authentic assessment is designed to improve the learning of the important ideas in a discipline in such a way that "students achieve a more integrated and in-depth understanding of important topics" (Peters, 1991, p. 590). By choosing assessment materials that have identifying broad themes, teachers can help students make links across topics within subject areas and across the disciplines. Authentic content or text is defined as material that represents real-world items (e.g., a computer manual), and material that has not been changed in content or form (e.g., original literature) (Harris & Hodges, 1995).

The following guidelines (Peters, 1991) are designed to help teachers select content for assessment.

1. Teachers should select materials that are consistent with the goals of the subject area curriculum.
2. Materials should reflect crucial themes and ideas, since these guide the integration of concepts, generalizations, and theories. To identify "themed" materials for assessment purposes, teachers might ask themselves the following questions:
   a. Does the text have essential (core) content or content related to one or several themes?
   b. Can questions be formulated to explain the themes and the content?
   c. What questions are critical to understanding the discipline?
3. Content selected should be rooted in real-world experiences and have applications outside the classroom.
4. The materials should involve students in higher-order thinking.
5. Teachers should choose content that is sensitive to students' developmental progression. In other words, the materials must be conceptually appropriate so that knowledge and skills transfer to new contexts.

Performance Standards

Performance criteria, benchmarks, and rubrics are guidelines that describe students' work in the subject areas, in reading, writing, listening, and in classroom talk. **Rubrics** are usually based on a scale that rates student performance from high to low. Words or phrases are used to describe the characteristics at each point in the scale.

How does a teacher or student use the rubric for assessment purposes and, in turn, to improve learning? First the scorer (a teacher or a student scoring his or her own work) needs an opportunity to examine scoring rubrics, and exemplary responses that fit in each of the categories. Then the scorer compares the student's work with the descriptions at each point in the rubric.

According to experts in the area of assessment (Jamentz, 1994; Valencia & Place, 1994), rubrics make expectations explicit for students, teachers, and parents. Rubrics set the standards, telling students what teachers think they should be able to do both at the in-process stage of a piece of work and at the final product stage. Standards provide students with criteria that they can internalize and then use to assess and improve the quality of their own work (Valencia & Place, 1994).

One example of a rubric can be seen in Box 11.1, which shows a scale for assessing the complexity of aesthetic response. The scale requires experience with reading and responding to stories (narratives). Wiseman, Many, and Altieri (1992, p. 287) suggest that the validity of the instrument might be examined not only with literature but also with oral, dramatic, or artistic responses. The scale is written in language appropriate to high-school students.

Criteria for Alternative Assessments

Several criteria (based on Herman, 1992, p. 76) need to be met to ensure the quality of different types of alternative assessments.

1. *Consequences*: Were plans made at the outset to evaluate the use and consequences of the assessment?
2. *Fairness*: Have cultural backgrounds and opportunities for learning been considered in the assessments?
3. *Credibility and trustworthiness*: Are the assessments appropriate and useful for their intended purpose? Are procedures outlined for data collection and standards for evaluating learning?
4. *Transferability and generalizability*: Do results support generalizations already made about students? Are they from consistent settings?

Box 11.1
The Assessment of Quality in Aesthetic Responses to Literature

Level 1: *Little or no evidence of story experience.* The book is referred to in broad general terms:

> I really liked the book it was neat it was fun to listen to I thought the tape player it went was darn good.

Level 2: *Slight evidence of story experience.* Certain literary features such as characters, theme, plot, or art media are mentioned without any elaboration or attempt to relate features to story events or actions.

> I liked the book.
> I liked the picetuers.
> I liked the houes.
> I liked the cereters.
> I liked the corloers.

Level 3: *Presentation of story events with little presence of aesthetic elements.* Story events are related or literary features may be identified without expressing personal story experiences.

> The first prnt the Lady go to the stoey.
> The sacend prnt the Lady walks out of the stoey and.
> The three prnt a blue man ran after her.

Level 4: *Some presence of aesthetic elements that directly relate to the story experience.* Story events are related and include a personal story experience such as mention of a favourite part or relationship to life experiences.

> I like went the ole wumn went She had heed be hind the theer and went the aewet came and stast the ole wummy tthrew the woods. The part I really like is when the monster was riding the skateborad after the bus.
> The book reminded me of the *Wizard of Oz* like the witch.

Level 5: *Detailed presence of aesthetic elements which give evidence of the personal significance of the story experience.* Presentation of story events is accompanied by reasons why specific aspects of the text were mentioned or by reference to the personal significance of events in the story.

(continued)

(continued)

> Sometimes My brother is Like Thomas. He is not scrard of nothing. I would be fun to be Thomas and get all that treser. I liked that ghost because he is Nice and Kind.

Level 6: *Highly inventive and mature presence of aesthetic elements that enhance the personal significance of the story experience.* Presentation of story events is accompanied by detailed and complex descriptions of reasons why specific aspects of the story were mentioned. Relationships between the story events and personal experiences are explicitly described.

> I am so happy that she got to win the dance and got a silver dollar. Boy I wish I was a great dancer like her. She musted of been very talented to do all those good dances. I thought she was pretty funny when when when't to the farm and when't under the table and when a veghtable fell off. She whould catch it and put them in her waggon. I wish she chould find her father that wen't away. She must of new him alot because she always thought of him. Mirandy and Brother Wind seem's pretty close to the story Ragtime tumpie because tumpie can seemerler dance like the wind.

Note: Aesthetic elements include: visualizing scenes or characters; making associations between the story and literary or life experiences; relating emotions evoked; putting self in character's shoes; passing judgements on characters' behaviour; discussing preferences; citing metacognitive awareness of living through the story; hypothesizing alternative outcomes; discussing personal relevance of story experience.

Source: From "Enabling Complex Aesthetic Responses: An Examination of Three Literary Discussion Approaches," by D.L. Wiseman, J.E. Many, and J. Altieri, in C. Kinzer & D.J. Leu (Eds.), 1992, *Literacy Research, Theory, and Practice: Views from Many Perspectives*, Chicago: National Reading Conference, pp. 283–90.

5. *Cognitive complexity*: Do the assessments assess higher-level thinking?
6. *Content validity*: Do the tasks reflect the most important concepts in the discipline and the most current understanding of the area of study? Are the tasks authentic?
7. *Content coverage*: Are the assessments representative of the entire curriculum?
8. *Meaningfulness*: Do the more meaningful, contextualized assessments contribute to greater student motivation and better educational experiences?
9. *Cost/efficiency*: How can the more labour-intensive, performance-based assessments be conducted more efficiently so that the demands on teacher time are not overwhelming?

Portfolio Assessment

Portfolios represent a philosophy that views assessment as an integral part of our instruction, and provide a process for teachers and students to use to guide learning. Portfolio assessment is an expanded definition of assessment in which a wide variety of learning indicators are gathered across many situations, before, during, and after instruction. It is a philosophy that honours both the process and the products of learning as well as the active participation of the teacher and the students in their own evaluation and growth (Valencia, 1990a, p. 340).

Portfolio assessment allows for the collaborative collection of a multidimensional profile of student progress (Flood, Lapp, & Monken, 1992). As a continuous collection of performances of authentic tasks, a portfolio can then be used by students to improve their learning and by teachers to improve their teaching. In this type of assessment, teaching and learning are directly connected, not separated as they are in traditional standardized assessment; teaching and learning are transactional with each other. Further, teacher reflectivity is increased (Dewitz, Carr, Palm, & Spencer, 1992). A portfolio, thus, is an aid for instructional purposes as well as for evaluative purposes (for parent–teacher conferences or for reporting progress to parents). Portfolio assessment takes somewhat different forms in different classrooms, as it is designed and accumulated by teachers, students, and even parents. Contents and formats reflect the diversity of purposes for assessment.

One important component of the portfolio is students' monitoring of their own growth and achievement though self-assessment. Such self-assessment gives evidence of students' ability to work collaboratively, to accomplish in a social learning context, to take ownership for learning, and to work independently. It is also a gauge of their knowledge of the process of becoming literate in each content area, and ability to evaluate that knowledge.

A portfolio should demonstrate all three aspects of Russell's (1954) description of vocabulary development: height (the number of different items in a portfolio), breadth (the variations of different items included), and depth (the demonstration of higher-order thinking skills in the various items). A portfolio also indicates the depth and breadth of the student's knowledge, not just the *what* in a subject area, but also the *how* and the *why* — and can reveal other information about the multidimensionality of the whole student (Flood, Lapp, & Monken, 1992). To achieve these purposes, students, teachers, and parents select information on processes, activities, and some products (performance-based assessments).

To meet these ends, the contents of a portfolio may include (and will change on a regular basis) any of the following: reports, reading and writing samples in various stages of development, projects, samples of daily work and classroom assignments, response logs, journals, self-evaluations, think-alouds (to capture metacognitive processes), attitude surveys, tests (teacher-made or standardized), surveys, checklists, inventories, and anecdotal notes made by a teacher during instruction in any of the content areas (Flood, Lapp, & Monken, 1992; Tierney, Carter, & Desai, 1991).

In portfolios, students can demonstrate different kinds of intelligences (Gardner, 1983; Hebert, 1992). Multiple dimensions of a student's learning can be demonstrated through art, music, drama, dance, and sculpting, which are not associated with traditional ways of assessing (Hebert, 1992). Some students who cannot perform as adequately on standardized tests or convey ideas in writing are better able to "convey a deep understanding of complex ideas and themes through . . . drawings" (Wolf, 1993, p. 518). Artistic talents can be used as "bridges" to advance written and oral language abilities (Wolf, 1993) and knowledge in the content areas. It is vital "that *alternate routes* to excellence . . . and alternate destinations of excellence" (Harman, 1992, p. 251) be allowed in content area classrooms and portfolios. Using classroom talk, drama, readers' theatre, and the visual arts as products to demonstrate what has been learned is referred to as **transmediation**. "Transmediation is a process of moving information from one communication system to another" (Hoyt, 1992, p. 580; Harste, Burke, & Short, 1988). Transmediation occurs when students translate their knowledge into motion, verbal interpretation, or artistic expression. In this way, the cognitive and affective aspects of learning are combined (Leland & Harste, 1994). "Classrooms that offer [students] a variety of communication systems facilitate learning in ways that stimulate the imagination, enhance language learning and deepen understanding" (Hoyt, 1992, p. 584). Evidence of all of these types of performances can be included in students' assessment portfolios.

Principles Underlying Portfolio Assessment

Portfolio assessment is guided by several principles drawn from research and instructional practice (Valencia, 1990a; Valencia, 1990b; Jordan, 1994). These principles are:

1. *Assessment is authentic.* The tasks given and the texts (content) used are drawn from instructional contexts (processes and products of classroom activities), and the assessment is conducted as part of the instructional process. Authentic content consists of material in the subject areas that goes to the heart of each discipline and allows for application of ideas in the real world (Peters, 1991).
2. *Assessment is continuous.* The process of learning/development is assessed over time. Students are continually observed and information is col-

lected continuously. Several indicators for each different goal are then collected, increasing the reliability of conclusions drawn.

3. *Assessment is multidimensional.* Because reading and learning are multi-faceted processes, sampling must include cognitive and affective responses across a wide range of texts and for different purposes.

4. *Assessment is collaborative.* Students need to evaluate how well they have learned and what they still need to learn. Teachers need to assess the effectiveness of their teaching so they can make further instructional decisions. As suggested earlier in this chapter, students and teachers should collaborate in assessment as partners in the learning process. "Collaboration precipitates meaningful dialogue about the criteria and process we use in evaluation and provides an important model for students as they become self-evaluators" (Valencia, 1990a, pp. 338–39).

5. *Assessment is trustworthy.* There should be clearly defined procedures for collecting information on students and clearly defined criteria for evaluating the information. In other words, there must be standards, expectations, or criteria that students should meet in terms of knowledge of content and ability to read, write, and talk about the content of the discipline. If all of this is accomplished, then the assessment can be deemed trustworthy.

When portfolios are used for classroom assessment, teachers have many indicators of students' work and know the conditions under which the work is produced. However, in large-scale assessments, tighter controls for collecting, scoring, and reporting are required (Valencia, Hiebert, & Afflerbach, 1994), undermining the original intent of portfolios (Jordan, 1994).

Beyond the classroom, administrators and other decision makers have expressed concerns that portfolio assessment is unreliable, inconsistent, and unequal across classrooms, schools, and whole school districts (Valencia, 1990a). A recent survey of portfolio practices (Calfee & Perfumo, 1992) has found that, despite intense commitment on the part of classroom teachers, the validity and reliability of portfolio assessment are seen to be untrustworthy (Valencia, 1990b); that is, results vary from teacher to teacher, school to school, district to district. This debate suggests a need for a balance between standardized testing and alternative assessments.

For Reflection 11.5

Describe your experiences with portfolio assessment when you were a student in secondary school.

Structure and Content of a Portfolio

Teachers using portfolios need to determine some management issues. These include: Who will be able to access the portfolios? Where will they be stored in the classroom and for use of future teachers? What form will the actual portfolio take (a file folder or a box)?

Portfolios can be large, expandable file folders containing (1) samples of the students' work (teacher-selected or student-selected); (2) the student's self-evaluations; (3) teachers' observational notes and comments; and (4) collaborative (teacher and student) notes on progress made. Unlike grade books, portfolios should be stored in an area of the classroom that provides easy access to students and teachers.

Organizational strategies (Valencia, 1990a) that make portfolios useful and manageable include the following:

1. *Plan for a portfolio.* Select representative items to include on the basis of curricular and instructional goals. Otherwise, the portfolio may become unfocussed. Identify the content and format for the assessment tasks. Many instructional activities (e.g., post-reading graphic organizers) can be used to assess students' understanding of content following reading and become part of the portfolio folder. Dialogue can be carried on with other teachers to build a common understanding of goals, tasks, and performance criteria.

2. *Organize the contents of the portfolio.* A two-layer organization would contain the actual work of the students and progress notes, and a summary sheet to synthesize the information. In this way progress can be conveyed to parents and others, and decision making is possible for future instruction. These items serve as supporting evidence for any synthesis of results and attend to consistency concerns.

3. *Use the portfolio for decision making.* The portfolio can be used
   a. at planning time by reviewing and reflecting on contents;
   b. for collaborative visiting by teacher and student every few weeks — to discuss progress, add items, or determine instructional/learning courses;
   c. by students themselves to visit individually or with a peer for interpersonal dialogue, to learn from each other, or compare items;
   d. at conference times with parents and administrators;
   e. at the end of the school year to determine which items remain permanently in the portfolio to be passed on to the next teacher and which items the student can take home.

The portfolio approach merely reflects what teachers and students have been doing in their classrooms intuitively in the past (Valencia, 1990a).

Portfolios in the Content Areas

Portfolios have been used successfully in such academic subjects as science, mathematics, and English and in multidisciplinary units across the curriculum. Two examples of portfolios follow.

Portfolios in Mathematics

Studies of portfolio use in mathematics show positive results (Knight, 1992). In these portfolios, students and teachers include daily class notes, long-term projects, scale drawings, journal entries, their best tests, their worst tests, problems of the week, and homework, as well as personal statements as to why each item included was important to the student's learning. Knight (1992) also presents questions teachers and mathematics departments should ask before they embark on portfolio assessment in mathematics (see Box 11.2).

Box 11.2
Questions to Ask about Math Portfolios

---

1. What is the difference between a folder of a student's work and a portfolio?
2. Can a portfolio of a limited number of pieces accurately reflect student growth over time in mathematics?
3. Should a student receive a grade for a portfolio, or would this double grading work?
4. Is it possible to use portfolio assessment in conjunction with current math teaching practices?
5. Must the grade of a portfolio correspond to what a student would attain under traditional grading standards?
6. If we use writing as a portion of math problem solving, will a student who is poor at written expression but skilled in math be penalized?
7. Could we standardize the format of portfolio assessment so that it would carry a universally understood meaning from site to site?
8. Should portfolios be scored by individual teachers or should a district-wide portfolio assessment group be formed?
9. Would standardized assessment criteria and grading of portfolios spoil portfolio assessment's special qualities?

Source: From "How I Use Portfolios in Mathematics," by P. Knight, 1992, *Educational Leadership, 49*(8), pp. 71–72. Reprinted by permission of the Association for Supervision and Curriculum Development. Copyright © 1992 by ASCD. All rights reserved.

For Reflection 11.6
How might portfolio assessment be used in your subject area specialization?

Multimedia Technology

Some schools (e.g., Conestaga Elementary School in Wyoming where a video of an assessment was transferred onto a laser disc, as described by Campbell, 1992) are combining laser disc technology with portfolios as a means of assessing students' work. Growth in verbal ability (e.g., reading), physical education, and art is documented on videotape and scanned onto laser disc. A multimedia system requiring a computer, a CD-ROM drive, an optical drive, a scanner, and a laser printer is required. With the laser disc, vast amounts of information can be stored or retrieved by any one student.

Some New Directions in Assessment

Co-operative Assessment in the Content Areas

Co-operative strategies for assessing students have recently been implemented in content area classrooms (Johnson & Johnson, 1991; Moje & Handy, 1995). A co-operative content assessment (as described by Moje and Handy, 1995) in chemistry would be set up in the following way.

Students in the content areas would be paired according to ability and personality traits. For example, students whose reading and mathematics abilities are somewhat different would be matched so that they could give each other support. They would also be paired based on their ability to work together collaboratively without competing or dominating during the interactions. While students prepare for the examination independently, they will work in pairs on the exam. The collaborative examination process, while an evaluative activity, is also viewed as a learning activity with partners having opportunities to play the role of both tutor and tutee as problems are worked out, solutions sought, and concepts addressed on a content examination.

A study of transcripts made during co-operative content examinations (Moje & Handy, 1995) revealed that students contribute in various ways: some students do "talk-alouds," while others monitor the thinking processes revealed; some correct their partners' miscalculations while others supply a needed test-taking strategy; some interpret materials for the other or negotiate interpretations while others provide steps needed to complete the calculation. For the teacher, just walking around the class listening to the pairs' conversations also provides numerous opportunities for assessment. The collaborative content test transforms a product orientation to a learning situation for both students and teacher.

In one co-operative content examination in mathematics, at a high school in Calgary, Alberta, students were matched on the basis of their average score in mathematics based on a number of teacher-made tests that students had completed independently. One of the lasting effects of the co-operative content examination experience was the positive feelings the students took away from the examinations. Gone was the sense of frustration, of feeling "put down" or "less than intelligent."

Several questions related to collaborative vs. individual assessment need to be addressed by teachers (Hiebert, Valencia, & Afflerbach, 1994): What understandings do students hold regarding collaboration in a test — is it "cheating" or "negotiating the answer" (the latter view is held in some real-world events)? How will the oral processes used in the collaboration be evaluated? How will scores be reported?

Panel Assessments

Some high-school mathematics teachers can use panel performance assessments as alternatives to pencil-and-paper tests in mathematics, particularly in assessing knowledge of complex problems, algebra, and pre-calculus (Haas & Lo Presto, 1994). In panel assessments students show their understanding of the concepts rather than regurgitate facts and knowledge. The process (Haas & Lo Presto, 1994) is as follows:

1. Several days before the mid-semester or semester exams, hand out to students six problems on important concepts in the course.
2. Allow students to work in collaborative learning groups (during and after class time) to work out solutions to the problems and to practise sharing their understandings with others in the group. Access to books and notes, teacher clarification, and parental assistance is permitted.
3. Recruit panels of judges from the community (several panels will be necessary). These will include people from the business and university communities as well as parents and administrators. One mathematics expert (a math teacher or engineer) and two laypeople who can help judge students' ability to explain mathematics in "everyday language" should also be on the panel.
4. Provide the panel judges with the problems, the answers, and the scoring criteria.
5. Allow student groups to go before the panel as a team. The assessment procedure is as follows:

For Reflection 11.7

Teachers in content areas other than mathematics might use a technique similar to panel assessment (Haas & Lo Presto, 1994). How might this technique be applied in other subject areas such as physical education, chemistry, English, or biology?

---

a. The judges randomly choose one of the problems and one team member to explain it. Each team member will then be asked to answer individually one of the six problems.

b. Judges may probe for more detail/explanation or allow other students on the team to take part in the discussion. Students may use visual aids in the communication process.

c. When the assessment is complete, each judge then evaluates individual students on their understanding, including the ability to relate the problem to real-world examples. A letter grade (based on a rubric) is assigned to each student, and written comments are provided by the judges.

Computerized Assessment in the Content Areas

One of the most exciting prospects for assessing students' literacy (reading, writing, and talk) as well as their content literacy lies in the area of interactive computer assessment. "With interactive assessment, the computer itself gathers the data by confronting the student directly with various kinds of reading [in the content area] tasks" (McKenna, 1991). Among the newer interactions of this kind are *hypertext* (links formed nonsequentially in weblike fashion to other texts for limitless associations) and *hypermedia* (branching to nonprint forms of information such as film, music, spoken text, pictures, icons, and animated graphics) (McKenna, 1991; Wepner, 1991). The two can be used in combination to track and then to analyze metacognitive processing. This would provide an account of a student's strategy use, interest in a topic, level of background knowledge, and performance self-assessment (McKenna, 1991; Pikulski, 1990; Wepner, 1991). In the content areas, comparisons of student performance could be made. For example, if a student who lacks the requisite background information and interest confuses two types of protozoa when reading in science, a videodisk presentation on these two types of protozoa might be assigned by the teacher (Wepner, 1991).

Assessment Techniques

This section describes forms of authentic assessment that can be used in the content areas. If portfolio assessment has been implemented by a content area teacher, some of these assessments could become the content of portfolios.

Assessing Reader Response

The transactional view of reading (and writing) suggests that comprehension should be assessed in a way that takes aesthetic response into account. We have already stated that different students can make different interpretations from the same reading of the same text because each reading is an evocation. As Rosenblatt (1989) has stated, individuals' responses are shaped by the feelings, images, attitudes, and ideas from their own experiences, language, culture, and the literature they have read. Their responses will also be shaped by the stance they take during reading.

An authentic instrument (consisting of a four-stage hierarchy and several levels of quality within each stage/category) to assess personal response, to direct teachers' instruction, and to guide students' self-assessment has been developed by Sebesta, Monson, and Doces Senn (1995) (see Table 11.1). The authors believe that "aesthetic response, to be authentic, necessitates a journey through these stages. Lacking evocation, the reader is unlikely to examine alternatives; lacking an examination of alternatives, the thoughtful reader is unlikely to arrive at a stage of reflection" (p. 445).

Although this instrument was developed mainly for use with literature, it lends itself to all content areas because it includes efferent responses. Students in the lower grades (4–6) responded more frequently at the evocation and alternatives levels, while students in the upper grades (7–10) had more responses at the reflective thinking and evaluation levels, suggesting that responses are developmental.

Assessing Comprehension Monitoring

In the other content areas teachers need to encourage a balance of efferent and aesthetic responses, as well as a shift in stance as the text and as their own experience direct them. Some texts in social studies, science, and art appreciation will trigger aesthetic responses. However, some content area textbooks do not capture the sense of wonder and adventure in science and history as do trade books on the same topic (Frager, 1993). As suggested in Chapter 2, to promote a balance of efferent and aesthetic reading, content area teachers should balance textbook reading with trade book reading (Frager, 1993).

Table 11.1

A Taxonomy of Aesthetic Response

	Minimal	Moderate	Complete

0. *Efferent response:*
Example: "The main characters in the story are the talking mule, the talking dog, the boy, and his father."

STAGE 1: EVOCATION (SUSPENSION OF CRITICAL JUDGEMENT, AND "LIVING THROUGH" THE TEXT)

1. *Relive the experience:* re-experience what happened as you read; includes acting out, telling, rereading a part that you, the reader, choose to reread.
Example: "When the mule spoke it was a surprise. I was thinking it was going to be a magical or in some way a special mule."

2. *Imagine or picture:* characters, setting, or events from the selection; elaborate on the basic idea.
Example: "The son was so scared that he almost had a heart attack. He screamed as loud as he could. Then he ran as far as he could."

(continued)

(continued)

	Minimal	Moderate	Complete

STAGE 2: ALTERNATIVES (COMPARING, CONTRASTING THE ORIGINAL EVOCATION)

3. *Apply own experience*: reconsider response by relating self.
Example: "This is a picture of all the people telling Bill what to do and where to go because it reminds me of my brother and everyone telling him what to do and him telling them NO!"

4. *Apply other reading or media to the work*: e.g., comparing folk tales.
Example: "This story reminds me of a story I was told when I was little about a king who had a chair that talked and nobody would believe him . . . "

5. *Apply other readers' views (as in book discussions) or re-examine your own views.*
Example: "I really liked the story. It was unpredictable and humorous . . . It was surprising when the dog started talking, too . . . It would be great to be able to talk to animals and have them talk back."

6. *Re-examine text from other perspectives*: including hypothesizing, considering another point of view, extrapolating.
Example: "I wonder why the mule hadn't talked before now? Why did he wait so long to say he was sick of being yelled at?"

(continued)

(continued)

	Minimal	Moderate	Complete

STAGE 3: REFLECTIVE THINKING (THEMATIC LEVEL, REQUIRING GENERALIZATION AND APPLICATION)

7. *Interpretation:* generalize about the meaning of the literary experience, with application to the reader's own life, hence extending #3 to application.

Example: "Finding out what animals thought would change the world. There may not be anymore eating beef or poultry. Yikes! I love a good leg of chicken."

STAGE 4: EVALUATION (CLASSIFIED ONLY AS AESTHETIC IF THE ABOVE CATEGORIES HAVE BEEN MET)

8. *Evaluating what you got from the transaction.*

Example: "If I were the boy I wouldn't trip out. I would go and talk to the animals. What harm can talking to a mule do? Most people chat with their pets anyways. It wouldn't make much difference if the pet talked back. It would actually be nice."

9. *Evaluating the "goodness" of the work itself:* in regard to criteria set by the reader.

Example: "I think this story really does not have any other point beside the fact that things are not always what they seem. Writing about this donkey might be a lot easier if the story was longer and more thought provoking."

Source: From "A Hierarchy to Assess Reader Response," by S.L. Sebesta, D.L. Monson, and H. Doces Senn, 1995, *Journal of Reading, 38*(6), pp. 444–50. Copyright © 1995 by the International Reading Association. All rights reserved.

One way to encourage transactions with text is to ask students to monitor their responses as they read sections of text. To get students to assess whether they are keeping a balance of efferent and aesthetic responses, teachers need to demonstrate through a talk-aloud or a think-aloud how to monitor responses. A comprehension monitoring strategy can serve as an authentic assessment measure. The following strategy (Frager, 1993) consists of students recording their responses during reading. Students use a code, which they write on strips of paper (coloured Post-it notes work well) and stick to the margins of the text they are reading. The code to use when reading a social studies chapter might be A = Agree; B = Bored; C = Confused; D = Disagree; M = Main Idea (Smith & Dauer, 1984). Students could add other codes such as H = Hope; D = Distrust; and An = Anger. For a chapter in science, the code might be A = Awesome; C = Clear; D = Difficult; I = Important; S = Surprising; U = Unbelievable. In this way students identify aesthetic and efferent responses in the process of comprehension/interpretation and note their obstacles to understanding (Frager, 1993).

The above strategy can be used in a discussion following the reading and then filed in a portfolio as part of a self-assessment of aesthetic and efferent response to content area reading.

Assessing Writing and Reading

Rubrics based on constructivism and on Rosenblatt's (1989) transactional model of reading and writing are beginning to emerge. Using ideas from Adams (1995), a rubric has been developed (see Table 11.2) in which reading and writing privilege efferent and aesthetic response and divergent and convergent thinking. Rubric descriptors (developed by Sheridan and Gordon for this text) are provided in Table 11.3.

Assessing Interdisciplinary Transactions

We have already discussed the importance of each subject area teacher encouraging students to make interdisciplinary transactions rather than compartmentalizing knowledge into subject areas. One of the best ways to integrate the curriculum is to have subject area teachers work together to develop interdisciplinary thematic units (Williams & Reynolds, 1993; Winograd & Higgins, 1994–95). Such integrative units go beyond segmenting topics/concepts into traditional subject area disciplines (see Figure 11.1). Instead, the theme serves as a hub with the spokes "no longer the academic subjects but rather living skills such as reflective thinking, critical ethics, problem-solving, valuing, building self-concept, social action skills, and searching for completeness and meaning" (Beane as paraphrased in Smith & Johnson, 1994, pp. 200, 204).

Table 11.2

Assessing Aesthetic and Efferent Response in Reading and Writing

Reading	Writing

AESTHETIC

Completeness: The reader engages the entire text, evoking images and making personal associations. Responses demonstrate a thorough understanding and interpretation of text.

Completeness: The writer engages the reader. The response shows audience awareness. The writer "reads his own writing."

Complexity: The response provides evidence of integration/interconnectedness from multiple sources.

Complexity: The writer provides evidence of interdisciplinary connections.

Risk-Taking: The reader acknowledges/evaluates the writer's craft, explores and reflects on multiple meanings, reads like a writer, and challenges self as a reader.

Risk-Taking: The writer evaluates her own craft, reads like a reader; and challenges self as a writer by "writing her own reading."

EFFERENT

Focus/Coherence: The reader understands the central ideas in the text in a coherent way and can make links across the curriculum.

Focus/Coherence: The paper is coherent and is focussed around main points or central ideas. Coherence is maintained by smooth transitions with no gaps.

Exploration of Ideas/Experiences: The reader understands the relevant and specific details.

Exploration of Ideas/Experiences: Main points are supported with numerous relevant and specific details.

Voice/Style: The reader uses style and voice of the text to enhance understanding and interpretation.

Voice/Style: The writing consistently engages the reader, showing that the writer is involved in the task. A natural, fluent, individual voice is present.

Control of Conventions: The reader demonstrates a clear grasp of reading skills and strategies to gain understanding of the main points and details in the text.

Control of Conventions: The writer demonstrates clear control of conventions. The paper may not be mechanically perfect, but errors are few and do not distract.

Source: Adapted from "Connections between Reading and Writing in Performance Assessment," by M.H. Adams, 1995, paper presented at the National Reading Conference, New Orleans, LA, December 1995.

Table 11.3

Key Rubric Descriptors

AESTHETIC (READING)	EFFERENT (WRITING)
Insightful interpretation	Well-developed whole
Personal connections	Significant details
Extensions	No gaps
Risk-taking	Strong, compelling voice
Challenging the author	Engaged reader

Key Rubric Descriptors

EFFERENT (READING)	AESTHETIC (WRITING)
Conceptual understanding	Awareness of pattern, shape, rhythm in textual language
Knowledge of detail	Grasp of "big picture"
Analytical understanding	Appreciation for detail
Understanding of logic	Risk-taking
Depth & breadth of new knowledge	Awareness of affective response as well as cognitive understanding

Source: Adapted from "Connections between Reading and Writing in Performance Assessment," by M.H. Adams, 1995, paper presented at the National Reading Conference, New Orleans, LA, December 1995.

However, it has also been pointed out that it is sometimes difficult to form interdisciplinary teams to plan and schedule such lessons in the time blocks at present available in many departmentalized secondary schools. A viable option for content area teachers is to use an interdisciplinary model that combines content areas by including concepts, skills, and questions from several disciplines when dealing with a topic in their own content area (see Figure 11.2). Such an approach is philosophically similar to Smith and Johnson's (1994) "interdisciplinary literature model," which weaves together content and skills while reinforcing the interrelationships among subjects. One teacher only would be required to plan for "interdisciplinary teaching" as it is proposed.

Figure 11.1

Integrative Literature Unit: Transitions*
Theme: Movement in U.S. History

SOCIAL ACTION SKILLS

- Develop timeline of the book according to when settlers banded together for survival (e.g., drought).
- Explore the handling of epidemics: What should a society do? (AIDS vs. scurvy).

REFLECTIVE THINKING

- Look at groups vs. individuals: the idea of connection vs. separation.
- Reflect on your own behaviours: toward parents, peers, and community — individualistic or team oriented?
- Study journals — those who keep them and what they say. Keep your own journal.

Transitions

PROBLEM SOLVING

- Graph conflicts in the book: Look at the intensity of seriousness of the problem; compare Constance's perspective with your own.
- Evaluate the strategies of problem solving: How effective were the Pilgrims' solutions?

Constance: A Story of Early Plymouth (Clapp, 1968)

CRITICAL ETHICS

- Look at the idea of "discovering" a land already inhabited.
- Study the ethics of the Native Americans and their relationship to the Pilgrims — actual and in the book.

CULTURAL DIVERSITY

- Study the Native Americans of the northeastern U.S.
- Research courtship behaviours of different societies and time periods (relate to book).

Understanding personal changes

Living in a changing world

VALUING

- Examine the "human condition."
- Look at publication dates of books: Note the issues/values expressed and compare to U.S. history. Correlate the view of the author to the social view of the day.

SELF-CONCEPT

- Look at the roles of men and women: Are they still accurate or necessary today?
- Compare the language of the Pilgrims with our own.

*Based on J. Beane's (1990) curriculum model.
Source: From "Models for Implementing Literature in Content Studies," by J.L. Smith and H. Johnson, 1994, *The Reading Teacher, 48*(3), Figure 3, p. 203.

Figure 11.2

Interdisciplinary Literature Unit
Theme: Movement in U.S. History

MATH CONCEPTS

- Study ratios and distance of Old World to New World.
- Make scale drawings of village or ship.
- Study directions in navigational terms.
- Graph distance and time.
- Study measurements: food per person (fractions).
- Study probability in reference to situations in the book

SCIENCE CONCEPTS

- Research scurvy and its causes; other diseases.
- Investigate food of the New World (plant life).
- Study the myth and lore of planting and healing (Native American).
- Learn navigation by the stars.
- Study cloud formations.
- Investigate drought and its effects.

Constance: A Story of Early Plymouth (Clapp, 1968)

SOCIAL STUDIES

- Develop timeline of movement in book.
- Determine cause and effect of moving to New World: What was happening in England?
- Research: People who came to New World — different beliefs and the interactions.
- Compare Native American rituals and religion to Pilgrims'.
- Map the area
- Study the economics and bartering of the New World.
- Compare gender roles.
- Research the connections of the Old and New Worlds.

READ OTHER BOOKS

- *The Serpent Never Sleeps* (O'Dell)
- *The Witch of Blackbird Pond* (Speare)

LANGUAGE ARTS

- Develop problem solving through drama.
- Write journal and reading responses.
- Write a diary from Elizabeth's perspective.
- Keep vocabulary book.
- Study the language and culture — compare with today.
- Discuss conflicts in the story.

RELATED ARTS

- Make models: Village or ship.
- Visit Williamsburg or other historical site established in 17th or early 18th century.
- Make baskets or Early American crafts.
- Illustrate scenes from the book.
- Listen to music from the 17th century.
- Study dances from the period.

Source: From "Models for Implementing Literature in Content Studies," by J.L. Smith and H. Johnson, 1994, *The Reading Teacher, 48*(3), Figure 2, p. 202.

Experts in interdisciplinary studies have proposed four stages of understanding that correspond fairly roughly to students' mental growth patterns (Gardner & Boix-Mansilla, 1994). These are:

1. *Common sense.* Novices consider generative questions by using their intuitive perceptions of the world (mind, matter, and life) (ages 5–6).
2. *Protodisciplinary knowledge.* Learners use knowledge gleaned from the media, peers, and some understanding of texts (e.g., differentiating between historical and literary accounts or recognizing prejudice) to understand the world.
3. *Disciplinary knowledge.* By middle school, once students are introduced to "disciplines" (social studies, science, math), they begin to learn by observing teachers or experts in the discipline, participating in exhibitions of knowledge in the discipline, and encountering concepts, theories, and methods in their own work.
4. *Beyond disciplinary knowledge.* This type of interdisciplinary work can only be done if students have already mastered portions of specific disciplines because it requires integration of some component disciplines. That is, it requires the asking and answering of generative questions that cut across various disciplines.

How does a teacher then evaluate whether interdisciplinary transactions have been made? Some general evaluation criteria (in the form of questions) are suggested for both teacher and student to assess the interdisciplinary linkages made. These are:

1. What connections have been made between the arts and the sciences? What interdisciplinary insights do students convey in their understanding expressed in writing?
2. What scientific concepts were grasped by students?
3. What political, social, or economic understandings are evident?
4. What types of authentic communication (speaking or writing) occurred?
5. What operations were used from mathematics? What mathematic concepts were acquired or applied?
6. At what level/stage is the student's understanding (common sense, protodisciplinary, disciplinary, or beyond disciplinary)?

Both teachers and students can be involved in evaluating such learning. They can reflect on learning as it occurs in each lesson. Some of the reflection can occur in small-group discussion, in whole-group discussion, and in informal talks with the teacher or peers.

Alternative assessments provide opportunities for teachers to assess the interdisciplinary connections made by students. In schools or individual classrooms where emphasis is placed on teaching a number of subjects in an inter-disciplinary fashion (through thematic units, by integrating several subjects, or in the manner proposed throughout this text), the goal is to assess in a way that reinforces or aligns with interdisciplinary teaching (Maeroff, 1991).

Assessing Reading Awareness

An inventory entitled the "Metacognitive Reading Interview" (Miholic, 1994) (see Box 11.3) can be used to help students become metacognitive in their use of learning strategies and thus achieve higher levels of comprehension in the content areas. "Comprehension monitoring, beyond being automatic when mastered, is a problem-solving process that invites critical, flexible, and insightful thinking. With this inventory, we are only bringing the assumed sub-conscious strategies to a concrete and conscious level" (Miholic, 1994, pp. 85–86).

Discuss the responses with students to heighten awareness rather than emphasize the score obtained. For scoring purposes, "correct" responses should be marked with a plus sign (+) and ambiguous or "incorrect" answers with a minus sign (–). Since there is more than one correct response for each number, students should be asked to choose the "most valuable strategies for each item" (Miholic, 1994).

Summary

The intended meaning of assessment is to "sit with" a student to find out what he or she really knows and means; it is "living through" an experience with a student as he or she transacts with texts, tasks, and the teacher. In this time of dramatic changes in how we assess students, we are moving closer to this intended definition of assessment. Authentic and performance assessment (both types of alternative assessments) are aspects of formative assessment, and grow out of and are part of the instructional process. Authentic assessments are informed assessments that require knowledgeable teachers, systematic observation and documentation, and multiple methods in many different contexts; they are continuous and conducted on meaningful learning activities.

An authentic assessment must be a quality assessment (Valencia, 1990a, 1990b). Good assessment is grounded in current theories of learning and cognition, and takes into account the skills that students will need for success at higher levels of education and in the work world (Herman, 1992). Good assessment highlights affective skills as well as cognitive and metacognitive

Box 11.3
Metacognitive Reading Interview

There's more than one way to cope when you run into difficulties in your reading. Which ways are best? For each question below, put a checkmark beside *all* the responses you think are effective.

1. What do you do if you encounter a word and you don't know what it means?
   a. Use the words around it to figure it out.
   b. Use an outside source, such as a dictionary or expert.
   c. Temporarily ignore it and wait for clarification.
   d. Sound it out.
2. What do you do if you don't know what an entire sentence means?
   a. Read it again.
   b. Sound out all the difficult words.
   c. Think about the other sentences in the paragraph.
   d. Disregard it completely.
3. If you are reading science or social studies material, what would you do to remember the important information you've read?
   a. Skip parts you don't understand.
   b. Ask yourself questions about the important ideas.
   c. Realize you need to remember one point rather than another.
   d. Relate it to something you already know.
4. Before you start to read, what kind of plans do you make to help you read better?
   a. No specific plan is needed; just start reading to complete the assignment.
   b. Think about what you know about this subject.
   c. Think about why you are reading.
   d. Make sure the entire reading can be finished as quickly as possible.
5. Why would you go back and read an entire passage over again?
   a. You didn't understand it.
   b. To clarify a specific or supporting idea.
   c. It seemed important to remember.
   d. To underline or summarize for study.
6. Knowing that you don't understand a particular sentence while reading involves understanding that
   a. The reader may not have developed adequate links or associations for new words or concepts introduced in the sentence.
   b. The writer may not have conveyed the ideas clearly.
   c. Two sentences may purposely contradict each other.
   d. Finding meaning for the sentence needlessly slows down the reader.

(continued)

(continued)

7. As you read a textbook, which of these do you do?
   a. Adjust your pace depending on the difficulty of the material.
   b. Generally, read at a constant, steady pace.
   c. Skip the parts you don't understand.
   d. Continually make predictions about what you are reading.
8. While you read, which of these are important?
   a. Know when you know and when you don't know key ideas.
   b. Know what it is that you know in relation to what is being read.
   c. Know that confusing text is common and usually can be ignored.
   d. Know that different strategies can be used to aid understanding.
9. When you come across a part of a text that is confusing, what do you do?
   a. Keep on reading until the text is clarified.
   b. Read ahead and then look back if the text is still unclear.
   c. Skip those sections completely; they are usually not important.
   d. Check to see if the ideas expressed are consistent with one another.
10. Which sentences are the most important in the chapter?
   a. Almost all of the sentences are important; otherwise, they wouldn't be there.
   b. The sentences that contain the important details or facts.
   c. The sentences that are directly related to the main idea.
   d. The ones that contain the most details.

Source: From "An Inventory to Pique Students' Metacognitive Awareness of Reading Strategies," by V. Miholic, 1994, *Journal of Reading*, 38(2), pp. 84–86. Reprinted with permission of Vincent Miholic and the International Reading Association. All rights reserved.

skills and provides opportunities for evaluation of learning in social contexts (in collaborative groups as well as independently).

Content area teachers need to clarify the goals of assessment to determine what type of assessment is needed. They should set performance standards for the multiple instruments/measures to be used. The results of assessment need to be interpreted and monitored in such a way that instruction and learning are improved. Management of authentic assessments and collaboration with other teachers are issues that still need to be addressed. To ensure the quality of alternative assessment, criteria such as fairness of assessments for all types of students, transferability and generalizability of results, cognitive complexity of tasks, trustworthiness, content validity and coverage, and cost and efficiency of the procedures need to be applied.

Portfolio assessment, a form of authentic assessment, includes evaluating the process and products of learning, self-assessment, assessment by peers and the teacher, as well as parental input. Portfolio assessment should adhere to the same guidelines that undergird all authentic assessment. Management and organizational issues for using portfolio assessment include planning on the basis of curricular and instructional goals, organizing the contents of a portfolio, and using the portfolio in instructional decision making. Portfolios have been used successfully in mathematics, science, English, and in multidisciplinary units across the curriculum.

Several recent developments in assessment include co-operative assessment in content area classrooms, panel assessments in high-school mathematics, and computerized assessment, the latter especially in English language arts. One type of authentic assessment being implemented in content area classrooms includes assessing reader response. A second type encourages comprehension monitoring in the content areas (as a form of self-assessment) by requiring students to balance efferent and aesthetic response and to shift stances as text and personal experience direct them. A third type, a rubric that privileges efferent and aesthetic response, can be used to assess reading and writing in the content areas. In a fourth type, questions need to be formulated to determine if interdisciplinary linkages have been made. Finally, the "Metacognitive Reading Interview" is a useful instrument for making students more aware of their ability and flexibility in strategy use as they read and learn in the content areas.

Questions for Further Reflection

1. Elaborate on what you now understand about the term *assessment*. What types of assessment do you think are needed in your subject area specialization to obtain a complete picture of students' learning? Why?
2. What difficulties need to be resolved before alternative types of assessment are adopted more widely in secondary schools?
3. Using guidelines for linking assessment to instruction (and for selecting the content for assessment), design a performance-based assessment in your content area specialization. Discuss it with your peers/colleagues.
4. Design an authentic assessment in your content area specialization. Discuss it with your peers/colleagues.
5. Develop performance standards to describe students' work in a specific topic in your subject area specialization.
6. What advantages would portfolio assessment offer your content area? Disadvantages?
7. Which new direction in assessment interests you most? Why? What other directions do you foresee assessment taking in the future?

8. Choose one of the specific assessment techniques provided in the chapter, administer it to a student, analyze the results, and reflect on the implications the results hold for instruction in a specific content area.
9. Who should be involved in student assessment? How can this involvement be transactional? Interdisciplinary?

Key Terms

Alternative assessment
Assessment
Authentic assessment
Evaluation
"Informed" assessment
Measurement
Outcome-based education
Paradigm shift
Performance assessment

Performance standards
Portfolio assessment
Portfolios
Rubrics
Self-assessments
Standardized norm-referenced tests
Traditional assessment
Transmediation

CHAPTER TWELVE

Evaluating Text to Bridge the Gap between Reader and Author

Questions to Consider for this Chapter

1. What is a reader–author relationship? What responsibilities do readers and writers have with respect to reading and writing text?

2. What are the responsibilities of creators of other types of texts (e.g., artwork, musical pieces, and environmental print)? How does a reader–writer or reader–artist relationship affect aesthetic or efferent response?

3. Why do teachers need to analyze the difficulty level of materials (i.e., specific chapters or entire texts) that they expect students to read for their courses?

4. What is the difference between the readability level and the comprehensibility level of a text? What factors that affect reading difficulty are considered in each?

5. What qualities in a reader make a text easy or difficult to read?

6. What are two predictive measures of the difficulty level of text, and what are the advantages of using each?

7. What is a performance measure of text difficulty and how is it different from a predictive measure of text difficulty?

Overview

This chapter opens with a discussion of what constitutes considerate text (print) and explores the responsibilities that readers and writers share in making sense of text or producing text. Reader-based and text-based attributes that contribute to text comprehensibility are then outlined. A review of the nature of content area texts and what makes them difficult enough to prevent an aesthetic or efferent reading precedes the discussion of the concept of text comprehensibility. The chapter discusses three procedures to assess the difficulty level of content area textbooks. These include text comprehensibility checklists, the cloze procedure, and readability formulas. Some instructional suggestions are provided for making textbooks more understandable to students. Using appropriate instructional techniques, teachers can intervene to offset any mismatch between the reader and the text.

What Is Considerate Text?

Reading is part of a larger communication process that involves the reader, the author, and the text. However, it is important to remember that *readers are not always at fault when comprehension difficulties arise or aesthetic or efferent response is not forthcoming.* Textbooks themselves can be one source of difficulty in response or comprehension. Readers are not likely to enter into an aesthetic or efferent relationship with text that is too difficult for them. Through instruction, the content area teacher needs to bridge the gap between what students know and what they will learn from the required readings or how they will experience text.

Considerate text is text that is "friendly" or understandable, be it a printed paragraph, an artist's interpretation of a concept or scene, a visual aid, or an oral presentation. Considerate text is clearly organized, uses appropriate vocabulary, and contains supplementary, explanatory features (Harris & Hodges, 1995).

Texts, particularly textbooks, are not always considerate — that is, "designed to enable the reader to gather appropriate information with minimal cognitive effort" (Anderson & Armbruster, 1984, p. 194). When texts are inconsiderate, the reader must put forth more effort, utilize a greater number of strategies, and possess more prior knowledge to comprehend the texts. **Inconsiderate text** is detrimental to effective aesthetic and efferent transactions. Along with the responsibilities that readers have during reading, authors share some responsibility in making texts comprehensible for their readers.

For Reflection 12.1

Think of texts that you have read and found to be considerate. What made them easy for you? Identify some texts that you have read that were inconsiderate. What made them difficult for you?

Shared Responsibilities of Readers and Writers

When composing a text, an author predicts the reader's background knowledge and experience (in content and language) on the topic and searches for words that will convey appropriate connotations and denotations. Examples, definitions, and elaborated explanations may be necessary if the reader is unfamiliar with the topic. The author will also predict the reader's familiarity with organizational structures and formats in a subject area.

A reader's comprehension and interpretation of the author's message will depend on such factors as background knowledge, interest in the topic, attitude toward reading, purpose (efferent or aesthetic) taken for reading, motivation for reading, linguistic and reading ability, and the reading situation (Richardson & Morgan, 1990). The physical environment, for example, may not be conducive to comprehension, or the reader's sociocultural background may influence what is understood and how it is understood. An examination of the relationship between author and reader in the communicative context reveals that both internal (e.g., use of appropriate vocabulary or paucity of examples by the author) and external (e.g., reader's interest or disinterest) factors are integral to the consideration of text for instructional purposes. "In short, the difficulty a text poses for a reader always stems from the relationship between the ability of the reader and the demands the text makes on the reader" (Estes, 1994, p. 978). Comprehensibility, therefore, is a relative rather than absolute concept. Thus, the match or mismatch between the author and reader is important in determining the extent to which a particular reading, chapter, or textbook will fit a particular audience.

Within this communicative context, authors as well as readers have responsibilities they must fulfil before a successful sharing of information can take place or before efferent and aesthetic transactions are possible. In many content areas, there may still be a mismatch between the author and reader, and thus the teacher has a mediative role to play.

For Reflection 12.2
Recall courses in secondary school when you felt that a text was too difficult. Was this the result of text variables, reader variables, or a combination of both? What steps do you recall teachers taking to bridge the gap between you, the learner, and the text?

Reader Attributes Contributing to Text Comprehensibility

Because text difficulty is a relative concept, it is important to mention briefly the qualities residing in a reader that affect the ease or difficulty with which text will be read.

What readers know before they even begin to read influences the ease or difficulty with which they will understand the text (Alvermann, 1987). This includes specific knowledge of text content, vocabulary used in the text, language and general world knowledge, as well as knowledge of the nature of reading processes, strategies, and tasks. Such knowledge will vary from student to student and lead to different interpretations. The author needs to make some assumptions about readers' knowledge.

If learners want to read-to-learn and believe there is a chance that investing time and effort will lead to success, their motivation will have an influence on the ease with which they comprehend text.

Students' purposes for reading and the stances taken also can make reading a text easier or more difficult. As mentioned throughout the foundational chapters, aesthetic reading can be a way into understanding some very difficult text, as a way into efferent reading.

A reader's interest in a particular topic can affect comprehension by enhancing motivation to read. While interest can affect text comprehensibility, interest-creating text features also play a role in how well different readers understand a text (Graves et al., 1991; Chambliss, 1993). These include certain topics (such as sex, power, the paranormal, death), verb choice, action, concrete detail, novelty, elements of surprise, and identification with a character in narration. Teachers can heighten readers' interest in a text by supplementing textbook materials with articles from popular magazines, newspapers, literature (trade books), as well as with videos, films, and brochures.

Content Area Texts and Learner Characteristics

A large percentage of learning at the secondary-school level occurs from the reading of textbooks. In order to teach students to be able to read effectively in the content areas, teachers need to be aware of the demands textbook authors place on students. They need to be able to determine the characteristics of content materials (especially nonfiction) that are most likely to create difficulties for students. Factors such as concept density (how many new concepts are packed into any one text), level of abstraction, technical vocabulary, sentence length, writing style, organizational patterns, and use of graphic aids can affect a student's comprehension in predominantly efferent reading. The lack of opportunities for aesthetic transactions adds to a text's difficulty level because learners cannot associate concepts with anything meaningful in their lives or bring their own feelings to their reading.

Because comprehensibility factors lie within the learner as well as within the text, teachers also need to acquire knowledge of their students' reading ability (in particular knowledge of their efferent and aesthetic strategies), background knowledge, and interest in and motivation for reading in the content areas. (Chapter 11 discusses assessment of students.)

To best meet students' instructional needs, teachers must be able to evaluate textbooks in terms of features that affect the difficulty of texts to be read. Comprehensibility then can be conceptualized as a transaction of text, reader, and teaching variables.

Three procedures that content area teachers can use to determine text difficulty are comprehensibility checklists, the cloze procedure, and readability formulas.

Features of Text Comprehensibility

As stated earlier, text **comprehensibility** (considerateness) refers to the ease or difficulty with which a text can be read. Experts state that several complex features contribute to making texts more or less comprehensible (Anderson & Armbruster, 1984; Chambliss, 1993; Clewell & Cliffton, 1983; Singer, 1986). Six critical features are presented below:

1. The degree to which the text takes into account a reader's background knowledge and experience (i.e., the congruence between a reader's actual store of knowledge on the topic and the knowledge the author assumes the reader to have);
2. The structure or organization of the text used to convey the author's purpose(s);
3. Coherence — the degree to which the relationships among ideas are logical and clear;
4. Unity, or the degree to which the author keeps to the topic and relates ideas to the major points;
5. The degree to which the author clarifies the use of different types of discourse (e.g., narrative, exposition, persuasion); and
6. The amount of metadiscourse (active dialogue with the reader) used by the author.

For Reflection 12.3
Which of these textbook features make reading especially easy or difficult for you?

The next sections will elaborate on each of the six aspects of text that can affect comprehension. A checklist to assess text comprehensibility will also be presented.

Reader's Knowledge and Experience

Sometimes called "**audience appropriateness**," this feature of text refers to both the reader's knowledge of the *content* of the text and the reader's familiarity with the sentence structure, vocabulary, and concepts in the text. Readers from culturally different backgrounds may have difficulty matching their linguistic knowledge with texts written in English. Research on the effects of prior knowledge on comprehension (e.g., Anderson, Reynolds, Schallert, & Goetz, 1977; and Pearson, Hansen, & Gordon, 1979) and on the relationship between vocabulary knowledge and comprehension (e.g., Anderson & Freebody, 1979) clearly shows the role of prior knowledge and vocabulary knowledge in enhancing comprehension of text.

Exercise 12.1
The Effect of Prior Knowledge on Reading Comprehension

Read the following two texts and indicate which one is more comprehensible, based on the extent to which the text takes into account a reader's prior knowledge.

Text 1

What Is the Theory of Continental Drift?

> One large island. Look at the map of the world. The large areas of land are called *continents* (KON-tuh-nents). Find North and South America, Africa, Europe, Asia, and Australia. Many scientists think that long ago there was only one continent. This piece of land had water all around it. Then the land broke into a number of pieces. The pieces slowly drifted apart. They became the continents we know today. Scientists believe the continents are still moving on the earth. The continents move only a few cen-

timeters each year. The idea that continents move is called the *the-ory of continental* (kon-tuh-NEN-tul) *drift.*

What do scientists think the continents are doing?

WORLD'S LARGEST JIGSAW PUZZLE

On your map, find the Atlantic Ocean. Look at the shape of the coast line of North and South America. Look across the ocean at the coast line of Europe and Africa. Notice that these two coast lines have the same shape. Both coast lines seem to fit together. Other places can be found that might have once fitted together. One reason for believing in continental drift comes from the shapes of land masses.

Source: From *Concepts and Challenges in Earth Sciences,* by L. Berstein, M. Schacher, A. Winkler, and S. Wolfe, 1979, Fairfield, NJ: Cebco Standard, p. 98.

Text 2

Continental Drift

Have you noticed how neatly the east edge of South America seems to match the west edge of Africa? Early in this century an Austrian geologist, Edward Suess, suggested that these conti-nents could be fitted together into one mass, similar to the parts of a jigsaw puzzle.

THEORY OF CONTINENTAL DRIFT

Alfred Wegener (1880–1930), a German meteorologist, pro-posed in 1912 the possibility that at one time continents were together in one supercontinent, which he called "Gondwana-land." He speculated that at some time during the last 200,000 years (since mid-Mesozoic time), this landmass broke into frag-ments (continents) that drifted apart. When this concept of drift-ing continents was presented, most geologists considered it to be mere speculation. However, in the light of recent discoveries of extensive crustal activities, the *Theory of Continental Drift* is now given serious study. Today, some geologists and geophysicists have modified Wegener's theory to include two initial supercon-tinents. They believe that one of the supercontinents, "Gondwana-land," broke into Africa, India, Australia, South America, and Antarctica. The other continent, "Laurasia," broke into Europe, Asia, and North America.

EVIDENCE OF CONTINENTAL DRIFT

One evidence of continental drift is the close fit of the continents into one or two supercontinents. However, to fit continents together, they must be fitted at the true edges of the continental blocks, not at the present shorelines. In many places today, shorelines are well inside the outer edges of the continents. Accordingly, computer studies show that if the 3,000 foot (915 m) depth is taken as the true boundary of the continents, the two sides of the North Atlantic fit exactly. A good fit between Africa and South America is also made when the edges at the 6,000 foot (1830 m) depth are matched. Furthermore, computer studies have demonstrated that all of the continents may be fitted neatly into two supercontinents.

Source: From *Earth Science*, by L. Goldthwait, 1972, Lexington, MA: Ginn, pp. 308–309.

You probably found the first text more comprehensible, or "friendlier." You'll notice that both texts relate the information to your prior knowledge (to familiar concepts such as the map and the jigsaw puzzle). The difference between the explanations, however, lies in (a) the assumptions made about the level of vocabulary and amount of concept knowledge you already possess and some of the inferences you will be able to make independently; (b) the number or density of concepts presented; (c) the definitions and examples provided; and (d) the syntactic complexity of the sentences.

Three guidelines for teachers and writers for increasing the match between a reader's knowledge and the text in order to improve comprehensibility (Anderson & Armbruster, 1984) are:

1. Take into account readers' background knowledge and experience, being sure that enough relevant information is included in the text to form a *complete* answer to the question implied in a title. If, for example, a text is titled "Theory of Continental Drift," it should supply the answer to a reader's question, "What is the theory of Continental Drift?"
2. Introduce technical terms or difficult vocabulary only if they are a necessary part of the content; provide clear definitions for such vocabulary, giving examples where necessary.
3. Use analogies, metaphors, and other kinds of figurative language but only if their referents will be clear to the readers.

Teachers should also assess the cultural sensitivity of instructional textbooks and materials. Textbooks that include only Eurocentric perspectives fail to take into account the needs of students from culturally different backgrounds and do not enable the teacher to use the textbook adequately to teach to diversity (Jackson, 1993–94). In fact, they make reading the text difficult because not all cultures learn to think in a linear, analytical, and logical way. Therefore, modelling is needed to share the underlying thinking processes

---

For Reflection 12.4

If textual information is incomplete and if technical or difficult words are not defined, consider what instruction or supplementary reading materials you would provide as teacher/mediator to make the text more comprehensible for students in your subject area specialization. (Specific strategies are provided in the chapters on vocabulary development and comprehension, should you require some suggestions.) What would you do to make the materials more appropriate for student diversity in your classroom?

---

required to master content in a particular subject area. The following criteria, adopted from Jackson (1993–94), can be used to assess the quality of cultural sensitivity in textbooks:

1. How accurate is the portrayal of the perspectives, attitudes, and feelings of the group being studied?
2. Are characters of different ethnic backgrounds included in fictional works?
3. Do references to ethnic groups avoid stereotypes?
4. How historically accurate are factual materials?
5. Is there opportunity for processing information in nonlinear ways, such as through intuitive learning?

Text Structure

The structure of a text refers to the pattern or arrangement of ideas and the relationships connecting the ideas. Research has shown that well-organized text has a positive effect on what is remembered and on how much is remembered (e.g., Englert & Hiebert, 1984; McGee, 1982a, 1982b; Meyer, Brandt, & Bluth, 1980). Think of text structure as providing the framework that students use to comprehend and remember the content of text in efferent reading.

When composing texts, authors first take stances and decide their purposes. The purpose can be in the form of a statement (imperative) or a question (interrogative). These purposes fall into general categories, and there is a particular organizational structure for each category. Authors then frame their content presentation in the organizational structure that is appropriate to the initial purpose. Reader's stance may or may not be influenced by a writer's stance. The types of author purposes and the corresponding **text structures** are presented in Table 12.1.

Several basic structures are commonly found within any one selection/chapter in subject area textbooks. These include description, enumeration (listing), temporal sequence, explanation or cause-effect, comparison-contrast,

Table 12.1

Types of General Author Purposes and Corresponding Text Structures

Author Purposes		Structure
IMPERATIVE FORM	INTERROGATIVE FORM	
Define A.	What is A?	Description
Describe A.	Who is A?	
List the features/ characteristics of A.	Where is A?	
Trace the development of A.	When did A occur (in relationship to other events)?	Temporal sequence
Give the steps of A.		
Explain A.	Why did A happen?	Explanation (cause–effect)
Explain the cause(s) of A.	How did A happen?	
Explain the effect(s) of A.	What are the causes/ reasons for effect/ outcomes/results of A?	
Draw a conclusion about A.		
Predict what will happen.	What will be the effects/outcomes/ results of A?	
Hypothesize about the cause of A.		
Compare and contrast A and B.	How are A and B alike and/or different?	Compare/contrast
List the similarities and differences between A and B.		
Define and give examples of A.	What is A, and what are some examples of A?	Definition/Examples
Explain the develop- ment of a problem and the solution(s) to the problem.	How did A get to be a problem and what is (are) its solutions?	Problem/solution

Source: From "Content Area Textbooks," by R.C. Anderson and B. Armbruster, 1984, in R.C. Anderson, J. Osborn, and R.J. Tierney (Eds.), *Learning to Read in American Schools: Basal Reader and Content Texts,* pp. 199–226. Copyright by Lawrence Erlbaum Associates, Inc.

definition-examples, and problem-solution. Each basic structure is illustrated below using examples from compositions by students following instruction on text structure (Gordon, 1990). Each of the passages was judged to be well organized and thus reader-friendly.

Description

The Year 2010

When the year 2010 comes, there will be baseball gloves that will open up when the ball is coming at you. The baseballs will have their own energy on which to travel. Cars will have octagon wheels and fly low to the ground. Houses, buildings and apartments will look like spaceships. New kinds of machines and complex technology will take over our planet.

Enumeration

Different Kinds of Books

There are many kinds of books in the library. The first and most popular kinds of books are fiction. They are exciting and sometimes funny. They are usually easy to read and some have some kind of message.

There is a second kind of book that is popular with many girls. It is a romance novel. These books tell about the funny, happy things that happen when someone is in love and the sad and disappointing things, too. Not all of these kinds of books have perfect situations in them. A perfect main character with no problems I think is quite unrealistic.

There are also animal stories. There are many, many about horses, dogs and cats. Some of these are fictional in that the animals talk to each other, but in others the animals have a real life with human beings.

Another kind of book is a mystery. These stories are sometimes scary but other times are not. They are exciting and keep you in suspense.

Temporal Sequence

How to Plant a Garden

When planting a garden, you must remember to do several things. The first step is to dig the soil so it is not all packed down. Then you might want to add some peat moss so that the soil holds the moisture better. Next, you make little rows where the little seeds will be planted. Finally you are ready to place the vegetable seeds in the little rows and to cover them with dirt.

The garden will need to be watered and have the warmth of the sun in order to grow.

Cause-Effect (Explanation)

Cheating: Causes and Effects

Some people cheat on tests. They cheat because they are afraid of failing. Usually students fail because they have not studied or listened to the teacher in class. They might also fail because the tests are too hard for them in the first place.

If students are caught cheating, they are given not only a failing grade for cheating but they are also punished. As a result of cheating, the school might expel them or they may have them write a whole new test to show how much they really know. Their parents are informed and then there is also some "price to pay" because the parents are upset at them for being dishonest.

There are different reasons for cheating on tests but none of them are good enough because you usually get caught.

Comparison/Contrast

Hair Styles of the Punk, the Typical and the Sophisticated

There are many differences between the hairstyles of the punk, the typical, and the sophisticated person.

One of the main differences is colour. Most punks dye their hair an unearthly and most unnatural colour such as blue, green or purple, whereas the typical person leaves his/her hair a natural, if somewhat dull, colour. Of course, the sophisticated persons have their hair beautifully coloured and highlighted to bring out the best tones.

Another difference among these types of people's hairstyles is the way the hair is cut. Punks, in the interests of science, have their heads shaved, their hair mohawked or spiked. Unlike the punks, the humdrum persons have their hair cut or trimmed in a "nice" style. Different from both of these types is the glamour girl or guy who has hair styled and cut in such a way that it frames the face beautifully, has class and thus grabs the attention of the opposite sex.

Each of these types takes pride in his/her hair. Let it be very different, just plain and natural, or sophisticated, it still reflects the person's character.

Definition-Examples

Fossils

Fossils are the impressions, remains or any evidence found in rocks of the existence of living things long ago. Examples of fossils are a thigh bone of the dinosaur, a fern imprint on a stone, or a piece of petrified wood.

Problem-Solution

Anne of Green Gables

We had some problems when we were producing Anne of Green Gables. One of these was that our school gym was too small. We could use the Jubilee

Auditorium but it was expensive. We had the choice of using the University Theatre but it would also cost money, $5.00 a person, and we would have to practice at the University a few times. But the school was too small so we used the University Theatre.

Another problem was deciding who would play the main roles. To solve this, the teachers practiced with us to see who was good for the part. Finally Susan was chosen for the part of Anne, Tom for the part of Gilbert, Sonya was to play Mirella and Sheri (a girl!) to play Matthew.

Each text type or structure typically contains certain kinds of relationships expressed as words or phrases. For example, to depict temporal sequence, authors use words like the following: *before, after, then, now, next, later, finally, previously, prior to, subsequently, first, second,* and *third.* In poorly organized text, the reader must infer relationships among ideas because they are neither explicitly stated nor logically presented.

Anderson and Armbruster (1984) present three guidelines that can be used by teachers in evaluating the structure of texts. These are:

1. Determine if the author's topic, purpose, or question is clearly evident to the readers from an examination of titles, headings, and/or topic sentences.
2. Determine if the actual structure matches the purpose (stance) of the author (as shown by titles, topics, and topic sentences).
3. Assess how consistently the structures are used in the chapter of the book so that the reader can form expectations about structure and content.

Because some expository texts in the content areas do not adhere to tight organizational structures, intervention by the teacher is necessary to enhance text comprehension and mastery of content. Under the guidance of a teacher, students might impose a structure on a text to make it better understood and remembered. The teacher could also ask structure-related questions to highlight some of the organizational patterns. Other teaching strategies are presented in the chapters in Part II.

Coherence

Coherence refers to the ways in which ideas are smoothly knit together. This aspect of text organization is sometimes called cohesiveness (a feature serving to tie together sentences, paragraphs, and chapters) (Singer, 1986). Coherent texts clearly show the relationships among ideas and enable a flow of meaning from one idea to the next. Coherence operates at two levels: local and global. At the local level, pronoun referents (such as *they, them, it*), connectives (such as *and, or, but*), and phrases (such as "following the series of sunspots") clarify temporal, causal, conditional, or spatial relationships, and help the reader integrate the information within and between sentences. Although the sentences with explicitly stated relationships tend to be longer, they reduce the number of inferences a reader needs to make. Research on the use of explicitly stated connectives versus connectives that have to be inferred by the reader shows that the use of connectives facilitates learning (e.g., Pearson, 1974–75). At the global level, titles, subtitles, diagrams, charts, tables, and other textual aids, and rhetorical devices such as previews and summaries, not only support and extend ideas in text but also enable the integration of the key ideas across the entire text (e.g., chapter). Research on titles and visual aids shows that they lend global coherence to content texts (e.g., Holliday, Brunner, & Donais, 1977).

Seven guidelines for evaluating text comprehensibility as it relates to coherence (Anderson & Armbruster, 1984; Clewell & Cliffton, 1983) are as follows:

1. Determine if the relationships among ideas are explicitly stated.
2. Determine if the references to pronouns (such as *they*, *it*), quantifiers (*few*, *many*, *some*), and other cohesive devices are clearly stated.
3. Determine if the time order in temporal sequences, processes, and explanations proceeds in one direction only (e.g., from earliest to latest) or is at least consistent in direction.
4. Determine if the illustrations, charts, headings, and other special features provide an overview or general impression of chapter content.
5. Determine if the special instructional aids such as the table of contents, overviews, chapter review questions and summaries, and italicized or boldfaced words reinforce or supplement (extend) key ideas and relationships in text.
6. Determine if the functions of the textual aids are clearly signalled through the captions, labels, and references within text.
7. Determine if the headings and subheadings are in themselves meaningful to readers and if they introduce clearly the information (content) that follows.

As a teaching/learning strategy, graphing the content of a chapter with students before having them read difficult texts will enhance efferent and aesthetic transactions.

Exercise 12.2
Assessing the Coherence of a Text

Below are two examples of texts written by students based on a selection they had read in their social studies text. Determine which one is more coherent at the local level and explain why. Use guidelines 1–3 above to assist you.

Text A

About the time of Confederation, more and more people found jobs in the factories of the growing Canadian cities. Before Confederation, Canada was largely a country of farms and villages. In 1851 only 13 percent of Canadians lived in towns or cities. Most Canadians were farmers raising their own food and making their own clothing. They had few machines to help them with their work. During the Industrial Revolution machines were invented that could do much of the work formerly done by human hands and muscles. Farmers began to use machinery and fewer workers were needed on the farms. They moved to the growing cities and towns looking for work in the factories. Immigrants were also coming to Canada. As a result of the growing numbers, there were soon many new problems.

Text B

At the beginning of its development, Canada was largely a country of farms and small villages. In 1851, for example, only 13 percent of Canadians lived in urban areas like large towns or cities. Most Canadians were farmers who raised their own food and made their own clothes. They did most of the work by hand because they had very few machines to help them with their work. About the time of Confederation (1867), this situation began to change because more and more people left the farms to find jobs in the factories. There are several reasons that brought this change but the most important reason was the invention and use of new machines during the Industrial Revolution (which began in England around 1760 and expanded to other countries later). Machines were invented that could do much of the work formerly done by human beings. Because more farmers began to use machinery, they needed fewer workers on the farms. Therefore, farm workers looking for work moved to the growing cities and towns and found work in factories. At the same time, large numbers of immigrants were coming to Canada. They too settled in the cities and found jobs in the factories. As a result, the number of factories grew and expanded in the cities and soon there were new problems such as the working conditions in the factories.

You may have noted that Text B is more coherent (and thus more comprehensible) because relationships have been made explicit, referents are clear, and the time order proceeds from earlier to more recent times.

Unity

Unity is the degree to which the author has addressed a single purpose, topic, or theme and has not strayed from that purpose. Theory supports the argument that the fewer ideas one holds in memory at any one time, the easier it is to integrate new information with what is already known. The author's use of titles, headings, and topic sentences should reinforce any structure imposed on the ideas (content) presented. Two guidelines (Anderson & Armbruster, 1984) that can be used to evaluate unity of texts are:

1. Determine if each idea in the text contributes directly to the author's purpose.
2. Determine if ideas that are peripherally related to the main purpose are or should be set aside in boxed-in areas or appendices.

As a teaching strategy, teachers need to point out, using explicit examples, when authors stray from the topic. Asking students to compose a short text with a single purpose also would enhance their awareness of a unified text.

Types of Discourse

Discourse types refers to the author's intention in writing the text, whether it be to inform (exposition), give directions (procedural text), tell a story (narration), or persuade (persuasion). Examples of these text types were provided in Chapter 8. Each text type makes different demands on the reader. If shifts from one type to another are not clearly signalled by the author, readers may experience some difficulty comprehending the content. Clearly signalled discourse shifts may contribute to a reader's shift in stance — from aesthetic to efferent and vice versa. The following guidelines (Clewell & Cliffton, 1983) assist in evaluating text comprehensibility according to discourse types.

1. Determine the types of discourse used.
2. Determine if the discourse types are suitable to the content and the author's purpose.
3. Determine if the shifts in discourse types are clearly signalled.

Notice the switch in discourse types in the text reproduced in Box 12.1.

Metadiscourse

Metadiscourse is "discourse that an author places in text to make sure the reader is aware of author perception and intention" (Shanahan & Tierney, 1990, p. 21). In other words, metadiscourse refers to the author's conversation with the reader about the information in the text (Crismore, 1983). This conversation reveals to the reader the purposes for which the text has been written, gives advice on how to learn the content of the text, assists the reader

Box 12.1
Example of Shifts in Discourse Types

Brenda and Frank Kunnuk: A Trapper Hunter Family

Brenda and Frank Kunnuk and their family live on Victoria Island in the Arctic. Their village is one of Inuit hunters and trappers. They are known for the seals, fox, and caribou that they hunt and for the arctic char they catch.

One of the biggest changes that has happened in the village is the use of snowmobiles rather than dog teams by hunters and trappers. A snowmobile can travel 160 to 240 km a day compared to 35–50 km by dog teams. This has meant that, with people living in the villages, hunters are able to hunt and trap hundreds of miles from home. This was important because the animals living near settlements were soon hunted or trapped. Snowmobiles allow the villagers to travel long distances to find the arctic char and caribou they eat.

The Kunnuk family makes their living hunting and trapping. The size of the family changes from year to year. It depends on which of the children are home with their families and which are not.

The first snow comes in early September. I repair machinery and my hunting equipment.

Our first hunting trapping trip of the year is to a lake, about 95 km north.

We catch enough arctic char for our family for the winter months.

We hunt tuktuk, small caribou, which are fat from summer feeding.

I set out 300 to 400 traps. It takes me about two weeks.

During the winter I spend a week at home and then 7–10 days checking my trapline. The trapping season ends in mid-May.

Our whole family moves to a summer camp on Iluvilik Island. There we hunt seals and ducks. On trips to nearby lakes we are able to catch trout.

At the end of August we return to the village. School opens and we return to village life.

Source: From *Canada: Its Land and People*, by D. Massey (with B. Conners), 1986, Edmonton, AB: Reidmore Pocoal Enterprises Ltd., p. 87.

in making appropriate links among chapters, and demonstrates the application of information gained. You will have noted that this text has involved a metadiscourse, or dialogue, between you and the writers. Questions are asked, encouraging you to reflect, link ideas across sections, chapters, and subject areas, involve yourself in activities, and then reflect on this involvement.

For Reflection 12.5
React to the metadiscourse in this textbook. Did you find it helpful in learning the content? In making connections across chapters? Why or why not? To what extent were interdisciplinary transactions enhanced? Share your reactions with your peers.

Metadiscourse contributes to making a text more reader-friendly. The following questions (Singer, 1986) can be used by teachers to evaluate the metadiscourse of textbooks:

1. To what extent does the author talk directly to the reader to enhance learning?
2. Does the author supply information that contextualizes the ideas presented?
3. Does the author link ideas previously presented in text and reader's prior knowledge and experience to the ideas under discussion?

If misused, metadiscourse can interrupt the reader's own train of thought and give a text a chatty tone where an impersonal academic tone might be more appropriate.

Comprehensibility Checklist

A comprehensibility checklist can be used to judge text difficulty according to the factors outlined above. While assessing text comprehensibility takes time, it has two advantages: (1) it increases awareness of the factors in a text that affect comprehension, and (2) it helps teachers plan for instruction while being cognizant of text (and learner) characteristics (Clewell & Cliffton, 1983).

The checklist in Table 12.2, a predictive measure of difficulty level, has been developed on the basis of several sources (Anderson & Armbruster, 1984; Clewell & Cliffton, 1983; Irwin & Davis, 1980; Singer, 1986; Vacca & Vacca, 1989). It incorporates an aesthetic approach to evaluating texts. Note the emphasis on both cognitive and affective factors in the checklist. The checklist takes into account not only text-related factors but also reader-related factors (e.g., reader's purpose for reading, interest, motivation, background knowledge, level of language). It summarizes the ideas presented thus far in the chapter and enables the evaluator to systematize subjective judgements about text comprehensibility and to plan instruction that takes into account the positive and negative features of a chapter or a unit of reading. The checklist can also guide the selection of one textbook over another.

Table 12.2

Comprehensibility Checklist

Directions: Read each question below and assess the chapter you are evaluating by placing a checkmark in the appropriate column to the right.

	YES	TO SOME EXTENT	NO

Audience Appropriateness

1. Does the passage provide clear and accurate answers to the questions implied in the titles and subtitles?

2. Do the students have sufficient background knowledge and experience with the topic to enhance aesthetic and efferent transactions?

3. Is the technical and specialized vocabulary likely to be understood by the readers? Are the words highlighted, defined, and clarified/explained and examples given?

4. Is the vocabulary load appropriate? For example, only one or two new or difficult vocabulary items are introduced per paragraph.

5. Is the writing style appealing and appropriate in terms of sentence length and structure? Is the style appealing from an aesthetic perspective?

6. Are terms and ideas integrated with other related ideas?

7. Are ideas and terms linked to students' prior knowledge and/or experiential background? Is there potential to excite students about the content?

8. Are important relationships, generalizations, and conclusions explicitly stated or is the reader expected to infer them from context?

(continued)

(continued)

	YES	TO SOME EXTENT	NO

9. Are analogies, metaphors, and other literary elements appropriate to the audience and are they easily identified in the text?

10. Are text features present that will add interest to the text?

11. Will the writing and format appeal to the students?

12. Does the text lead to motivating activities? Are accompanying activities motivating to the students?

13. Does the text help develop visual and sensory images?

Text Structure

1. Are there clear, explicit purposes for each chapter or section of text and can the reader follow them through?

2. Are the relationships among topics and subtopics clear and logical?

3. Are the relationships made apparent to the reader through the use of text structures appropriate to the content, the genre, and to the reader's purpose?
   a) chronological (time) order
   b) description
   c) explanation
   d) enumeration
   e) comparison and contrast
   f) cause and effect
   g) problem and solution

(continued)

(continued)

YES   TO SOME EXTENT   NO

4. Are there clues (titles; subheads; signal/cue/key words; connectors; clear referents; introductory, transitional, and summary words or statements) to identify the text structure and to interrelate ideas?

5. Does the text itself or do the end-of-chapter questions lead to different levels of comprehension (literal, interpretive, applied, evaluative, appreciative)? Is there potential to look at the topic from an aesthetic perspective (getting students to see, hear, feel, and think)?

Coherence

1. Are the relationships among ideas explicitly stated at the local level (within and between sentences and between paragraphs)?

2. Are ideas presented in a unidirectional order or in a consistent direction (in ascending or descending order)?

3. Are the pronouns and nouns clearly referenced?

4. Do overviews, chapter headings, and subheadings provide a good overview of chapter content? (Are they meaningful in and of themselves to the reader and do they clearly indicate the information that follows?)

5. Do textual aids such as graphs, charts, illustrations support and/or extend the text? Do they enable vizualization? Evoke aesthetic transactions?

6. Are textual aids clearly integrated with text through captions, labels, and in-text references?

(continued)

(continued)

	YES	TO SOME EXTENT	NO

Unity

1. Does each idea in the text contribute to the author's purpose?
2. Does the text contain irrelevant details? Are these ideas set aside in appendices or boxed-in areas? Do these ideas encourage aesthetic transactions?

Types of Discourse

1. Are several types of discourse (narrative, expository, procedural, persuasive) used in the text?
2. Are discourse types suitable to the content and purpose of the text?
3. Are shifts in discourse types clearly signalled to enhance aesthetic and efferent transactions?

Metadiscourse

1. Does the author speak directly to the reader to reinforce important concepts, relationships, and generalizations?
2. Does the author explicitly point out relationships to ideas previously presented in text and/or to the reader's background knowledge? Does the author personalize learning?
3. Does the author effectively raise questions of, and provide imperatives for, the reader? Are any of these questions on the aesthetic dimension?
4. Does the author provide a context for ideas and events?
5. Does the author actively dialogue with the reader through activities in the text?

Cloze Procedure

An alternative way to assess the difficulty level of text in order to plan for instruction is the cloze test procedure. **Cloze** is considered a performance measure or a user-involvement technique because the students (the prospective users) must actually read excerpts of text taken from the chapter (or the book) before the teacher is able to evaluate the difficulty level of the text (Roe, Stoodt, & Burns, 1987). Note that when using a comprehensibility checklist it is the teacher who reads the text, but in the cloze procedure the students must read the text and show how they perform on the materials. In this way students provide information to the teacher on the difficulty level of the text. (In readability formulas, to be discussed later in this chapter, neither teacher nor students need to read the text at all in order to ascertain text difficulty level.)

In the cloze procedure, students read a 250–275-word passage (taken from a chapter, for example) that they have not previously read or studied and replace words that have been systematically deleted — usually every fifth word according to the Bormuth (1968) procedure. The deletion of every seventh word is recommended when cloze is applied to social studies content. For junior or senior high-school students reading below the fourth-grade level, only every tenth word should be deleted (Chance, 1985).

The cloze procedure assesses a reader's sensitivity to vocabulary and syntax. The cloze activity draws on students' prior knowledge of the topic, as well as their interest in and knowledge of language. The procedure is also sensitive to concept load (idea complexity), coherence, and organization. The percentage of words correctly replaced by students indicates the extent of the match between the students' comprehension and the material, permitting the teacher a better basis for planning instructional procedures and for selecting materials.

The following are guidelines for preparing, administering, scoring, and interpreting a cloze test. The teacher must first explain the cloze task to the students by working through several examples. Without sufficient practice, students' scores will not give a true indication of how well they can handle the materials.

1. Select a representative passage, or passages, of content material you wish to evaluate, usually about 275 words if every fifth word is deleted.
2. Leave the first sentence intact. Then omit every fifth word in order to obtain 50 blanks (for intermediate grade levels, 25 blanks might be sufficient). The blanks in the material should be of uniform length. (If every seventh word is omitted, longer passages will be required to obtain 50 blanks.) Leave the final sentence free of omissions.
3. When administering the cloze test, inform the students that they cannot use their textbooks or work together.

4. Assure the students that they will not be graded on their performance on this exercise. Stress that the information will help in the selection of materials and planning of instruction. Students are to guess, on the basis of context (semantic, syntactic), the exact word that was omitted. Synonyms are not accepted. (When cloze is used for instructional purposes, however, students should be encouraged to suggest synonyms.)
5. Allow students ample time to complete the cloze task.
6. When scoring, count every *exact* word replacement as correct. You might also provide a key for correct answers and have the students score their own cloze inventories, showing percentage of correct replacements. A generic formula for calculating percentage correct is:

$$\frac{\text{Number of correct responses}}{\text{Total number of blanks}} \times 100 = \text{percentage score}$$

7. In interpreting scores on materials written in a fairly easy narrative style, it is recommended that teachers use Bormuth's (1968) criteria for functional reading levels. These are summarized below:

% correct	Corresponds to	Means
58–100	Independent reading level (90% on traditional question/answer tests)	The student can read without guidance.
44–57	Instructional reading level (75% on traditional tests)	The student can read with some guidance.
0–43	Frustration reading level (below 75% on traditional measures)	Too difficult for reading without a great deal of guidance; material is likely unsuitable for those students scoring at frustration.

If the material is basically expository, it is suggested that teachers use the following criteria as guidelines:

% correct	Corresponds to
54–100	Independent level
39–53	Instructional level
0–38	Frustration level

None of the scores should be treated as rigid cut-off points, as they are based on the means of cloze scores derived from a number of cloze research studies. Because teaching of new vocabulary is assumed in the content areas, students may be unable to replace deleted content words not yet taught. Students' anxiety about criteria for successful performance (and the nonacceptance of synonyms) may be alleviated by explaining that approximately 55–60 percent represents successful performance.

8. Record the performance for each class, grouping the names under three categories, as shown in Box 12.2.

Box 12.2
Record of Cloze Performance

Subject or Course: _____

Text: _____

INDEPENDENT LEVEL PERFORMANCE	INSTRUCTIONAL LEVEL PERFORMANCE	FRUSTRATION LEVEL PERFORMANCE
(can read text on their own)	(need reading guidance)	(need much reading guidance or alternate text)
Names of students	Names of students	Names of students

Exercise 12.3
A Sample Cloze Task

In the cloze passage that follows, every fifth word has been deleted. Try this task yourself. List your responses on a separate sheet of paper and then check your accuracy with the key provided. Calculate your performance level on this passage.

An Archaeological Find

In the fall of 1991, the body of a 4000-year-old leather-clothed man was found in an Austrian glacier. Scientists will use high-technology _1_ to study the prehistoric _2_ from Bronze Age Europe _3_ hopes of finding out _4_ people in those days _5_ and kept themselves. While _6_ skeletons and artifacts have _7_ found from this period _8_ 2000 to 700 B.C., _9_ civilization shifted from stone _10_ use to metalworking, a _11_ has never been found. _12_ dry cold of the _13_ preserved the body in _14_ storage when the man _15_ 2000 years B.C.

The _16_ and tattooed man is _17_ to be between 20 _18_ 40 years old, about _19_ feet in height and _20_ in leather trousers and _21_ stuffed with straw for _22_ warmth. Artifacts discovered near _23_ body included a bronze _24_, a bow, a stone _25_, a wooden backpack and _26_ leather pouch full of _27_ for light-ing fires. A _28_ by Innsbruck scientists to _29_ glacier sight in the _30_ produced a leather quiver _31_ with arrows. Researchers speculate _32_ the man was probably _33_ miner searching the mountains _34_ the rich deposits of _35_ used in the bronze _36_ of the period. Copper _37_ the region's economy and _38_ to the establishing of _39_ routes with other areas.

_40_ technology tools such as _41_ microscopes and biological probes _42_ enable researchers to examine _43_ skin for chemicals left _44_ the tattoos, the hair, _45_ cells for signs of _46_ like tuber-culosis and the _47_ in search of variations _48_ genetic material.

Scientists are _49_ about the prospect of _50_ glaciers offering up other evidence of prehistoric man. According to archaeologists, the possibility of finding a Neolithic or Neanderthal is most exciting.

Source: Based on "A four thousand year old find opens up Bronze Age," by Richard Saltus, Sept. 27, 1991. Used courtesy of the Boston Globe.

Answers

1. methods	14. bacteria-free	27. flint	40. High
2. man	15. died	28. return	41. electron
3. in	16. clean-shaven	29. the	42. will
4. how	17. thought	30. Alps	43. the
5. lived	18. to	31. filled	44. by
6. numerous	19. five	32. that	45. body
7. been	20. dressed	33. a	46. diseases
8. of	21. jacket	34. for	47. DNA
9. when	22. added	35. copper	48. in
10. tool	23. the	36. industries	49. excited
11. body	24. axe	37. underlay	50. melting
12. the	25. necklace	38. led	
13. glacier	26. a	39. trade	

For Reflection 12.6
What is your reaction to the rule for not using synonyms in the cloze passage? What role do aesthetic transactions play in cloze and in determining the difficulty level of text?

Thus far we have seen that many factors influence the difficulty level of printed materials. To summarize, these include (1) reader variables, such as background knowledge, interest, enjoyment, and motivation, and (2) text factors, such as number of abstract concepts, concept density, underlying organization of the text, unity, and coherence. To augment their own subjective judgements of text difficulty and to supplement the evaluations made by using the comprehensibility checklist and the cloze procedure, teachers might want to use a readability formula as an additional measure.

Readability Formulas

Readability formulas are based on difficulty of vocabulary and sentence length and provide a predictive estimate of text difficulty. Although many researchers have pointed out the limitations of scores obtained by this method, the formulas remain popular (Lange, 1982). They are relatively quick and easy to use, and employ an identifiable number or grade level (e.g., 2.5 or 10.7) to denote the text's readability. The number can be used to match approximately the student's assessed reading level to appropriate textbooks. Teachers can use the formulas without any specialized training or knowledge about reading-to-learn or content literacy (Davison, Lutz, & Roalef, 1981). Another advantage of readability formulas is that they do not require students to be present; thus teachers can test and select textbooks before a course begins.

One problem is that readability formulas use only two factors — vocabulary and sentence length — to determine the difficulty level of a text. Yet some researchers argue that these two factors are the most important in predicting readability. Although these two factors are important, they are insufficient in and of themselves, as noted earlier in this chapter under the heading "Features of Text

---

For Reflection 12.7
Have you ever used a readability formula? What is your reaction to this procedure?

Comprehensibility." Difficulty of vocabulary in a readability formula is judged in one of two ways: either through a syllable count, or by using a comparison against a "hard word" list. Difficulty of sentences is usually measured by average sentence length or by the average number of sentences per 100 words.

Readability formulas ignore many of the reader-based and text-based factors mentioned earlier. Therefore, assumptions on which readability formulas are based have to be considered carefully. First, is it always true that the longer a word, the more difficult it is? Take "id," for example, a very short word in terms of number of syllables but a word for which only a few people know the meaning. Second, is it always true that the longer the sentence, the more difficult the text? Many longer sentences supply connectors that make explicit relationships among ideas and decrease the number of inferences a reader has to make, thus making the sentence easier to understand.

There are other arguments against the indiscriminate use of readability formulas. Readability formulas violate much of the current knowledge we have about the reading process (for example, they do not address the transaction between the reader and text in the process of reading) (Bruce, Rubin, & Starr, 1981). In addition, they have a shaky statistical basis in that they are poorly supported mathematically (each formula was validated in terms of an earlier formula and the flaws are perpetuated) and are difficult to generalize.

However, the major problem with readability formulas is that they do not consider readers' emotional, cognitive, and linguistic backgrounds as they transact with texts. While formulas might assist a teacher by showing the approximate match between reader and text, they do little to reveal what aspects in the reader and text are responsible for a student's success or failure and where the teacher might direct instructional emphasis. In addition, different readability formulas applied to the same passage yield different levels of difficulty. Why do these inconsistencies occur? They happen because (1) each formula applies different criteria to measuring vocabulary difficulty and sentence length; (2) text sampling methods vary (for example, only three samples may be taken from a text); and (3) formulas are not meant to be precise indicators of text difficulty level. Hence, readability formulas are probably most useful in judging the difficulty level of library books and periodicals for school purchase (Rush, 1985). Content area teachers must also recognize that text difficulty level prediction through the use of a readability formula is only one part of a total text assessment. Readability formulas "create a one-dimensional picture of text difficulty" (Estes, 1994, p. 979).

Over 30 readability formulas are available, some of which are also available as computer programs. The most popular and easy-to-use is the Fry Readability Graph (Fry, 1977) (see Figure 12.1). Content area teachers may find the formula useful as an additional measure of text difficulty to help them match or assign students to a content area text. It provides little instruction in preparing students for, guiding them through, or reinforcing the content read.

Figure 12.1

Fry Readability Graph

GRAPH FOR ESTIMATING READABILITY — EXTENDED

by Edward Fry, Rutgers University Reading Center, New Brunswick, N.J. 08904

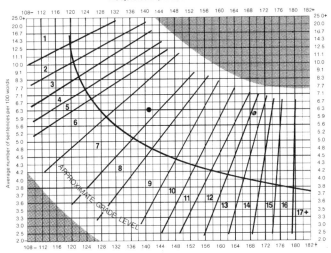

Expanded Directions for Working Readability Graph

1. Randomly select three (3) sample passages and count out exactly 100 words each, beginning with the beginning of a sentence. Do count proper nouns, initializations, and numerals.
2. Count the number of sentences in the hundred words, estimating length of the fraction of the last sentence to the nearest one-tenth.
3. Count the total number of syllables in the 100-word passage. If you don't have a hand counter available, an easy way is to simply put a mark above every syllable over one in each word, then when you get to the end of the passage, count the number of marks and add 100. Small calculators can also be used as counters by pushing numeral 1, then push the + sign for each word or syllable when counting.
4. Enter graph with *average* sentence length and *average* number of syllables; plot dot where the two lines intersect. Area where dot is plotted will give you the approximate grade level.
5. If a great deal of variability is found in syllable count or sentence count, putting more samples into the average is desirable.
6. A word is defined as a group of symbols with a space on either side; thus, *Joe, IRA, 1945,* and *&* are each one word.
7. A syllable is defined as a phonetic syllable. Generally, there are as many syllables as vowel sounds. For example, *stopped* is one syllable and *wanted* is two syllables. When counting syllables for numerals and initializations, count one syllable for each symbol. For example, *1945* is four syllables, *IRA* is three syllables, and *&* is one syllable.

Note: This "extended graph" does not outmode or render the earlier (1968) version inoperative or inaccurate; it is an extension. (REPRODUCTION PERMITTED—NO COPYRIGHT)

Source: From "Fry's Readability Graph: Clarifications, Validity, and Extension to Level 17," by E. Fry, 1977, *Journal of Reading, 21* pp. 242–52.

The Fry Readability Graph was designed to determine a grade level score for materials Grade 1 through college. The two standard factors — word length and sentence length — are used to calculate the difficulty of text. According to Fry, three 100-word samples should be used from a textbook. The grade level scores obtained on each passage can then be used to determine overall readability of a chapter or of a textbook (if samples are taken from the beginning, middle, and end of the book). Figure 12.1 showing the Fry Graph includes expanded step-by-step directions for its use. It must be remembered that the Fry Graph only provides estimates within a year of grade level, generally underestimating difficulty level.

Exercise 12.4
Estimating Text Difficulty Using Three Procedures

For the first portion of a chapter on weathering from a Grade 8 textbook (see Box 12.3), use the Fry Readability Graph, the cloze procedure, and the comprehensibility checklist to estimate the difficulty level of the text.

First begin with the easiest and quickest method, the Fry Graph. Take a 100-word sample from the narrative-type introduction and then a sample from the expository text and calculate a readability level. Which sample of text was easier? Why? Was the overall readability (an average of the two calculations) appropriate for students reading at Grade 8 level? Did you find out specifically what you can do as a teacher to bridge the gap between learner and text? Probably not, but calculating a readability level gave you a ballpark figure as to the difficulty level of the text.

Next develop a cloze selection on the passage by following the instructions presented earlier. Administer it to an eighth grade student, score, and interpret it. What did you find out? You learned the functional level (independent, instructional, or frustration) at which your student placed and whether he or she would need guidance in reading this particular text. An analysis of the responses on the cloze test could give you two kinds of additional information: (1) whether the student has adequate vocabulary knowledge on the topic in that content area, and (2) whether the student uses his or her knowledge of language (word order) to make sense of the material read. If the student used synonyms appropriately, you might discuss with the student his or her knowledge of the vocabulary. A discussion with the student would also enlighten you as to his or her interest in the topic and motivation for learning about the topic. A student might volunteer his or her personal response to the text or might be asked for such a response.

Last, apply the comprehensibility checklist to the passage. Determine how this portion of the chapter rates on audience appropriateness, text structure, coherence, unity, use of discourse types, and metadiscourse.

To check your evaluation against the evaluation of someone else (without going through the checklist item by item), let me share just a few of the key strengths and weaknesses of these pages of text on the basis of an evaluation using the comprehensibility checklist.

Box 12.3
Text for Estimating Difficulty Level

Weathering

Most people have to learn things the hard way. Take Janet, for example. She finally had to give up on her flower bed. Pieces of concrete from the wall next to the flower bed kept falling on the plants. A daisy would have to wear a helmet to take that for long.

On their way to a vacation spot along the coast, Steve and Peg had to drive through a desert area. Suddenly a violent sandstorm came up. When it finally died down, they found to their surprise that the windshield was pitted and scratched.

Mr. Morris, a local clergyman, has a real problem. Last winter a fire destroyed all the town records. He can only replace the oldest ones by copying information from old gravestones. But the oldest stones have been worn almost completely smooth. Minerals in the newer stones have rusted and run down over the letters. Mr. Morris will never be able to make out all the names and dates.

Even the mayor is in trouble. Many town sidewalks need to be replaced this year. He didn't plan on sidewalk repairs in the town budget. Guess the mayor thought the sidewalks would last forever.

You have to feel sorry for Tom, too. His mother has a small garden with stones around the edge. The moss she planted alongside the stones keeps growing up over them. So she makes Tom trim it back. You should see what the moss does to the stones — makes them all rough. You guessed it! He gets blamed for not taking care of the stones "Polish those stones," his mother yells. "And water the moss." All in the same breath. What a grouch!

ROCKS MUST WEATHER

What do the falling cement, the pitted windshield, the aging gravestones, the rusting minerals, the flaking sidewalks, and the rough garden stones all have in common? The answer is weathering. Weathering is breaking down of earth materials into smaller pieces or changing them chemically. What results may be the same as the original material or may be changed into a new material. Without weathering there would be no soil. There would be no sandy beaches. All home cellars would have to be dug with dynamite.

So far you have learned about changes on the earth that build up the landscape. Volcanoes pile up new rock. Movements in the earth's crust raise up new mountains. But rocks and mountains must be broken down at nearly the same rate somewhere else. Otherwise the earth would become only new rock and all mountains.

(continued)

(continued)

WEATHERING RESULTS FROM NATURAL DISORDER

When we look around us, many things seem to be in the process of becoming disordered. This "mixed-up-ness" happens all the time. In spite of the fact that weathering has helped to give us the soil we depend on for growing food, weathering is one of those things that annoys us. Like rain that brings an end to a picnic, watches that run down, pizza that gets cold before we can get it home, and rooms that have to be cleaned once a week, there seems to be no way to stop it from happening. And the reason is quite simple. Weathering is just another one of those things following the natural tendency for things in the universe to lose energy and become disordered.

Weathering causes the earth to become disordered. It happens naturally, without the aid of people. The things that do the actual weathering, called weathering agents, break down the hard rock. Weathering agents are usually water, wind, plants, animals (including man), and chemicals. Then a force like gravity moves the weathered particles so that fresh particles will be exposed to the agents. The work of gravity can easily be seen at the foot of a cliff. The pile of rock that collects there is called a talus (Taylus).

Anyway, Steve and Peg's windshield, Mr. Morris's gravestones, and the mayor's sidewalks were simply "doing what comes naturally."

DID YOU GET THE POINT?

Weathering breaks down earth materials and may change them into new materials.

Weathering happens naturally and causes the earth to become more disordered.

Weathering is caused by water, wind, chemicals, and plants and animals.

CHECK YOURSELF

1. Certain governments have put together "time capsules," containing information about our civilization. They hope that this information in the form of tape recordings, pictures, and diaries can be preserved for study by future civilizations, no matter what happens to us. How would you go about preparing and storing such a time capsule so that weathering could not destroy the information?
2. If a scientist wants a piece of rock that is unchanged since it was formed, he digs deep into the earth for it or breaks open other rocks. Why?

Source: From "Weathering," by J.H. Jackson and E.D. Evans, 1976, *Spaceship Earth: Earth Science*, Boston: Houghton-Mifflin, pp. 333–36. Reprinted by permission of McDougal Littell Inc.

First of all, I applaud the author's attempt to access students' prior knowledge of weathering and to liken weathering to topics previously studied (e.g., changes on the earth that build landscapes). Some of the examples will mirror experiences of students and enable aesthetic responses. The difficulty is that the author did not make explicit the relationship of the examples of weathering within and between the narrative section and the expository section that follows. It might have been useful to move the three points from "Did You Get the Point?" at the end of this section to the beginning of the chapter on weathering. Students would thus be assisted in making the links. In addition, a discussion activity prior to reading on the topic or before the teacher "walks the students through" the text would help to access and engage students' prior knowledge, and would help them make links to weathering. The teacher should also bring the shift in discourse type, made by the author, to the students' attention.

I admired the attempt to link the content presented to the examples given at the beginning, but was it done explicitly enough?

How does the introduction of a difficult concept like the force of gravity affect difficulty level? An examination of the textbook from which the excerpt on *Weathering* was taken reveals that gravitational force is studied later in the instructional sequence, that is, after the study of *Weathering*. A teacher-led discussion on gravity would therefore be beneficial.

With respect to structure, students are going to have difficulty understanding the intent and content of the first two subtitles under *Causes of Weathering*. What does "Rocks Must Weather" have to do with the causes of weathering and why is the definition of weathering placed under this subtitle? Under "Weathering Results from Natural Disorder," the causes of weathering are finally presented. Yet some pre-service teachers (in our content area courses over the years) with a science specialization argued vehemently against the link between weathering and the natural tendency for things to become disordered. They were uncomfortable with the other examples of disorder — pizza that gets cold, rooms that need to be cleaned. Do you then see some major problems with unity and coherence or even with accuracy of content? Do you see any provisions for an aesthetic response as a "way into" an efferent reading? Following a discussion of these points, students might be asked to rewrite some paragraphs under the guidance of the teacher.

The illustration provided in the original text does little to enhance the comprehension of agents of weathering but might help develop the meaning of the word talus. The teacher might elaborate on the illustration and discuss its possible links to the text.

Having completed an evaluation of the text on weathering, the teacher needs to use that information to make some instructional decisions. Some instructional activities were suggested as part of the assessment of this text. However, a teacher will need to think about purposes for reading the text and the kind of activities students will need to accomplish the following: relate their prior knowledge and experience to the text; respond personally to the text; use the existing text structure or modify it to read, organize, and remember the content; create an organizational structure that can be better used to understand the text; understand and reinforce vocabulary; use the textual aids

---

For Reflection 12.8
How did your use of the readability formula, the cloze procedure, and the comprehensibility checklist assist you in making instructional decisions?

---

provided in the text. Instructional procedures might occur before, during, and after the reading.

Instructional Suggestions to Bridge the Gap between Readers and Texts

Teachers who are skilled in assessing expository materials will choose better textbooks and other materials for use in the classroom. By eliminating textbooks that are less than comprehensible, teachers increase students' chances of reading with competence. Teachers will choose textbooks that invite personal associations, that stimulate visual images, that encourage the use of the senses, and that excite students about scientific, mathematical, or historical concepts. Such qualities increase text comprehensibility by promoting aesthetic transactions. Teachers also can provide instruction to help students capitalize on well-designed composition for comprehension purposes (Chambliss, 1993). One way is to teach students to detect the structure of well-designed passages while working in co-operative learning groups.

If faced with prescribed texts that contain poorly crafted exposition, teachers will need to provide instructional support after the analysis of the text. Chambliss (1993) provides several suggestions:

1. Use other reading materials in place of particularly "less-than-well-organized" passages in the textbook, or use them instead of or as advance organizers before reading the textbook sections.
2. Capitalize on students' background knowledge and experience by brainstorming with them and helping them organize the ideas before the textbook passages or chapters are assigned. Build on any background knowledge that may be lacking. Use supporting texts such as pictures, brochures, or electronic image-texts (films, videotapes, and television programs).
3. If the passage lacks a coherent structure, help students impose one by diagramming or rewriting the passage.
4. Use small discussion groups and collaborative activities, rather than assigned individual reading assignments (for school or as homework), to help students talk and write their way into the content.

Summary

Expository text, whether it is material presented in a textbook, a lecture, or a chart, is not necessarily considerate or reader-friendly. Although writers have a responsibility to make text comprehensible for readers and readers have a responsibility to approach the text strategically, there is sometimes a mismatch between reader and text that makes it difficult to respond efferently and/or aesthetically. In order to bridge the gap between reader and text, content area teachers must evaluate the texts for comprehensibility.

Several key features contribute to making texts easy or difficult to understand. These include the degree to which the reader's interest, prior knowledge, and experience are taken into account in vocabulary use and syntactic structures; coherence, unity, text structure, and types of discourse present in the text; and the amount and type of metadiscourse included.

Procedures to assist teachers in determining text comprehensibility and planning for better instruction include the text comprehensibility checklist, the cloze procedure, and readability formulas. The comprehensibility checklist, which requires the teacher to read the text and to make subjective judgements, encompasses many reader and text factors that research has shown make text difficult or easy to read. The advantage of using the cloze procedure is that students actually transact with samples of text that they will be required to read. Readability formulas, limited in the information they can provide as guides for instruction, have been criticized on a number of fronts and therefore should be used with caution.

Questions for Further Reflection

1. What are the teacher's responsibilities in mediating between reader and author?
2. When there is a mismatch between reader and text, why does teacher mediation enhance efferent and/or aesthetic response to text?
3. What is the difference between the terms *readability* and *comprehensibility*?
4. What are the key features of comprehensible text?
5. What information about students is particularly important when determining whether a text is difficult or easy?
6. How does the cloze procedure assess students' transactions with text?
7. Why would you use or not use a readability formula?
8. What factors in the secondary school might impede teachers' use of procedures to evaluate text difficulty?

9. What did your high-school teachers do to make difficult texts easier for you to understand? What are some instructional techniques you would want to use?

Key Terms

Audience appropriateness
Cloze
Coherence
Comprehensibility
Considerate text
Discourse types

Inconsiderate text
Metadiscourse
Readability formulas
Text structures
Unity

REFERENCES

Adams, M.H. (1995, December). *Connections between reading and writing in performance assessment.* Paper presented at the National Reading Conference, New Orleans, LA.

Allen, S. (1987). Attitudes of preservice teachers toward teaching reading in content areas. *Reading-Canada-Lecture, 5*(2), 96–103.

Almasi, J.F. (1996). A new view of discussion. In L.B. Gambrell & J.F. Almasi (Eds.), *Lively discussions: Fostering engaged reading.* Newark, DE: International Reading Association.

Almasi, J.F., & Gambrell, L.B. (1994). Sociocognitive conflict in peer-led and teacher-led discussion of literature. (Reading Research Report No. 12). Athens, GA: Universities of Maryland and Georgia, National Reading Research Center.

Alvermann, D.E. (1986). Discussion versus recitation in the secondary classroom. In J.A. Niles & R.V. Lalik (Eds.), *Solving problems in literacy: Learners, teachers and researchers.* Rochester, NY: National Reading Conference.

Alvermann, D.E. (1987). Learning from text. In D.E. Alvermann, D.W. Moore, & M.W. Conley (Eds.), *Research within reach secondary school reading* (pp. 33–51). Newark, DE: International Reading Association.

Alvermann, D.E., Dillon, D.R., & O'Brien, D.G. (1987). *Using discussion to promote reading comprehension.* Newark, DE: International Reading Association.

Alvermann, D.E., & Hayes, D.A. (1989). Classroom discussion of content area reading assignments: An intervention study. *Reading Research Quarterly, 24*(3), 305–35.

Alvermann, D.E., & Moore, D.W. (1991). Secondary school reading. In R. Barr, M.L. Kamil, P. Mosenthal, & P.D. Pearson (Eds.), *Handbook of Reading Research* (Vol. II, pp. 951–83). New York: Longman.

Alvermann, D.E., O'Brien, D.G., & Dillon, D.R. (1990). What teachers do when they say they're having discussions of content area assignments: A qualitative analysis. *Reading Research Quarterly, 25*, 296–322.

Alvermann, D.E., & Phelps, S.F. (1994). *Content reading and literacy: Succeeding in today's diverse classrooms.* Boston: Allyn & Bacon.

Anders, P.L., Bos, C.S., Filip, D. (1984). The effect of semantic feature analyses on the reading comprehension of learning disabled students. In J.A. Niles & L.A. Harris (Eds.), *Changing perspectives on research in reading language processing and instruction.* Thirty-third yearbook of the National Reading Conference (pp. 162–66). Rochester, NY: National Reading Conferences.

Anderson, D.J. (1990). Parallel processes in the reading and writing of sixth graders. *Reflections on Canadian Literacy, 8*(2–3), 98–104.

Anderson, J. (1993). Journal writing: The promise and the reality. *Journal of Reading, 36*(4), 304–9.

Anderson, R. (1994). The role of the reader's schema in comprehension, learning and memory. In R. Ruddell, M. Rapp-Ruddell, & H. Singer (Eds.), *Theoretical models and processes of reading* (pp. 469–82). Newark, DE: International Reading Association.

Anderson, R.C., & Freebody, P. (1979, August). *Vocabulary knowledge* (Reading Education Report No. 11). Urbana, IL: University of Illinois, Center for the Study of Reading. (ERIC Document Reproduction Service No. ED 177 470)

Anderson, R.C., & Freebody, P. (1981). Vocabulary knowledge. In J.T. Guthrie (Ed.), *Comprehension and teaching: Research reviews* (pp. 77–117). Newark, DE: International Reading Association.

Anderson, R.C., & Freebody, P. (1985). Vocabulary knowledge. In H. Singer and R.B. Ruddell, (Eds.), *Theoretical processes and models of reading* (3rd ed.) (pp. 343–71). Newark, DE: International Reading Association.

Anderson, R.C., Reynolds, R., Schallert, D., & Goetz, E.T. (1977). Frameworks for comprehending discourse. *American Educational Research Journal, 14*, 367–81.

Anderson, T.H., & Armbruster, B. (1984). Content area textbooks. In R.C. Anderson, J. Osborn, R.J. Tierney (Eds.), *Learning to read in American schools: Basal readers and content texts* (pp. 193–226). Hillsdale, NJ: Laurence Erlbaum Associates.

Anderson, W. (1995). *The truth about truth*. New York: G.P. Putnam's Sons.

Applebaum, S.H., Beckman, M.D., Boone, L.E., & Kurtz, D.L. (1990). *Contemporary Canadian business*. Toronto: Holt, Rinehart and Winston.

Applebee, A. (1984). *Contexts for learning to write: Studies of secondary school instruction*. Norwood, NH: Ablex.

Applebee, A.N. (1981). Writing in the secondary school: English and the content areas (NCTE Research Report No. 21), Urbana, IL: National Council of Teachers of English.

Applebee, A.N., Langer, J., Durst, R.K., Butler-Nalin, K., Marshall, J.D., & Newell, G.E. (1984). *Contexts for learning to write: Studies of secondary school instruction*. Norwood, NJ: Ablex.

Aries, P. (1960). *Centuries of childhood: A social history of family life*. New York: Vintage Books.

Armstrong, T. (1994). Multiple intelligences: Seven ways to approach curriculum. *Educational Leadership, 52*(3), 26–28.

Aschbacher, P.R. (1991). Humanities: A thematic curriculum. *Educational Leadership, 49*(2), 16–19.

Athey, I. (1985). Reading research in the affective domain. In H. Singer & R.B. Ruddell (Eds.), *Theoretical models and processes of reading* (pp. 527–57). Newark, DE: International Reading Association.

Atlantic Science Curriculum Project. (1990). *Science Plus: Technology and Society 8*. Toronto: Harcourt Brace Jovanovich.

Atwell, N. (1987). *In the middle: Writing, reading and learning with adolescents*. Portsmouth, NH: Heinemann.

Atwell, N. (1991). *Side by side: Essays on teaching to learn*. Portsmouth, NH: Heinemann.

Aulls, M. (1992). Teaching comprehension strategies as common knowledge. In C.J. Gordon, G.D. Labercane, & W.R. McEachern (Eds.), *Elementary Reading: Process and Practice* (pp. 227–44). New York: Ginn Press.

Bagwell, T. (1989). Turn and return: The image of deconstruction. *Diacritics, 19*(1), pp. 97–115.

Bailey, N. (1988). S-RUN: Beyond SQ3R. *Journal of Reading, 32*, 170–71.

Baker, L., & Brown, A. (1984). Metacognitive skills and reading. In P.D. Pearson (Ed.), *Handbook of reading research* (pp. 353–394). New York: Longman.

Bakhtin, M.M. (1981). *The dialogic imagination.* Austin, TX: The University of Texas Press.

Ballah, J. (Ed.). (1995). *Insights: Understanding war.* Toronto: Harcourt Brace.

Ballah, J. (Ed.). (1996). *Insights: Technology and change.* Toronto: Harcourt Brace.

Ballah, J., Kirkland, G., & Terpening, J. (1995). *Insights: Relationships and responsibility.* Toronto: Harcourt Brace.

Ballheim, C., Cheverie, M., Danbrook, C., Leddy, F., Romiens, T., Sands, A., and Warren, M. (1994). *Math Plus 9.* Toronto: Harcourt Brace.

Ballheim, C., Cheverie, M., Danbrook, C., Leddy, F., Romiens, T., Sands, A., & Warren, M. (1995). *Math Plus 8.* Toronto: Harcourt Brace.

Baloche, L., & Platt, T.J. (1993). Sprouting magic beans: Exploring literature through creative questioning and cooperative learning. *Language Arts, 70*(4), 264–71.

Barnes, D. (1972). Language and learning in the classroom. In *Language in education: A source book* (pp. 112–118). London: Routledge & Kegan Paul in association with Open University Press.

Barnes, D. (1973). Styles of communication and thinking in the classroom. In *Language in the classroom* (pp. 14–17). ED 262, Block 4, Milton Keynes, England: Open University Press.

Barnes, D. (1976). *From communication to curriculum.* Harmondsworth: Penguin.

Barnes, D., Britton, J., & Rosen, H. (1971). *Language, the learner and the school.* Harmondsworth: Penguin.

Barnitz, J.G. (1994). Discourse diversity: Principles for authentic talk and literacy instruction. *Journal of Reading, 37*(7), 586–91.

Barron, R.F., & Melnick, R. (1973). The effects of discussion upon learning of vocabulary meanings and relationships in tenth grade biology. In H.L. Herber & R.F. Barron (Eds.), *Research in reading in the content areas: Second year report* (pp. 46–52). Syracuse, NY: Syracuse University, Reading and Language Arts Center.

Barton, J. (1995). Conducting effective classroom discussions. *Journal of Reading, 38*(5), 346–50.

Baumann, J.F., & Kameenui, E.J. (1991). Research on vocabulary instruction: Ode to Coltaire. In J. Flood, J.M. Jensen, D. Lapp, & J.R. Squire (Eds.), *Handbook on teaching the English language arts* (pp. 602–32). New York: Macmillan.

Beane, J. (1991). The middle school: the natural home of integrated curriculum. *Educational Leadership, 49*(2), 9–13.

Beane, J. (1990). *A middle school curriculum: From rhetoric to reality.* Columbus, OH: National Middle School Association.

Bean, T.W., & Zulich, J. (1990). Teaching students to learn from text: Preservice content teachers changing view of their role through the window of student–professor dialogue journals. In J. Zutell & S. McCormick (Eds.), *Literacy theory and research: Analyses from multiple paradigms* (pp. 171–78). Chicago: National Reading Conference.

Beck, R.H., Copa, G. H., & Pease, V.H. (1991). Vocational and academic teachers work together. *Educational Leadership, 49*(2), 29–31.

Bembridge, T. (1994). A multi-layered assessment package. In E.H. Hiebert, S.W. Valencia, & P.P. Afflerbach (Eds.), *Authentic Reading Assessment: Practices and Possibilities* (pp. 167–84). Newark, DE: International Reading Association.

Bennett, T. (1990). *Popular fiction: Technology, ideology, production, reading.* New York: Routledge.

Bereiter, C. (1995) A dispositional view of transfer. In A. McKeough, J.L. Lupart, & A. Marini (Eds.), *Teaching for transfer: Fostering generalization in learning.* Hillsdale, NJ: Erlbaum.

Bereiter, C., & Scardamalia, M. (1985). Cognitive coping strategies and the problem of "inert knowledge." In S.F. Chipman, J.W. Segal, & R. Glaser (Eds.), *Thinking and learning skills, vol. 2: Research and open questions* (pp. 65–80). Hillsdale, NJ: Erlbaum.

Berger, A. (1980). *Film in society.* New Brunswick, NJ: Transaction Books.

Berger, A. (1991). *Media Research Techniques.* London: Sage Publications.

Berger, J. (1977). *Ways of seeing.* New York: Viking Penguin.

Berghoff, B. (1993). Moving toward aesthetic literacy in the first grade. In D.J. Leu, C.K. Kinzer, L.M. Ayre, J.A. Peter, & S. Bennett (Eds.), *Examining central issues in literacy research, theory, and practice* (pp. 217–26). 42nd Yearbook of The National Reading Conference. Chicago: National Reading Conference, Inc.

Berliner, D., & Casanova, U. (1986). How to make cross-age tutoring work. *Instructor, 95*(9), 14–15.

Berstein, L., Schacter, M., Winkler, A., & Wolfe, S. (1979). *Concepts and challenges in earth science.* Fairfield, NJ: Cebco Standard.

Birrell, J.R., & Ross, S.K. (1996). Standardized testing and portfolio assessment: Rethinking the debate. *Reading Research and Instruction, 35*(4), 285–97.

Blachowicz, C.L. (1985). Vocabulary development and reading: From research to instruction. *Journal of Reading, 38*(9), 876–81.

Blachowicz, C.L. (1986). Making connections: Alternatives to the vocabulary notebook. *Journal of Reading, 29*(7), 643–49.

Blachowicz, C.L., & Lee, J.J. (1991) Vocabulary development in the whole literacy classroom. *The Reading Teacher, 45*(3), 188–95.

Blachowicz, C.L., & Zabroske, B. (1990). Context instruction: A metacognitive approach for at-risk readers. *The Journal of Reading, 33*(7), 504–8.

Bohning, G. (1982). A resource guide for planning, implementing, and evaluating peer and cross-age tutoring. *Reading Improvement, 19*(4), 74–78.

Bonds, C.W., Gant Bonds, L., & Peach, Q. (1992). Metacognition: Developing independence in learning. *Clearing House, 66*(1), 56–59.

Bone, J. & Johnston, R. (1991). *Understanding the film: An introduction to film appreciation.* Lincolnwood, IL: NTC Publishing.

Bormuth, J.R. (1968). Cloze test readability: Criterion reference scores. *Journal of Educational Measurement, 5,* 189–96.

Boughton, D. (1986). Visual Literacy: implications for cultural understanding through art education. *Journal of Art & Design Education, 5*(1–2), 125–42.

Boyd, D. (1989). *Film and the interpretive process.* New York: Peter Lang.

Bragstad, B., & Stumpf, S. (1987). *A guidebook for teaching study skills and motivation*. Needham, MA: Allyn and Bacon.

Brandt, R. (1991). On interdisciplinary curriculum: A conversation with Heidi Hayes Jacobs. *Educational Leadership, 49*(2), 24–26.

Brent, R., & Anderson, P. (1993). Developing children's classroom listening strategies. *The Reading Teacher, 47*(2), 122–26.

Britton, J. (1970). *Language and learning*. Harmondsworth, Middlesex: Penguin.

Britton, J. (1984). Viewpoints: The distinction between participant and spectator roles in language research and practice. *Research in the Teaching of English, 14*, 320–31.

Britton, J., Burgess, T., Martin, N., MacLeod, A., & Rosen, H. (1975). *The development of writing abilities* (11–18). London: MacMillan Education Ltd.

Brody, C.M. (1995). Collaborative and cooperative learning: Complimentary [sic] practices for instructional reform. *The Journal of Staff, Program, & Organization Development, 12*(3), 133–43.

Brophy, J., & Alleman, J. (1991). A caveat, curriculum integration isn't always a good idea. *Educational Leadership, 49*(2), 66.

Brown, A. (1980). Metacognitive development and reading. In R.J. Spiro, R.C. Bruce, & W.F. Brewer (Eds.), *Theoretical issues in reading comprehension* (pp. 453–81). Hillsdale, NJ: Erlbaum.

Brown, A., Collins, J.S., & Duguid, P. (1989). Situated cognition and the culture of learning. *Educational Research, 18*(1), 32–42.

Brown, A.L., Campione, J.C., & Day, J. (1981). Learning to learn: On training students to learn from texts. *Educational Researcher, 10*, 14–21.

Brown, J.E., Phillips, L.B., & Stephens, E.C. (1993). *Toward literacy: Theory and applications for teaching writing in the content areas*. Belmont, CA: Wadsworth.

Brozo, W., & Simpson, M. (1991). *Readers, teachers, learners: Expanding literacy in the secondary school*. Toronto: Collier Macmillan.

Bruce, B., Rubin, A., & Starr, K. (1981). *Why readability formulas fail* (Reading Education Report No. 28). Urbana: Center for the Study of Reading, University of Illinois.

Bruffee, K. (1984). Collaborative learning and the "conversation of mankind." *College English, 46*(7), 635–52.

Bruner, J. (1966). *Toward a theory of instruction*. Cambridge, MA: Harvard University Press.

Bruner, J. (1986). *Actual minds, possible words*. Cambridge, MA: Harvard University Press.

Brunette, P. & Wills, D. (1989). *Screen/Play: Derrida and film theory*. Princeton, NJ: Princeton University Press.

Burch, R. (1986). Confronting technophobia: A topology. *Phenomenology and Pedagogy, 4*(2), 3–21.

Calfee, R.C., Dunlap, K.L., & Wat, A.Y. (1994). Authentic discussion of texts in middle grade schooling: An analytic–narrative approach. *Journal of Reading, 37*(7), 546–56.

Calfee, R.C., & Perfumo, P.A. (1992). *A survey of portfolio practices*. Berkeley, CA: Center for the Study of Writing, University of California, Berkeley.

Calgary Herald. (1996, February 24 and March 2). In Sci bites: Daffy definitions, B5.

Calkins, L. (1986). *The art of teaching writing*. Portsmouth, NH: Heinemann.

Campbell, J. (1986). *Lifestyle 3*. Markham, ON: Globe/Modern Curriculum Press.

Campbell, J. (1992). Laser disk portfolios: Total child assessment. *Educational Leadership, 49*(8), 69–70.

Caputo, J. (1988). Beyond aestheticism: Derrida's responsible anarchy. *Research in Phenomenology, 18*, 59–73.

Carr, E., & Wixson, K.K. (1986). Guidelines for evaluating vocabulary instruction. *Journal of Reading, 29*(7), 588–595.

Carrier, C. (1988). Notetaking research: Implications for the classroom. *Journal of Instructional Development, 6*(3), 19–25.

Case, R. (1992). *The mind's staircase: Exploring the conceptual underpinnings of children's thought and knowledge*. Hillsdale, NJ: Lawrence Erlbaum Associates.

Case, R., Bleiker, C., Henderson, B., Krohn, C., & Bushey, B. (1993). The development of central conceptual structures in adolescence. In R. Case (Ed.), *The role of central conceptual structures in the development of children's numerical, literary and spatial thought*, (pp. 104–28). Final report submitted to the Spencer Foundation.

Case, R., & McKeough, A. (1990). Schooling and the development of central conceptual structures: An example from the domain of children's narrative. *International Journal of Education, 13*, 835–55.

Chafe, W., & Danielewicz, J. (1987). Properties of spoken and written language. In R. Horowitz, & S.J. Samuels (Eds.), *Comprehending oral and written language* (pp. 83–113). London: Academic Press.

Chambers, I. (1991). *Border dialogues: Journeys in postmodernity*. New York: Routledge.

Chambliss, M. (1993). Assessing instructional materials: How comprehensible are they? In C.J. Gordon, G.D. Labercane, & W.R. McEachern (Eds.), *Elementary reading: Process and practice*, (pp. 319–41). Needham Heights, NY: Ginn Press.

Chance, L. (1985). Use cloze encounters of the readability kind for secondary school students. *Journal of Reading, 28*, 690–93.

Chatman, S. (1990). *Coming to terms: The rhetoric of narrative in fiction and film*. Ithaca, NY: Cornell University Press.

Chomsky, N. (1977). *Language and responsibility*. New York: Panther Books.

Cintorino, M.A. (1993). Getting together, getting along, getting to the business of teaching and learning. *English Journal, 82*, 23–32.

Clapp, P. (1968). *Constance: A story of early Plymouth*. New York: Penguin.

Clewell, S.F., & Cliffton, A.M. (1983). Examining your textbook for comprehensibility. *Journal of Reading, 27*, 219–25.

Cohen, E.G. (1994). *Designing groupwork: Strategies for the classroom*. New York: Teachers College Press.

Cohn, A.L. (Ed.). (1993). *From sea to shining sea*. New York: Scholastic.

Collins, A., Brown, J.S., & Newman, S.E. (1989). Cognitive apprenticeship: Teaching the crafts of reading, writing, and mathematics. In L.B. Resnick (Ed.), *Knowing, learning, and instruction: Essays in honor of Robert Glaser*, (pp. 453–94). Hillsdale, NJ: Lawrence Erlbaum Associates.

Cook, P. (1985). *The cinema book: A complete guide to understanding the movies*. New York: Pantheon Books.

Cooper, J. (1993). *Literacy: Helping children construct meaning*. Toronto: Houghton Mifflin.

Cowan, P. (1982). The relationship between emotional and cognitive development. In D. Cicchetti & P. Hesse (Eds.), *New directions for child development: Emotional development*. No. 16. San Francisco: Jossey-Bass.

Craik, F., & Lockhart, R. (1972). Levels of processing: A framework for memory research. *Journal of Verbal Learning and Verbal Behavior, 11*, 671–84.

Crane, S. (1991). Integrated science in a restructured high school. *Educational Leadership, 49*(2), 39–41.

Crawley, S., & Mountain, L. (1995). *Strategies for guiding content reading*. Boston: Allyn and Bacon.

Crismore, A. (1983, May). *Interpersonal and intentional metadiscourse in learning from text*. Paper presented at the International Reading Association, Anaheim, CA.

Crist, B.I. (1975). One capsule in a week — A painless remedy for vocabulary ills. *Journal of Reading, 19*(58), 147–49.

Crowhurst, M. (1989). Writing to learn in content area. *Reading-Canada-Lecture, 7*(4), 181–90.

Crowhurst, M. (1990). Teaching and learning the writing of persuasive/argumentative discourse. *Canadian Journal of Education, 15*(4), 348–59.

Culler, J. (1981). *Pursuit of signs: Semiotics, literature, deconstruction*. Ithaca, NY: Cornell University Press.

Culler, J. (1982). *On deconstruction: Theory and criticism after deconstruction*. Ithaca, NY: Cornell University Press.

Cullinan, B. (1993). Introduction. In B.E. Cullinan (Ed.), *Children's voices: Talk in the classroom* (pp. 1–5). Newark, DE: International Reading Association.

Curry, J. (1989). The role of reading instruction in mathematics. In D. Lapp, J. Flood, & N. Farman (Eds.), *Content area reading and learning* (pp. 187–197). Englewood Cliffs, NJ: Prentice Hall.

Dale, E. (1965). Vocabulary measurement: Techniques and major findings. *Elementary English, 42*, 895–901.

Dandies, D. (1973). *A primer of visual literacy*. Cambridge, MA: MIT Press.

D'Arcy, P. (1984). Keeping options open: Writing in the humanities. In N. Martin (Ed.), *Writing across the curriculum: Pamphlets from the schools council: London Institute of Education*, (pp. 86–124). NJ: Boynton/Cook Publishers Inc.

D'Arcy, P. (1989). *Making sense, shaping meaning: Writing in the context of a capacity-based approach to learning*. Portsmouth, NH: Heinemann.

Davison, A., Lutz, R., & Roalef, A. (1981). *Text readability: Proceedings of the March 1980 conference* (Technical Report No. 213). Urbana: Center for the Study of Reading, University of Illinois.

Delpit, L.D. (1988). The silenced dialogue: Power and pedagogy in educating other people's children. *Harvard Educational Review, 58*(3), 280–98.

Denner, P.R., & Rickards, J.P. (1987). A developmental comparison of the effects of provided and generated questions on text recall. *Journal of Educational Psychology, 12*, 135–46.

Derrida, J. (1976). *Of grammatology* (Gayatri Spivak, Trans.). Baltimore: Johns Hopkins University Press.

Derrida, J. (1978). *Writing and difference*. Trans. Alan Bass. Chicago: University of Chicago Press.

Derrida, J. (1979). Living on: Borderlines. In H. Bloom et al. (Eds.), *Deconstruction and criticism*. New York: Seabury Press.

Derrida, J. (1981). *Positions* (A. Bass, Trans.). Chicago: University of Chicago Press.

Derrida, J. (1984). Deconstruction and the other. In R. Kearney (Ed.), *Dialogues with contemporary continental thinkers*. Manchester: Manchester University Press.

Descartes, R. (1980). *Discourse on method & meditations on first philosophy* (2nd ed.) (D.A. Cress, Trans.). Indianapolis: Hackett Publishing Company.

Devine, T. (1987). *Teaching study skills: A guide for teachers* (Rev. ed.). Needham, MA: Allyn and Bacon, Inc.

Devine, T. (1991). Studying: Skills, strategies, and systems. In J. Flood, J. Jensen, D. Lapp, & J. Squire. *The handbook of research on teaching the English language arts* (pp. 743–53). New York: Macmillan.

Dewey, J. (1897/1959). My pedagogic creed 9. In M.S. Dworkin (Ed.), *Dewey on education: Selections* (pp. 19–42). New York: Teachers College Press.

Dewey, J., & Bentley, A.F. (1949). *Knowing and the known*. Boston: Beacon.

Dewitz, P., Carr, E.M., Palm, K.N., & Spencer, M. (1992). The validity and utility of portfolio assessment. In C. Kinzer, & D. Leu (Eds.), *Literacy research, theory, and practice: Views from many perspectives* (pp. 153–60). Forty-first Yearbook of the National Reading Conference. Chicago, IL: National Reading Conference.

Dillon, J.T. (1981). Duration of response to teacher questions and statements. *Contemporary Educational Psychology, 6*, 1–11.

Dillon, J.T. (1982). Cognitive correspondence between question/statement and response. *American Education Research Journal, 19*, 540–51.

Dillon, J.T. (1984). Research on questioning and discussion. *Educational Leadership, 42*, 50–56.

Dixon, R.C., & Jenkins, J.R. (1984). An outcome analysis of receptive vocabulary knowledge. Unpublished manuscript, University of Illinois, Champaign, IL.

Donovan, T.R., Poole, M.C., & Yack, D.J. (1995). *Chemicals in action*. Toronto: Holt, Rinehart and Winston.

Drake, SM. (1991). How our team dissolved the boundaries. *Educational Leadership, 49*(2), 20–22.

Dreher, M.J. (1990). The role of affect in the reading process. *Literacy: Issues and Practices, 7*, 20–27.

Dreher, M.J., & Singer, H. (1986). *Affective processes involved in reading comprehension*. Paper presented at the Eleventh World Congress on Reading, London, England.

Duffy, G., & Roehler, L.R. (1987). Teaching reading skills as strategies. *The Reading Teacher, 40*, 414–18.

Duncan, B. (1988). *Mass media and popular culture*. Toronto: Harcourt Brace.

Duncan, B., et al. (1989). Eight key concepts of media literacy. *Media Literacy Resource Guide*. Toronto: Ontario Ministry of Education.

Dunkley, R.G. (Ed.). (1988). *Finite Mathematics*. Toronto: Holt, Rinehart and Winston.

During, S. (1990). Postmodernism or post-colonialism today. In A. Milner et al. (Eds.), *Postmodern conditions*. New York: Berg Press.

Eagleton, T. (1983). *Literary theory: An introduction*. Minneapolis: University of Minnesota Press.

Eanes, R. (1997). *Content area literacy: Teaching for today and tomorrow*. Toronto: Delmar Publishers.

Early, M. (1989). Using key visuals to aid ESL students' comprehension of content area texts. *Reading-Canada-Lecture, 7*(4), 202–12.

Ehri, L.C. (1991). Development of ability to read words. In R. Barr, M.L. Kamil, P. Mosenthal, & P.D. Pearson (Eds.), *Handbook of reading research*: Vol II (pp. 381–417). White Plains, NY: Longman.

Eisner, E.W. (1978). Reading and the creation of meaning. In E.W. Eisner (Ed.), *Reading, the arts and the creation of meaning* (pp. 12–21). Reston, VA: National Art Education Association.

Elbow, P. (1973). *Writing without teachers*. London: Oxford University Press.

Ellis, M. "Theory and practical work in media education." *English Quarterly, 25*(2–3), pp. 28–34.

Emig, J. (1983). *The web of meaning*. Upper Montclair, NJ: Boynton/Cook.

Englert, C.S., & Hiebert, E.H. (1984). Children's developing awareness of text structures in expository materials. *Journal of Educational Psychology, 76*, 65–75.

Enright, D.S., & McCloskey, M.L. (1988). *Integrating English: Developing English language and literacy in the multi-lingual classroom*. Reading, MA: Addison-Wesley.

Estes, T.H. (1994). Readability. In A. Purves (Ed.), *Encyclopaedia of English studies and language arts* (Vol. II, pp. 978–980). New York: Scholastic & NCTE.

Faigley, L. (1986). Competing theories of process: A critique and a proposal. *College English, 48*(6), 527–42.

Farquhar, W., Krumboltz, J., & Wrenn, C. (1960). *Learning to study*. New York: Ronald Press.

Field Enterprises Educational Corporation. (1976). *Childcraft: The how and why library, vol. 6. The green kingdom*. Chicago: Author.

Fielding, L., & Pearson, P.D. (1994). Reading comprehension: What works. *Educational Leadership, 51*(5), 62–68.

Fillion, B. (1979). Language across the curriculum: Examining the place of language in our schools. *McGill Journal of Education, 14*(1), 47–60.

Fillion, B. (1983). Let me see you learn. *Language Arts, 60*, 702–10.

Fiske, J. (1982). *Introduction to communication studies*. London: Methuen.

Flavell, J.H. (1976). Metacognitive aspects of problem-solving. In L.B. Resnick (Ed.), *The nature of intelligence* (pp. 231–35). Hillsdale, NJ: Erlbaum.

Flavell, J.H. (1979). Metacognition and cognitive monitoring: A new area of cognitive-developmental inquiry. *American Psychologist, 34*(10), 906–911.

Flood, J., Lapp, D., & Monken, S. (1992). Portfolio assessment: Teachers' beliefs and practices. In C. Kinzer & D. Leu (Eds.), *Literacy research, theory, and practice: Views from many perspectives*. Forty-first Yearbook of the National Reading Conference (pp. 119–27). Chicago, IL: National Reading Conference.

Flower, L. (1994). *The construction of negotiated meaning: A social cognitive theory of writing*. Carbondale: Southern Illinois University Press.

Flower, L., & Hayes, J. (1981). A cognitive process theory of writing. *College Composition and Communication, 32*, 365–87.

Flower, L., Stein, V., Ackerman, J., Kantz, M., McCormick, K., & Peck, W. (1990). *Reading-to-write: Exploring a cognitive and social process.* New York: Oxford.

Flowers, B. (1981). Madman, architect, carpenter, judge: Roles and the writing process. *Language Arts, 58*(7), 834–36.

Fogarty, R. (1991). Ten ways to integrate curriculum. *Educational Leadership, 49*(2), 61–65.

Foster, H. (1985). *Postmodern culture.* London: Plato Press.

Frager, A. M. (1993). Affective dimensions of content area reading. *Journal of Reading, 36,* 616–22.

Frank, A. (1995). The diary of a young girl. In J. Ballah (Ed.), *Insights: Understanding war.* Toronto: Harcourt Brace.

Frith, K. (1990). *Undressing the ad: A method for deconstructing advertisements.* Presented to the Association for Education in Journalism and Mass Communication Annual Conference, Minneapolis, MN.

Fry, E. (1977). Fry's readability graph: Clarifications, validity, and extension to level 17. *Journal of Reading, 21,* 242–52.

Gambell, T. (1989). Linguistics and literacy teaching. *Reading-Canada-Lecture, 7*(1), 4–15.

Gambrell, L.B. (1996). What research reveals about discussion. In L.B. Gambrell & J.F. Almasi (Eds.) *Lively discussion: Fostering engaged reading* (pp. 25–38). Newark, DE: International Reading Association.

Gardner, H. (1959). *Art through the ages.* New York: Harcourt, Brace & Co.

Gardner, H. (1983). *Frames of mind: Teaching for Multiple Intelligences.* New York: Basic Books.

Gardner, H., & Boix-Mansilla, V. (1994). Teaching for understanding: Within and across disciplines. *Educational Leadership, 51*(5), 14–18.

Garner, R. (1987). *Metacognition and reading comprehension.* Norwood, NJ: Ablex.

Garner, R. (1992). Metacognitive activity and learning from text: Following Martha around during one school day. In C.J. Gordon, G.D. Labercane, & W.R. McEachern (Eds.), *Elementary reading: Process and practice,* (pp. 19–28). Needham Heights, MA: Ginn Press.

Gaskins, I., Satlow, E., Hyson, D., Osterlag, J., & Six, L. (1994). Classroom talk about text: Learning in science class. *Journal of Reading, 37*(7), 558–65.

Gauthier, L.R. (1990). Helping middle school students develop language facility. *Journal of Reading, 33*(4), 274–76.

Gillet, J., & Kita, M.J. (1979). Words, kids and categories. *The Reading Teacher 32*(5), 538–42.

Gillet, J.W., & Temple, C. (1986). Instructor's manual to accompany *Understanding reading problems: Assessment and instruction* (2nd ed.). Boston: Little, Brown & Company.

Giroux, H. (1992). Resisting difference: Cultural studies and the discourse of critical pedagogy. In L. Grossberg, C. Nelson, and P. Treicher (Eds.), *Cultural studies.* New York: Routledge.

Glaser, B., & Strauss, A. (1967). *The discovery of grounded theory: Strategies for qualitative research.* Chicago: Aldine.

Glasgow, J. (1994). Teaching visual literacy for the 21st century. *Journal of Reading, 37*(6), 494–99.

Goldthwait, L. (1972). *Earth science*. Lexington, MA: Ginn.

Gordon, C.J. (1990). Context for expository text structure use. *Reading Research and Instruction, 29*, 55–72.

Gordon, C.J. (1991a). Literacy events: Always social or occasionally solitary. *Reflections on Canadian Literacy, 9*, 32–33.

Gordon, C.J. (1991b). Socializing the writing process through collaboration. *Canadian Journal of English Language Arts, 12*, 3–15.

Gordon, C.J. (1993). Writing to learn; Writing to understand. In C.J. Gordon, G.D. Labercane, & W. McEachern (Eds.), *Elementary Reading: Process and Practice* (pp. 274–286). New York: Ginn & Co.

Gordon, C.J. (1994). Metacognition: Enabler or immobilizer of learning. In F.D. Oliva & D.R. McGaw (Eds.), *Annual Distinguished and Anniversary Lectures* (Vol. II, pp. 116–51). Calgary: Faculty of Education, University of Calgary.

Gordon, C.J. & Hunsberger, M. (1990). Preservice teachers' conceptions of content area literacy instruction. Paper presented at The National Reading Conference, Miami Beach, Florida, December, 1990.

Gordon, C.J., & Hunsberger, M. (1991). Preservice teachers' conceptions of content area literacy instruction. In S. McCormick & J. Zutell (Eds.), *Learner factors/teacher factors: Issues in literacy research and instruction* (pp. 399–407). Chicago, IL: National Reading Conference.

Gordon, C.J., & MacInnis, D. (1993). Using journals as a window on students' thinking processes in mathematics. *Language Arts, 70*, 33–38.

Gould, S.J. (1980). *The panda's thumb: More reflections in natural history*. New York and London: W.W. Norton & Company.

Graham, K., & Robinson, H. (1984). *Study skills handbook: A guide for all teachers*. Newark, DE: International Reading Association.

Graves, D. (1983). *Writing: Teachers and children at work*. Exeter, NH: Heinemann.

Graves, M. (1987). The role of instruction in fostering vocabulary development. In M.G. McKeown & M.E. Curtis (Eds.), *The nature of vocabulary acquisition* (pp. 165–84). Hillsdale, NJ: Erlbaum.

Graves, M., & Hammond, H.K. (1980). A validated procedure for teaching prefixes and its effect on students' ability to assign meaning to novel words. In M.L. Kamil & A.J. Moe (Eds.), *Perspective on reading research and instruction*, Twenty-ninth Yearbook of the National Reading Conference (pp. 184–88). Washington, DC: National Reading Conference.

Graves, M.F., Prenn, M.C., Earle, J., Thompson, M., Johnson, V., & Slater, W.H. (1991). Commentary: Improving instructional texts — some lessons learned. *Reading Research Quarterly, 26*, 110–22.

Greenberg, K. (1994). Writing evaluation. In A. Purves (Ed.), *Encyclopaedia of English studies and language arts* (Vol. II, pp. 1307–9). New York: NCTE and Scholastic.

Guskey, T.R. (1994). What you assess may NOT be what you get. *Educational Leadership, 51*(6), 51–54.

Haas, N.M., & Lo Presto, S. (1994). Panel assessments: Unlocking math exams. *Educational Leadership, 51*(5), 69–70.

Habermas, J. (1983). Modernity — An incomplete project. In Hal Foster (Ed.), *The anti-aesthetic: Essays on postmodern culture*. Seattle, WA: Bay Press.

Hafner, L. (1967). Using context to determine meanings in high school and college. *Journal of Reading, 10*(7), 491–98.

Hairson, M. (1982). The winds of change: Thomas Kuhn and the revolution in the teaching of writing. *College Composition and Communication, 33*(1), 76–88.

Halliday, M.A.K. (1978). *Language as social semiotic.* London: Edward Arnold.

Halliday, M.A.K. (1987). Spoken and written modes of meaning. In R. Horowitz & S.J. Samuels (Eds.), *Comprehending oral and written language* (pp. 55–82). London: Academic Press.

Hamann, L.S., Schultz, L., Smith, M.W., & White, B. (1991). Making connections: The power of autobiographical writing before reading. *Journal of Reading, 35*(1), 24–28.

Hannan, E., Hannan, E., Quigley, G., & Wintrob, R. (1990). *Perspectives One.* Toronto: Harcourt Brace Jovanovich, Canada.

Hansen, J., & Rubin, A. (1984). *Reading and writing: How are the first two "r's" related?* Reading Education Report #51. Champaign, IL: University of Illinois Center for the Study of Reading.

Harker, W.J. (1990). Reader response and the interpretation of literature: Is there a teacher in the classroom? *Reflections on Canadian Literacy, 8,* 69–73.

Harman, S. (1992). Snow White and the seven warnings: Threats to authentic evaluation. *The Reading Teacher, 46*(3), 250–52.

Harrell, L.E. Jr. (1957). An inter-comparison of the quality and rate of the development of the oral and written language of children. *Monographs of the Society for Research in Child Development, 22,* 35–60.

Harris, T.L., & Hodges, R.E. (Eds.) (1995). *The literacy dictionary.* Newark, DE: International Reading Association.

Harste, J.C. (1984). *The winds of change: Examining assumptions in instructional research in reading comprehension.* Paper presented at the National Council of Teachers of English Conference, Detroit, MI.

Harste, J., Burke, C., & Short, K. (1988). *Creating classrooms for authors.* Portsmouth, NH: Heinemann.

Harste, J.C., Woodward, V.A., & Burke, C.L. (1984). Examining our assumptions: A transactional view of literacy and learning. *Research in the Teaching of English, 18,* 84–108.

Hayes, J., & Flower, L. (1980). Identifying the organization of writing processes. In L. Gregg & E. Steinberg (Eds.), *Cognitive processes in writing* (pp. 3–30). Hillsdale, NJ: Erlbaum.

Heath, S.B. (1991). The sense of being literate: Historical and cross-cultural features. In R. Barr, M. Kamil, P. Mosenthal, & P.D. Pearson (Eds.), *Handbook of reading research* (Vol. II, pp. 3–25). New York: Longman.

Hebdige, D. (1988). *Hiding in the light: On images and things.* New York: Routledge.

Hebert, E.A. (1992). Portfolios invite reflection — from students *and* staff. *Education Leadership, 49*(8), 58–61.

Hentze, T. (1989). Language arts with junior high school grade nines — a sheer delight. *Reading-Canada-Lecture, 7,* 71–81.

Herman, J. (1992). What research tells us about good assessment. *Educational Leadership, 49*(8), 74–78.

Herman, P.A., Anderson, R.C., Pearson, P.D., & Nagy, W.E. (1987). Incidental acquisitions of word meanings from expositions with varied text features. *Reading Research Quarterly, 22*(3), 263–84.

Hermann, B.A. (1990). Cognitive and metacognitive goals in reading and writing. In J. Duffy (Ed.), *Reading in the Middle School* (pp. 81–96). Newark, DE: International Reading Association.

Hidi, S., & Anderson, V. (1986). Producing written summaries: Task demands, cognitive operations and implications for instructions. *Review of Educational Research, 56*, 473–94.

Hiebert, E.J., Valencia, S.W., & Afflerbach, P.P. (1994). Definitions and perspectives. In E.J. Hiebert, S.W. Valencia, & P.P. Afflerbach (Eds.), *Authentic Reading Assessment: Practices and Possibilities*, (pp. 6–21). Newark, DE: International Reading Association.

Hlynka, D., & Yeaman, R. (1992). *Postmodern educational technology*. ERIC Digest No. EDO-IR-92-5. Syracuse, NY: ERIC Clearinghouse on Information Resources.

Holbrook, H.T. (1987). Writing to learn in the social studies. *The Reading Teacher, 41*(2), 216–19.

Holliday, W.G., Brunner, L.L, & Donais, E.L. (1977). Differential cognitive and affective responses to flow diagrams in science. *Journal of Research in Science Teaching, 14*, 129–38.

Holmes, J.A. (1960). The substrata-factor theory of reading: Some experimental evidence. In J. Figurel (Ed.), *New Frontiers in Reading* (pp. 115–21). Proceedings of the Fifth Annual Conference of the International Reading Association. New York: Scholastic.

Horowitz, R. (1991). Studies of orality and literacy: Critical issues for the practice of schooling. *Text, 2*(1), Special Issues.

Horowitz, R. (1994). Written and oral English. In A. Purves (Ed.), *Encyclopaedia of English studies and language arts* (Vol. II, pp. 1327–28). New York: NCTE and Scholastic.

Hoyt, L. (1992). Many ways of knowing: Using drama, oral interactions, and the visual arts to enhance reading comprehension. *The Reading Teacher, 45*(8), 580–84.

Hunsaker, R.A. (1990). *Understanding and developing the skills of oral communication: Speaking and listening* (2nd ed.). Englewood, CO: Morton.

Irwin, J.W., & Davis, C.A. (1980). Assessing readability: The checklist approach. *Journal of Reading, 24*, 124–30.

Jackson, F.R. (1993–94). Seven strategies to support a culturally responsive pedagogy. *Journal of Reading, 37*(4), 298–303.

Jackson, J.H., & Evans, E.D. (1976). *Spaceship earth*. Boston: Houghton-Mifflin.

Jacobs, H.H. (1991). Planning for curriculum integration. *Educational Leadership, 49*(2), 27–28.

Jagodzinski, J. (1995). Curriculum as felt through six layers of an aesthetic embodied skin. In W. Pinar (Ed.), *Understanding Curriculum*, (pp. 159–81). New York: Peter Lang.

Jalongo, M.R. (1991). *Strategies for developing children's listening skills*. Phi Delta Kappa Fastback Series #314. Bloomington, IN: Phi Delta Kappa Educational Foundation.

Jamentz, K. (1994). Making sure that assessment improves performance. *Educational Leadership, 51*(6), 55–57.

Jenkins, J. (1979). Four points to remember: A tetrahedral model of memory experiments. In L.S. Cermak & F.I.M. Craik (Eds.), *Levels of processing and human memory*, (pp. 429–46). Hillsdale, NJ: Erlbaum.

Johnson, D.W., & Johnson, R.T. (1991). Group assessment as an aid to science instruction. In G. Kulm, & S.M. Malcolm (Eds.), *Science assessment in the service of reform*, (pp. 283–89). Washington, DC: American Association for the Advancement of Science.

Johnson, D.W., & Johnson, R.T. (1993). Gifted students illustrate what isn't cooperative learning. *Education Leadership, 50*(6), 60–61.

Johnson, D.W., Johnson, R.T., & Holubec, E.J. (1991). *Cooperation in the classroom.* Edina, MN: Interaction Books.

Johnson, S. (1977). *Cross-age tutoring handbook.* Corcoran, CA: Corcoran Unified School District. (ERIC Document Reproduction Service No. ED 238 826).

Johnston, P.H. (1995, December). *Response to symposium presentations entitled "Statewide Writing Assessments: Lessons from Kentucky, Indiana, and Vermont."* Presented at the National Reading Conference, New Orleans, LA.

Jongsma, E., & Farr, R. (1993). A themed issue on literacy assessment. *The Journal of Reading, 36*(7), 516–17.

Jordan, S. (1994). Portfolio assessment. In A. Purves (Ed.), *Encyclopaedia of English studies and language arts* (Vol. II, pp. 928–29). New York: Scholastic and NCTE.

Kagan, S. (1992). *Cooperative learning.* Laguna Nigual, CA: Kagan Cooperative Learning.

Kahn, N. (1984). *More learning in less time: A guide for effective study.* Upper Monclair, NJ: Boynton/Cook Publishers.

Kameenui, E.J., Dixon, D.W., & Carnine, R.C. (1987). Issues in the design of vocabulary instruction. In M.G. McKeown & M.E. Curtis (Eds.), *The nature of vocabulary acquisition* (pp. 129–45). Hillsdale, NJ: Erlbaum.

Karpinski, E.C., & Lea, I. (1993). *Pens of Many Colours: A Canadian Reader.* Toronto: Harcourt Brace.

Kelly, B., & Holmes, J. (1979). The guided lecture procedure. *Journal of Reading, 31*, 602–4.

Kesey, K. (1962). *One flew over the cuckoo's nest.* New York: Viking Press.

Kiewra, K., & Frank, B. (1988). Encoding and external storage effects of personal lecture notes, skeletal notes, and detailed notes for field-independent and field-dependent learners. *Journal of Educational Research, 81*(3), 143–48.

Kirkland, G., Roy, K., & Terpening, J. (1996). *Insights: Technology and Change.* Toronto: Harcourt Brace.

Kletzien, S.B., & Baloche, L. (1994). The shifting muffled sound of the pick: Facilitating student-to-student discussion. *Journal of Reading, 37*(7), 540–45.

Knight, P. (1992). How I use portfolios in mathematics. *Educational Leadership, 49*(8), 71–72.

Knoeller, C.P. (1993). *How talk enters writing: A study of 12th graders discussing and writing about literature.* Unpublished doctoral dissertation, University of California, Berkeley.

Knoeller, C.P. (1994). Negotiating interpretations of text: The role of student led discussions in understanding literature. *Journal of Reading, 37*(7), 572–79.

Kogawa, J. (1993). What do I remember of the evacuation? In E.C. Karpinski & I. Lea (Eds.), *Pens of Many Colors.* Toronto: Harcourt Brace.

Konopek, B.C. (1988). Effects of inconsiderate vs. considerate text on secondary students' vocabulary learning. *Journal of Reading Behavior, 20,* 25–41.

Konopek, B., Martin, B., & Martin, S. (1987). Reading and writing: Aids to learning in the content areas. *Journal of Reading, 31,* 109–17.

Korchinski, D. (1991, June 23). A losing proposition. *Calgary Herald Sunday Magazine,* pp. 14–16.

Krueger, R., Corder, R., & Koegler, J. (1991). *This land of ours: A new geography of Canada.* Toronto: Harcourt Brace Jovanovich.

Kucer, S.L. (1985). The making of meaning: Reading and writing as parallel processes. *Written Communication, 2,* 317–36.

Lange, B. (1982). Readability formulas: Second looks, second thoughts. *The Reading Teacher, 35,* 858–61.

Langer, J. (1981). From theory to practice: A pre-reading plan. *Journal of Reading, 25*(2), 152–56.

Langer, J. (1986). *Children's reading and writing: Structures and strategies.* Norwood, NJ: Ablex.

Langer, J.A., & Applebee, A.N. (1987). *How writing shapes thinking: A study of teaching and learning.* Research Report No. 22. Urbana, IL: National Council of Teachers of English.

Lasch, C. (1979). *The culture of narcissism.* New York: Warner.

Leal, D. (1993). The power of literary peer discussions: How children collaboratively negotiate meaning. *The Reading Teacher, 47*(2), 114–20.

Lehr, F. (1984). Promoting vocabulary development. *Journal of Reading, 27*(7), 656–58.

Lehr, F. (1985). Instructional scaffolding. *Language Arts, 62,* 667–72.

Leitch, V. (1983). *Deconstructive criticism: An advanced introduction.* New York: Columbia University Press.

Leland, C.H., & Harste, J.C. (1994). Multiple ways of knowing: Curriculum in a new key. *Language Arts, 71*(5), 337–45.

Lindfors, J. (1994). Classroom interaction. In A.C. Purves (Ed.), *Encyclopaedia of English studies and language arts* (Vol. I, pp. 187–89). New York: Scholastic & NCTE.

Loban, W. (1963). *The language of elementary school children.* (National Council of Teachers of English Research Report No. 1). Urbana, IL: National Council of Teachers of English.

Loban, W. (1976). *Language development: Kindergarten through grade twelve.* (Research Report 18). Urbana, IL: National Council of Teachers of English.

Lynch, J. (1983). *Film education in the secondary schools: A study of film use and teaching in selected English and film courses.* New York: Garland Publishing.

Lyotard, J. F. (1989). *The postmodern condition: A report on knowledge.* Trans. G. Bennington and B. Massumi. Minneapolis: University of Minnesota Press.

MacDonnell, R. (1992). *A study of the humanities programme at St. Francis High School, Calgary, Alberta, Canada.* Unpublished manuscript, University of Calgary.

McFadden, C.P., & Morrison, E.S. (1990). *Science plus: Technology and society (8)*. Toronto: Harcourt Brace Jovanovich.

McGee, L.M. (1982a). Awareness of text structure: Effects on children's recall of expository text. *Reading Research Quarterly, 17*, 581–90.

McGee, L.M. (1982b). The influence of metacognitive knowledge of expository text structure on discourse recall. In J.A. Niles & L.A. Harris (Eds.), *New inquiries in research and instruction: Thirty-first yearbook of the National Reading Conference* (pp. 64–70). Rochester, NY: National Reading Conference.

MacGinitie, W. (1984). Readability as a solution adds to the problem. In R. Anderson, J. Osborn, & R. Tierney (Eds.), *Learning to read in American schools* (pp. 141–52). Hillsdale, NJ: Erlbaum.

McKenna, M.C. (1991). Computerized reading assessment: Its emerging potential. *The Reading Teacher, 44*(9), 692–93.

McKenna, M.C., & Robinson, R.D. (1990). Content literacy: A definition and implications. *Journal of Reading, 34*(3), 184–86.

McKeough, A. (1995). Teaching narrative knowledge for transfer in the early school years. In A. McKeough, J. Lupart, & A. Marini (Eds.), *Teaching for transfer: Fostering generalization in learning*. Hillsdale, NJ: Erlbaum.

McLaren, P. (1989). *Life in schools*. New York: Longman.

McLaughlin, M.W. (1991). Test-based accountability as a reform strategy. *Phi Delta Kappan, 73*, 248–51.

McMahon, S.I. (1992, April). *Classroom discourse during social studies: Students' purposes and topics of interest in peer-led discussion groups*. Paper presented at the annual meeting of the American Educational Research Association, San Francisco, CA.

Maeroff, G.I. (1991, December). Assessing alternative assessment. *Phi Delta Kappan, 73*(4), 273–81.

Malczewski, C.L. (1991). Toward a theory of ownership through the dramatic process. *Reflections on Canadian Literacy, 9*, 182–86.

Malicky, G. (1990). Parallel processes in reading and writing: Further implications. *Reflections on Canadian Literacy, 8*, 104–5.

Malicky, G. (1994). Learning modality/style. In A.C. Purves (Ed.), *Encyclopaedia of English studies and language arts* (Vol. II, pp. 725–26). New York: Scholastic & NCTE.

Manzo, A.M., & Sherk, J. (1971–72). Some generalizations and strategies to guide vocabulary acquisition. *Journal of Reading Behavior, 4*, 78–79.

Marland, M. (1977). *Language across the curriculum*. London: Heinemann Educational Books.

Martin, N. (1977). Writing. In N. Marlan (Ed.), *Language across the curriculum* (pp. 145–68). London: Heinemann Educational Books.

Martin, N. (1984). Introduction. In N. Martin (Ed.), *Writing and learning across the curriculum: Pamphlets from the school council: London Institute of Education* (pp. 1–3). Portsmouth, NH: Boynton/Cook Publishers.

Martin, N., D'Arcy, P., Newton, B., & Parker, R. (1976). *Writing and learning across the curriculum*, pp. 11–16. London: Ward Lock Educational.

Martin, N., Medway, P., Smith, H., & D'Arcy, P. (1984). Why Write? In N. Martin (Ed.), *Writing and learning across the curriculum: Pamphlets from the school council: London Institute of Education* (pp. 34–59). NJ: Boynton/Cook Publishers, Inc.

Marzano, R. (1994). Lessons from the field about outcome-based performance assessments. *Educational Leadership, 51*(6), 44–50.

Marzano, R., & Marzano, J. (1988). A theoretical base for vocabulary instruction. *A Cluster Approach to elementary vocabulary instruction* (pp. 1–14). Newark, DE: International Reading Association.

Massey, D., & Conners, B. (1986). *Canada: Its land and people.* Edmonton, AB: Reidmore Pocol Enterprises.

Masterman, L. (1993). Media Education: What should be taught? From fragmentation to coherence. *English Quarterly, 25*(2–3), pp. 5–7.

Mathewson, G. (1985). Towards a comprehensive model of affect in the reading process. In H. Singer & R. Ruddell (Eds.), *Theoretical models and processes of reading* (3rd ed.) (pp. 841–856). Newark, DE: International Reading Association.

May, S.A. (1993). Redeeming multi-cultural education. *Language Arts, 70*(5), 364–372.

Mazzoni, S.A., & Gambrell, L.B. (1996). Text talk: Using discussion to promote comprehension of informational texts. In L.B. Gambrell & J.F. Almasi (Eds.), *Lively discussions: Fostering engages reading* (pp. 134–48). Newark, DE: International Reading Association.

Meyer, B.J.F., Brandt, D.M., & Bluth, G.J. (1980). Use of top-level structure in text: Key for reading comprehension of ninth-grade students. *Reading Research Quarterly, 16*, 72–103.

Meyer, C.A. (1992). What's the difference between *authentic* and *performance* assessment? *Educational Leadership, 49*(8), 39–40.

Mickelson, N. (1992). Whole language: philosophy, implementation, and evaluation. In C.J. Gordon, G.D. Labercane, & W.R. McEachern (Eds.), *Elementary reading: Process and practice.* Needham Heights, MA: Ginn Press.

Miholic, V. (1994). An inventory to pique students' metacognitive awareness of reading strategies. *Journal of Reading, 38*(2), 84–86.

Moffat, J.M. (1968). *Teaching the universe of discourse.* New York: Houghton Mifflin.

Moje, E.B., & Handy, D. (1995). Using literacy to modify traditional assessments: Alternatives for teaching and assessing content understanding. *Journal of Reading, 38*(8), 612–25.

Monahan, J., & Hinson, B. (1988). Content area reading-learning strategies. *New directions in reading instruction.* Newark, DE: International Reading Association.

Moore, D.W., Readence, J.E., & Rickelman, R.J. (1986). An historical exploration of content area reading instruction. In E.K. Dishner, T.W. Bean, J.E. Readence, & D.W. Moore (Eds.), *Reading in the content areas: Improving classroom instruction* (pp. 4–27). Dubuque, IA: Kendall/Hunt.

Morrison, E.S. (Ed.). (1994). *Science plus 9.* Toronto: Harcourt Brace & Co., Canada.

Mulcahey, P.I., & Samuels, S.J. (1987). Problem solving schemata for text types: A comparison of narratives and expository text structures. *Reading Psychology, 8*, 247–56.

Murray, D.M. (1982). The feel of writing — and the teaching of writing. In D.M. Murray, *Learning by teaching: Selected articles on writing and teaching* (pp. 42–49). Montclair, NH: Boynton Cook.

Murray, D. (1985). *A writer teaches writing*. Boston: Houghton Mifflin.

Murray, D. (1986). *Read to write: A writing process reader*. New York: Holt, Rinehart & Winston.

Myers, J.W. (1984). *Writing to learn across the curriculum* (Fastback 209). Bloomington, IN: Phi Delta Kappa Educational Foundation. (ERIC Reproduction Service No. ED 248 532).

Nagy, W.E., Herman, P.A., & Anderson, R.C. (1985). Learning words from context. *Reading Research Quarterly, 20*(3), 233–53.

Nagy, W.E., Herman, P.A., Anderson, R.C., & Pearson, P.D. (1984). *Learning words from context* (Tech. Rep. No. 319). Urbana: University of Illinois, Center for the Study of Reading.

National Assessment of Education Progress. (1985). *The reading report card*. (Report No. 15-R-01). Princeton, NJ: Educational Testing Service.

National Association for the Teaching of English. (1976). *Language across the curriculum: Guidelines for schools*. London: Ward Lock Educational.

Nelson-Herber, J. (1986). Expanding and refining vocabulary in content areas. *Journal of Reading, 29*(7), 626–33.

Newell, G. (1986). Learning from writing: Examining our assumptions. *English Quarterly, 19*(4), 291–301.

Newkirk, T. (1991). *The high school years*. In J. Flood, J.M. Jensen, D. Lapp, & J.R. Squire (Eds.), *Handbook of research on teaching the English Language Arts*, (pp. 331–42). New York: MacMillan.

Newton, E.G. (1991). Developing metacognitive awareness: The response journal in college composition. *Journal of Reading, 36*, 476–78.

Noden, H., & Moss, B. (1994). Perceiving discussion as Eskimos perceive snow. *The Reading Teacher, 47*(6), 504–6.

Noden, H., & Vacca, R. (1994). *Whole language in middle and secondary classrooms*. New York: Harper Collins.

Norman, M., & Norman, E. (1968). *Successful reading*. New York: Holt, Rinehart and Winston.

Norris, C. (1982). *Deconstruction: Theory and practice*. London: Methuen.

Norris, C. (1985). *Derrida*. Cambridge, MA: Columbia University Press.

Norris, C., & Benjamin, A. (1988). *What is deconstruction?* New York: St. Martin's.

Norris, S.P., & Phillips, L.M. (1994). The relevance of a reader's knowledge within a perspective view of reading. *Journal of Reading Behavior, 26*, 391–412.

Nystrand, M. (1986a). A social interactive model of writing. *Written Communication, 6*(1), 66–85.

Nystrand, M. (1986b). *The structure of written communication*. New York: Academic Press.

Nystrand, M. (1989). A social-interactive model of writing. *Written Communication, 6*(1), 66–85.

O'Brien, D., Stewart, R., & Moje, E. (1995). Why content literacy is difficult to infuse into the secondary school: Complexities of curriculum, pedagogy, and school culture. *Reading Research Quarterly, 30*(3), 442–63.

O'Dell, S. (1987). The serpent never sleeps: A novel of Jamestown and Pocahontas. New York, NY: Fawcett Juniper.

O'Donnell, R. (1994a) Criterion- and domain-referenced tests. In A. Purves (Ed.), *Encyclopaedia of English studies and language arts* (Vol. I, pp. 314–15). New York: Scholastic and NCTE.

O'Donnell, R. (1994b). Norm-referenced tests. In A. Purves (Ed.), *Encyclopaedia of English studies and language arts* (Vol. II p. 882). New York: Scholastic and NCTE.

O'Donnell, R. (1994c). Norms. In A. Purves (Ed.), *Encyclopaedia of English studies and language arts* (Vol. II, p. 883). New York: Scholastic and NCTE.

Ogle, D.M. (1986). K-W-L: A teaching model that develops active reading of expository text. *The Reading Teacher, 39*, 564–70.

Ogle, D. (1996). Study techniques that ensure content area reading success. In D. Lapp, J. Flood, and N. Farnan, (Eds.), *Content area reading and learning*. Toronto: Allyn and Bacon.

O'Neil, J. (1992). Putting performance assessment to the test. *Educational Leadership, 49*(8), 14–19.

Onore, C. (1990). Negotiation, language, and inquiry: Building knowledge collaboratively in the classroom. In S. Hynds, and D. Rubin (Eds.), *Perspectives on talk and learning*, (pp. 57–72). Urbana, IL: National Council of Teachers of English.

Ontario. Ministry of Education. (1989). *Media literacy resource guide*. Toronto: Government of Ontario Printing Services.

Orr, D. (1993). Schools for the twenty-first century. *Resurgence, 160*, 16–19.

Pace, A., Marshall, N., Horowitz, R., Lipson, M., & Lucido, P. (1989). When prior knowledge doesn't facilitate text comprehension: An examination of some of the issues. In S. McCormick & J. Zutell (Eds.), *Cognitive and social perspectives for literacy research and instruction* (pp. 213–24). Rochester, NY: National Reading Conference.

Palmatier, R.A. (1973). A note-taking system for learning. *Journal of Reading, 17*, 36–39.

Palmer, R., & Pope, C. (1984). *Braintrain: Studying for success*. London: E. & F.N. Spoon.

Palmquist, M. (1994). Writing across the curriculum and computers. In A. Purves (Ed.), *Encyclopaedia of English studies and language arts* (Vol. II, pp. 1303–4). New York: NCTE and Scholastic.

Paris, C., Lipson, M., & Wixson, K. (1983). Becoming a strategic reader. *Contemporary Educational Psychology, 8*, 293–316.

Paris, S., Oka, E., & DeBritto, A. (1983). Beyond decoding: Synthesis of research in reading comprehension. *Educational Leadership, 41*, 78–83.

Paris, S.G., & Winograd, P. (1990). How metacognition can promote academic learning and instruction. In B. Jones and L. Idol (Eds)., *Dimensions of thinking and cognitive instruction* (pp. 15–52). Hillsdale, NJ: Laurence Erlbaum Associates.

Pauk, W. (1974). *How to study in college* (2nd ed.). Boston: Houghton Mifflin.

Pauk, W. (1978). A notetaking format. Magical but not automatic. *Reading World, 16*, 96–97.

Pearson, P.D. (1974–75). The effects of grammatical complexity on children's comprehension, recall and conception of certain semantic relations. *Reading Research Quarterly, 10*, 155–92.

Pearson, P.D. (1982). The new buzz word in reading is schema. *Instructor, 91*, 46–48.

Pearson, P.D. (1993). Teaching and learning reading: A research perspective. *Language Arts, 70*(6), 502–11.

Pearson, P.D., Hansen, J., & Gordon, C.J. (1979). The effect of background knowledge on young children's comprehension of explicit and implicit information. *Journal of Reading Behavior, 11*, 201-209.

Pearson, P.D., & Johnson, D. (1978). *Teaching reading comprehension.* New York: Holt, Rinehart and Winston.

Perkins, D.N. (1991). Educating for insight. *Educational Leadership, 49*(2), 4–8.

Peters, C.W. (1991). You can't have authentic assessment without authentic content. *The Reading Teacher, 44*(8), 590–91.

Petrosky, A.R. (1982). From story to essay: Reading and writing. *College Composition and Communication, 33*, 11–36.

Phillips, L. (1988). Young readers' inference strategies in reading comprehension. *Cognition and Instruction, 5*, 193–222.

Piaget, J. (1926). *The language and thought of the child.* London: Routledge & Kegan Paul.

Pikulski, J. (1990a). The role of tests in a literacy assessment program. *The Reading Teacher, 43*(9), 686–88.

Pikulski, J.J. (1990b). Statewide reading tests: The present and the future. *The Reading Instruction Journal, 33*(3), 5–13.

Plecha, J. (1992). Shared inquiry: The great books methods of interpretive reading and discussion. In C. Temple & P. Colins (Eds.), *Stories and readers: New perspectives on literature in the elementary classroom* (pp. 103–14). Norwood, MA: Christopher Gordon.

Pollack, L. (1983). *Forgotten children.* Cambridge: C.U. Press.

Poole, M.C., Pilkey, G., & Johnson, E.C. (1992). *Biology in Action.* Toronto: Harcourt Brace Jovanovich.

Postman, N. (1992). *Technopoly: The surrender of culture to technology.* New York: Alfred A. Knopf.

Poter, A., Archibald, D., & Tyree Jr., A. (1990). Reforming the curriculum: Will empowerment policies replace control? *Politics of Education Association Yearbook,* (pp. 11–36).

Probst, R.E. (1990). Dialogue with a text. In T. Newkirk (Ed.), *To compose* (pp. 163–76). Portsmouth, NH: Heinemann.

Proett, J., & Gill, K. (1986). *The writing process in action: A handbook for teachers.* Urbana, IL: National Council of Teachers of English.

Rafoth, B.A. (1994). Writing/speaking relationships. In A. Purves (Ed.), *Encyclopaedia of English studies and language arts* (Vol. II, pp. 1325–26). New York: NCTE and Scholastic.

Rafter, M. (1996, September 26). Watching the Web. *Calgary Herald*, p. D13.

Rapp-Haggard, M. (1986). The vocabulary self-selection strategy: Using student interest and world knowledge to enhance vocabulary growth. *Journal of Reading, 29*(7), 634–42.

Rapp-Haggard Ruddell, M. (1992). Integrated content and long-term vocabulary learning with the vocabulary self-selection strategy. In E.K. Dishner, T.W. Bean,

J.E. Readence, & D.W. Moore (Eds.), *Reading in the content areas: Improving classroom instruction* (3rd ed.) (pp. 190, 195). Dubuque, IA: Kendall/Hunt.

Ray, M. (1990). *Working cinema.* Belmont, CA: Wadsworth.

Readence, J., Baldwin, R.S., & Bean, T. (1981). *Content area reading: An integrated approach.* Dubuque, IA: Kendall/Hunt.

Rekrut, M.D. (1994). Peer and cross-age tutoring: The lessons of research. *Journal of Reading, 37*(5), 356–361.

Reynolds, R., Wade, S., Trathen, W., & Lapan, R. (1989). The selective attention strategy and prose learning. In M. Pressley, C. McCormick, and E. Miller (Eds.), *Cognitive Strategies Research*, (pp. 159–90). New York: Springer-Verlag.

Ricci, M.N. (1985). *Writing across the curriculum: Strategies for social studies.* Paper presented at the 4th annual meeting of the National Council of the Teachers of English Spring Conference, Houston, TX.

Ricco, G.L. (1989). Daedalus and Icarus within: The literature/art/writing connection. *English Journal, 78,* 14–23.

Richardson, J., & Morgan, R. (1994). *Reading to learn in the content areas.* Belmont, CA: Wadsworth.

Richek, M.A. (1988). Relating vocabulary learning to world knowledge. *Journal of Reading, 32*(3), 262–67.

Richgels, D.L., McGee, L.M., Lomax, R.B., & Sheard, C. (1987). Awareness of four text structures: Effects on recall. *Reading Research Quarterly, 22,* 177–96.

Robinson, F. (1970). *Effective study* (4th ed.) New York: Harper and Row.

Roe, B., Stoodt, B., & Burns, P. (1991). *Secondary school reading instruction: The content areas.* Boston: Houghton Mifflin Company.

Roehler, L.R., Duffy, G.G., & Meloth, M. (1984). What to be direct about in direct instruction: Content-only versus process-into-content. In T. Raphael (Ed.), *The contexts of school-based literacy* (pp. 79–95). New York: Random House.

Rogoff, B. (1990). *Apprenticeship in thinking: Cognitive development in social context.* Oxford: Oxford University Press.

Rosenblatt, L.M. (1938). *Literature as explanation.* New York, NY: Appleton-Century.

Rosenblatt, L.M. (1969). Towards a transactional theory of reading. *Journal of Reading Behavior, 1*(1), 31–49.

Rosenblatt, L.M. (1978). *The reader, the text, the poem: The transactional theory of the literary work.* Carbondale, IL: Southern Illinois University Press.

Rosenblatt, L.M. (1980). What facts does this poem teach you? *Language Arts, 57,* 386–88.

Rosenblatt, L.M. (1985). Viewpoints: Transaction versus interaction — A terminological rescue operation. *Research in the Teaching of English, 19,* 96–107.

Rosenblatt, L.M. (1989). Writing and reading. The transactional theory. In J.M. Mason (Ed.), *Reading and writing connections* (pp. 153–76). Boston: Allyn & Bacon.

Rosenblatt, L. M. (1991). Literature — S.O.S.! *Language Arts, 60,* 444–48.

Rothman, W. (1988). *The "I" of the camera: Essays in film criticism, history, and aesthetics.* New York: Cambridge University Press.

Rousenau, P.M. (1992). *Post-modernism and the social sciences: Insights, inroads, and intrusions.* Princeton, NJ: Princeton University Press.

Roy, K. (Ed.). (1996). *Insights: Identity and learning.* Toronto: Harcourt Brace.

Ruddell, R., & Unrau, N. (1994). Reading as a meaning-making construction process: The reader, the text, and the teacher. In R. Ruddell, M. Rapp-Ruddell, & H. Singer (Eds.), *Theoretical models and processes of reading* (pp. 996–1056). Newark, DE: International Reading Association.

Ruddell, R.B., & Rapp-Ruddell, M. (1994). Language acquisition and literacy processes. In R.B. Ruddell, M. Rapp-Ruddell, & H. Singer (Eds.), *Theoretical models and processes of reading* (pp. 83–103). Newark, DE: International Reading Association.

Rush, R.T. (1985). Assessing readability: Formulas and alternatives. *The Reading Teacher, 39*, 274–83.

Russell, D. (1954). *The dimensions of children's meaning vocabularies in grades 4 through 12*. Berkeley: University of California.

Saliani, D. (1995). *Insights: Immigrant experiences*. Toronto: Harcourt Brace.

Sanacore, J. (1993). Supporting a literature-based approach across the curriculum. *Journal of Reading, 37*(3), 240–44.

Santa, C. (1992). Comprehending and studying in the content areas. In C. Gordon, G. Labercane, and W.R. McEachern (Eds.), *Elementary reading: Process and practice* (pp. 245–62). New York: Ginn Press.

Santeusanio, R. (1988). *A practical approach to content area reading*. Reading, MA: Addison-Wesley.

Sapon-Shevin, M., & Schniedewind, N. (1993). Why (even) gifted children need cooperative learning. *Educational Leadership, 50*(6), 62–63.

Sarup, M. (1989). *An introductory guide to post-structuralism and postmodernism*. Athens: University of Georgia Press.

Scardamalia, M., & Bereiter, C. (1986a). Research on written composition. In M. Wittrock (Ed.), *Handbook of research on teaching* (pp. 778–803). New York: McMillan.

Scardamalia, M., & Bereiter, C. (1986b). Writing. In R. Dillon & R. Sternberg (Eds.), *Cognition and instruction* (pp. 59–81). Orlando, FL: Academic Press.

Schifini, A. (1996). Discussion in multilingual, multicultural classrooms. In L.B. Gambrell, & J.G. Almasi (Eds.), *Lively discussions: Fostering engaged reading*. Newark, DE: International Reading Association.

Schnitzer, S. (1993). Designing an authentic assessment. *Educational Leadership, 50*(7), 32–35.

Schumacher, G.M., & Nash, J.G. (1991). Conceptualizing and measuring knowledge change due to writing. *Research in the Teaching of English, 25*, 67–96.

Schwartz, J. (1991). Let them assess their own learning. *English Journal, 80*, 67–73.

Schwartz, R.M. (1988). Learning to learn vocabulary in content area textbooks. *Journal of Reading, 32*(2), 108–17.

Schwartz, R.M., & Raphael, T.E. (1985). Concept of definition: A key to improving students' vocabulary. *The Reading Teacher, 39*(2), 198–204.

Scott, J.A., & Nagy, W.E. (1994). Vocabulary development. In A. Purves (Ed.), *Encyclopaedia of English studies and language arts* (Vol. II, pp. 1242–44). New York: Scholastic.

Sebesta, S.L. (1995). Reader response. In T.L. Harris & R.E. Hodges (Eds.). *The literacy dictionary* (pp. 209–10). Newark, DE: International Reading Association.

Sebesta, S.L., Monson, D.L., & Doces Senn, H. (1995). A hierarchy to assess reader response. *Journal of Reading, 38*(6), 444–50.

Seminoff, N.W. (1983). Organizing the secondary classroom for language learning: A practical approach. In U.H. Hardt (Ed.), *Teaching reading with the other language arts* (pp. 135–58). Newark, DE: International Reading Association.

Shanahan, T. (1994). Assessment, theory and practice. In A. Purves (Ed.), *Encyclopaedia of English studies and language arts* (Vol. I, pp. 93–97). New York: Scholastic and NCTE.

Shanahan, T., & Tierney, R.J. (1990). Reading–writing connections: The relations among three perspectives. In J. Zutell & S. McCormick (Eds.), *Literacy theory and research: Analysis from multiple paradigms* (pp. 13–34). Chicago, IL: National Reading Conference.

Silberman, A. (1989). *Growing up writing: Teaching children to write, think and learn.* Toronto: Random House.

Silverman, H. (1990). *Postmodernism — Philosophy and the arts.* New York: Routledge.

Simmons, J.S. (1991). The junior high school years. In J. Flood, J.M. Jensen, D. Lapp, & J.M. Squire (Eds.), *Handbook of research on teaching the English language arts* (pp. 320–30). New York: MacMillan Publishing Co.

Simons, S. (1989). PSRT — A reading comprehension strategy. *Journal of Reading, 32,* 419–27.

Simpson, M. (1987). Alternative formats for evaluating content area vocabulary understanding. *Journal of Reading, 31*(1), 20–27.

Simpson, M. (1989). PORPE: A writing strategy for studying and learning in the content areas. *Journal of Reading, 29,* 407–14.

Simpson, M., et al. (1988). An intial validation of a study strategy system. *Journal of Reading Behavior, 20,* 149–80.

Sinatra, R. (1986). *Visual literacy connections to thinking, reading, and writing.* Springfield, IL: Charles C. Thomas.

Singer, H. (1986). Friendly texts: Description and criteria. In E.K. Dishner, T.W. Bean, J.E. Readence, & D.W. Moore (Eds.), *Reading in the content areas: Improving classroom instruction* (pp. 112–28). Dubuque, IA: Kendall/Hunt.

Singer, H., & Bean, T.W. (1986). Ability to learn from text, background knowledge, and attitudes towards learning are predictive of freshmen achievement in the University of California and the California State University systems. *The California Reader, 19,* 35–38.

Singer, H., & Donlan, D. (1989). *Reading and learning from text* (2nd ed.). Hillsdale, NJ: Erlbaum.

Smart, B. (1992). *Modern conditions, postmodern controversies.* New York: Routledge.

Smith, C., & Bean, T. (1980). The guided writing procedure: Integrating content reading and writing improvement. *Reading World, 19,* 290–98.

Smith, D. (1988). Brighter than a thousand suns: Facing pedagogy in the nuclear shadow. In T. Carson (Ed.), *Toward a renaissance of humanity: Rethinking and reorienting curriculum and instruction.* Edmonton, AB: University of Alberta.

Smith, F. (1971). *Understanding reading.* New York: Holt Rinehart and Winston.

Smith, J.L., & Johnson, H. (1994). Models for implementing literature in content studies. *The Reading Teacher, 48*(3), 198–208.

Smith, L.J., & Smith, D.L. (1994). The discussion process: A simulation. *Journal of Reading, 37*(7), 582–85.

Smith, R.J., & Dauer, V.L. (1984). A comprehension monitoring strategy for content area teachers. *Journal of Reading, 28*, 144–47.

Smith-Burke, M.T. (1982). Extending concepts through language activities. In J.A. Langer and M.T. Smith-Burke (Eds.), *Reader meets author/Bridging the gap* (pp. 163–79). Newark, DE: International Reading Association.

Speare, E. (1958). *The perilous road.* New York, NY: Harcourt Brace Jovanovich.

Sperling, M. (1994). Rubrics. In A. Purves (Ed.), *Encyclopaedia of English studies and language arts* (Vol. II, pp. 1052–1053). New York: Scholastic and NCTE.

Sperling, M. (1996). Revisiting the writing–speaking connection: Challenges for research on writing and writing instruction. *Review of Educational Research, 66*(1), 53–86.

Spires, H.A., & Stone, P.D. (1989). The directed note-taking activity: A self-questioning approach. *Journal of Reading, 33*, 36–39.

Spiro, R.J. (1988). Cognitive flexibility theory: Advanced knowledge acquisition in ill-structured domains (Tech. Report No. 441). Champaign: University of Illinois, Center for the Study of Reading.

Stahl, S.A., & Vancil, S.J. (1986). Discussion is what makes semantic maps work in vocabulary instruction. *The Reading Teacher, 40*, 62–69.

Staton, T. (1954). *How to study.* Nashville, TN: McQuiddley Printing Co.

Stayter, F. (1994). Assessment and evaluation in reading and writing. In A. Purves (Ed.), *Encyclopaedia of English studies and language arts* (Vol. I, pp. 88–92). New York: Scholastic and NCTE.

Sternglass, M.S. (1987). Instructional implications of three conceptual models of reading/writing relationships. *English Quarterly, 20*, 184–93.

Stetson, E. (1981). Improving textbook learning with S4R: A strategy for teachers, not students. *Reading Horizons, 22*, 129–35.

Stewart-Dore, N. (1982). Where is the learning we have lost in information?: Strategies for effective reading in content areas. Paper presented at the 9th World Congress in Reading, International Reading Association, Dublin, Ireland, July, 1982. (ED 322 138).

Stotsky, S. (1983). Research on reading/writing relationships: A synthesis and suggested directions. *Language Arts, 60*, 627–42.

Straw, S. (1990). Reading and response to literature: Transactionalizing instruction. In S. Hynds, and D. Rubin, (Eds.), *Perspectives on talk and learning* (pp. 129–148). Urbana, IL: National Council of Teachers of English.

Strother, D.B. (1985). Adapting instruction to individual needs: An eclectic approach. *Phi Delta Kappan, 67*, 308–11.

Stubbs, M. (1976). *Language, schools and classroom.* London: Methuen.

Suzuki, D. (1990). Views and values. *Perspectives: One.* Toronto: Harcourt Brace Jovanovich.

Tchudi, A., & Yates, J. (1983). *Teaching writing in the content areas: Senior high school.* Washington: National Education Association.

Teaching Professor, The. (1995). Collaborative and cooperative learning: Definitions and differences. A review of Brody (1995). *The Teaching Professor, 9*(7), 3–4.

Terpening, J. (Ed.). (1996). *Insights: Cultures.* Toronto: Harcourt Brace.

Thaiss, C.J. (1983). *Learning better, learning more: In the home and across the curriculum.* The talking series, K–12: Successful classroom practice. (ERIC Document Reproduction Service No. ED 233 833). Washington, DC: Dingle Associates.

Thomas, E., & Robinson, H. (1972). *Improving reading in every classroom.* Boston, MA: Allyn and Bacon.

Thomas, L. (1979). *The medusa and the snail: More notes of a biology watcher.* New York: Viking.

Tierney, R. (1994). Dissension, tensions, and the models of literacy. In R. Ruddell, M. Rapp-Ruddell, & H. Singer (Eds.), *Theoretical models and processes of reading* (pp. 1162–82). Newark, DE: International Reading Association.

Tierney, R., Carter, M., & Desai, L. (1991). *Portfolio assessment in the reading–writing classroom.* Norwood, MA: Christopher-Gordon.

Tierney, R., & Lapp, D. (1979). *National assessment of educational progress.* Newark, DE: International Reading Association.

Tierney, R.J., & LaZansky, J. (1980). *The rights and responsibilities of readers and writers: A contractual agreement* (Reading Education Report No. 15). Urbana: University of Illinois, Center for the Study of Reading.

Tierney, R.J., LaZansky, J., Raphael, T., & Cohen, P. (1987). Author's intentions and reader's interpretation. In R.J. Tierney, P. Anders, & J. Mitchell (Eds.), *Understanding readers' understanding,* (pp. 205–226). Hillsdale, NJ: Erlbaum.

Tierney, R.J., Mosenthal, J., & Kantor, R.N. (1984). Classroom applications of text analysis: Toward improving text selection and use. In J. Flood (Ed.), *Promoting reading comprehension* (pp. 139–60). Newark, DE: International Reading Association.

Tierney, R., & Pearson, P.D. (1983). The composing model of reading. *Language Arts, 60,* 568–80.

Tierney, R., & Shanahan, T. (1991). Research on the reading–writing relationship: Interactions, transactions, and outcomes. In R. Barr, M.L. Kamil, P. Mosenthal, & P.D. Pearson (Eds.), *Handbook of reading research* (Vol. II, pp. 246–80). White Plains, NY: Longman.

Tipton, J. (1991). Extending context clues to composition and cooperative learning. *Journal of Reading, 35*(1), 50.

Ulmer, G. (1985). Textshop for post(e)pedagogy. In G. Atkins and M. Johnson (Eds.), *Writing and reading differently.* Lawrence KA: University of Kansas.

Vacca, R., & Vacca, J. (1989). *Content area reading.* Glenview, IL: Scott, Foresman & Co.

Vacca, R., & Vacca, J. (1996). *Content area reading.* New York: Harper Collins.

Valencia, S.W. (1990a, January). A portfolio approach to classroom reading assessment: The whys, whats and hows. *The Reading Teacher, 43*(4), 338–40.

Valencia, S. (1990b, September). Alternative assessment: Separating the wheat from the chaff. *The Reading Teacher, 44*(1), 60–61.

Valencia, S.W., Hiebert, E.H., Afflerbach, P.P. (1994). Realizing the possibilities of authentic assessment: Current trends and future issues. In E.J. Hiebert, S.W. Valencia, & P.P. Afflerbach (Eds.), *Authentic Reading Assessment: Practices and Possibilities* (pp. 286–300). Newark, DE: International Reading Association.

Valencia, S.W., & Place, N. (1994). Portfolios: A process for enhancing teaching and learning. *The Reading Teacher, 47*(8), 666–69.

Valencia, S., & Stallman, A.C. (1989). Multiple measures of prior knowledge: Comparative predictive validity. In S. McCormick & J. Zutell (Eds.), *Cognitive and social perspectives for literacy research and instruction* (pp. 427–36). Chicago, IL: National Reading Conference.

Valeri-Gold, M., Olson, J.R., & Deming, M.P. (1991–92). Portfolios: Collaborative authentic assessment opportunities for college developmental learners. *Journal of Reading, 35*(4), 298–305.

Van Manen, M. (1982). Phenomenological pedagogy. *Curriculum Inquiry, 12*(3), 283–99.

Van Manen, M. (1990). *Researching lived experience: Human science for an action sensitive pedagogy.* London, ON: Althouse Press.

Van Manen, M. (1991). *The tact of teaching: The meaning of pedagogical thoughtfulness.* London, ON: Althouse Press.

Vars, G.F. (1991). Integrated curriculum in historical perspective. *Educational Leadership, 49*(2), 14–15.

Villaume, S., Worden, T., Williams, S., Hopkins, L., & Rosenblatt, C. (1994). Five teachers in search of a discussion. *The Reading Teacher, 47*(6), 480–87.

Vygotsky, L. (1962). *Thought and language* (E. Hanfmann & G. Vakar, Trans.). Cambridge, MA: MIT Press. (Original work published 1934.)

Vygotsky, L. (1978). *Mind in society* (M. Cole, V. John-Steiner, S. Scribner, & E. Soubermann, Eds. & Trans.). Cambridge, MA: Harvard University Press.

Vygotsky, L. (1986). *Thought and language* (Rev. ed.) (A. Kozulin, Trans. & Ed.). Cambridge, MA: MIT Press.

Walker, A. (1988). Writing-across-the-curriculum: The second decade. *English Quarterly, 21*, 93–103.

Walker, B.J. (1996). Discussions that focus on strategies and self-assessment. In L.B. Gambrell & J.F. Almasi (Eds.), *Lively discussion: Fostering engaged reading* (pp. 286–96). Newark: DE: International Reading Association.

Watson, J. 1968. *The double helix: A personal account of the discovery of the structure of DNA.* New York, NY: New American Library, Inc.

Watson, M., Baardman, S., Straw, S.B., & Sadowy, P. (1992). Collaboration and the curriculum: An investigation of six grade twelve students' responses to novels in a collaborative classroom. *Reflections on Canadian Literacy, 10*(4), 160–67.

Wepner, S.B. (1991). On the cutting edge with computerized assessment. *Journal of Reading, 35*(1), 62–65.

Wertheim, M. (1995). *Pythagoras' trousers: god, physics and the gender wars.* New York and Toronto: Times Books, Random House.

Wertsch, J.V. (1984). The zone of proximal development: Some conceptual issues. In B. Rogoff & J. Wertsch (Eds.), *Children's learning in the zone of proximal development,* (pp. 7–18). San Francisco: Jossey-Bass.

Wertsch, J.V. (1991). *Voices of the mind.* Cambridge, MA: Harvard University Press.

Wiencek, B.J. (1996). Planning, initiating and sustaining literature discussion groups: The teacher's role. In L.B. Gambrell & J.F. Almasi (Eds.), *Lively discussion: Fostering engaged reading* (pp. 206–23). Newark, DE: International Reading Association.

Wiggins, G. (1989, May). A true test: Toward more authentic and equitable assessment. *Phi Delta Kappan, 70*(9), 703–713.

Wilkinson, A. (1965). *Spoken English*. Birmingham, UK: University of Birmingham.

Williams, J., & Reynolds, T.D. (1993). Courting controversy: How to build inter-disciplinary units. *Education Leadership, 50*(7), 13–15.

Williams, William Carlos. (1963). *The Selected Poems of William Carlos Williams*. New York, NY: New Directions Publishing Corp.

Willis, J., Stephens, E., & Matthew, K. (1996). *Technology, reading, and language arts*. Toronto, ON: Allyn and Bacon.

Wilson, P.T., & Anderson, R.C. (1986). What they don't know will hurt them: The role of prior knowledge in comprehension. In J. Orasanu (Ed.), *Reading comprehension: From research to practice* (pp. 31–48). Hillsdale, NJ: Erlbaum.

Winchester, I. (1990). The standard picture of literacy and its critics. *Comparative Education Review, 34*(1), 21–40.

Winograd, K., & Higgins, K.M. (1994–95). Writing, reading, and talking mathematics: One inter-disciplinary possibility. *The Reading Teacher, 48*(4), 310–17.

Winograd, P. (1994). Developing alternative assessments: Six problems worth solving. *The Reading Teacher, 47*(5), 420–23.

Winograd, P., Paris, S., & Bridge, C. (1991). Improving the assessment of literacy. *The Reading Teacher, 45*(2), 108–16.

Wiseman, D.L., Many, J.E., & Altieri, J. (1992). Enabling complex aesthetic responses: An examination of three literary discussion approaches. In C. Kinzer & D.J. Leu (Eds.), *Literacy Research, Theory, and Practice: Views from Many Perspectives*, (pp. 283–90). Chicago: National Reading Conference.

Wolf, D., Bixby, J., Glenn, J., & Gardner, J.H. (1991). To use their minds well: Investigating new forms of student assessment. In G. Grant (Ed.), *Review of research in education* (Vol. 17). Washington, DC: American Educational Research Association.

Wolf, K. (1993). From informal to informed assessment: Recognizing the role of the classroom teacher. *The Journal of Reading, 36*(7), 518–23.

Wood, D. (1988). *How children think and learn*. Oxford: Basil Blackwell.

Wood, K.D., & Muth, K.D. (1991). The case for improved instruction in the middle grades. *Journal of Reading, 35*(2), 84–90.

Wood, P., Bruner, J., & Ross, G. (1976). The role of tutoring in problem-solving. *Journal of Child Psychology and Psychiatry, 17*, 89–100.

Worsnop, C. (1996). *Assessing media*. Mississauga, ON: Wright Communications.

Wurzer, W. (1990). *Filming and judgment: Between Heidegger and Adorno*. Atlantic Highlands, NJ: Humanities Press International.

Wurzer, W. & Silverman, H. (1990). Filming: Inscriptions of Denken. In H. Silverman (Ed.), *Postmodernism — Philosophy and the arts*. New York: Routledge.

Zinsser, W. (1988). *Writing to learn*. New York: Harper & Row.

INDEX

READER REPLY CARD

We are interested in your reaction to *Content Literacy for Secondary Teachers,* by Christine J. Gordon, Mary Sheridan, and W. James Paul. You can help us to improve this book in future editions by completing this questionnaire.

1. What was your reason for using this book?

   ☐ university course ☐ continuing education course ☐ personal interest

   ☐ college course ☐ professional development ☐ other _____

2. If you are a student, please identify your school and the course in which you used this book.

3. Which chapters or parts of this book did you use? Which did you omit?

4. What did you like best about this book?

5. What did you like least about this book?

6. Please identify any topics you think should be added to future editions.

7. Please add any comments or suggestions.

8. May we contact you for further information?

Name: _____

Address: _____

_____

Phone: _____

(fold here and tape shut)

Larry Gillevet
Director of Product Development
HARCOURT BRACE & COMPANY, CANADA
55 HORNER AVENUE
TORONTO, ONTARIO
M8Z 9Z9